Cinepaternity

Cinepaternity

Fathers and Sons in Soviet and Post-Soviet Film

EDITED BY

Helena Goscilo & Yana Hashamova

INDIANA UNIVERSITY PRESS

Bloomington & Indianapolis

This book is a publication of

Indiana University Press
601 North Morton Street
Bloomington, IN 47404-3797 USA

www.iupress.indiana.edu

Telephone orders   800-842-6796
Fax orders   812-855-7931
Orders by e-mail   iuporder@indiana.edu

♾The paper used in this publication
meets the minimum requirements of
the American National Standard for
Information Sciences—Permanence
of Paper for Printed Library Materials,
ANSI Z39.48-1992.

Manufactured in the United States of
America

Library of Congress Cataloging-in-
Publication Data

Cinepaternity : fathers and sons in
Soviet and post-Soviet film / edited by
Helena Goscilo and Yana Hashamova.
      p. cm.
   Includes bibliographical references and
index.
   ISBN 978-0-253-35458-7 (cloth) —
ISBN 978-0-253-22187-2 (pbk.) 1.
Fathers and sons in motion pictures. 2.
Motion pictures—Russia (Federation)—
History—20th century. I. Goscilo,
Helena, [date]– II. Hashamova, Yana.
   PN1995.9.F42C56 2010
   791.43'65251—dc22

2009036049

1 2 3 4 5 15 14 13 12 11 10

For Josie,

With loving gratitude for two decades of friendship and countless happy memories of times spent together in Bethesda, London, and Pittsburgh

and

with affection and admiration for work that has guided and inspired generations of Russian film scholars

CONTENTS

· PREFACE · ix

INTRODUCTION   CINEPATERNITY: THE PSYCHE AND ITS
HERITAGE · 1

ONE   THAW, STAGNATION, PERESTROIKA

1   The Myth of the "Great Family" in Marlen
Khutsiev's *Lenin's Guard* and Mark Osep'ian's
Three Days of Viktor Chernyshev ·
Alexander Prokhorov · 29

2   Mending the Rupture: The War Trope and the
Return of the Imperial Father in 1970s Cinema ·
Elena Prokhorova · 51

3   Models of Male Kinship in Perestroika Cinema ·
Seth Graham · 70

TWO   WAR IN THE POST-SOVIET DIALOGUE WITH PATERNITY

4   The Fathers' War through the Sons' Lens ·
Tatiana Smorodinskaya · 89

5   War as the Family Value: Failing Fathers and
Monstrous Sons in *My Stepbrother Frankenstein* ·
Mark Lipovetsky · 114

6   A Surplus of Surrogates: Mashkov's Fathers ·
    Helena Goscilo · 138

THREE   RECONCEIVING FILIAL BONDS

7   Resurrected Fathers and Resuscitated Sons:
    Homosocial Fantasies in *The Return* and *Koktebel* ·
    Yana Hashamova · 169

8   The Forces of Kinship: Timur Bekmambetov's *Night
    Watch* Cinematic Trilogy · *Vlad Strukov* · 191

9   Fathers, Sons, and Brothers: Redeeming Patriarchal
    Authority in *The Brigade* · *Brian James Baer* · 217

FOUR   AUTEURS AND THE PSYCHOLOGICAL/PHILOSOPHICAL

10   Fraught Filiation: Andrei Tarkovsky's
    Transformations of Personal Trauma ·
    Helena Goscilo · 247

11   Vision and Blindness in Sokurov's
    Father and Son · *José Alaniz* · 282

·   CONTRIBUTORS · 311
·   INDEX · 315

PREFACE

We conceived of *Cinepaternity* several years ago during a conversation about topics in Russian cinema that were begging for analysis, yet unaccountably seemed to have escaped critical notice. A focal preoccupation throughout Russian culture, male filiation has enjoyed a conspicuously vigorous revival on the post-Soviet screen, troping a series of cultural and sociopolitical dilemmas that followed the dissolution of the Soviet Union. Fathers and sons therefore struck us as a "natural" choice for investigation, particularly given our long-standing commitment to gender studies. Our decision to extend the collection's purview to encompass Soviet cinema from the Thaw through perestroika sprang from our awareness of the phenomenon's historical dimension; only practical considerations of length dictated our exclusion of the Stalin era. Although we predictably focus on Russian film and culture, the growing body of scholarship on masculinity and paternity in the Western cinematic context suggests that masculine passions and identifications generate corresponding images beyond national borders.

We thank our contributors, from whom we solicited chapters according to their personal or professional interests and periods of specialization, for their responsiveness not only to the invitation but also to our critical reactions and suggestions regarding earlier versions of their work. Since our original decision to assemble this collection, several Russian critics have published articles on the subject, notably in a 2005 issue of the film journal *SEANS,* and we express our appreciation of their scholarship, which *Cinepaternity* happily engages.

Our sincerest gratitude to the Graduate Dean's office at the University of Pittsburgh, which underwrote our illustrations, and to Jane K. Behnken, the *simpatica* film editor at Indiana University Press, whose flexibility and professionalism eased the process of publication.

We dedicate *Cinepaternity* to Josephine Woll, a much-loved friend and colleague with brains and heart whose death is mourned so profoundly because her life was such a rich gift to all who knew her.

Cinepaternity

INTRODUCTION

Cinepaternity: The Psyche and Its Heritage

We apparently aspire to persist in ourselves through the perseverant links of fathers and sons: links like those woven in blood by the prophets all the way back to the bosom of Abraham.

ALBERTO MANGUEL, *FATHERS AND SONS*

Indeed, the whole progress of society rests upon the opposition between successive generations.

SIGMUND FREUD, "FAMILY ROMANCES"

The common man cannot imagine [. . . a benevolent] Providence otherwise than in the figure of an enormously exalted father.

SIGMUND FREUD, *CIVILIZATION AND ITS DISCONTENTS*

RUSSIAN PATERNITY AS ABSENCE

While "the metaphysics of presence," according to Jacques Derrida, wields incalculable force, paternity in Russian culture demonstrates how "the metaphysics of absence" exerts its own empirical and discursive power. The significance of such a metaphysics was eloquently conveyed in Moscow on 15 September 2007, when author and host Viktor Erofeev devoted the entire hour of his radio show, *Encyclopedia of the Russian*

Soul [*Entsiklopediia russkoi dushi*], to the topic of Russian fathers.[1] The impassioned three-way discussion between Erofeev[2] and his guests, the poet Tatiana Shcherbina and the journalist Vladimir Chernov, proved remarkable for its critical consensus, notwithstanding the participants' diverse backgrounds and professional trajectories. All declared paternity an acute, endlessly ramifying problem in post-Soviet society, rooted in the passivity, self-indulgence, and fecklessness of men raised by single or divorced mothers who dote on their sons. Russian fathers, the trio insisted, are essentially absent. They either abandon their families for other women or simply abrogate traditional paternal responsibilities. Since sons iterate that pattern upon attaining adulthood, perpetuation by successive generations has naturalized the legacy of lack.

Attributing the contemporary epidemic of "fatherlessness" to the catastrophic loss of male lives in World War II, Chernov maintained that during the Soviet postwar era the country's leaders and screen personalities functioned as compensatory virtual fathers. Shcherbina concurred, recounting how, in 1980, at the funeral of the gravel-voiced singer/poet/actor Vladimir Vysotskii, she overheard one of the mourners confess, "For me Vysotskii was a father" ["Vysotskii byl dlia menia otets"]. Today even that surrogacy has evaporated. Whereas in contemporary Western Europe, just as in nineteenth-century Russia, "real" fathers command respect and inculcate decent values [*"poriadochnost'"*] in their offspring, with whom they forge intimate relations through companionship, guidance, and support, late-Soviet society supplanted familial bonds and obligations with the appreciably less exacting ties of friendship. That trend continues to flourish today. In general, Erofeev contended, the history of the Russian family is not one of intimacy but of violence, and sociological studies, anecdotal evidence adduced by Chernov, and the reported ubiquity of battered wives and children would seem to confirm that judgment.[3]

Attuned though he is to prevailing tendencies,[4] Erofeev is not the first Russian male to have identified fatherhood as a major dilemma in post-Soviet culture. That distinction belongs to filmmakers and their critics. Two related, thought-provoking articles about celluloid male filiation appeared in 2005 under the rubric "Otets i syn: Novyi geroi" ["Father and Son: The New Hero" 197] in an issue of the major Russian film journal *SEANS*. While Pavel Kuznetsov's "Ottsy i synov'ia" ["Fathers and Sons" 206–17] surveys European and American directors' images of paternity over several decades, Aleksandr Sekatskii's revealingly titled "Ottsepriimstvo"[5] focuses on current Russian cinema's persistent fascination with failed or flawed paternity (199–205). "*Ottsepriimstvo*," Sekatskii clarifies, "is an attempt to eliminate the existential deficit that has arisen there, where the transformation of a boy into a man traditionally transpired" (199). Recent Russian cinema's intense preoccupation with sundry forms of that deficit not only symptomatizes post-Soviet Russia's crisis of identity, but also culminates decades of conflicts and troubled negotiations between generations of males—similarly reflected in post-Soviet theater.[6]

Kuznetsov briefly prefaces his condensed but penetrating scrutiny of twenty-four international films—ranging from Vittorio De Sica's *Bicycle Thieves* [*Ladri di bicicletti* 1948] and Elia Kazan's *East of Eden* (1954) to the Canadian Denys Arcand's award-winning *Barbarian Invasions* [*Les invasions barbares* 2003]—by remarking on their inseparability from biblical, Greek, and Freudian narratives of fraught father-son constellations. As he contends, "Rebellion, hatred, patricide, filicide, orphanhood, and wandering [*skital'chestvo*] are immemorial archetypes of human history" (206) that conceptually structure the majority of films in his purview.[7] Indeed, amid the welter of negative or defective screen types spotlighted in his survey, Kuznetsov finds only one instance of "the father as an image of perfection" [*otets kak obraz sovershenstva*]—in Ishtvan Szabo's *Father* [*Apa* 1966]. Inasmuch as the father in Szabo's film perished in World War II and survives as an ideal exclusively in the son's subjective recollections, such an exemplar, Kuznetsov concludes, can exist solely in our imagination (210). Indeed, the prerequisite of death for paternal elevation to iconic status or even mere acceptance, familiar from Freud's classic formulation in *Totem and Taboo* (1913), implicitly underpins not only Szabo's narrative but also such post-Soviet films as Pavel Chukhrai's *Vor* [*The Thief* 1997], Andrei Zviagintsev's *Vozvrashchenie* [*The Return* 2003], and Vladimir Mashkov's *Papa* (2004). Death, however, is not the ultimate absence, for the idealized image can persist and preserve its immaculacy through memory. More traumatic, perhaps, is the psychological/existential absence of the paternal in the father who is physically present yet fundamentally inaccessible.

As figures of priority and authority, fathers tend to script sons' lives, fruitfully or fatally.[8] Ideally fathers bond with beloved sons, benignly facilitating their maturation into manhood through openness, wise counsel, and the provision of a behavioral model premised on identification and continuity. This utopian dyad informs not only Szabo's film but also Alberto Manguel's retrospective perception of his son's birth: "His appearance in the world, the only *true* act of creation I can say I've witnessed, moved me more than anything I have ever experienced. From that moment, his existence demanded a relationship, the building of bridges and walls and the marking of common land between us" (8). Yet, as Kuznetsov's commentary emphasizes, that land all too often becomes contested terrain. Ancient myths of origin and succession universally narrate volatile power struggles between generations of males, whereby authoritarian fathers who fear usurpation slaughter sons, and ambitious and rebellious sons butcher or emasculate fathers.

Kuznetsov recognizes that father-son relations in contemporary culture draw on some of the earliest Western paradigms of patricide and filicide, where "home" conflicts culminate in brutal homicide. In Hesiod's *Theogony* (ca. 700 BC), which charts the genealogies of early Greek mythological divinities, Kronos[9] castrates his tyrannical father, Ouranos, in a symbolic act of disempowerment so as to depose him, only to be overthrown in turn by his own son, Zeus, who proceeds to arrogate the Olympian throne—a narrative that Freud borrowed for his template of primal parricide in *Totem and Taboo*. As Freud theorized, "The inclination to aggression is an original, self-subsisting disposition in man, [. . .] constitut[ing] the greatest impediment to civilization" (*Civilization* 69), and "the regulations of civilization can only be maintained by a certain degree of coercion" (*Future* 8). What Freud calls the primordial ambivalence toward the father (on the one hand, love and fear; on the other, hatred), which inspires violent resistance to his authority, breeds guilt, the "fatal inevitability" that impedes happiness and constitutes the most significant hindrance to the development of civilization (*Civilization* 79, 81; *Future* 24). In contrast to the daughter's recognition of "my mother, myself," the son, "far more inclined to feel hostile impulses towards his father than towards his mother" ("Family Romances" 75), repudiates his biological sire as both respected progenitor and emulative ideal. Yet how can the son abandon yearning for the man whose paternal identity his own birth created and who, symbolically or empirically, represents an omnipotent authority culturally codified since time immemorial and essential to his "transformation [. . .] into a man" (Sekatskii 199)?

INDEFINABLE IDENTITY AND AUTOMATIC AUTHORITY

As Sekatskii's article argues, the complexities of biological and surrogate fatherhood, though hardly ignored in West European and Soviet film, have acquired unusual prominence in post-Soviet cinema (199), triggered by the radical rupture in Russia's historical continuity and the concomitant crisis in masculinity and paternity. Unavoidably generations play a key role in the struggle to construct a new identity on the ashes of discredited long-standing values and traditions. An affective paradigm for troping contentious or unverifiable identities, the father/son dyad taps into the classic dilemma (predating DNA tests) of establishing fatherhood and its attendant issue of legitimacy. Unlike the unassailable identity of the mother, biological paternity traditionally has been uncertain ("pater semper incertus est")—a circumstance that facilitates targeting the father as the disavowed parent in the dynamic of the family romance (1909: Freud 1950, 76) and justifies the embrace of surrogates.[10] Such substitutions frequently result in the son's psychological oscillation between the fantasized Ideal and the ostensibly Real. Recognition and acceptance of the absent-but-returned father necessitates an act of faith, for what can vindicate his prolonged physical or psychological absence, both of which render him a phantom, a figment of the desirous imagination that may suddenly become embodied in what is essentially a stranger, as in Zviagintsev's *Vozvrashchenie*? The dynamic of recognition and acceptance operates in both directions. If, as Shakespeare put it, "It is a wise father that knows his own child,"[11] what does the father's rejection of his paternal accountability by refusing to acknowledge or "know" his son signify? Valerii Todorovskii's chilling *Moi svodnyi brat Frankentshtein* [*My Stepbrother Frankenstein* 2003] investigates precisely such a resistance to cross-generational blood kinship and its lethal consequences.

Sekatskii distinguishes between literal absence and a more profound, existential absence—not of physical being but of definition and communication, most dramatically rendered in Zviagintsev's film, where sons struggle for a discursive link with the "alien" who claims and immediately asserts paternal authority over them (199–200). Ancient myths, religion, history, and psychoanalysis all testify to the limitless and often arbitrary nature of that power—which Carl Jung called "demonic" when exercised by the archetype of the negative, devouring father ("The Significance of the Father" 314). In the ancient myths so central to both Jung and Freud, Kronos/Chronos, "devouring father Time," negates his natural successors by literally swallowing them to forestall usurpation. Eager to please the gods he is hosting, Tantalus cooks his son, Pelops, and serves him in a stew to his divine guests.[12] Biblical narratives likewise reveal paternal willingness to spill sons' blood—though for ostensibly admirable ends: in the Old Testament's most famous example, Abraham unhesitatingly prepares to obey Yahweh's command to sacrifice his son, Isaac,[13] while the New Testament God mandates the crucifixion of his only son. Such scenarios provided inspiration for *Nochnoi dozor* [*Night Watch* 2004], the first film in Timur Bekmambetov's *Dozor* trilogy, which opens with a father's endeavor to abort his son, whom he subsequently fails to recognize and who spurns him for a surrogate. "The iniquity of the fathers" (Exodus 20:5), Bekmambetov demonstrates, cripples the lives of the sons, and the majority of post-Soviet films chart sons' struggles to surmount the dilemma of iniquitous, indifferent, or absolutist fathers—for whom, custom and law decree, sons must demonstrate dutiful respect. In short, current Russian cinema, Sekatskii aptly maintains, teems not with prodigal sons but with prodigal fathers.

The categorical imperative of filial reverence and obedience doubtless stems from the analogy between man as progenitor and God as creator, captured in Shakespeare's maxim, "To you, your father should be as a god."[14] Indeed, according to Plato, respect and fear should both govern sons' relationships with fathers and define pious veneration of the gods: "We should be quick to appreciate how very relevant [. . .] the subject of worshipping gods will be to the respect or disrespect in which we hold our father and mother" (Plato, *Laws*, XI, 930e, 446). Those commentators who interpret Andrei Tarkovsky's oeuvre as a profound spiritual statement perceive just such an equation between the father and the Heavenly Father in his films, an equation that Aleksandr Sokurov's *Otets i syn* [*Father and Son* 2003] strives to recuperate primarily through aesthetics.

While prescriptive aggrandizing parallels function as desiderata, deviations are what preponderate in modern narratives. Violation of the prescribed ideal through incestuous patricide in Sophocles' *Oedipus Rex* (ca. 430 BC)[15] provided the basis for Freud's thesis about universal human desire and identity formation, whereby the male child's sexual desire for his mother leads him to wish for his father's death. This triangular Oedipal structure, which Freud deemed fundamental to maturation and adult sexuality, is resurrected in the *Dozor* trilogy, Chukhrai's *Vor* [*The Thief* 1997], and Kirill Serebrennikov's *Izobrazhaia zhertvu* [*Playing the Victim* 2006]. The French psychoanalyst Jacques Lacan's subsequent revision of Freud retains the triadic constellation in mapping the child's transition from the Imaginary (mother) to the Symbolic order (Law of the Father), arguing that a third term—The Name of the Father—is a requisite "interference" in the sense-based attachment/identification between child and mother (or any primary caretaker) in the child's introduction to the Law (prohibitions, lack, and Symbolic castration). In Soviet and post-Soviet films that explore father-son relations Lacan's emphasis on the centrality of the father's role in the individual's socialization translates into the relegation not only of the mother but of any female presence to the periphery, most conspicuous in Sokurov's *Otets i syn* and Aleksei Popogrebskii and Boris Khlebnikov's *Koktebel'* (*Koktebel*) (2003).

RESISTING AND EMBRACING TRADITIONAL DOMINION AND DISCOURSE

Cinematic and literary works in Russia that replay patrilinear conflicts illustrate Freud's notions about the consequences of civilization: with time, censoring mechanisms inhibit patricidal/filicidal impulses, interiorizing enmity. Hostility expresses itself in mediated and reduced forms of alienation and resentment: freighted silences, passive-aggressive behavior, and determination on the son's part to carve out a life remote from the father's.[16] Whereas filicide tainted early Russian history, strained relations between fathers and sons in nineteenth-century Russian literature found more muted ("civilized") expression in rebellion and feelings of guilt, inferiority, neglect, suffocation, and rivalry. The frequency of paternal surrogates in various narratives partially anticipated Freud's theory of the family romance (1897, 1909), whereby children who feel slighted by their parents replace them with fantasized, incomparably better parents of more exalted status.[17] Such substitutions, which according to Freud spring from estrangement and a rejection of parental authority en route to the universal process of maturation,[18] proliferate in Mashkov's *Papa,* where the posthumous triumph of the biological father at film's end coincides with the repentant son's belated recognition of his "filial betrayal."

Since the Soviet regime shared Plato's investment in the stability of the state, its official doctrine of socialist realism required that metaphorical paternity directly facilitate sons' ideological maturation. Accordingly, in exemplary canonical texts on page[19] and screen, "enlightened" mentors function as surrogate father figures for the "spontaneous" positive heroes in what are essentially political *Bildungsromane* and stories of secular conversion.[20] More overtly sociopolitical than their nineteenth-century predecessors, these relationships develop in a homosocial environment that typifies Soviet narratives of legitimate succession, inasmuch as they prize ideological allegiances over blood ties. Stalinism, in fact, evidenced the triumph of trope (Stalin as Father) over lived reality (the biological father). The Stalinist concept of the country as the Big Family united through a single, communal worldview conspired to make a highly publicized national hero of the fifteen-year-old Pavlik Morozov, the schoolboy who in 1931 demonstrated his ostensive devotion to the "the common good" by denouncing his father to the secret police for falsifying documents. As a reward for conformity to the Father's Law, he earned the title of Hero-Pioneer of the Soviet Union. Elsewhere he doubtless would have been vilified as a contemptible patricide who transgressed the laws of nature and most religions.[21] In his comments on the extant segment of Sergei Eisenstein's screen version of these events, *Bezhin lug* [*Bezhin Meadow* 1935–37], Kuznetsov notes that it casts the Morozov plot as an Oedipal drama that simultaneously invites a religious reading—as divine retribution for the son's infraction of biblical interdictions (208).

Whereas religion posits God as the ultimate, heavenly Father, His earthly equivalent and representative in Orthodox Russia was the tsar. Indeed, Russia's centuries-old historical and political tradition construed the figure of its ruler as the "father of the nation."[22] The mythic preeminence of the "*batiushka tsar*'"—his profoundly revered authoritarian stature—was entrenched in the Russian collective imagination, which conveniently ignored notorious instances of filicide by two of its most autocratic rulers in scenarios recalling Hesiod's *Theogony*. In a fit of rage, Ivan IV killed his son and heir to the throne,[23] and Peter the Great had his son tortured to death, allegedly participating in the process.[24] Yet the seemingly ecumenical longing for a positive father figure (one, moreover, "blessed by God") bred the populace's trust in and loyalty to its patriarchal autocrats, for the relationship between "father" and "son" "has been the model for conceptualizing Western political authority" (Borneman 4), and Russia certainly was no exception to this rule.[25]

Twentieth-century Russian totalitarianism embraced the supremacy of the paternal ruler, with only slight, primarily secularizing, modifications. The paternal image positioned the leader—Lenin and Stalin—as an omniscient divinity with absolute power, an image amply illustrated in Soviet visual culture, which drew on religious iconography for its representation of the two addressing multitudes "from above," dispensing "blessings," and withdrawing into sacred solitude to contemplate ways of improving the lot of the masses.[26] This mythology, which propagated Lenin's purported single-minded devotion to the masses and Stalin's tireless work on their behalf, necessarily operated on desire and selectivity. Stalin's canny exploitation of familial rhetoric proclaimed him not only Father of the People, but Father of virtually everyone and everything in sight. And the populace responded with the sort of fearful idolatry that children nurture for the domineering, arbitrary, but charismatic father they idealize. As Schoeberlein phrases it, Stalin "was held with that *characteristic* mixture of feeling with which fathers are often held, blending awe, esteem, fear, and submission" (205; emphasis added). In some quarters that awed and terrified adulation of Stalin persists to this day and represents an ideal of authority for those prepared to overlook the mass murder of Soviet citizens to further his paranoid cause.[27]

After Stalin's death, however, the leader's paternal function weakened and the Communist Party's First Secretaries dwindled from inspirational role models to impotent government functionaries—not wise and vigorous fathers but somnolent grandfathers. The impotence of these geriatric leaders, as well as the staggering number of male casualties in World War II and in concentration camps, surely accounts for the disappearance of virile, influential fathers in various cultural genres from the mid-1950s to the 1990s. Part of Vladimir Putin's popularity, in fact, may be ascribed to the reverse transformation of his image—from party functionary to energetic leader and, in the eyes of the major-ity, protective if youthful guardian of the nation. Not unlike Stalin, though on a more modest scale and in a less lethal mode, Putin has inspired a cult of personality mounted by both old and young (e.g., the ultra-conservative group Nashi [Ours]), powerful and populist, men and women—who create songs, novels, portraits, slogans, handicrafts, and various marketable items (calendars, watches, T-shirts) devoted to his persona/image, lauding the sober, dependable, self-confident authority he exudes in a recognizable discourse of paternal power. A report in 2007 (*Izvestiia* [News]) indicated that Putin was "the only politician trusted by the overwhelming majority of people."[28] That perception partly ac-counts for Russians' electing as president the candidate endorsed by Putin, whose imprimatur ensured and naturalized the succession of his "ideological son."

CELLULOID FILIATION IN MULTIPLE MODES

Several of the chapters in this volume, which investigates father-son re-lations in post-Stalinist and post-Soviet Russian film, inevitably engage Freud (the Oedipal complex, the family romance), Lacan (the Law of the Father), and contemporary theories of masculinity, all of which at-tempt to illuminate the psychological and social bases of what long ago solidified into recognizable patterns of identification, disavowal, and displacement in male filiation.[29] Like recent Western European films, such as *The Full Monty* (Peter Cataneo 1997), *TwentyFourSeven* (Shane Meadows 1997), *Character* (Mike Van Diem 1997), *Billy Elliot* (Stephen Daldry 2000), and *Gabriel and Me* (Udayan Prasad 2001),[30] the Russian films analyzed in this collection explore not only the obsession with absent or ineffectual father figures but also the perceived pressure on homosocial bonds and territories. Since the trope of paternity in the transfer of power from "Grandfather Lenin" to "father Stalin"[31] and the latter's comprehensive elaboration of the paternal image as icon inform countless Soviet films, Stalinist paradigms inevitably figure as a back-ground or point of departure for some of the chapters analyzing legiti-mate succession and historical rupture. That backward glance, moreover, has an empirical basis, for Stalin continues to surface in contemporary debates about a strong Russia and Russians' nostalgia for empire.

Unavoidably sons in Thaw cinema represent the young generation's reaction to the Stalinist era, during which fathers embraced the Great Leader as their mythological exemplar—inspiring but necessarily unattainable and unique, for the state father "stands above the nation—loving it, looking after its needs, and arbitrating its destiny" (Schoeberlein 205). As numerous biographies and memoirs attest, Stalin's mode of leadership was supremely militaristic, the "connotations of military order" helping to sustain the paradoxical image of the father who is "of us" yet "above us" (Schoeberlein 201). Ever vigilant in detecting "enemies," quick to execute perceived competitors and opponents, and brooking no "insubordination" or challenge to his supreme control, Stalin favored terror, violence, and punishment as the most effective policy of governance, while playing the role of soldiers' "caring father" in the model of the army as family (Schoeberlein 202). Chukhrai's *Vor*, according to Helena Goscilo (chapter 6), captures the ambiguous complexity of the alluring and powerful but brutal father figure derived from the simulacrum of Stalin as intrepid military genius. As a reduced imitation of Stalin, the eponymous thief Tolian initiates his pseudo-son, Sania, into the Law of the Father by teaching him the value of remorseless force, and thereby preparing him for conditions of war—the supreme measure of masculinity during the Stalinist period.

Thaw film, however, as Alexander Prokhorov maintains in chapter 1 of this volume, distanced itself from Stalin's methods and his charisma, as evident in *Zastava Il'icha* [*Il'ich's Guard*, Marlen Khutsiev 1962] and *Tri dnia Viktora Chernysheva* [*Three Days of Viktor Chernyshev*, Mark Osep'ian 1968]. In commemorating a lost generation of fathers who perished in the war or in Stalin's prison system, *Zastava Il'icha* reinvigorates the trope of the Big Family but discredits Stalinist authority, which it indicts for betraying the revolutionary ideals embodied in Lenin and nurtured by the grandfathers.[32] The film's visual dynamism and its optimistic faith in a young, ebullient generation capable of restoring earlier ideals contrast dramatically with the pacing and mood of *Tri dnia Viktora Chernysheva*. Unlike Khutsiev, who conveys the promise of transformative, affective energy, Osep'ian details the devastating effects of Stalinism on the succeeding generation: sons without fathers suffer from anomie and cultural amnesia, aimlessly going through the motions of living while suspended in a vacuum.

Whereas Osep'ian underscores Viktor Chernyshev's fundamental indifference to everything around him, other films of the period portray orphaned boys desperately seeking surrogate paternal figures among the often traumatized veterans who survived World War II but likewise lost their families and homes, and suffered psychic wounds in battle that only an emotional bond could heal. Such is precisely the scenario of two key Thaw films, Marlen Khutsiev's *Dva Fedora* [*Two Fedors* 1958] and Sergei Bondarchuk's *Sud'ba cheloveka* [*Fate of a Man* 1959], released several years after the death and subsequent denunciation of the Soviet Union's historical Father and the cult of personality that deified him. While acknowledging male psychological needs, the Thaw, however, merely adjusted instead of jettisoning the military-based misogyny of the Stalinist era. Its continued focus on homosocial ties relegated women to the role of bystanders or impediments to the emotional union of vulnerable boys and tender, needy veterans who adopted them in a spirit of compassionate identification.[33]

Casualties, not lustrous causes, mark men's on-screen struggles during this period, and though most of Andrei Tarkovsky's oeuvre belongs to the Stagnation period, his debut Thaw-era feature film, *Ivanovo detstvo* [*My Name Is Ivan* 1962], likewise mourns the fate of a boy orphaned by World War II whose hatred for the Germans maims his existence. As a scout in the Soviet resistance, Ivan courts constant danger but resists soldiers' affectionate efforts to replace his dead parents, and ultimately suffers capture, interrogation, and death by hanging. Through the boy's psychological and physical torments Tarkovsky explores the trauma of national and personal bereavement instead of glorifying male derring-do. Yet his scenario here, as elsewhere, also trivializes women or locates them on the periphery of historical processes.

If the Thaw tended to demythologize war, however timidly, Elena Prokhorova, in chapter 2, makes a persuasive case for Stagnation's return to a prior military discourse in order to affirm the authority of the paternal signifier as a guarantor of continuity. The 1970s revitalized melodramatic machismo in efforts to legitimate the regime through stirring accounts of a heroic national history that collapsed Russia's imperial era into the Soviet Union's "revolutionary" past. Despite the blatant stylistic and tonal contrasts in Vladimir Motyl"'s flamboyant *Beloe solntse pustyni* [*White Sun of the Desert* 1969] and Vladimir Rogovoi's nakedly ideological *Ofitsery* [*Officers* 1971], both films idealize dashing masculinity and male filiation in a patriotic vein. The Law of the Father reigns supreme as biological and surrogate fathers "show the way" to sons, providing blueprints of Soviet manhood in narratives confirming stability through several generations' unflagging devotion to nation and the military ethos. Typically Tarkovsky's late-Stagnation films explore precisely the reverse—the son's endeavors to fashion an existence devoid of a father, blighted by the latter's emotional aloofness or the son's incapacity to forge a meaningful link with his sire. Unlike his fellow directors, Tarkovsky drew directly on autobiographical family experience to overcome, by creative means, his childhood trauma—Arsenii Tarkovsky's abandonment of the family for another woman, from which his son evidently never recovered.

Though perestroika's reassessment and restoration of entire periods in the Soviet Union's past superficially seemed to resemble the Thaw's cautious recasting of Stalinism, cultural production under Gorbachev actually confronted an incomparably weightier phenomenon: the imminent wholesale disavowal of the Soviet system and the incalculable ramifications of that *volte-face*. Invoking the traditional trope of filiation as well as other modes of kinship, film directors during the late 1980s tackled both the moral burden of an increasingly discredited legacy and the generational estrangement that by the 1990s would culminate in a decisive historical rupture. Attempts to assimilate and cope with revelations about the Stalinist terror, as Seth Graham shows in chapter 3, yielded several major films, including Tengiz Abuladze's milestone *Pokaianie* [*Repentance* 1984, released 1986], in which richly grotesque and surrealistic segments capture the rewards of collaboration and the horrors of resistance in two contrasting families along patrilinear lines, and Vadim Abdrashitov's *Pliumbum, ili opasnaia igra* [*Lead, or A Dangerous Game* 1986]. Unsurprisingly both directors exposed the bankruptcy of Stalinism as a system of values rooted in literal and metaphorical death—wholesale murder and suicide in *Pokaianie*,[34] and the Pavlik Morozov brand of filial betrayal in *Pliumbum*.

These and similar reappraisals in perestroika feature films had their counterpart in such documentaries as Tofik Shakhverdiev's *Stalin s nami?* [*Is Stalin with Us?* 1989] and Semen Aronovich's *Ia sluzhil v okhrane Stalina* [*I Was Stalin's Bodyguard* 1989], which strove to unravel the enigma of the populace's prolonged attachment to the venerated Father who killed approximately twenty million of his children/fellow countrymen so as to vouchsafe their eventual happiness. In the midst of sociopolitical upheaval, the vital issues of tracing historical origins and mapping possible futures found expression not only in film but also in literature, theater, and journalism. By the end of the decade, the disintegration of the Big Family left trans-generational masculinity unmoored and threatened by new paradigms of non-homosocial kinship.

MILITARY DISCOURSE AS PATRIOTIC PATERNAL LEGACY

Yet, despite the demise of the Soviet Union, Stalin's "paternal" shadow continues to loom over Russia, as attested by countless films not only revisiting his era (Petr Todorovskii's *Ankor, eshche ankor!* [*Encore! Again, Encore!* 1992], Ivan Dykhovichnyi's *Prorva* [*Moscow Parade* 1992], Sergei Livnev's *Serp i molot* [*Hammer and Sickle* 1994], Pavel Chukhrai's *Vor* [*The Thief* 1997], Aleksei German's *Khrustalev, mashinu!* [*Khrustalev, My Car!* 1998], and Vladimir Mashkov's *Papa* [2004]),[35] but also repeatedly recuperating in a critical vein the single most significant, mythologized moment of Soviet unanimity—World War II. Signally called the Great Patriotic/Fatherland War [*Velikaia otechestvennaia voina*], the German invasion of 1941 and its cost-heavy repulsion by Soviet forces holds a unique place in Russian collective memory: through shared national pride it unites people who may disagree about all other aspects of life but celebrate victory over the Nazis as a superhuman, specifically Russian feat of *moral* resistance against a numerically and technologically superior army. This is the single moment in (post)Soviet history that elevates fathers and grandfathers to a heroic stature celebrated in annual parades, even if at first glance their values seem alien to a young generation reared on entrepreneurial conventions.

Screen narratives of that watershed event nonetheless clearly demarcate the perspectives of directors who actually participated in combat from those who experienced the war as children or only secondhand. A comparison of such canonical Soviet screen representations as Aleksandr Stolper's *Zhdi menia* [*Wait for Me* 1943], Lev Arnshtam's *Zoia*

[1944], Sergei Gerasimov's *Molodaia Gvardiia* [*The Young Guard* 1947], and Mikhail Chiaureli's *Padenie Berlina* [*The Fall of Berlin* 1949] with the postwar generation's distanced view of the war's trials, triumphs, and compromises reveals, as Tatiana Smorodinskaya contends in her essay in this volume (chapter 4), their sons' remoteness from the grandiloquent claims of the fathers' highly selective, patriotic mythmaking.

Discussing post-violence trauma, Borneman, in his inquiry into the anthropology of ends, maintains that the "temporally delayed and repeated suffering of these events [. . .] can only be grasped retrospectively" (Borneman 1). Whereas Soviet-era war films, by definition, underscored national solidarity, leaders' (and especially Stalin's) tactical wisdom, individual and collective bravery, fearless resistance in occupied territory, and the cowardly savagery of the invaders, 'sons' have tended to dwell on common soldiers' fear and uncertainty, fatal errors in the midst of battle, cases of collaboration with the occupying Nazis, and, in the extraordinary case of Aleksei German Jr.'s *Poslednii poezd* [*The Last Train* 2004], compassionate, bewildered Germans at odds with Hitler's policies of extermination.[36] Contemporary Russian directors, as Smorodinskaya contends in her contribution to this volume, must negotiate between two incompatible imperatives: on the one hand, a regard for history, which demands investigation of, inter alia, degrading realities as Russians struggled for survival amid tragic circumstances, and, on the other, a respect for what Smorodinskaya calls the populace's "sensitivities" and the state's expectations of patriotic glorification congruent with its official perspective on the war. While some young directors have chosen to explore and expose less edifying aspects of Soviet wartime activities, others have folded military violence and machismo into the genre of mainstream action film entertainment. Nikolai Lebedev's remake (2002) of Aleksandr Ivanov's *Zvezda* [*The Star* 1949] epitomizes this widespread trend, which reflects the "director-sons'" concern with box office receipts.

Military discourse, reinforced by the Cold War, remains sedimented in Russian culture and above all in the collective memory of its older population, while also kept alive for anyone tracking the wars in Afghanistan (1979–89) and Chechnya (1994–96, 1999–), inasmuch as it still permeates official documents, pronouncements, and interviews with government representatives. That discourse seems ineradicable, solidly entrenched in officially endorsed precedents that enjoyed a revival under Putin: starting with the late 1940s, participation in World War II elevated veterans to a position of moral and historical authority that nowadays few dare challenge and that to some extent has been recuperated in such imperialistic celluloid fare as Lebedev's *Zvezda*, Aleksei Balabanov's *Voina* [*War* 2002], and Fedor Bondarchuk's *Deviataia rota* [*The Ninth Regiment* 2005]. Putin's enthusiastic endorsement of Bondarchuk's enormously popular paean to macho bonding during the war in Afghanistan indicates the extent of the Kremlin's enduring cathexis to a wounded but militaristic identity.[37] Many post-Soviet films indifferent to the dream of empire, however, query the basis and legitimacy of more recent wars— notably those waged to preserve the communist regime (in Afghanistan) or to assert Russian control over contested territory (in Chechnya).

War in Valerii Todorovskii's *Moi svodnyi brat Frankenshtein* impresses Mark Lipovetsky, the author of chapter 5, as a "family value." One of the most original and disturbing cinematic achievements of the new century, *Moi svodnyi brat Frankenshtein* examines the consequences of the protracted, disastrous war in Chechnya. More generally, however, it tackles the failure of contemporary Russian society to confront its past, present, and future. The disciplined, chilling narrative dramatizes the psychic damage of an unacknowledged illegitimate son and veteran of the Chechen war, Pavlik (the obverse of Pavlik Morozov), who unexpectedly materializes on the doorstep of his unsuspecting father and the latter's family. Pavlik's combat training and his rapidly unfolding paranoia—consonant with the Soviet Union's and to some extent contemporary Russia's presupposition of ubiquitous enemies—prompt him to assume the guise of paternal protector against phantom threatening forces, with disastrous consequences. The biological father's inability to enact strong, emulation-inspiring masculinity within and outside the household and Pavlik's readiness to "take care" of the family ineluctably result in a role reversal, symbolized in part by the father's disavowal of his son and that son's insistence on "saving the children." War, Todorovskii shows, creates vulnerable monsters who perceive everyday reality as military conflict, while those who colluded in their terrifying creation disengage themselves from their Frankensteinian offspring. Whereas the state and the population revered World War II veterans as exemplars of stalwart honor and courage, returnees from the war in Chechnya face indifference and rejection, for the older generation shirks its account-ability for demobilized young soldiers physically and psychologically maimed by the horrors of war. The film metaphorically confirms Croe-sus's famous dictum, "In peace the sons bury their fathers, but in war the fathers bury their sons."

ENABLING THROUGH STRENGTH AND WEAKNESS

The proliferation of both authoritarian and ineffectual fathers on the Russian screen during the 2000s stems from the widespread post-Soviet disorientation that characterized the roller-coaster 1990s, when the country was groping its uncertain, crime-riddled way to some sem-blance of a market economy under Yeltsin's rapidly deteriorating lead-ership. Through sheer force of experience, self-confidence, and mystery that readily translates into mystique, strong or domineering paternal figures in Chukhrai's *Vor*, Zviagintsev's debut film *Vozvrashchenie*, and Sokurov's *Otets i syn* exert a decisive formative influence on sons ne-gotiating a transition to manhood. Ultimately enigmatic, in all three films the father enables the son's painful but successful consummation of the universal rite of passage into the Symbolic—a process, as Yana Hashamova points out in chapter 7, simultaneously revealing the fis-sures in the Real. Whereas both Chukhrai and Zviagintsev dwell on the afflictive aspects of maturation, which hinges on the father's figura-tive or literal death, Sokurov tends to rhapsodize over the loving filial bond. As José Alaniz maintains in chapter 11 of this volume, Sokurov marshals all available means of representation (painting, cinema, and music) so as to "(re)construct, (re)affirm and (re)revivify the post-Soviet father—to rebuild him in palpable, yet 'spiritual' flesh." Drawing on biblical sources and art to fashion a father immemorially authoritative, yet also alluring and beloved, the film casts him as a seductive object of desire not only for the numerous "sons" he encounters and spellbinds but also, presumably, for members of the audience seeking the consum-mate *pater noster*. Despite the flimsy military overlay of the film, not violence but physically demonstrated tenderness and mutuality govern father-son relations, enabling Sokurov to make the best of both worlds in a markedly homosocial key that unsurprisingly elicited gay readings by Western critics.

Sokurov's idealized father could hardly contrast more starkly with the weak or flawed paternal figures in Aleksei Popogrebskii and Boris Khlebnikov's *Koktebel'*, as well as *Nochnoi dozor* [*Night Watch* 2004] and *Dnevnoi dozor* [*Day Watch* 2006]—the first two installments of Bekmambetov's frenetically-paced *Dozor* trilogy. Adhering to the post-Soviet habit of consigning women to the periphery, *Koktebel'* traces a boy's coming of age, interweaving that zigzag trajectory with the gradual revelation of his inept, widowed father's alcoholism and haplessness in a bleak world requiring survival skills that he sorely lacks. As in the *Bildungsroman*, countless fairy tales, and Zviagintsev's *Vozvrashchenie*, the journey tropes the inner evolution to a more mature self. Temporizing and backsliding, the father nonetheless constitutes the single weightiest formative influence on the son's development. In the film's final scenes, his lessons about flight and birds—symbols of aspiration and transcendence—bear fruit in the cruel "mastery" over an aggressive seagull by the son who independently "finds his way" to their envisioned destination, and confronts the open waters of the unknown as an individual in his own right. Though indispensable to his son's earlier psychological growth, at film's end the father seems superfluous, his status and the film's inconsistencies symptomatizing what Hashamova justly perceives as "cracks in the desire for the return of the omnipotent father." While the directors do not explicitly conceive of maturation as generational usurpation, the father's inadequacies manifestly accelerate the son's access to adulthood.

The Freudian/Lacanian elements latent in *Koktebel'* flaunt themselves in Bekmambetov's films, which, as Vlad Strukov argues in chapter 8, transparently revisit the Oedipal myth/complex in identity formation. Dualism (Night/Day; Good/Evil, human/vampire, etc.) structures not only the films' narratives, but also the social, psychological, and moral makeup of the characters, and none more so than Anton and his son, Egor. "Fated" to be the Great One who, according to prophecy, will determine the future—and here Bekmambetov borrows lavishly from ancient Greek scenarios of potentially superannuated fathers who commit filicide to preempt usurpation or annihilation by their ambitious offspring—Egor becomes the battleground for three problematic paternal figures: his biological sire (Anton), unaware of his status; the imagined illegitimate father falsely identified by the sorceress urging

Egor's abortion, which Anton sanctions in a reversal of Oedipal non-recognition; and Zavulon, the surrogate ideological father, driven by his compulsion to control the future. Emphasizing the primacy of legitimate cultural lineage, Bekmambetov resurrects the Greek myths of sanguinary generational succession along Freudian and Lacanian lines to expose, in Strukov's phrase, "filicide and cannibalism/vampirism as a divine patriarchal prerogative." As Egor's "blood father" and Geser's spiritual son, Anton overcomes his initial symbolic impotence so as to restore social order through the balance advocated by Geser—a balance that ultimately acknowledges generational continuity as the bedrock of cultural vitality and holds out the promise of national unity. Communal validation ultimately supersedes vampiric self-perpetuation. A figure of disciplined authority endowed with self-awareness and a potentiating vision, the films suggest, can prevail over the chaos that constituted Russia's lawless, self-vitiating 1990s. It requires little imagination to read Bekmambetov's trilogy as a paean to Putin's restoration of "order" in the ensuing decade—"order" unfailingly touted as the single supreme achievement of Putin's presidency, whatever the casualties of its institution.

An analogous corpse-strewn transition from the volatility of a nation-enfeebling Imaginary to the Symbolic/Law of the Father (1989–2000) maps Aleksei Sidorov's vastly popular TV mini-series *Brigada* (2002–2004), propelled, Brian Baer astutely notes in his essay, by the long-sustained but eventually resolved tension between the horizontal bonds of brotherhood and the vertical ties of patriarchal authority (chapter 9). That tension is finally defused by Sasha Belov, ethical hoodlum and disillusioned veteran of the Afghan war. Throughout the series he battles enemies and treacherous allies in a world of corruption, greed, and cynicism, in the process metamorphosing from criminal to elected member of the State Duma. Belov's particular combination of rule and paternity illustrates the possibility of strong leadership without tyranny, of a father loyal to his brothers—a message that begs to be parsed, in Baer's words, "as an apologia for the centralization of powers and the 'verticalization of government' carried out by Vladimir Putin."

More than two centuries ago Alexander Pope's *Essay on Criticism* wittily captured the psychology of "natural succession" over time: "We think our fathers fools, so wise we grow; / Our wiser sons, no doubt, will think us so" (ll. 438–39). Pushkin likewise embraced an organic view of the life cycle, which he regularly compared to the seasons, as did Tolstoi in such meditations on temporality as *Voina i mir* [*War and Peace* 1869], particularly in the moving conclusion preceding the essay on history. Soviet cinema, however, like the Soviet regime, attributed extraordinary discursive and political authority to age and to sundry symbolic fathers, and though the post-Soviet period has replaced its series of superannuated leaders with younger, more vigorous presidents, has disempowered pensioners and disenfranchised the ubiquitous *babushka* as the fabled, unofficial arbiter of proper conduct, numerous Soviet traditions continue to hold sway, particularly in the sphere of cultural discourse. Whether the newly elected President Medvedev, Prime Minister Putin's ideological son and political "creation," will bend to the paternal will or elaborate an independent agenda has already bred considerable speculation.[38] To what extent the orchestrated transfer of official power will leave traces in Russian cinema's articulation of father-son relations remains to be seen—on screen.

NOTES

1. *Encyclopedia of the Russian Soul* is also the title of a prose collection by Erofeev published by ZebraE in Moscow in 2002.

2. Several of Erofeev's publications ruminate on the nature of masculinity and filial relations. See, especially, his *Muzhchiny* [*Men* (Moscow: Dom "Podkova," 1998)] and *Khoroshii Stalin* [*The Good Stalin* (Moscow: ZebraI, 2004)]. The latter, which attempts to assess the significance of Erofeev's "good" Stalinist father in his life, opens with the sentence, "V kontse kontsov ia ubil svoego ottsa" ["Ultimately I killed my father," 7].

3. On domestic violence in Russia and efforts by activists, institutions, and organizations to combat its many manifestations, see the recent study by Janet Elise Johnson, *Gender Violence in Russia* (Bloomington: Indiana University Press, 2009).

4. As the host of the show *Apokryf* on the TV channel "Kul'tura," Erofeev regularly invites representatives of contemporary culture to debate key questions that often lead to revelatory polemics.

5. It is impossible to translate the neologism adequately into standard English, for the term (in the context of the article) has the sense of "accepting the father" or "the father," but with both metaphysical and Freudian overtones.

6. According to John Freedman, Russian theater, currently experiencing an exciting renaissance, is also tackling "such relevant topics as the generation gap, the increase in violence in Russian society, alienation" ("New Voices in a Shifting Age: Recent Russian Drama and Theater," *Kennan Institute Meeting Report* 26, no. 6 [2009]: n.p.).

7. "Bunt, nenavist', ottse-i synoubiistvo, sirotstvo i skital'chestvo—izvechnye arkhetipy chelovecheskoi istorii."

8. In a study based on interviews, Robert Meister posits a typology of paternity consisting of six categories: "distant, silent," "seductive," "tyrannical, demanding," "idealized," "macho, competitive," and "eccentric, bizarre." He arrives at the disputable conclusion that "children who idealize their fathers are most likely to achieve stable, unharmed lives, even if the fathers are unworthy of idealization by objective standards" (*Fathers* [New York: R. Marek, 1981], 14).

9. Kronos, also known as Cronus, often merges with Chronos, the implacable, sickle-carrying god of time—a merger that suggests the inevitable succession of generations, frequently resisted by the superannuated paternal authoritarian.

10. The socioeconomic and political consequences of paternity's questionable status led to the invention of the chastity belt in the nineteenth century, whereby a husband would literally "lock up" his wife's sexual organs to forestall the danger of offspring fathered by other men (while men's "hydraulic equipment" enjoyed "free circulation").

11. William Shakespeare, *The Merchant of Venice* (II.2.73). On the dilemma of illegitimacy and paternal indeterminacy, see Margaret Bożenna Goscilo, *The Bastard Hero in the Novel* (New York: Garland, 1990), especially 3–52.

12. This is not the only case of serving cooked children as meals to their parents in ancient Greek culture, for that grisly strategy also is found in Aeschylus's *Oresteia*, where Atreus prepares a collation for his brother Thyestes comprising the bodies of the latter's two sons. Another myth has Lycaon's sons preparing a dinner of their brother Nyctimus's body for Zeus in Arcadia (Graves 2, 25).

13. This episode, which has elicited controversies in biblical interpretations, also has generated a sizable body of art, primarily paintings and sculptures by Donatello, Raphael, Caravaggio, Rembrandt, Tiepolo, and Chagall. Philosophers have attempted to rationalize the paradox of paternal filicide yet righteous father, most notably Søren Kierkegaard in *Fear and Trembling*.

14. William Shakespeare, *A Midsummer Night's Dream* (I.1.50).

15. Seneca modeled his *Oedipus* on this, the first of Sophocles' two Oedipus tragedies.

16. In *The Future of an Illusion* Freud observes, "It is in keeping with the course of human development that external coercion gradually becomes internalized; for a special internal agency, man's super-ego, takes it over and includes it among its commandments" (11).

17. Originally (1897) identifying the family romance as symptomatic of pathology, by 1909 Freud posited this transference fantasy as a universal wish fulfillment.

18. Mainstream Russian narratives that dramatize the traumas and ramifications of male filiation along Oedipal lines or those of the family romance—and in several instances feature illegitimate sons—include Aleksandr Pushkin's *Kapitanskaia dochka* [*The Captain's Daughter* 1836]; Nikolai Gogol''s *Taras Bul'ba* [1835]; Sergei Aksakov's *Semeinaia khronika* [*The Family Chronicle* 1856]; Ivan Turgenev's "Pervaia liubov'" ["First Love" 1860], *Ottsy i deti* [*Fathers and Sons* 1862], and *Nov'* [*Virgin Soil* 1877]; Lev Tolstoy's "Dva gusara" ["Two Hussars" 1856] and *Voina i mir* [*War and Peace* 1869]; Fyodor Dostoevsky's *Podrostok* [*The Adolescent* 1875], *Besy* [*The Possessed/Demons* 1877], and *Brat'ia Karamazovy* [*The Brothers Karamazov* 1880]; Saltykov-Shchedrin's

Gospoda Golovley [*The Golovlevs* 1972–76]; Andrei Belyi's *Peterburg* [*Petersburg* 1922]; Iurii Olesha's *Zavist'* [*Envy* 1927]; Andrei Bitov's *Pushkinskii Dom* [*Pushkin House* 1978]; and Viktor Erofeev's "Popugaichik" ["The Parakeet" 1988].

19. For instance, Dmitrii Furmanov's *Chapaev* (1923), Aleksandr Fadeev's *Razgrom* [*The Rout* 1927] and *Molodaia Gvardiia* [*Young Guard* 1946], Nikolai Ostrovskii's *Kak zakalialas' stal'* [*How the Steel Was Tempered* 1934], and Boris Polevoi's *Story of a Real Man* [*Povest' o nastoiashchem cheloveke* 1946]. For their cinematic adaptations, see Mikhail Utevskii, ed., *Domashniaia sinemateka: Otechestvennoe kino, 1918–1996* (Moscow: Dubl'-D, 1996).

20. Although socialist realism as the official artistic method of Soviet literature was mandated only in 1934, earlier works were recognized as representative *avant la lettre,* including the prototype, Maksim Gor'kii's *Mat'* [*Mother* 1906]. For a revisionist, Lacanian treatment of the socialist realist hero, see Lilya Kaganovsky, *How the Soviet Man Was Unmade: Cultural Fantasy and Male Subjectivity under Stalin* (Pittsburgh: Pittsburgh University Press, 2008).

21. Curiously, recent scholarship has posited resentment at the father's abandonment of the family for another woman as the motivation for Pavlik Morozov's betrayal of his biological father. For a detailed account of the Morozov phenomenon, see Yuri Druzhnikov, *Informer 001: The Myth of Pavlik Morozov* (New Brunswick, N.J.: Transaction, 1997).

22. The concept of the ruler as divinely ordained was widespread in Europe, as attested by the expression "the divine right of kings," which reflected the religious and political doctrine of political absolutism, whereby the monarch's legitimacy and authority derived from God's will.

23. Il'ia Repin's painting (1885), which captures the irascible Ivan holding his blood-spattered, dead son in his arms, has helped to wrest this act of filicide from oblivion.

24. An ironic summary of the filicidal strain in Russian culture and its consequences appears in a poem by Dmitrii Prigov:

> Petor Pervyi zlodei
> Svoego synochechka
> Posredi Rossii Vsei
> Muchil chto est' mochi sam
> Tot Terpel, terpel, terpel
> I v kraiu berezevom
> Cherez dvesti strashnykh let
> Pavlikom Morozovym
> Otmstil.

25. For various models of rule and kinship as related to the father-son relationship, see Borneman 1–31.

26. Even a cursory glance at Aleksandr Gerasimov's *Lenin at the Rostrum* (1929) and *Stalin's Report* (1944), Isaak Brodskii's *Lenin in Smol'nyi* (1930), Fedor Reshetnikov's *Generalissimo I.V. Stalin* (1948) and *The Great Oath* (1949), and Viktor Koretskii's *The Great Stalin Is the Banner of the Friendship of Soviet Peoples* (1950) suffices to corroborate the metaphysical nature of this iconography, later parodied by Komar and Melamid in *Lenin Proclaims the Victory of the Revolution* (1981–82) and similar works. For additional images in this vein and for analyses of them, see http://images

.library.pitt.edu/s/stalinka (accessed 26 June 2009); Matthew Cullerne Bown, *Socialist Realist Painting* (New Haven, Conn.: Yale University Press, 1998).

27. The durability of Stalin's constructed image is extraordinary: According to a recent poll, 29 percent of Russian respondents in December 2004 credited him with the Soviet Union's survival and victory in World War II, though his tactical misjudgments and opposition to the fighting retreat cost thousands of Soviet lives. Similarly, 21 percent of those polled deemed Stalin a "wise leader" who built a "mighty, flourishing" country (Allen).

28. Polls conducted by the Public Opinion Foundation revealed concern by 46 percent of those polled about Putin's future. See "Russian press review," *International Herald Tribune* (14 August 2007), http://www.iht.com/articles/2008/08/14/europe/14russiapress-review.php accessed (14 August 2007). And there can be no doubt that the March 2008 election of the unremarkable Dmitrii Medvedev as Russian president constituted support of Putin as Medvedev's Frankenstein and future prime minister—the "power behind the throne."

29. Also central in American literature, such constellations served as the theoretical underpinnings for Harold Bloom's influential study *The Anxiety of Influence* (1973).

30. For more on these films, see James Leggott.

31. In his astute discussion of the two leaders' public images, Schoeberlein cites examples from children's informal discourse and adults' amateur poems expressing affection for "Grandfather Lenin" and exalting Stalin the Father, respectively: "'He who is the creator of all that is wonderful, / The masterful architect, our friend and father / Comrade Stalin. We are Stalin's children" (205). According to Sheila Fitzpatrick, pilots addressed Stalin as "father" (72).

32. During perestroika, which witnessed various revelations about formerly suppressed aspects of Soviet history, writers likewise insisted on the distinction between Stalin's murderous methods and Lenin's elevated principles—a critical stance undermined by subsequent examinations of Lenin's policies and practices. See Helena Goscilo, "Introduction: A Nation in Search of Its Authors," in *Glasnost: An Anthology of Literature under Gorbachev*, ed. Helena Goscilo and Byron Lindsey, xvii–xxi (Ann Arbor, Mich.: Ardis, 1990).

33. Caring males, in fact, usurped the traditional maternal function of women, whom the Thaw portrayed as flawed or more invested in romance than motherhood.

34. A twinning of self-elimination and Stalin has an empirical basis, given the wealth of suicides (motivated by disillusionment or simply the decision to preempt execution by Stalin's order) among those "close" to him, including his second wife and the son he repudiated, and such "intimates" as the Politburo member Grigorii Ordzhonikidze.

35. See Susan Larsen, "Melodramatic Masculinity, National Identity, and the Stalinist Past in Postsoviet Cinema" in *Russian Culture of the 1990s*, ed. Helena Goscilo, special issue of *Studies in 20th Century Literature* 24, no. 1 (winter 2000): 85–120.

36. For a comprehensive list of Soviet and post-Soviet war films, see Youngblood, 241–53; for a more selective overview, see Antropov, Shkliaruk, and Medvedev 2005.

37. Putin reportedly declared the Russian film industry "reborn" after seeing this Russian/Ukrainian/Finnish collaboration subsidized by the ministry of culture (Holson and Myers).

38. For instance, the journalist Andrei Zolotov noted the "perhaps too active" role of the outgoing president in Medvedev's inauguration, wondering whether the incoming president will be "a self-sufficient head of state, or a cover-up for continued Putin's [sic] rule." The record seven vice premiers recently proposed by Putin as prime minister are "avowed Putin loyalists" and members of his old team at the Kremlin, suggesting that Putin desires to prolong the profile of his administration under the new president, according to Dmitry Babich.

REFERENCES

Allen, Nick. "Why Russia is putting Stalin back on to his pedestal." *The Telegraph*, 21 April 2005. Available at http://www.telegraph.co.uk/news/main.jhtml?xml=/news/2005/04/20/wsta120.xml (accessed 16 June 2006).

Antropov, Vladimir, Aleksandr Shkliaruk, and Armen Medvedev. *Sto fil'mov o voine*. Moscow: Kontakt-Kul'tura, 2005.

Babich, Dmitry. "Putin's New Ark: Russia Now Has a Record Number of Vice Premiers." *Russia Profile*, 12 May 2008. Available at http://www/russiaprofile.org/page/php?pageid=Politics&articleid=al (accessed 14 May 2008).

Borneman, John, ed. *Death of the Father: An Anthropology of the End in Political Authority*. New York: Berghahn, 2004.

Caldwell, Richard. *The Origin of the Gods: A Psychoanalytical Study of Greek Theogonic Myth*. New York: Oxford University Press, 1989.

Downing, Christine. "Sigmund Freud and the Greek Mythological Tradition." *Journal of the American Academy of Religion* 43, no. 1 (March 1975): 3–14.

Erofeev, Viktor [host]. "Russkie ottsy." *Entsiklopediia russkoi dushi*. Moscow: Radio Svoboda, 15 September 2007.

Fitzpatrick, Sheila. *Everyday Stalinism*. New York: Oxford University Press, 1999.

Freud, Sigmund. *Civilization and Its Discontents*. Translated and edited by James Strachey. New York: W. W. Norton, 1961.

———. "Dostoevsky and Parricide." In *Character and Culture*, ed. Philip Rahv, 274–93. New York: Collier Books, 1963.

———. "Family Romances." *Collected Papers*. Edited by James Strachey. Vol. 5. London: Hogarth, 1950 [1909], 74–78.

———. *The Future of an Illusion*. Translated and edited by James Strachey. New York. W. W. Norton, 1961.

———. "Reflections upon War and Death." In *Character and Culture*, ed. Philip Rahv, 107–34. New York: Collier Books, 1963.

"From disorder to order: The Olympic mythical archetype." *International Association of Sports Law*, 1999. Available at http://iasl.org/modules.php?name=News&file=article&sid=36 (accessed 16 June 2007).

Graves, Robert. *The Greek Myths*. 2 vols. Harmondsworth, Middlesex: Penguin Books, 1955/1969.

Hashamova, Yana. *Pride and Panic: Russian Imagination of the West in Post-Soviet Film*. Bristol, U.K.: Intellect Books, 2007.

Hesiod. *Theogony. Works and Days. Testimonia*. Translated and edited by Glenn W. Most. Cambridge, Mass.: Harvard University Press, 2006.

Holson, Laura M., and Steven Lee Myers. "The Russians Are Filming! The Russians Are Filming!" *New York Times*, 16 June 2006. Available at http://www.nytimes .com/2006/7/16/business/your money/16russia.html (accessed 17 July 2006).

Jung, Carl Gustav. "The Significance of the Father in the Destiny of the Individual." In C. G. Jung, *The Collected Works of C.G. Jung*, trans. R. F. C. Hull, 4:301–23. New York: Pantheon Books, 1961.

Jung, C. G. *Memories, Dreams, Reflections*. Recorded and edited by Aniela Jaffé. Translated by Richard and Clara Winston. New York: Vintage Books, 1961/1963.

Kuznetsov, Pavel. "Ottsy i synov'ia." *Seans* 21/22 (2005): 206–17.

Lacan, Jacques. *Écrits: A Selection*. Translated by Alan Sheridan. New York: W. W. Norton, 1977.

Leggott, James. "Like Father? Failing Parents and Angelic Children in Contemporary British Social Realist Cinema." In *The Trouble with Men: Masculinities in European and Hollywood Cinema*, ed. Phil Powrie, Ann Davies, and Bruce Babington, 163–76. London: Wallflower Press, 2004.

Manguel, Alberto. *FATHERS & SONS: An anthology*. San Francisco: Chronicle Books, 1998.

Meister, Robert. *Fathers*. New York: R. Marek, 1981.

Plato. *Laws*. Translated by R. G. Bury. 2 vols. Vol 2. Cambridge, Mass.: Harvard University Press, 1984.

———. *The Republic*. Translated by B. Jowett. New York: Vintage Books, 1900.

Schoeberlein, John S. "Doubtful Dead Fathers and Musical Corpses: What to Do with the Dead Stalin, Lenin, and Tsar Nicholas?" In *Death of the Father: An Anthology of the End in Political Authority*, ed. John Borneman, 201–19. New York: Berghahn Books, 2004.

Sekatskii, Aleksandr. "Ottsepriimstvo." *Seans* 21/22 (2005): 197–205.

Youngblood, Denise J. *Russian War Films: On the Cinema Front, 1914–2005.* Lawrence: University Press of Kansas, 2007.

Zhu, Rui. "What if the Father Commits a Crime?" *Journal of the History of Ideas* 63, no. 1 (January 2002): 1–17.

Zolotov, Andrei, Jr. "Inauguration Augurs: The Inauguration Ceremony Took Place in a Tsarist Atmosphere." *Russia Profile*, 8 May 2008. Available at http://www.russia profile.org/page.php?pageid=Politics&articleid=al (accessed 14 May 2008).

PART ONE

Thaw, Stagnation, Perestroika

ONE

The Myth of the "Great Family" in Marlen Khutsiev's *Lenin's Guard* and Mark Osep'ian's *Three Days of Viktor Chernyshev*

ALEXANDER PROKHOROV

In his recent monograph, *Telling October,* Frederick Corney contends that the institutionalization of official Soviet memory of the Revolution played an essential part in establishing Soviet political mythology (Corney 11). Since communal commemoration of this official historical narrative was one of Stalinist cinema's central functions, the major genres of that cinema became the historical and historico-revolutionary film. At the core of these films was the ritual of paying due respect to the Revolution or the events that, according to the canonical account of not only Russian but also world history, led to the October Revolution as a key episode of world-historical significance. In the course of such screen narratives, the father-leader passed on to his sons the sacred knowledge to be preserved by them, the positive heroes of socialist realism. Spectators were presumed to identify with the filial characters and therefore to participate in commemorating the official story of origins.

Khrushchev-era de-Stalinization, known as the Thaw, revived Soviet utopianism by releasing both repressed recollections of Stalinist-era crimes and the martyrs who had preserved the memories and spirit of the Leninist Revolution. Reacting to decades of Stalinist rhetoric, writers and filmmakers of the Thaw presented these martyrs as the generation of true fathers (not their false Stalinist counterparts), whom characters of the Thaw generation never saw because they either had died during the Great Patriotic War—the official Soviet name for World War II—or disappeared in Stalinist camps. Thaw cinema, according to its makers, restored the ideal values associated with the name of the lost father.

Ideologically these father figures often evoked the image of Lenin either in their name (for instance, Ul'ian in *Ispytatel'nyi srok* [*The Probationary Period*, Gerasimov 1960]) or in their biographical experience (such as the fateful encounter of the narrator's father with Lenin in *Kommunist* [*Communist*, Raizman 1957]).

Lack of the father and the quest for the ideal associated with his name are a recurring motif in Thaw films. Fathers are absent usually because they perished during the Great Patriotic War, and their heroic deaths in combat partially explain their sons' troubled childhood, criminal behavior, and resultant prison experience (as in *Nochnoi patrul'* [*Night Patrol*, Sukhobokov 1957] or *Delo pestrykh* [*The Case of Many Colors*, Dostal' 1958]). Unable to address directly the theme of Stalinist camps, where their own fathers had disappeared, many Thaw cinema filmmakers and scriptwriters invoked it indirectly by connecting the prison, crime, or war themes with the theme of fatherlessness.[1] Few pictures made the sons' actual imprisonment the result of their crimes. For example, in *Delo Ruminatseva* [*Rumianstev's Case*, Kheifits 1955], the fatherless protagonist ends up in jail because he is set up by his criminal boss (the false father), and the investigator (another false father) is a bureaucrat and is indifferent. To my knowledge, the only picture that dared to link directly the imprisonment of the father figure with Stalinist policies, namely, Stalin's imprisonment of Soviet POWs, was Grigorii Chukhrai's *Chistoe nebo* [*Clear Sky* 1961]. Marlen Khutsiev and Feliks Mironer, whose fathers died in the Stalinist purges, avoided a frontal attack on Stalin and his crimes, and preferred instead to focus on the new generation: characters orphaned by the Great Patriotic War, now restoring the memory and values of their late fathers. Perhaps by refusing to deal with the crime at the heart of the nation's historical and personal trauma Khutsiev was able to preserve the utopian *élan* of his picture, essential for establishing the continuity between the generation of fathers and the generation of sons. Though the father died during the war, he saved the state created by Lenin, and now the sons will complete Lenin's project by finishing the construction of the communist utopia.

By commemorating the heroic paternal past, the sons ensure the continuity of the Great Family myth in post-Stalinist society. In her discussion of the Soviet novel, Katerina Clark contends that the myth of the Great Family constitutes the fundamental kinship metaphor of Stalinist culture.[2] This family not only includes the paternal ideological mentor and the son/positive hero, but it also provides the main ideological community of the socialist-realist masterplot (Clark 255–60). I contend that commemorating the father in Khutsiev's *Zastava Il'icha*[3] [*Il'ich's Guard* 1962],[4] one of the political manifestoes of the generation of the sixties, is central for reviving Soviet political mythology during the Thaw, and above all the myth of the Great Family. My claim rests on the conviction that this mythology weakened during late Stalinism, whereas Thaw filmmakers reenergized the myth of the Great Family by striving to commemorate accurately the stories of the Revolution and the Great Patriotic War. Whereas under Stalin the great leader was proclaimed the sole heir of Lenin who had saved the Revolution from numerous traitors, Thaw cultural producers portrayed Lenin's Revolution as betrayed by Stalin, who eliminated many Leninist fathers, and whose sons would complete their work on the revolutionary utopia.[5]

During the late Stalinist period, the received truth about the Great Patriotic War featured the central role of Stalin's genius in the victory over the Nazis. In other words, the Great Patriotic War was central to the epic cult of the Great Father. The country celebrated not Victory Day but Stalin's birthday.[6] Thaw filmmakers, however, reimagined the Great Patriotic War as the central event en route to communism, in which the key role belonged to the idealized image of their own fathers and the sons' commemoration of them. Thus the veneration of Stalin ceded to the veneration of the spirit of the warrior-fathers who had perished. It is no accident that, during the Thaw, Victory Day became the key Soviet holiday, an essential ritual in the "rehabilitation" of fighting fathers. Khutsiev made Victory Day a symbolic conclusion in his late-Thaw picture *Iiul'skii dozhd'* [*July Rain* 1966)] and borrowed the victorious days of May 1945 as a time frame for his last Thaw film, *Byl mesiats mai* [*It Was the Month of May* 1970].

In contrast, Mark Osep'ian in his directorial debut, *Tri dnia Viktora Chernysheva* [*Three Days of Viktor Chernyshev* 1968], showed the protagonist's inability to commemorate the sacred past, incarnated above all in the father figure. That incapacity is symptomatic of the crisis in Soviet culture and, above all, in Thaw cultural values. My discussion focuses on the two young protagonists' strategies—for commemorating the father in *Il'ich's Guard*[7] and for dealing with the trauma of amnesia in the *Three Days of Viktor Chernyshev.*[8]

Khutsiev starts his picture with the return of the protagonist, Sergei (Valentin Popov), to Moscow after his stint in the army. The opening evokes the plot of many early postwar films about the generation of fathers returning from the war, with *Vozvrashchenie Vasiliia Bortnikova* [*The Return of Vasilii Bortnikov,* Pudovkin 1953] the most memorable instance during that era. In *Il'ich's Guard,* the son replicates his father's steps in order to continue his interrupted life's path.

From the very beginning of *Il'ich's Guard* the son's individual identity dissolves in communal identities. He becomes a part of the modern urban community. He rejoins his circle of friends, the community of his apartment building's courtyard, his girlfriend's social acquaintances (at the *vecherinka* [party]), and the poetry community at a Polytechnic Museum concert. The concert epitomizes the power of communal identity as the creative force in the film. To naturalize the communal experience of creativity, the filmmaker represents the poetry reading in the documentary style of "direct cinema" (Mikhalkovich 132–33). The observational camera of the director of photography, Margarita Pilikhina, dissolves the line between the staged event and life caught unawares as she captures the outpouring of emotions during the poetry reading and the discussion that follows.

Imitating "direct cinema" stylistics, the director and his camerawoman succeeded in creating the effect of a non-staged event. The action unfolds in front of the camera and looks unpredictable, spontaneous, following its own natural flow. Khutsiev reinforces the documentary effect of the scene by mixing his characters with bona fide celebrity figures who "play" themselves: Bella Akhmadulina, Evgenii Evtushenko, Bulat Okudzhava, Robert Rozhdestvenskii, Boris Slutskii, and Mikhail Svetlov, whose role in the diegesis is that of contemporaries of the two main characters, Sergei and Ania. Thus the story of Khutsiev's protagonists appears to cross the border of the fictional world and spill into the daily life of 1960s Moscow. This illusion is so strong that since the second release of the film in 1988 the scene at the Polytechnic Museum has often appeared in television programs as documentary footage of Moscow's cultural life of the era.[9]

Paying homage to the importance of communal identity, Khutsiev carefully negotiates the value of the individual as part of that identity.

In fact, the film's culmination—Sergei's conversation with his father's ghost—deals with the dialectics of the individual and the communal. After the party at his friend's apartment, Sergei finds himself in the chronotope of the Great Patriotic War—in his father's dugout, where the father and his unit rest before the morning attack, during which they will be killed. Notably the father is not just an individual, but is also part of his military unit (Figure 1.1).

A military uniform de-individualizes his body, making him a representative of his generation, an allegory of martyrdom, an incarnation of fatherhood. Whereas the communal identity dominates the father's individual identity, his son's identity is a compromise between the two. We see Sergei, unlike his father, operating in multiple social roles. Though he venerates his father's memory and martyrdom, he is more complex and multifaceted than his father, for the tunnel-vision teleology of the Stalinist era has been replaced by different, and more differentiated, values. That transformation explains why the father cannot offer Sergei sage counsel when he compares their ages: Sergei and his generation represent a complex compromise of communal and individual identities, beyond the scope of what the father ever knew and experienced.

The scene of the son's exchange with his father's ghost caused a major controversy in Soviet culture of the era. Khrushchev was outraged by the scene, because the protagonist asks his father's ghost how to live and the father refuses to give advice, having died at the age of twenty-one; his son, already twenty-three at the time of their conversation, presumably knows more about life than his father. Khrushchev interpreted this scene as an attack on official patriarchy, as the sons' rebellion against the fathers. During a March 1963 exchange with the intelligentsia, the Soviet leader devoted considerable time to castigating the film for downplaying the role of fathers as sons' ideological mentors:

> The meeting between the hero of the film and the ghost of his father killed in the war raises serious ideological objections. When the son asks how he should live, the ghost in turn asks how old he is. And when the son answers, "Twenty-three," the father says, "And I'm twenty-one," and disappears. You really want us to believe that this could be true? No one would believe it! . . . Can anyone believe that a father wouldn't answer his son's question and wouldn't help him by advising him to find the right path in life?

There is more to this than meets the eye. It has a particular meaning. The idea is to impress upon children that their fathers cannot be their teachers in life, and there is no point in turning to them for advice. The film-makers think that young people ought to decide for themselves how to live, without asking their elders for counsel and help.[10]

In my view, however, the logic of the film implies that the sons only continue the project of their fathers, interrupted by the fathers' untimely deaths in the war—a not so subtle euphemism for the fathers' fate under Stalin. In fact, I contend that the protagonist's conversation with his father's ghost incorporates the communal experience of the fathers' generation into the collective memory of the sons, giving a sense of dynamism to the Thaw-era version of the Great Family myth revitalized in the process of de-Stalinization.

Moreover, when Sergei's father refuses to give his son guidelines for his future life, he implies the impossibility of simply replicating the experience of the fathers and the necessity of mapping out one's own life journey while preserving via personal doubts and choices the freshness of the socialist project. Sergei and his friends reinvent the communist dream of Lenin's guards and warrior-fathers within the framework of the new values, reformulating the myth of the Great Family more flexibly: it embraces the sincerity, lyricism, intimacy, and romance of the post-Stalin years. In this respect, the communal reciting/listening of lyrical poetry or the performance of Bulat Okudzhava's song provides a successful visual and aural representation of the Thaw era's Great Soviet Family. Perhaps this is why Russian collective memory preserved the segment of the poetry reading as one of the iconic images of the Thaw.

The Cult of Personality, the official name retrospectively given by the Communist Party to the crimes of the Stalinist regime, effectively summarizes how Khutsiev represents Stalinism—as an aberration of communal utopian identity. The filmmaker offers a new paradigm of communal and individual identity: communal events such as the poetry reading and the parade enable Sergei to further his relations with Ania, his romantic interest. In stark contrast to the protagonist's individuality, which harmonizes with collective identities, are the scenes evoking the Stalinist past: the attempt by a colleague to recruit Sergei's friend, Nikolai, as a secret police informer, and the conversation between the protagonist and his girlfriend's Stalinist father. In both scenes the conversations take place in secluded locations. The negative characters try to corrupt the protagonist and his friend while they are isolated from their communities. The logic of the film links Stalinism with isolation and with the splintering of the individual from the communal body of the modern city and the collective of young Soviets. When Nikolai rejects the offer to become a stool pigeon, he escapes into the communal body of modern Moscow. After his conversation with the Stalinist false-father figure, he replenishes his spiritual forces by joining the community of participants in the poetry evening.

Khutsiev juxtaposes what he sees as the genuine communist sense of the collective to the Stalinist perversion of communal identity by emphasizing unmediated human contact within Sergei's communities, on the one hand, and, on the other, the alienating power of the media, which permeates the mise-en-scène during Sergei's conversation with Ania's father. The protagonist and his ideological opponent argue in the "false father's" apartment, the walls of which are covered with old, perhaps Stalinist, newspapers. Ania's father, in fact, does not want to hear Sergei's opinion and lectures him about the dangers of self-reflexivity and the need to struggle for a better future. Like Dostoevsky's Grand Inquisitor, he claims to know how to guarantee the people's happiness (through complete control and obedience), while Sergei's martyr-father later chooses to remain silent and let Sergei make his own choices.

The audience hears the false father's words against the background of the TV set, with its uniformed Young Pioneers singing in chorus (Figure 1.2). Television images of officially garbed and infantilized collectivity are juxtaposed to the representations of communal identity in the Polytechnic Museum sequence, where characters are part of the collective but preserve their individual uniqueness (Figure 1.3). Their voices are projected in their full spontaneity and immediacy, not controlled and processed by official media. Notably the audience and the poets are in dialogue in this scene, whereas the conversation between Ania's father and Sergei is primarily a monologue by the former.

Similarly the filmmaker emphasizes the immediacy and intimacy of dialogue in the scene of Sergei's conversation with his "true" father. No sound or media-induced background noise interferes as two individuals speak in a genuine, spiritually oriented dialogue that suspends the linearity of historical time in favor of the simultaneous co-presence of the past and the present in the utopian union of father and son. The power of the son's commemoration establishes a different kind of utopian time—that of intimacy and what Mikhail Bakhtin would identify as "deep time," which offers timeless, transcendent insight, as opposed to Stalinist teleological progressive time.

In depicting the redefined communal ideal, Khutsiev tries to naturalize narrative time and space, avoiding any narrative strategies that would betray the artifice of the plot. *Il'ich's Guard* narrates one annual cycle in the life of the city. Pilikhina's hidden camera, as if randomly, alights on the scenario's heroes from the city crowd, catching unaware the three ordinary Muscovites: Sergei, Slavka (Stanislav Liubshin), and Nikolai (Nikolai Gubenko).

Finally Khutsiev attempts to enhance the "authenticity" of the three friends by modeling them on his own personal experiences. As the filmmaker noted in 1990:

> All three characters, each in his own way, expressed my own experience, emotional state, and attitude toward life. I had just had a son and was running around with milk bottles, just like Ivan.[11] I dreamt of being like Kol'ka, easy-going, brave, capable of joining any conversation, establishing contact. And, just like Sergei, I have been struggling with the question of the meaning of life.[12]

The filmmaker maintains that the myth of the Great Family is universal and natural for all Soviet society and that the protagonist's act of remembering is equal to the act of remembering by communities—circles of friends, creative communities of poets and their audiences—and eventually intimated by the state itself. The state and the protagonist's contemporary communities share the sacred memories of the revolution and the war, in which the protagonist's father perished. According to the film, during Stalin's era only the carriers of the myth of the Great Family, but not the myth itself, perished. The sons regenerate the myth via the act of commemorating the generation of fathers and that generation's fathers—Lenin's revolutionary guards, referenced in the film's title.

Visually the motif of memory's power to link seamlessly several generations of Soviet society is reinforced by the constant presence within the diegesis of three human figures, at times revolutionary Red Guards, at times Great Patriotic War soldiers, and most of the time the three young comrades, the focal characters of Khutsiev's picture.[13]

The film opens with three revolutionary Red Guards walking through contemporary Moscow: they are the grandfathers of Sergei, Slavka, and Nikolai. After Sergei's imaginary conversation with his father, we see three soldiers in World War II uniforms walking down a contemporary Moscow street: they are the fathers of the main heroes. Finally, at film's end, three guards approach Lenin's Mausoleum, the heart of utopia, where past, present, and future are co-present in the miraculous immortality of the leader of the Revolution. The viewer sees Lenin's literal guards and, enabled by the film's editing, infers the meaning of the communal identity of the three main heroes. One can hardly disagree with Aleksandr Timofeevskii, who noted about Khutsiev's picture, "It is difficult to imagine a more Soviet, more Communist, more Khrushchev-era film than Marlen Khutsiev's picture. He poured young wine into an old wineskin and, moreover, unquestionably did so with talent and sincerity."[14] Khutsiev creates an ideal memory vehicle, in which the Great and nuclear family stories collapse into a highly personal quasi-documentary about a revived Soviet utopia.

In contrast, the creators of *Three Days of Viktor Chernyshev* do not view memories of the official and of the small family as one. The film's scriptwriter, Evgenii Grigor'ev,[15] a student of Khutsiev, offers a world in which official memory of the Great Family differs from the vernacular memory of the nuclear family.[16] The protagonist, Viktor (Gennadii Korol'kov), remembers neither his nuclear family's story nor the official story of the Great Family. The filmmaker presents fragmentation and the gradual forgetting of the official story of origins as Viktor's formative identity experience.

Osep'ian's film rejects the naturalizing chronotope of *Il'ich's Guard* (one year in the life of three friends, alter egos of the filmmaker, in tune with the life of the modern city) in favor of the chronotope of liminality, in which the protagonist loses memories of a personal and historical past, and instead succumbs to anxious uncertainty about his individual and communal identity. The film covers three days (Saturday, Sunday, and Monday morning) between two workweeks, which the protagonist spends mostly on the street corner between the factory where he works and his home, which he avoids because he feels alienated from his older sister and his mother. Viktor spends his Sunday (in Russian, *voskresen'e; voskresenie* means "resurrection") on the road, between Moscow, where he currently lives, and the village, where he travels to help local peasants harvest potatoes. He feels at home in neither place. Existing essentially in the future, he waits for his eighteenth birthday, when he will be drafted into the army, where he hopes to acquire a stable individual and communal identity.

Despite his longing for a communal identity, which in the Soviet context means an ideological family, Viktor experiences only alienation and solitude. If in *Il'ich's Guard* the moral ideals associated with the absent father are the guiding ideology for the generation of sons, in *Three Days of Viktor Chernyshev* Viktor cannot or does not want to remember the values embodied in the absent paternal figure. Having no knowledge of his biological father and the world of rural Russia that he used to represent, Viktor finds paternal surrogates at work who speak a meaningless official language irrelevant to his life.

In depicting the vernacular recollection of Viktor's small family, Osep'ian follows the narrative logic of village prose, whereby Viktor is the son of a father-migrant who moved from the village to the city, lost his original rural identity, and eventually perished in the war. A central scene in the film is the conversation over dinner between Viktor and his uncle, who comes from his father's native village to visit Viktor and his mother. This sequence ironically echoes Sergei's conversation with his father's ghost in *Il'ich's Guard*. Ideologically the uncle emerges as a quasi-father figure, but Viktor scarcely remembers his blood ties with the uncle and, unlike Sergei, poses no questions about the meaning of life.

Instead, the uncle bombards his nephew with such questions as, "Do you remember?" "Do you remember me? Grandfather?" When Viktor automatically responds in the affirmative, his uncle tells him that he cannot remember his grandfather because he never even saw him. Viktor is not so much embarrassed that he says things without thinking, as he is confused because he does not understand how he is expected to respond in a situation when the ritualistic phrase does not correspond to reality. He presumes that he must remember his relatives because such is the rule of the game, not because he remembers anybody. When he admits to himself that his memories are but empty shells, containing neither emotions evoked by a visceral sense of the past nor stories establishing any historical continuity between him and his ancestors, he feels disoriented and guilty.

The scene culminates in a conversation about Viktor's father. The uncle tells the mother that Mit'ka, Viktor's father, made a big mistake moving to the city, where, according to the uncle, Mit'ka lost his unique identity, especially his particular talent for arts and crafts, and eventually he died. Viktor jokes that if this Mit'ka was so good in arts and crafts, he should have returned to the sticks, not realizing that he is speaking about his late father. The father's name means nothing to the son. When the uncle interrupts, saying that this Mit'ka was actually his father, Viktor's mother is terrified, but Viktor once again feels merely embarrassed, disoriented, and alienated, realizing that his late father is even more remote from him than he had assumed.

When Viktor takes his uncle to the railway station, in a desperate attempt to repair the broken continuity of generations he gives his uncle his wristwatch to pass on to his grandfather. Transferred from one stranger to another, the watch serves as a token of displacement and alienation rather than mending bridges between generations and value systems: Viktor never saw his grandfather and most likely will never see him. The liminal space of the railroad station is the place closest to Viktor's native village, which he will never visit, and he is relieved to return to his urban environment. An indispensable part of his "rootless" cosmopolitan milieu is the speech of foreign, notably German, tourists, who are apparently much closer to Viktor than is his rural, Russian-speaking uncle.

Osep'ian ends the scene at the station with a device rare for sound film but effective: an intertitle that provides information about Viktor's father. Since the son will never visit his father's village and meet his father's relatives, this insertion is compensatory, reestablishing the memory link between father and son for the viewer (Figure 1.4).

Whereas Viktor feels at least fleeting pain at the severed ties with his relatives, his friend Anton (Lev Prygunov) feels nothing but the desire to exploit and manipulate his father when he meets him after many years of separation. Lacking the aura of both a war hero and a victim of Stalin's policies, Anton's father left his mother for another woman and now confesses to his son that he committed a terrible mistake and has always loved only Anton and his mother. This confession belongs to the familiar discourse of Thaw cinema sincerity, the rebuilding of authentic human relations and nuclear families. Anton appears willing to understand, forgive, and embrace his prodigal father, and the two discuss how after his imminent marriage Anton will create a new and strong family and will never repeat his father's mistakes. The scene unfolds in a sun-lit outdoor coffee shop against the background of a bicycle track, a site of youthful energy and renewal. Seated at a table next to Anton and his father, Viktor eavesdrops on what seems to be the reunion of father and son after years of estrangement—precisely the opposite of his own situation, for his ties with his father's kin are irrevocably severed (Figure 1.5).

Yet after his father leaves, Anton approaches Viktor's table and asks him how he liked the performance that Anton staged for him. Viktor and the viewer suddenly realize that the entire conversation had different meanings for the father and the son. While the father continued to regurgitate Thaw-era narratives, Anton simply manufactured the story of his wedding and a new family because he knew that such plans would disarm his father, prompting him to give Anton cash—for a new scooter. Anton notes in conclusion, "I acted so well. I almost started crying myself."

Anton's filial project is revenge: he wants his father to discover his son's deception, feel hurt, and realize that a confession and cash cannot compensate for twenty years of separation. The reunification of the nuclear family by an outburst of sincerity is nothing but a ritual, a manipulative technique practiced not only by Anton but also, he suspects, by his father. Whereas in Khutsiev's film confessional discourse, nuclear family bonds, and commemoration of the father are the very fabric of the revolutionary utopia to be restored, in Osep'ian's film this fabric shreds into a set of devices that can be performed on demand but fails to produce a coherent, meaningful narrative.

Anton is not a scoundrel who refuses to know and remember his guilt-ridden father. Like Viktor, he suffers from the lack of an ideal paternal figure, and while Khutsiev shows the young generation drawing upon such a figure, Osep'ian emphasizes the break between generations. When Viktor asks Anton not to take money from his father, Anton is confused and angry rather than manipulative and cynical, as in the scene with his father. Osep'ian conveys the discrepancy between ideal and actual by contrasting the psychological isolation of the two youths with a "narrative about community" that they overhear in the background: a TV broadcast of the Stalin-era fairy-tale film *Zolotoi kliuchik* [*The Golden Key*, Ptushko 1939], based on Aleksei Tolstoi's class-conscious remake of Carlo Collodi's *Pinocchio*. In Ptushko's film, Buratino (the Soviet Pinocchio) ultimately attains the communist fairy-tale land, significantly with the help of his father, Papa Karlo. Osep'ian projects on the TV screen the famous shot in which the magic flying ship carries Buratino, his father, and his friends to the paradisiacal communist future. Within the diegesis of *Three Days of Viktor Chernyshev,* this image of a vanishing magic ship visually inscribes the dissolution of the dream world of the Soviet utopia and the inspiring memory of the father on which this utopia rested. The foundational ideal of *The Golden Key,* partly recuperated in *Il'ich's Guard,* has vanished, and Anton and Viktor's friendship will neither provide a much-needed continuity nor transform the world.

While vernacular memory exists as the unknown story of Viktor's biological father and his small communal identity, official memory survives as the frustrated socialist realist plot set against a traditional industrial setting. The ideal world of the official Great Family, which at the beginning of the film emerges as the factory collective, appears troubled by institutional amnesia and a failing narrative of collectivism and generational continuity. When Viktor completes his daily quota, he discovers that somebody in management forgot to send the correct blueprints, and the measurements for the parts he was making were changed. The foreman tells him to throw away everything that he made over the course of the day, promising that he will still be paid for the work done, even though he produced nothing of any use during his workday. Clearly the industrial collective does not function productively.

After this introductory snapshot of institutional culture, the focus shifts to a Komsomol meeting, where the potential socialist realist story turns into a scandalous scene. Debated at the emergency meeting is a worker's refusal to help retrain the new engineer, a woman with a college degree but no hands-on knowledge of her profession. Instead of helping her, the worker swears at the incompetent engineer, she in turn slaps him, and he wipes her face with oily rags. The edifying Soviet formula of the proletariat reeducating the intellectual degenerates here into an ugly fight between a man and a woman. Pointing out that the engineer should have learned her trade, the worker denounces the system of tolerating incompetence as abuse of the people.

Again, as in the scene of Viktor's dinner with his uncle, Osp'ian invokes the ideological assumptions of village prose. The worker—played by Vasilii Shukshin, a key figure in village prose traditions—defines the system's mistreatment of the people in terms of the state abusing the patience of Russian peasants: "Nichego, muzhichki vse vyterpiat" ("Don't worry. Russian peasants can put up with anything"). In contrast to the impassioned worker, who raises his voice, the party leader remains calm; he tries to "reeducate the worker" and, on his example, the meeting's attendees. Watching the worker argue with the factory's party and Komsomol leaders, the audience (including Viktor) is silent: this official game of the engineer's reeducation by the spontaneous worker and the latter's by the party leader is simply a boring ritual, nothing to do with the group's lives. They wait patiently until the performance is over, allowing them to go home. Notably this ritualistic performance within the Great Family in no wise differs from the Thaw-inspired performance of sincerity within the nuclear family, as exemplified by Anton and his confessional father.

Rather than ending in a resolution, the conflict between the worker and the engineer indicates that in the diegetic world of the film nobody is going to reeducate anybody. The meeting concludes in a stalemate. As everyone prepares to depart, the party leader suddenly remembers that the local party office has arranged the funeral of a Communist Party veteran who participated in the revolution, and asks the workers to attend the funeral on Sunday. For the first time the collective grows agitated, shouting that the deceased revolutionary was not from their factory and they see no need to attend a stranger's funeral. The party leader's heated response recalls the worker's earlier tirade as he roars that the party veteran spilled his blood for the future of everyone there, yet they all refuse to commemorate the revolutionary soldier at his funeral. Under coercion, without remorse, the group reluctantly agrees to fulfill another meaningless ritual. No one is reformed by the party leader's words or touched by his invocation of the revolution.

Lacking both the Great Family and the small one, Viktor has an alternate ideological community: his buddies, with whom he aimlessly spends days on the street corner before his anticipated draft into the army. This street gang parodies the close-knit circle of the three comrades from Khutsiev's *Il'ich's Guard*. Osep'ian replaces Khutsiev's trope of mobility with that of stasis. Still inspired by a vibrant utopian ideology, Khutsiev's Thaw friends walk, fly, explore, and travel by train, whereas Viktor's buddies stand at the street corner or hang out in dark and dirty streets, as though providing a visual epigraph for the coming political stagnation. Even the title of Osep'ian's film, compared to those of the Thaw, denotes a lack of energy and motion, as illustrated by the titles of several famous Thaw pictures—*Letiat zhuravli* [*Cranes Are Flying*, Kalatozov 1957], *Chelovek idet za solntsem* [*A Man Walks after the Sun*, Kalik 1961], *Ia shagaiu po Moskve* [*I Walk around Moscow*, Daneliia 1964]. Even the three days mentioned in Osep'ian's title are too long for the protagonist: he wastes days waiting for someone—anyone—to give him a sense of direction.

The Russian critic Valeriia Gorelova has noted that the concluding part of Osep'ian's film appears to be a direct parody of Khutsiev's *Il'ich's Guard* (435). For the utopian community of poets-fathers and poets-sons at the Polytechnic Museum concert, Osep'ian substitutes a scandal scene, in which the sons thrash the father figure for a bottle of vodka. While buying vodka, the friends quarrel with an older man who insists that they wait their turn in line. The buddies ambush the old man in a dark street in order to beat him up but, after humiliating him, condescendingly dismiss him. The older man, who, significantly, wears World War II medals, calls them fascists. When he announces that he killed scum like them during the war, the young men beat the veteran to a pulp and end up in a police station. Yet again, Viktor and his friends not only fail to recognize the father figure, but in a profane version of the Oedipal denouement, degrade and almost erase a representative of their fathers' generation.

In the sequence at the police station, which serves as a carnivalized version of the conversation with the father's ghost in *Il'ich's Guard*, Viktor is interrogated by a paternal police officer about his values and the meaning of life. This final conversation about the ideals of fathers and sons reveals the enormous gap that emerged over time since the release of the censored version of Khutsiev's film under the title *Mne dvadtsat' let* [*I Am Twenty* 1964]. Seeking some common ground, the officer asks Viktor what he liked to do as a child, to which Viktor replies that he played in a school production based on the novel *The Young Guard* [*Molodaia gvardiia* 1945]. This canonical socialist realist text by Aleksandr Fadeev about a heroic anti-fascist Komsomol underground during World War II, adapted to the screen by Sergei Gerasimov, was familiar to every Soviet citizen. Relieved and excited, the officer tries to guess which Soviet war hero Viktor played in the production, only to learn that Viktor played not a Soviet but a Romanian soldier, and did so upon instructions. Viktor's response reveals that he barely recollects anything about *The Young Guard,* for the official Great Family and the fathers' values associated with it are as alien to Viktor as the vernacular memories of his nuclear family.

Finally, Osep'ian engages Khutsiev's film in his last narrative title: "It was Monday. The beginning of the workweek." Whereas in *Il'ich's Guard* viewers hear the sound of the clock on the Kremlin's main tower and the voice-over buoyantly pronouncing, "Monday! The first workday of the week!" while the screen shows the Moscow skyline with the Kremlin at its center, Osep'ian's narrative title appears on the screen in total silence against the background of a shabby street with three young men standing purposelessly on the street corner.

Osep'ian's film is a bridge text, a product of late Thaw and a harbinger of stagnation. The filmmaker parodies Khutsiev's picture, calling attention to the crisis of the Great Family mythology as it was redefined during the Thaw in the films of Raizman (*Kommunist* and *Tvoi sovremennik* [*Your Contemporary* 1967]), Saltykov (*Predsedatel'* [*Chairman* 1964]), and, above all, Khutsiev. That predicament manifests itself in the splintering of the family narrative into two stories, that of the official and that of the nuclear family. Most important, Osep'ian's protagonist is unable to perform the acts of commemoration that ensure the continuity of generations and the stability of both the official identity conferred by the state and the individual identity rooted in the nuclear family. Osep'ian's work inaugurates the social problem film that explores the symptoms of the systemic crisis in Soviet ideology during the Brezhnev era. Such films explored characters' inability to rely on the mythic story of the past, in which the father figure, legitimated and sanctioned by the state, remained the master signifier. They expressed the acute need for new meanings, ones that contested the two-dimensional heroicization of the past and were anchored in alternative mnemonic father figures.

NOTES

1. See, for example, *Delo bylo v Pen'kove* [*It Happened in Pen'kovo*, Rostotskii 1957], *Ispravennomu verit'* [*Trust the Reformed Man*, Zhilin 1959], *Drug moi, Kol'ka!* [*My Friend, Kol'ka!* Saltykov and Mitta 1961], *Ver'te mne, liudi* [*Trust Me, People*, Berenshtein, Gurin, and Lukov 1964]. In the case of Ivan Pyr'ev's last film, a 1968

THE MYTH OF THE "GREAT FAMILY" · 45

three-part adaptation of Dostoevsky's *Brothers Karamazov,* the story of fatherless-ness, crime, and imprisonment acquires elements of a quasi-religious parable.

2. "Like Germany and several other countries in this period, the Soviets focused on the primordial attachments of kinship and projected them as the dominant symbol for social allegiance. Soviet society's leaders became 'fathers' (with Stalin as the patri-arch); the national heroes, model 'sons'; the state, a 'family' or 'tribe.' . . . The metaphor also served the needs of the Stalin faction in its 'struggles': it provided formulas for a symbolic legitimation of the actual leadership (the succession of generations in the 'family' stands in for the succession of political leaders and for Stalin's accession to power after Lenin's death in particular), for the way forward (through the evolution of ever greater sons), and for the unquestioning loyalty of citizens (blood is thicker than water)" (Clark 114–15).

3. Khutsiev uses Lenin's patronymic in the title of his picture, thus invoking Lenin as the ideological father of his generation. This generation claimed to embrace the spirit of the Leninist Revolution and to restart the construction of the communist utopia.

4. The film's title is more commonly translated as *Il'ich's Gate.* This transla-tion points to the name of the working-class neighborhood on the eastern outskirts of Moscow. I opted for *Il'ich's Guard* as the translation, however, to emphasize the second meaning of the word *zastava,* which points to the function of the young protagonists in Khutsiev's picture. They serve as the guards and heirs of Leninist revolutionary ideals. In Russian, the title of Khutsiev's film is a poetic interplay of meanings, the name of the proletarian neighborhood, the birthplace of the characters, and the reference to the major characters' mission in life.

5. Thaw culture's reinvention of the myth of the Great Family became part of a bigger project of refurbishing the cultural and political mythology inherited from Stalinism. For further discussion of how Thaw literature and cinema reinstantiated the key tropes of Stalinist culture, see Prokhorov, *Unasledovannyi diskurs: paradigmy stalinskoi kul'tury v literature i kinematografe "ottepeli."*

6. In 1947 Stalin abolished Victory Day as an official state holiday. V Day became a holiday again only in 1965. For further discussion, see Youngblood 87, Tumarkin 104.

7. Both films had difficult release histories. *Il'ich's Guard* was completed in 1962, and after Khrushchev's official criticism, the filmmaker had to rework the film, which received a belated release in 1965 under the title *I Am Twenty.* In the original version and under the original title the picture was re-released only in 1988. The release his-tory of *Il'ich's Guard* is discussed in great detail by Woll, *Real Images: Soviet Cinema and the Thaw* 146–50; Woll, "Being 20, 40 Years Later; Marlen Khutsiev's *Mne dvadt-sat' let* [*I Am Twenty* 1961]"; Zorkaia 386–92; Khlopliankina; and in several articles in the June 1988 issue of *Iskusstvo kino* [*The Art of Cinema*] associated with the second release of the film during perestroika.

8. *Three Days of Viktor Chernyshev* was not banned, and even received the an-nual award of the Central Committee of the Komsomol in 1968. This did not mean, however, that the authorities approved of the film. They merely used a less overt way of suppressing it by releasing it in a very limited number of prints (Gorelova 435). Since the picture was virtually unknown to viewers, the Conflict Commission released the film again, together with other banned films.

9. The film continues to maintain a cult status among Russian intellectuals. Russian historian Andrei Levandovskii, for example, notes that the picture captured

the spiritual atmosphere of the 1960s with iconic precision ("Posledniaia zastava," 249–50).

10. Cited in Woll 147.

11. In the film this character will become Slavka.

12. "Vse tri geroia, kazhdyi po-svoemu, vyrazhali moe togdashnee sostoianie, kharakter, otnoshenie k zhizni. U menia v tu poru kak raz rodilsia syn, i ia tozhe begal s molochnymi butylkami, kak Ivan. Ia mechtal byt' takim zhe, kak Kol'ka, raskovannym, smelym, sposobnym s khodu vmeshat'sia v razgovor, zaviazat' znakomstvo. I ia, podobno Sergeiu, tozhe muchilsia voprosami, kak zhit'" (cited in Khlopliankina 24).

13. Critics (Anninskii 117, Mikhalkovich 118–22) also point out that intertextually Khutiev's characters are linked with the characters of Erich Maria Remarque's *Three Comrades*, a cult novel for the Thaw intelligentsia. Like Remarque's characters, Khutsiev's three comrades value the authenticity of human relations above all social conventions and view their friendship as the core of their communal identity.

14. "Trudno sebe predstavit' bolee sovetskii, bolee kommunisticheskii, bolee khrushchevskii fil'm, chem kartina Marlena Khutsieva. On vlil-taki molodoe kino v starye mekhi, prichem sdelal eto nesomnenno talantlivo i stol' zhe nesomnenno iskrenne" (Timofeevskii 62).

15. Viktor Filimonov discusses Grigor'ev's screenplay for Osep'ian's picture as a part of an entire cycle of screenplays dealing with the evolving role of the Soviet cinematic hero in the 1960s and 1970s.

16. In *Remaking America* John Bodnar distinguishes between official and vernacular memory:

> Official culture relies on "dogmatic formalism" and the restatement of reality in ideal rather than complex or ambiguous terms. . . . Cultural leaders [the creators of official memory—A.P.], usually grounded in institutional and professional structures, envisioned a nation of dutiful and untied citizens which undertook only orderly change. These officials saw the past as a device that could help them attain these goals and never tired of commemoration to restate what they thought the social order and citizen behavior should be. . . . Defenders of [vernacular] cultures are numerous and intent on protecting values and restating views of reality derived from firsthand experience in small-scale communities of a large nation . . . normally vernacular expressions convey what social reality feels like rather than what it should be like. Its very existence threatens the sacred and timeless nature of official expressions. . . . Vernacular memory was derived from the lived or shared experiences of small groups. Unlike official culture which was grounded in the power of larger, long-lasting institutions. (Bodnar, 13–14, 245, 247)

REFERENCES

Bodnar, John. *Remaking America: Public Memory, Commemoration, and Patriotism in the Twentieth Century*. Princeton, N.J.: Princeton University Press, 1992.

Clark, Katerina. *The Soviet Novel: History as Ritual*. 3rd ed. Bloomington: Indiana University Press, 2001.

Corney, Frederick. *Telling October: Memory and the Making of the Bolshevik Revolution*. Ithaca, N.Y.: Cornell University Press, 2004.

Filimonov, Viktor. "Opravdanie dolga, ili o proiskhozhdenii zhanra. (K fenomenologii stsenarnogo tvorchestva Evgeniia Grigor'eva)." *Kinovedcheskie zapiski* 66 (2004): 73–124.

Gorelova, Valeriia. "Tri dnia Viktora Chernysheva." In *Rossiiskii illiuzion*, ed. L. M. Budiak, 435–40. Moscow: Materik, 2004.

Khlopliankina, Tat'iana. *Zastava Il'icha*. Moscow: Kinotsentr, 1990.

Levandovskii, Andrei. "Posledniaia zastava: fil'my Marlena Khutsieva *Zastava Il'icha i Iiul'skii dozhd'* kak istochnik dlia izucheniia ischezaiushchei mental'nosti." In *Istoriia strany. Istoriia kino*, ed. S. S. Sekirinskii, 240–63. Moscow: Znak, 2004.

Mikhalkovich, Valentin. *Izbrannye rossiiskie kinosny*. Moscow: Agraf, 2006.

Prokhorov, Aleksandr. *Unasledovannyi diskurs: paradigmy stalinskoi kul'tury v literature i kinematografe "ottepeli."* St. Petersburg: Akademicheskii proekt, DNK, 2007.

Timofeevskii, Aleksandr. "Poslednie romantiki." *Iskusstvo kino* 5 (1989): 59–66.

Tumarkin, Nina. *The Living and the Dead: The Rise and Fall of the Cult of World War II in Russia*. New York: Basic Books, 1994.

Woll, Josephine. "Being 20, 40 Years Later: Marlen Khutsiev's Mne dvadtsat' let (I Am Twenty, 1961)." *kinoeye* 1, no. 8 (10 December 2001). Available at http://www.kinoeye.org/01/08/woll08.php (accessed 24 February 2007).

———. *Real Images: Soviet Cinema and the Thaw*. London: I. B. Tauris, 2000.

Youngblood, Denise. *Russian War Films. On the Cinema Front, 1914–2005*. Lawrence: University Press of Kansas, 2007.

Zorkaia, Neia. *Istoriia sovetskogo kino*. St. Petersburg: Aleteiia, 2005.

FILMOGRAPHY

Tri dnia Viktora Chernysheva [*Three Days of Viktor Chernyshev*]. Dir. Mark Osepyan. Gorky Film Studios, 1968.

Zastava Il'icha [*Il'ich's Guard*]. Dir. Marlen Khutsiev. Mosfilm, censored version released in 1964 under the title *Mne dvadsat' let* [*I Am Twenty*]. Director's cut under the original title released in 1988.

Figure 1.1. The Thaw-era son seeks advice from his father's ghost.

Figure 1.2. The Young Pioneers' chorus.

Figure 1.3. Camaraderie of individuals at the Polytechnic Museum.

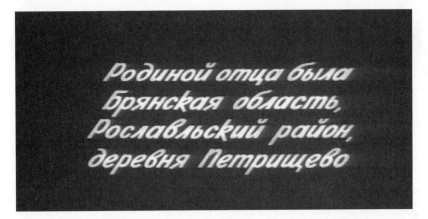

Figure 1.4. Intertitle documenting the fate of Viktor's father, one of countless victims in Stalin's camps.

Figure 1.5. Viktor eavesdrops on Anton and his father.

TWO

Mending the Rupture:
The War Trope and the Return of the
Imperial Father in 1970s Cinema

ELENA PROKHOROVA

In Vladimir Motyl''s film *Beloe solntse pustyni* [*White Sun of the Desert* 1969], the Red Army soldier Sukhov, about to be killed by the gang of the warlord Abdullah, is saved at the last moment by the lone warrior Said. "What are you doing here?" Sukhov asks him. "Streliali [There was shooting]," answers Said. This exchange, which by now has become part of Russian folklore, captured the fundamental shift in the raison d'être of the war genre, releasing male bonding from its excessive Soviet baggage. This essay argues that by the late 1960s ideological meanings of the father-son paradigm had become fully conventionalized genre formulas that expressed cultural rituals. Within the familiar space of the war trope, buttressed as it was by ideological commonplaces, filmic relationships in male genres that traditionally "uphold the values of social order"[1] acquired more flexibility, ultimately challenging the narrowly construed "Soviet identity."

Soviet cinema, which from the moment of its revolutionary birth was conceived as an ideological weapon, considered the war trope an indispensable part of film's symbolic structure. The relationship of fathers and sons was at the heart of the Soviet utopian imagination, asserting historical and ideological continuity between generations, while also marking moments of traumatic rupture and transition. Peacetime relationships were usually marked by children's rebellion against fathers, the disowning of the latter's values by the "sons"—a paradigm conspicuously absent from Soviet cinema until perestroika[2]—whereas wartime strengthened filial bonds, both literal and metaphorical. War narratives not only brought generations together against a common enemy in the space of legitimate male authority—the battlefield—but also gave a boost to the continuity paradigm. Killed, missing, or otherwise absent men (both fathers and sons) personified the family's and the community's trauma, opening up a space for new filial and political configurations. Such was the case with Khrushchev-era Soviet cinema, which mapped both the decimation of several generations of men and, with Stalin's death, the trauma of the absent Father. The symbolic, utopian dimension of the father-son relationship was the backbone of a number of outstanding films of the period.[3] In fact, Thaw culture owes its historical optimism largely to the flexibility of the father-son metaphor, particularly its inherent potential to connect the reconfigured private/family issues with the changing public/social issues.[4]

In his contribution to the recent discussion of cinematic father-son relationships published in the journal *SEANS*, Aleksandr Sekatskii comments on the new paradigm emerging in post-Soviet cinema. According to the author, the new Russian cinema manifests not only a challenge to the bond between fathers and sons but also the absence of a language to describe these relations.[5] In contrast, Sekatskii argues, the traumatic experiences of the past century ensured the semiotic stability of the "father-sign":

> The wartime and post-war fatherlessness periodically experienced by humankind did not damage the father figure. The father's place remained unshakable. [. . .] A boy or an adolescent who had lost his father at least knew exactly *what* (and of course *who*) was missing in his life. In some sense, the negative experience of absence left as deep an imprint as a normal relationship of father and son, passed through generations. (199–200)[6]

The unchallenged *place* of the father here implies that the ideological variables of male filiation remained stable, easily translatable into a clear comment on the social situation or, more precisely, into an affirmation of the status quo. The normal *Soviet* relationship of father and son was, above all, a part of the authoritative discourse of historical progress; within this discourse war provided a major setting and reference point. Yet the "progress via enlightenment" model had been largely exhausted during the Thaw:[7] the sons who grew up in a peaceful and more prosperous time suffered from amnesia and had little appreciation of—let alone shared ideals with—their self-sacrificial Soviet fathers.

If political metaphors did indeed guide the rest of the Soviet semiotic universe, Soviet leaders provided the model for paternal meanings. Roughly speaking, Lenin stood for equality, Stalin for expansion and protection, Khrushchev for renewal. Within this paradigm, the "stability" of Brezhnev's leadership seems to have failed to bring any radical changes into the paternal discourse. As Alexei Yurchak writes:

> Authoritative language became citational during late socialism [. . .] because it was built on a deep foundation of prior temporalities: all types of information, new and old, were presented as knowledge previously asserted and commonly known. The temporal organization anchored the rhetorical structure of this language, making it possible to convey new ideas and facts only by coding them in terms of prior ones. (61)

This very exhaustion of the potential for innovation, however, constituted the foundation of the mystery of the 1970s, the "last Soviet generation" in Yurchak's apt expression, as, simultaneously, the profoundly conservative culture that brought to a halt Khrushchev-era reforms and the period that spearheaded the fundamental shift from the Soviet identity model to the imperial Russian one.

The beginning of the 1970s marked the last attempt to rescue Soviet mythology from collapsing under the weight of mounting economic problems, political apathy, growing consumerism, and the fading of men's symbolic and social status, which mirrored the waning of Soviet mythology. The "de-heroization" of Soviet cinema became a major concern of the film administration, especially troublesome in historical-revolutionary films and films about World War II that were expected to set models of a "usable past" (Youngblood 144) and heroic patriotism. A number of epic films about the war were released, among them *Osvobozhdenie* [*Liberation* 1969–71], *Blokada* [*The Blockade* 1974–78], and *Soldaty svobody* [*Soldiers of Freedom* 1977], which brought back the war of the generals, the epic scale of production, and even the figure of Stalin as the Father of the nation. Fathers became the Soviet regime's main asset in rescuing both heroic history and strong masculinity. War veterans provided the bridge from a heroic and sacrificial past to a stable present, albeit one devoid of the heroic.

I argue that Brezhnev-era cinema introduced a new mythology of the imperial father as a symbol of stable identity and jettisoned the myth of the son as the socialist realist positive hero, blurring the border between Russian and Soviet identity. Many films of the time use the war setting as a familiar and conventional backdrop for exploring other issues or developing other genres. Unlike Khrushchev-era films, late-1960s and 1970s cinema shuns both stylistic innovation and political metaphors. But by exchanging the illusion of cinema as an "organic expression" for the sobering "iconographic code" (or the citational mode), to use Noel Carroll's terms,[8] the films of the era use the war trope both as a parody and an homage to the ideological clarity of the Soviet war narratives, while at the same time expanding the boundaries of identity those narratives offered. The barely outlined, yet transparent, war narrative serves as a background for male relationships that faithfully reproduce "authoritative discourse" even as they transcend the canonical Soviet dynamic of the father-son paradigm and redefine the genres that embody it.

Cinema and television of the time feature an astounding number of films and serial productions that strive to revitalize militaristic macho genres—from straight war epics and adventure films to spy thrillers and various fictionalized "institutional histories" (of the military, the KGB, and the police).[9] Legitimation of the regime through a recounting of the "heroic pages" of Soviet history was, of course, the primary political goal of these productions. But both the origins of this legitimacy and its very nature were fundamentally different. First, more often than not, history did not start with the Revolution; rather, the hero was portrayed as the product of both Russian imperial and Soviet experiences. His identity was thus enriched without compromising the "core" Soviet model.[10] Second, popular genres portrayed wartime in terms of a male utopia—as the time of male bonding and of purifying violence at the heroic service of the strange cinematic hybrid of the Russian Empire and the Soviet state.

Two notable examples of this trend are Vladimir Rogovoi's *Ofitsery* [*Officers* 1971] and Vladimir Motyl''s *Beloe solntse pustyni* [*White Sun of the Desert* 1969]. In most respects, these films are complete opposites. *Officers* has all the signs of a patriotic epic: its narrative spans fifty years, seen through the prism of several Soviet-era wars and exemplified in a multigenerational military family. Both in its representation of Soviet history and its idealistic portrayal of the military, *Officers* is a bona fide Soviet propaganda *lubok* [folk painting]. In contrast, *White Sun of the Desert* is a playful version of a Soviet civil war Western (or, more precisely, "Eastern") populated by clichéd heroes and portraying the civil war as the rescue of a harem comprising a local warlord's wives. The film has enjoyed an almost unprecedented—and unexpected—popularity with several generations of viewers. It is also an established tradition that Russian cosmonauts watch this film the day before the launch from the Baikonur Cosmodrome.

For film critics and viewers alike, *Officers* is, above all, Soviet propaganda, which draws a false, "prettified" picture of Soviet history, the army, and society in general,[11] whereas *White Sun of the Desert* offers a "de-ideologized" patriotic message (Bogomolov). Yet it is precisely at the level of ideology that this dichotomy proves false. Neither film questions the Soviet mythos; in fact, both feature the fully internalized Soviet authoritative discourse of heroic masculinity and father-son relations. Yet this "performative replication of the precise forms of authoritative representation" (Yurchak 60) is what enables the films to introduce unexpected meanings and configurations, while the very mythology of a heroic male utopia becomes material for a melodramatic or comedic narrative. Both films focus on several generations of men who defend Russia. The focus on normative masculinity leads to cross-class filiation, while the patriotic message is embedded in a conventional war setting and therefore remains valid despite the dominating melodramatic or ironic mode.[12] In both films the heroic tradition of strong masculinity transcends the strict boundaries of Soviet ideology: the Russian Empire and the Soviet Empire are linked through the theme of patriotism and anchored in the catchphrases that have wide cultural circulation: "There is such a profession—to defend your Motherland" ["est' takaia professiia—zashchishchat' Rodinu," *Officers*] and "My heart bleeds for the empire" ["Za derzhavu obidno," *The White Sun*].[13] The Soviet referent of both "Motherland" and "Great Power" is confirmed by the films' familiar coding, yet neither word is reducible to the Soviet idea. In Russian cultural mythology, which constitutes the playing field in both films, the Motherland is invoked (or is most emotionally charged) in times of war—as a *female* entity to be protected by *men*. "Derzhava" is an almost untranslatable fusion of state, nation, and empire, and although the word is a feminine noun, the image it projects is one of power and (imperial) pride. In both cases the speaker is a former imperial officer, a "class enemy," who shares love and concern for Russia with his Soviet heirs. Although relying heavily on the settings, tropes, and genre conventions of Soviet war film, the films thus eschew being construed as *ideologically* Soviet. In response to idealistic, youthful, and profoundly Soviet Thaw-era culture, these films offer a sober narrative with "father surplus." Fathers guarantee both the stability of the Great Power and cinematic genre memory, whereas sons are dispensable.

Officers is a heroic saga of the professional Russian military, focusing on three generations of Aleksei Trofimov's family. The title of the film suggests that its agenda is not the Soviet idea but the strong state and its defenders. Officers are a caste, an honor-driven breed, whether this honor concerns their service to the state, their friendship, or their love. The second plot line concerns Trofimov's forty-year friendship with Ivan Varrava—and Varrava's forty-year-long love for Trofimov's wife, Liuba. The film begins when Trofimov and his young wife arrive at a remote outpost in Central Asia during the civil war. The frontier setting invokes civil war mythology while also providing the perfect symbolic site for new allegiances to form. Here the couple meets Varrava, who in five minutes defeats a small *basmach* army and helps rescue Liuba when she is kidnapped in revenge. Here, in the barracks, the Trofimovs also conceive their only child. And, finally, here Trofimov receives the blessing of his own symbolic father—the former tsarist officer who became a Red Army officer. When Trofimov remarks that after the civil war is over he will study to acquire a profession, the Russian officer tells him, "There is such a profession—to defend your Motherland," the key ideological slogan of the film. The senior officer's cigarette holder has an inscription acknowledging his courageous service to the Russian Empire and celebrating his noble origins. After the commander is killed protecting Liuba, his lighter—and his name—become symbolic objects in the film. Trofimov names his son Egor (a Russified Georgii or "St. George"—the patron saint of Russia) in memory of his imperial mentor. The film not only establishes continuity between the Russian imperial and Soviet armies but holds the former as a model of military honor and patriotism.

By abruptly cutting from one war to another, the film emphasizes the significance of war in the identity formation of the father-son community, relegating peacetime moments to the status of annoying, confusing, and effeminate transitions. War transforms a boy into a man, normalizes family relations, and straightens the vertical father-son paradigms. The film races through Soviet history with breathtaking speed, ending in the late 1960s. The ascetic, fragmented, barely outlined plot is held together, on the one hand, by the idea of service to the Motherland as a "family project" and, on the other, by references to iconic settings. The sequences set during the civil war in Central Asia are modeled on Soviet Westerns (or "Easterns") à la *Chapaev*. During the 1931 Japanese invasion of Manchuria, Varrava works undercover as a Chinese official—a nod to the spy thrillers ("films about Soviet agents") that proliferated in the late 1960s.[14] The end of the film—the armored division lovingly greeting General Trofimov—recalls the Soviet defense film of the 1930s.[15] Finally, several scenes in the middle of the film feature iconic devices of World War II melodrama, with Trofimov's son, Egor, using the mirror-reflected sunbeam as a signal to a girl, or Egor and Masha posing for a photograph before their separation on the eve of the Nazi invasion. The soundtrack supports the eclectic visual structure of the film, punctuated by both diegetic and extradiegetic Soviet hit songs belonging to various historical periods but united by their wartime origins: the revolutionary song "Nash parovoz" ["Our Steam Engine"], the civil war song "Ukhodili komsomol'tsy" ["Komsomol Members Were off to the Civil War"], and the World War II song "Prifrontovoi val's" ["Wartime Waltz"]. The visual and the soundtrack substitute nostalgic genre memory for direct representation of the war: the Civil War segment at the beginning remains the only action scene in *Officers*.

In the absence of battle scenes, the film inscribes an epic dimension into the male relationships within one family. *Officers* is filled with machines—symbols of progress, heroic utopia, and historical optimism. These "epic machines" are the symbolic sites of characters' *private* lives: Trofimov's son, Egor, is born on the train and dies from wounds on the train; Egor's wife, Masha, leaves her baby son to Liuba while the latter is traveling on a train; Varrava admits his love for Liuba beside an airplane; and, finally, old General Trofimov is greeted by an entire tank division, which roars past his car containing the fractured family: grandparents and a grandson, with the middle generation missing, but plenty of symbolic surrogate sons-soldiers.

The passing of the baton from father to son is the backbone of the plot, and yet the father-son relationship in the film is entirely symbolic. Liuba raises Egor alone, for her husband is always absent. Egor is eventually killed without even learning that he has a son—news that is conveyed to the viewer in a scene that takes place on a train where Liuba—now a doctor—transports wounded soldiers. As she signs death certificates, the nurse gives her one from a badly burned tankman, who has only a photo to identify him. Liuba recognizes the picture of her son, Egor, and his Masha. The Trofimovs thus adopt Egor and Masha's son, and learn about Egor's death almost simultaneously. Just like little Boris, who appears in Mikhail Kalatozov's *Letiat zhuravli* [*Cranes Are Flying* 1957] in the nick of time to save Veronika, so does Ivan appear in the film as an impossible coincidence, a miracle orphan. But where Kalatozov's film is openly melodramatic, using Bor'ka as just another symbolic device to orchestrate Veronika's rebirth and redemption, little Ivan does not need to redeem anyone, because his only function is to continue the family's military tradition.

Trofimov's grandson, Ivan, is burdened with a number of conflicting meanings. He represents the military dynasty of the Trofimov family. But Ivan is also Varrava's symbolic son, not only because he is named after him but also because without Ivan this strange military ménage-à-trois has no children. As an orphan Ivan represents the sacrifices of the war, its human trauma and personal dimension. The final shot of the pseudo-documentary sequence that closes the film, however, is a flash forward to Ivan, now a paratrooper officer, who signifies the myth of the heroic Russian military.

Next to Trofimov's multigenerational—if fragmented—family, we have the character of Ivan Varrava, whose entire life is defined by his repressed love for his friend's wife. Unlike the idealistic portrayal of Aleksei and Liuba's relationship (an *intelligentka* and, as her fluent French suggests, a woman of noble origins, she, like the Decembrists' wives, follows him wherever he goes, sacrificing her comfort, education, and desire for a comfortable urban life), Varrava and Liuba's relationship is punctuated by a melodramatic eruption of feeling and awkward moments. When Liuba gives birth to Aleksei's child, it is Varrava who jumps off the moving train, picks wild flowers, and leaves them on Liuba's pillow. When, later in the film, Liuba is called to the airport and sees

Varrava, who travels there specifically to catch a glimpse of her, she is terrified to think that something may have happened to her husband. Their shared realization of the incongruity—she thinks only of her husband, while he makes a *faux pas* because he cannot contain his feelings for her—resolves itself in his words: "I have nobody apart from you . . . and Aleksei." The viewer last sees General Varrava as an old, lonely man, slowly ascending a stairway, his back to the camera.

The lonely, repressed, single-minded Varrava is the epitome of Soviet masculinity, whereas Trofimov's family offers a healthy combination of Russian social types: a peasant and a noble woman, the people and the national elite. Unlike the childless Varrava, the Trofimovs can procreate, even though their Soviet offspring perishes in the war. Egor's death symbolizes the sacrificial aspect of state service but folds the Soviet generation of the military family into the overarching Russian identity. The film privileges Russian over Soviet identity in yet another way: Trofimov and Varrava are equal in rank at the end of the film—they are both generals. Varrava, however, is an army bureaucrat, a representative of the Moscow Central Headquarters. In that capacity, he is officially superior to Trofimov, but, unlike the latter, he has no connection to real people and is growing old in the sterile environment of an office. Trofimov, on the other hand, has both a natural and an army family. The narrative ends with totalitarian sentimentality and a public display of emotion: the tank division professing its love for its father-commander Trofimov, who chooses a nomadic army life over a cushy teaching job in Moscow.

Next to Trofimov's archetypically Russian name, Varrava's stands out and engages the biblical story, unexpected in a Soviet patriotic epic. Varrava bears clear resemblance to Barabbas, the riotous "bandit" whom the Jerusalem crowd chooses to pardon instead of Jesus Christ. Jesus Christ and Barabbas are closely linked historically for both were "rioters": Barabbas sought to overthrow Rome by violence, whereas Jesus prophesized a spiritual illumination at odds with Roman values. Although the association of the Russian Trofimov with Christian symbolism and the Soviet Varrava with the "wrong choice" might seem far-fetched, the film clearly keeps the split focus, ending with a collage of documentary footage and fictional shots that both reestablish the continuity between past and present on the *mythological* level and signal the trauma on the *personal* level. The final sequence is linked to the film's patriotic, heroic message and resembles a propaganda reel interpolated from Ivan Pyr'ev's *Tractor Drivers* [*Traktoristy* 1939]. Yet the main narrative's heroic progression, its linking the heroes' lives with the country's history, is counterposed at the end by the *narrative of losses.* The final collage of images fast-tracks us back in time, filling in the blanks of the narrative: the wounded Varrava on a stretcher, Egor's burning body, Masha's execution by the Nazis. This second narrative is one of martyrdom and suffering, an indispensable component of the Russian Idea.

All these meanings come together in the melancholy and low-key song with epic content—a typical Brezhnev era song: "Of the heroes of the past / Sometimes not even names are left. / Those who engaged in deadly combat / Became earth and grass. / Only their formidable valor / Found a home in the hearts of the living. / This eternal fire/Bequeathed to us / We preserve inside."[16] The patient service to the state by every generation of Russian men constitutes the raison d'être for the father-son bond, according to *Officers,* and the picture visualizes this state-endorsed utopia dream of Russian history.

Whereas in Rogovoi's film patriotism bridges the divide between melodramatic masculinity and the triumphant and epic modernity, Motyl''s film blends the two, reducing them to a bare parody of tropes. Male relationships are central to the film's narrative, confirmed as they are by the civil war setting. As in *Officers,* the canonical narrative of establishing Soviet power in Central Asia functions as a familiar chronotope that requires no comment.[17] If in *Officers* the frontier outpost serves as the site of male bonding and the passing of the baton, Motyl''s film uses the frontier setting to act out a commercial genre formula. However, both the ideological dimension of the civil war narrative and the related issues of authority and legitimacy of male power and filiation remain stable parameters of the war narrative. If rescuing a harem sounds like a playful premise for a civil war film, one only need remember that the discourse of women's liberation as the major achievement of the Soviet power in Central Asia was at the center of Soviet mythology of the civil war. In its most propagandistic, if also poetic, form, this narrative appeared in Dziga Vertov's *Tri pesni o Lenine* [*Three Songs about Lenin* 1934]. Yet, as befits a war film, women in *White Sun of the Desert* are part of the landscape, an excuse for violence and eventual male bonding.

White Sun of the Desert opens where *Officers* ends—with a dream. Red Army soldier Sukhov narrates an unwritten letter to his wife, and we see her portrayed as a stereotypically Russian peasant beauty—full-bodied, round-faced, her hair covered with a red scarf and her skirt modestly but suggestively lifted as she crosses the stream. The *lubok* origins of the dream are confirmed by the contrasting primary colors: red, green, and so on, juxtaposed to Sukhov's washed-out, faded uniform and the blinding whiteness of the desert. Sukhov's dream may be symbolically motivated, but it has no place in the film's civil war narrative. The film's male characters wander around the desert, where modernity's conflicts are being played out, killing one another, driven by the "obvious" historical necessity that sidesteps the need for motivation.

Sukhov is a fairy-tale soldier who can outsmart the devil; he is indestructible, but he cannot reach home or settle down. The soldier's narrative is one of homeless wandering and brief encounters. Sukhov's local counterpart and "magic helper" is Said (Spartak Mishulin), whom Sukhov saves after finding him buried up to the neck in sand. Said returns the favor by appearing (twice) in the nick of time to save Sukhov from the villain Abdullah. While these scenes offer some action and suspense, both Sukhov and Abdullah are iconic figures who symbolize archetypal narratives rather than function as full-fledged characters. Sukhov's narrative is the road home; Abdullah's is the revenge for his father's death.

Yet just as Sukhov is not destined to reach his home and form a natural family with "Katerina Matveevna," so, too, is Said continually delayed in finding the elusive "Dzhavdet" and avenging his father. These recurring words function not as personal names but as magical incantations, marking the moments when the characters are diverted from their epic journeys by the political exigencies of the civil war. The tropes embodied by the two names—the road as teleology and the father as homeland—frame the civil war narrative and re-mythologize it as an archetypal heroic tale. At the film's end, as the "liberated women of the East" share a meal with Red Army troops, the commander suggests that Sukhov and Said stay with them and continue fighting the counterrevolution. Neither man accepts. Said asks, "Who will then take vengeance on Dzhavdet?" and Sukhov resumes his endless journey to "Katerina Matveevna."

The film makes full use of its frontier setting. Classes, cultures, and ideologies indeed collide here, but these conflicts are neither essential to characters' motivations nor do they constitute the focal points of the action. Instead, the border facilitates male bonding. The film brims with father figures: from Sukhov to the old museum keeper to village elders who in the course of the film never move or say a word—and only one son. The young soldier Petrukha, a cinematic heir of Chapaev's valiant machine-gunner and sidekick Pet'ka (and the folk puppet Petrushka), has a plethora of potential fathers in the film: Sukhov, the old customs officer Vereshchagin, and the local warlord Abdullah. Petrukha does indeed look as though he needs a father figure in his life: he is puny, confused, and more interested in chasing girls than in his revolutionary duty. These "fathers" teach him three things that have little to do with ideology but are essential for a "real man": to fight, to drink, and to die. Petrukha is assigned to Sukhov in order to help him with his assignment—to protect Abdullah's wives. As the temporary commander of this "army of one," Sukhov is Petrukha's father and teacher—or at least he is slated to fulfill those functions in a traditional war narrative. Sukhov, who has his hands full protecting the Oriental beauties and dreaming of his Russian wife, does little to teach Petrukha anything or to save his life. Instead, Petrukha becomes a toy in the hands of his other two fatal "mentors."

One of them, Vereshchagin, is a veteran of the imperial service and a decorated customs officer whose name used to instill fear in the hearts of smugglers. With the civil war raging in Central Asia, both the borders and the relationships have been redefined, however. Now retired, Vereshchagin has exchanged most of his large arsenal of weapons for peacocks that stroll free in his garden—an oasis in the desert—and spends his days drinking moonshine, which he accompanies with spoonfuls of beluga caviar, the only food available in the war-ravaged Caspian region. The exchange of "weapons for peacocks" may be grotesque, and the irony of anybody's being sick and tired of eating caviar is a knowing wink to contemporary, Brezhnev-era audiences. Nevertheless the film treats Vereshchagin with a noticeable degree of reverence and imperial nostalgia. It is not accidental that the film's theme song—Bulat Okudzhava's "Your Majesty, Madame Luck"—is performed by the old tsarist officer. The camera, too, privileges the customs officer and, through him, the mythology of loyalty and patriotism. After Petrukha is kidnapped by Vereshchagin and before we are introduced to him personally, the tracking shot of the wall in his house supplies a visual summary of his life and service: a sabre and a picture of young Vereshchagin dressed in an elegant officer's uniform, posing with his young wife. Vereshchagin, whose son is dead, "adopts" Petrukha simultaneously as a son, a drinking buddy, and a symbolic atonement for the sin of relinquishing the responsibilities of a customs officer and border guard for the tranquility of family bliss.

As in *Officers*, character naming is far from accidental. The "dry," that is, childless, Sukhov is less than a perfect father to his "Petka." Abdullah's and Said's names are archetypically "ethnic" and "oriental." It is not surprising, then, that the film's most revered character bears the name of the famous Russian imperial artist Vasilii Vereshchagin. The latter not only specialized in battlefield epics but personally took part in several campaigns with the Russian army, from the war with the Ottoman Empire in the Balkans in 1877–78 to the colonial adventures of the Russian Empire in Central Asia and the Far East. He is therefore simultaneously a symbol of Russian military glory and of war horrors. One of Vereshchagin's most famous paintings, *The Apotheosis of War* (1871), depicts a pile of skulls in the middle of a desert.

Initially Vereshchagin refuses to support either Sukhov or Abdullah, not for the lack of desire to reenter "boys' games" but in compliance with his wife's tearful request. Vereshchagin's fatal decision to join Sukhov in fighting Abdullah is motivated by what Iurii Bogomolov describes as a shared "vague idea of state interests and a clear sense of duty. Their hearts bleed for the Great Power. And, strangely enough, they do not care for which power: Red or White. They are both on the same side of the frontline."[18] Yet, if class ideology is indeed blurred in the film, it is more than compensated for by the ideology of state service, which combines ideally with the family trope (revenge for Petrukha) and male bonding. After all, Vereshchagin tests "Comrade Sukhov" by offering him a smoking piece of dynamite to light his cigarette—a test Sukhov passes with flying colors.

Petrukha's death at Abdullah's treacherous hand brings into the film a peculiar Freudian motif. The young soldier is attracted to Abdullah's youngest wife, Giul'chatai, because she is as "feisty" as he is, yet she refuses to lift her *burka* to a man who is not her husband. Sukhov warns Petrukha not to chase after Giul'chatai because in doing so, the young soldier will have to barge into the "women's quarters" and cause panic among the women. Ironically, Sukhov himself does precisely that, with the significant difference that the women accept him as the new "husband." Sukhov's order thus amounts to paternal interdiction of incest. Notably this is the only instance when Sukhov teaches his adoptive son anything, and the latter's disobedience leads to his death. Having tricked and murdered Giul'chatai, Abdullah uses her dress as a disguise to kill Petrukha. "Revealing" his face to the enamored soldier, Abdullah punishes him for the Oedipal transgression: after all, Petrukha is attracted to Abdullah's wife. The screwball comedy scenario—an older man, the father or the older suitor, creating obstacles for the young couple's love—resolves in a shocking demonstration of the "father's" phallic power. Abdullah grabs Petrukha's rifle and thrusts the bayonet into the young man's heart.

Abdullah's act of double murder confirms his status as a villain, formally illustrating the ideologically correct story of the civil war while at the same time reinforcing patriarchal hierarchy. In the space of the narrative, however, Sukhov, Vereshchagin, and Abdullah are equal both as "fathers" and as "real men." In short, they are the "three bogatyrs": Vereshchagin is a Russian imperial man, Sukhov an epic Red man, Abdullah an imperial villain who conveniently combines political, ethnic and moral "otherness." It is not accidental that in the script, after killing Abdullah, Sukhov praises him as a real warrior—an attitude that was unacceptable to the class-minded members of the Film Commission.[19] Next to these three epic warriors, who define war utopia and male glory, Petrukha is a weak and unnecessary son, foisted onto the film by the waning Thaw culture and socialist realist canon. He is killed as soon as he attempts to usurp his father's right to own women.

In contrast to the machine-filled world of *Officers*, *White Sun* completely lacks technology, with the notable exception of the patrol boat, which has a dual significance. On the one hand, Vereshchagin learns about Petrukha's death by Abdullah's hand and acquires a "family" reason to join Sukhov in fighting the bandits. On the other hand, the boat is a symbol of the customs officer's patriotic duty and former heroic service to guard the Great Power's property. Vereshchagin's struggle with the gangsters-smugglers begins as slapstick, proceeds as a fairy-tale battle of the Russian bogatyr against the thrice-stronger enemy, and ends in tragedy when the dynamite bomb (planted there earlier by Sukhov and Petrukha) explodes in the boat, killing both the wounded Vereshchagin and several smugglers.

The succession of generations within one military family in *Officers* spans the entire history of twentieth-century Russia, capturing the glory, heroism, and nobility of the Russian military—and of Russian men. The film's extreme fragmentation, its focus on symbolic scenes at the expense of transitions, the disregard for motivation and reliance on the established structures of meaning—all this marks the film as a utopian project. In *White Sun*, the generations are co-present in the space, rather than time, of utopia. Class distinctions and other ideological divisions ultimately collapse, revealing the bare structure of male relationships.

In *Officers*, the generation of sons—the only purely Soviet generation—is wiped out, but its memory is the point of intersection of Russian military glory and the Soviet utopia.[20] *White Sun of the Desert* altogether dispenses with the core issue of the civil war—conflict between classes—by killing all ideological characters: the Red Army soldier Petrukha, the tsarist army officer Vereshchagin, and the *basmatch* Abdullah, together with the ideology they represent. The survivors embody the elements of both male fantasy (Oriental beauties) and the purified myth of male warrior honor (Said) and imperial valor (Sukhov).

Whereas the popularity of Motyl''s film never faded, *Officers* led a fairly inconspicuous existence, occasionally rerun on TV, until it acquired a new life at the beginning of the twenty-first century. For many young Russians, the film came to represent a patriotic ideal in its "pure," that is, non-political, form.[21] In post-Soviet culture, *Officers* had two postscripts. In 1994 sixty-eight-year-old Georgii Iumatov, who played Trofimov in the film, shot and killed a thirty-three-year-old Azeri man, who (at least according to the official version) remarked that Soviet soldiers should have fought on the side of Nazi troops during World War II.[22] The second postscript is less tragic but also typically post-Soviet. In 2006 Russian television broadcast the mini-series *Officers: The Last Soldiers of the Empire*, which is both a sequel to the film and its remake, with the patriotic plot and even the love triangle now in line with the openly nationalistic Russian agenda. The series is advertised as an "action thriller" about an elite counterintelligence squad. The surviving member of the duo of officers, Vasilii Lanovoi appears in the films as the old general, who now has a son by a woman whom he did not love and who by now is conveniently dead. The series capitalizes on everything that the Soviet-era film promised but could not deliver: two good-looking Russian warriors with jumbo biceps emphasized by new Western-style uniforms; war as the ultimate space for male bonding, youthful escapades, and a testosterone rush; the rescue of dumb blond Russian beauties threatened by the barbarians' white slavery in the desert; and, at the foundation of it all, numerous imperial father figures—Russian security service officers. If the film *Officers* timidly reestablished the continuity between prerevolutionary and Soviet Russia, the series boldly bridges the Soviet war in Afghanistan and post-Soviet heroic secret missions of Russian special forces in various trouble spots of the world in the name of Great Russia, the power for which the heroes' "hearts bleed." Brezhnev-era culture, which used debilitated Soviet tropes to revitalize Russian identity, continues to serve as a model to post-Soviet Russia—which largely shares the same agenda. After the Wild West decade of the 1990s, when gangster "sons" ran amok amid newly discovered freedom, the return to imperial identity, positive past models, and fathers' authority is an anticipated reaction.

NOTES

1. Thomas Schatz, *Hollywood Genres* (Boston: McGraw-Hill, 1981), 29. See also the discussion of Soviet and Russian film genres in Birgit Beumers, "Soviet and Russian Blockbusters: A Question of Genre," *Slavic Review* 62, no. 3 (fall 2003): 441–454.

2. Thaw cinema offers a telling demonstration of the limits of the "rebellious" discourse in Soviet culture. Although young people often hold the moral high ground against the older generation and its values in such different films as Iosif Kheifits's *Delo Rumiantseva* [*Rumiantsev's Case* 1955] or El'dar Riazanov's *Karnaval'naia noch'* [*The Carnival Night* 1956], the positive father figure is never far away. The good father both corrects the young protagonist's erratic behavior (the police colonel of Kheifits's film) and authorizes the "rebellion" (the party boss in Riazanov's film). Equally revealing is the Thaw part of Vladimir Men'shov's *Moskva slezam ne verity* [*Moscow Does Not Believe in Tears* 1980], where a young poet attacks an older man at the dinner table on the topic of his generation's complicitous silence during the Stalin-era purges. "We wouldn't have been silent," the poet exclaims. But the film problematizes the moral righteousness of the young generation. At this party the female protagonist, Katia, gets involved with Rudol'f, a TV cameraman (likewise claiming the superiority of the new technology and the young generation), who not only abandons the pregnant Katia but is exposed as a "mama's boy," sending his mother to pay Katia off.

3. See, for example, Josephine Woll, *Real Images: Soviet Cinema and the Thaw* (London: I. B. Tauris, 2000).

4. The same is true of European "new wave" cinema: Vittorio de Sica's *Bicycle Thieves* (1948) and François Truffaut's *400 Blows* (1959) use filial relationships to renew the film form while simultaneously probing family and social issues.

5. In his discussion of Andrei Zviagintsev's *Vozvrashchenie* [*The Return* 2003], Sekatskii notes that the two boys feel that their life has changed with the father's appearance, and yet they neither know what it means to have a father nor can adequately express their feelings. "D'you see what kind of guy he is?" (Vidal, kakoi?)—"Yeah" (199). One might add to this that the father's heroic status in the film is unmotivated (he appears out of nowhere) except as the boys' compensatory fascination with his *presence*.

6. Bezottsovshchina voennykh i poslevoennykh let, periodicheski nastigavshaia chelovechestvo, ne nanosila ushcherba figure ottsa. Mesto ottsa ostavalos' nezyblemym [. . .] Mal'chik ili podrostok, okazavshiisia bez ottsa, po krainei mere tverdo znal, *chto* imenno (i, razumeetsia, *kto* imenno) otsutstvuet v ego zhizni. Negativnyi opyt otsutstviia v kakom-to smysle ostavlial stol' zhe glubokii sled, kak I normal'noe, peredannoe po estafete pokolenii sodruzhestvo ottsa i syna.

7. See Alexander Prokhorov's essay in this collection, chapter 1.

8. Noel Carroll, *Interpreting the Moving Image* (Cambridge: Cambridge University Press, 1998), 244, 261.

9. For example, Edmond Keosaian's *Neulovimye mstiteli* [*Elusive Avengers* 1966] and its sequels; a number of television series also follow this pattern: Evgenii Tashkov's *Ad"iutant ego prevoskhoditel'stva* [*His Majesty's Aide* 1966]; Grigorii Kokhan's *Rozhdennaia revoliutsiei* [*Born in the Revolution* 1976]; Boris Stepanov's *Gosudarstvennaia granitsa* [*State Border* 1980].

10. *His Majesty's Aide* exemplifies this trend with utmost clarity. The young boy from an aristocratic military family, who becomes an orphan during the civil war, has at least two adoptive fathers: a White Army colonel and a Red agent who has infiltrated the White Army headquarters. Notably, *both* are patriots of Russia, and both are portrayed sympathetically in the film. Although the viewer's primary identification is with the Red agent whose death ensures the passing of the ideological baton to his adoptive son, the boy's noble origins and his questioning of the morality of spying for the sake of an idea complicate the conventional class-driven picture of the Revolution.

11. The documentary film *The Fate of Officers*, which was broadcast in 2003 on Russian television on the Day of the Defenders of the Fatherland (23 February, formerly the Day of the Soviet Army), included interviews with both the creators of the film and critics whose job was to deconstruct the film's falsity. The newspaper *Sovetskaia Rossiia* answered with an article, suggestively titled "The Stagnant Well," attacking the unpatriotic commentators.

12. The recent *History of Russian Cinema* [*Istoriia otechestvennogo kino* 2005] mentions *Officers* among 1970s lyrical films, "stories about acquiring and losing love."

13. The Soviet state was directly involved in both film projects. *Officers* was commissioned by then Minister of Defense Andrei Grechko, who also reportedly suggested the phrase. See Slava Taroshchina, "Gospoda Ofitsery," *Gazeta* 35 (27 February 2007). Available at http://www.gzt.ru/culture/2007/02/26/220148.html (accessed 26 February 2007). In case of *White Sun of the Desert*, the head of Goskino Vladimir Baskakov not only commissioned an "eastern" but also inspired another catchphrase: "The East is a subtle matter" ["Vostok—delo tonkoe"].

14. E.g., Veniamin Dorman's *Oshibka rezidenta* [*Resident's Mistake* 1968] and Vladimir Basov's *Shchit i mech'* [*Shield and Sword* 1968].

15. For instance, *Esli zavtra voina* [*If There Is War Tomorrow* 1938, Lazar' Antsi-Polovskii and Georgii Berezko].

16. Ot geroev bylykh vremen / Ne ostalos' poroi imen. / Te kto priniali smertnyi boi / Stali prosto zemlei i travoi / Tol'ko groznaia doblest' ikh/Poselilas' v serdtsakh zhivykh. / Etot vechnyi ogon' / Nam zaveshchanyi odnim / My v grudi khranim.

17. In his interview, scriptwriter Valentin Ezhov recounts that he and Andrei Konchalovsky, who started working on the film, were given the "assignment" to shoot a Western "no worse than American ones." Since neither of them had ever lived in Central Asia, where the film was set, they invited the young scriptwriter Rustam Ibragimbekov to work on the desert mise-en-scène. As it turned out, Ibragimbekov knew nothing about the desert either, but, Ezhov remarks, "What was there to know about the desert? After all, it's just that—desert." After Konchalovsky withdrew from the film, the search for a new director focused on the right combination of genres. The cause for rejecting Iurii Chuliukin was his desire to make a pure comedy. Zhalakia-vichus saw *White Sun* as an action movie. Eventually Vladimir Motyl' satisfied both scriptwriters by agreeing to shoot a generically hybrid film (interview with Ezhov on the DVD release). Notably absent among the considerations was a concern about the authenticity of the civil war setting.

18. ". . . tumannaia ideia gosudarstva i poniatnoe chuvstvo dolga. Im oboim za derzhavu obidno. I kak ni stranno, dlia nikh ne vazhno, za kakuiu: za Krasnuiu ili za Beluiu."

19. Valentin Ezhov's interview on the Ruscico DVD release of the film.

20. Another genre that reconfigures the "us" versus "them" paradigm along patri-otic-imperial, rather than class, lines is the spy thriller. The hero of *Resident's Mistake*, for instance, is the son of a Russian émigré who works for Western intelligence. When the father attempts to quit his job, apparently because of his newly awakened patri-otic feelings, he is killed. The son—also a Western spy—thus has conflicted feelings about his mission in the Soviet Union. The sequence of the protagonist and his Soviet counterpart—a KGB agent—wandering around the Palace Square in Leningrad, the cradle of the Russian Empire rather than the Revolution, visually marks the turning point for the protagonist (he "turns" against his Western bosses) and for the narrative ("Great Russia" takes precedence over "Soviet Russia").

21. See, for instance, viewers' responses at http://www.kinomost.ru/index.asp ?case=19&num=12988 (accessed 14 March 2007).

22. Evgenii Buzni, "Zatkhlyi kolodets: Sud'ba *Ofitserov* na TVC," *Sovetskaia Ros-siia* 23 (1 March 2003). Available at http://www.sovross.ru/2003/023/023_8_03.htm (accessed 14 March 2007).

REFERENCES

Beumers, Birgit. "Soviet and Russian Blockbusters: A Question of Genre." *Slavic Review* 62, no. 3 (fall 2003): 441–54.

Bogomolov, Iurii. "Muzhskoe i zhenskoe." *Rossiiskaia gazeta* (1 March 2005). Available at http://www.rg.ru/2005/03/01/televidenie.html (accessed 1 November 2006).

Budiak, L. M., ed. *Istoriia otechestvennogo kino*. Moscow: Progress-Traditsiia, 2005.

Buzni, Evgenii. "Zatkhlyi kolodets: Sud'ba *Ofitserov* na TVC," *Sovetskaia Rossiia* 23 (1 March 2003). Available at http://www.sovross.ru/2003/023/023_8_03.htm (accessed 15 October 2006).

Carroll, Noel. *Interpreting the Moving Image*. Cambridge: Cambridge University Press, 1998.

Clark, Katerina. *The Soviet Novel: History as Ritual*. Bloomington: Indiana University Press, 2000.

Schatz, Thomas. *Hollywood Genres: Formulas, Filmmaking, and the Studio System*. Boston: McGraw-Hill, 1981.

Sekatskii, Aleksandr. "Ottsepriimstvo." *SEANS* 21/22 (2006): 198–205.

Taroshchina, Slava. "Gospoda Ofitsery." *Gazeta* 35 (27 February 2007). Available at http://www.gzt.ru/culture/2007/02/26/220148.html (accessed 28 February 2007).

Youngblood, Denise J. *On the Cinema Front: Russian War Films, 1914–2005*. Lawrence: University Press of Kansas, 2007.

Yurchak, Alexei. *Everything Was Forever, Until It Was No More: The Last Soviet Generation*. Princeton, N.J.: Princeton University Press, 2006.

FILMOGRAPHY

Beloe solntse pustyni [*White Sun of the Desert*]. Dir. Vladimir Motyl'. Mosfilm (Experimental Creative Unit), 1969.

Ofitsery [*Officers*]. Dir. Vladimir Rogovoi. Gorky Film Studios, 1971.

THREE

Models of Male Kinship in Perestroika Cinema

SETH GRAHAM

Among the vast arsenal of Soviet themes that became vulnerable to critical reevaluation during the perestroika period (1985–91) were numerous tropes of male familial relations, by which I mean those categories of maleness defined by blood or marital relationships to others—father, son, brother, grandfather, uncle—and the varieties of symbolic value attached to them. Such roles, of course, had figured prominently in the metaphorical lexicon of the evolving official mythos for decades: Stalin as the Father of Peoples [*otets narodov*]; "Thank you, Comrade Stalin, for our happy childhood!"; Soviet head of state Mikhail Kalinin as the "All-Union Elder" [*vsesoiuznyi starosta*]; Grandfather (or Uncle) Lenin; The Great Fatherland War (World War II); and the "fraternal" [*bratskie*] countries of the Eastern bloc (who occasionally needed a bit of "fraternal aid" [*bratskaia pomoshch'*], delivered by Soviet tanks), to name just some of the most canonical formulations.

Familial metaphors figured prominently in the textual manifestations of Soviet ideology in part because they were easily "marketed": they had an innate (in the most direct sense of that word) emotional appeal to the intended recipients of the ideology—Soviet citizens—and to their direct experience with family relationships. The appeal to a seemingly obvious biological/biographical fact tells only part of the story, of course; the deployment of kinship metaphors by the Soviet culture industry was also strategic to a central goal of Soviet social reengineering: to abduct the primary concepts of collectivity and loyalty from the biological to the sociopolitical realm. In other words, the aim was to plant in Soviet hearts and minds a dual connotation of "father" (and "son," "mother," etc.)—one civic and one personal—accompanied by the strong implication that the civic version was the more significant of the two.[1]

The explicitly familial metaphors used in the service of the Revolution supplemented the more abstract models of Soviet ideological enlightenment that drew on and modified existing motifs of intergenerational (especially male) impartation of skills, knowledge, and values. On a synchronic level, the mentor-initiate relationship, which Katerina Clark identifies as a crucial dynamic in socialist-realist narratives, is the "Great Family" analogue to the literal parent-child relationship in the biological family (114–35).[2] A more broadly scoped concept, the cult of personality, draws on traditional structures of patriarchy and heredity, and smacks of ritualistic, secret wisdom handed down a successive line of anthropomorphic embodiments of a value system. Soviet leader-cultism was, in fact, a re-mythologized version of monarchic succession in its pre-Enlightenment, divine-right form: Marxist shaman-kings with a direct link back to the cultural progenitor, Lenin, and even beyond to Marx-Engels and (along a parallel line, with an ostensibly negative valence) to the tsars. Such paternalistic political symbolism implicitly defined power-subject relations in a particular way, casting citizens as children,[3] with all the attendant connotations (powerless "dependents," receptacles for the impartation of knowledge, etc.).

Although the paternal paradigm after Stalin never regained its original prominence, subsequent Soviet leaders attempted to draw on it more or less explicitly. Nikita Khrushchev's own aspirations to be a more folksy (and less punitive) father figure to his people than Stalin were problematic, of course, given the official program of de-Stalinization, and, moreover, were not taken seriously, as the flood of jokes such as the following demonstrates: "On a visit to a collective farm Khrushchev is chatting paternally [po-otecheski] with the farmers. 'So how's life?' Nikita Sergeevich jokes. 'Life's great!' the farmers joke back." Even Leonid Brezhnev, remembered more as a feeble grandfatherly figure, drew on his status as a member of the paternal generation that had fought and won the Great Fatherland War as a source for both credibility and authority.[4]

Significantly the Soviet leaders who were never the subjects of personality cults or officially characterized by paternal imagery—the aforementioned Khrushchev and his fellow Kremlin reformer Mikhail

Gorbachev—ruled during periods in which the ideology and its symbolic vocabulary and iconography underwent extensive revision. During such moments of ideological correction and critical attention on the part of one "generation" of leaders toward their predecessors/"ancestors," metaphors of fatherhood and sonhood acquired a sudden, problematic multivalence, and their utility as signifiers in mass-media narratives underwent analogous reevaluation. Both Khrushchev's Thaw and Gorbachev's perestroika were cultural moments when the question of generational transition was especially thorny. As elements within the evolving Soviet Master Narrative, the figures of speech and symbolic associations of male kinship relations served, in turn, as further metaphors and were used in the (little-n) narratives of Soviet mass culture, including film, and the cinematic output of both those frequently compared eras reflected the unstable nature of filial tropes. Such images, perhaps more so than others, did double duty in Soviet culture; on the level of plot, they illustrated the effects of history on "typical" (but literal) families in the Soviet Union, and, more broadly, they served as metaphors for the officially defined socialist commonweal, frequently represented, again, as a Great Family.

The recalibrations of paternal and filial paradigms by Soviet filmmakers during perestroika were many and varied, but the overall impression is one of multifarious crises. Perhaps predictably for a cultural moment so strongly defined by the impulse to expose previously hidden social abscesses and historical traumas, representations of families during the Gorbachev years typically emphasized their dysfunctionality (to put it euphemistically). This is not to claim that analogous representations in previous Soviet cinema did not also frequently depict broken or traumatized families; they certainly did, as discussed by several of the other contributors to this volume. The pre-perestroika cinematic family, however, when broken, was almost invariably portrayed as such owing to a clearly defined historical process or event, most commonly the Great Fatherland War or the Russian civil war. Absent fathers were (so to speak) ever-present in Soviet war films and revolutionary-historical films, for reasons that are far from mysterious. Moreover, the familial ruptures in such films as Nikolai Ekk's *Putevka v zhizn'* [*Road to Life* 1931], Mikhail Kalatozov's *Letiat zhuravli* [*Cranes Are Flying* 1957], Grigorii Daneliia and Igor' Talankin's *Serezha* [*A Summer to Remember*

1960], Sergei Bondarchuk's *Sud'ba cheloveka* [*Fate of a Man* 1959], and Nikolai Gubenko's *Podranki* [*Orphans* 1976] were typically depicted so they could then be repaired by the establishment of new family units (with adoptive or stepparents), or alleviated by the formation of alternative communities (e.g., residents of communal apartments, children in schools, or orphanages). Such narrative arcs demonstrated both the possibility of overcoming obstacles via adherence to Soviet values and the historically determined progression from strictly biological to other types of intimate collectives.

The denial and obsolescence of this restorative motif was a hallmark of representations of Russian families in perestroika cinema, with its aggressively (and sometimes nihilistically) revisionist position vis-à-vis both (big-H) history and Soviet cinematic tradition. The ruptured families that filled Soviet screens in the 1980s and early 1990s most often figured as victims of, and metaphors for, comprehensive systemic failure, rather than isolated, externally caused, temporary anomalies in an otherwise stable and functional social order. In the words of Andrew Horton and Michael Brashinsky, the underlying message of many perestroika-era films was "that it is not merely *something* that is rotten in the state of the Soviet Union, but everything" (78; emphasis in original). It was a time of crisis even for the alternative, small collectives to which citizens had retreated during the Stagnation period, following the disappointingly abortive collective enthusiasm of the Thaw. To extend Horton and Brashinsky's metaphor of physical corruption: the social wasting disease by the mid-1980s was depicted as having infected the social organism on the cellular (i.e., familial) level.

In what follows, I examine various ways in which perestroika filmmakers represented the sociopolitical moment by deploying concepts of paternity and filiation. I draw my examples from several films: Tengiz Abuladze's *Pokaianie* [*Repentance* 1984, released 1986], Abdrashitov's *Pliumbum*, Vasilii Pichul's *Malen'kaia Vera* [*Little Vera* 1988], Ol'ga Narutskaia's *Muzh i doch' Tamary Aleksandrovny* [*The Husband and Daughter of Tamara Aleksandrovna* 1988], and Nikita Mikhalkov's *Urga: Territoriia liubvi* [*Urga: Territory of Love* (also known in English as *Close to Eden*) 1991].

The celebrated "first swallow of perestroika" (Woll and Youngblood 1), *Repentance* is centrally concerned with paternal legacies, both symbolic (historical, extra-textual, national) and literal (lyrical, diegetic, biological). The film depicts three generations of the Aravidzes (a Georgian surname that means something close to "son of nobody" or "son of everybody"): the recently deceased dictator Varlam, his middle-aged son, Abel, and Abel's teenage son, Tornike.[5] The relationship of Abel (whose name evokes a different, biblical kinship narrative) and Tornike, and the effect on that relationship of revelations concerning the Stalinesque crimes of their common progenitor, Varlam, is the main theme of this complex film's climax. Initially Abel and Tornike are united in their grief at Varlam's passing and, soon thereafter, in their outrage at the anonymous vandal who keeps unearthing the old man's corpse and propping it in sight of the Aravidze house. Tornike stakes out the cemetery and catches the grave-robber in the act: it is Keti Barateli, the daughter of an artist who was executed decades before, during Varlam's reign of terror.

At her trial, Keti tells the long story of the tyrant's rise to power and his crimes against the population of the unnamed city-state.[6] The vivid and harrowing tale, which makes up an extended flashback that occupies the central third of the film, devastates Tornike's sense of family and self, ultimately leading him to commit suicide with a rifle that had been given to him by his grandfather. Abel, now both fatherless and sonless, himself disinters Varlam's body and, with a cry of rage and anguish, throws it off a cliff to the carrion-birds, a symbolic act of parricide and partial suicide that is underscored by the fact that the same actor portrays both Abel and Varlam.

The characters in this family drama are mappable onto the generations faced with the legacy of historical guilt and trauma that largely defined perestroika: the "remains" of the Stalinist past refuse to remain buried, and it is the collective burden of those in the present to decide what to do with the corpse (and its still-present odor). The political-historical allegory is enhanced if we add an ethnic dimension: the Georgian film is also an implicit engagement with the status of Stalin (né Dzhugashvili) himself as a "son" of Georgia.[7] That the legacy of the past and the problem of dealing with that legacy represent a predominantly male concern is implicit in the fact that the only two main characters who do not waver in their views are female: Keti, who speaks and acts for Varlam's victims, and Abel's wife, Guliko, who is Varlam's staunchest defender and, in fact, engineers Keti's ultimate fate of being declared insane by the tribunal (a clear analogy to a tactic used against Soviet dissidents in the Brezhnev-era USSR). By contrast, all three generations of the male Aravidzes, including Varlam, experience moments of doubt or other psychic dissonance. For instance, in a daydream Tornike has during Keti's trial, Varlam is thoroughly infantilized, his chubby features enhanced by a white dressing gown and his nonsensical behavior and speech.

Tornike is the one who eventually takes adult responsibility for his family's sinister history and collective guilt, by apologizing to Keti in her jail cell. His subsequent suicide seems to suggest that genuine redemption, if not repentance, is impossible, at least for his generation, the "grandsons"—that is, that the curse of history called into being by Varlam is a multigenerational curse. The image of powerless youth, doomed not only by the crimes of their grandfathers but also by the passivity and complicity of their fathers, was a common motif in perestroika treatments of generational dynamics. In another, in most respects completely different, film, Savva Kulish's *Tragediia v stile rok* [*Tragedy in the Style of Rock* 1988], a teenage boy in the 1980s experiments with various extreme subcultures before committing suicide and leaving a taped message to the older generations, a method that articulates a sentiment that Tornike implicitly shares: "Children raised on lies cannot be moral" (Horton and Brashinsky 78). The issue of the relationship between morality and truth in *Pokaianie* is one aspect of the film's complicated engagement with religion. Abuladze's linkage of spirituality and politics is also apparent in the film's title, in the explicit thematic treatment of the revolutionary destruction of churches, and in the crucifixion imagery used to depict the execution of Keti's artist father, Sandro Barateli. One of the most striking uses of religious imagery in the film is a sequence near the end in which Abel has a vision in which he unburdens himself to an initially unseen confessor, who is revealed to be the ghost of Varlam, who graphically devours a fish during the meeting.

The perestroika-era deployment of the biblical sentiment "the sins of the fathers will be revisited on the sons" is also apparent in Abdrashitov's *Pliumbum,* which, like *Pokaianie,* allegorizes the late-Soviet encounter with the Stalinist past as an intra-familial dynamic, albeit in quite different ways than in Abuladze's film, visually, narratively, and otherwise. The psychological climax of Abdrashitov's film is a contemporary reworking of the Pavlik Morozov story—a boy is so loyal to his larger, symbolic family, the state, that he informs on a member of his biological family, his own father. Pliumbum (from the Latin for "lead") is the alias of sixteen-year-old Ruslan Chutko, a schoolboy who works as an undercover operative for the police. He is the image of a model (if fledgling) secret policeman [*chekist*]: self-disciplined, unwavering in his devotion to the letter of the law, and unbiased in his enforcement of it and his desire to "clean up society." Ruslan's code name indicates both his Stalinist tendencies (lead—steel [*stal'*, the root of the adopted name Stalin]) and his inadequacy in the role (lead is among the *softest* of metals).

Ruslan/Pliumbum's militarism and statism are motivated neither by inattentive parenting nor, indeed, by anything on the surface of the film, indicating the organic and insidious nature of the *chekist* psychopathology that would be so thoroughly interrogated during perestroika. He is surrounded by father figures, including his own biological father. Their relationship is one of mutual love and respect; they greet each other with the seemingly flattering pseudo-vocatives "Hail to the Father!" ["Ottsu!"] and "Hail to the Son!" ["Synu!"], even in the scene where the son arrests his father. The police inspector for whom Ruslan works undercover is a potential mentor in the socialist-realist sense, but the protégé's enthusiasm for the task at hand seems excessive even to the mentor (who is the model of a cynical, Stagnation-era bureaucrat, like Abel in *Pokaianie*). Ruslan's place in his family, too, is marked as aberrational. In one scene the three members of the Chutko family sit in their living room singing a bard song. Although the family is literally in harmony, Ruslan is visually displaced from his position in the biological hierarchy: sitting on the back of the sofa, he looms above both his parents in the frame.

The visual manifestation of Ruslan's status as a self-styled Nietzschean superman and generationally displaced "guardian" of his own parents is repeated in the key scene in which he chases down and tackles a fleeing fish poacher, who turns out to be his own father. At the subsequent interrogation, Ruslan, impeccably pro forma, asks his father/arrestee for basic biographical information that Ruslan, of course, already knows: "Last name, first name, patronymic?" he repeats, as his father's initially bemused attitude to the situation disappears as he realizes just what his son has become. He then offers a psycho-sociological analysis of Ruslan's behavior:

Maybe you just like power? Be careful, that's dangerous! Yesterday there was an article in *Izvestiia* that I put aside especially for you to read. It's about what a dangerous thing power is when a person's still morally immature. Or maybe you consider yourself mature? Have you really seen that much evil in your life? Where? When? I don't get it. (Mindadze 370)[8]

The scene is not merely an illustration of the coldly terrifying, anti-human effect of blind faith in the civic (public) at the expense of the familial (private); it is also a parody of one of the primary functions of the father-son dynamic: the passage of family history and accumulated knowledge from one generation to the next. Pliumbum's stoic indifference to his father's appeal to intimacy and emotion is also an implicit rebuke to the liberal values of the generation to which Ruslan's parents belong; they are clearly marked as having come of age in the Thaw of the 1960s, with its premiums on authenticity and sincerity. Pliumbum's "career" as an undercover informant represents a clear rejection of those central Thaw values. The interrogation scene is also explicitly male-centered; at the end of the questioning, Ruslan's father asks his son not to tell his mother about what has happened, suggesting, as in *Pokaianie,* that perestroika artists read the Soviet period primarily as a failure of men and, perhaps, masculinity itself. Ruslan eventually falls asleep, indicating his distance from his father, a distance born of his unwillingness to consider any mitigating circumstances when it comes to the law. The scene contrasts the Stagnation-era penchant for bureaucratism and pedantry to the faith in genuineness and truth of the "sixties generation." Thus the episode affirms the argument in the article Pliumbum's father mentions about power in the hands of a naïf.

A scene near the end of the film shows Ruslan meeting with two detectives as they play the Russian version of skittles, *gorodki* [little cities]. Ruslan is the pin boy, setting up the progressively more elaborate block formations, which the men then must knock over by throwing a bat. Ruslan here is a symbolic builder, or tireless rebuilder, a force of energy, while the representatives of the older generation are symbolic destroyers. The gap between the earnest young defender of the system and his would-be mentors is underscored still later, after the policemen betray Ruslan by imprisoning a man he turned in with the understanding that the man (the fiancé of Ruslan's adult female friend/mother figure) would provide information on other, more powerful criminals but not be prosecuted himself. In fact, though Ruslan/Pliumbum does not acknowledge it himself, the experience is a displaced object lesson regarding his own betrayal of his father. The last scene of the film, in which Ruslan chases a boy (whom he recognizes as the thief of his cassette player before the action of the film began) onto a rooftop, is a final visual placement of Ruslan above other members of society, the scene's tragic conclusion validating his father's warnings about the danger of "immature" exercises of power. Ruslan's school friend, Sonia, follows him onto the roof, where she slips and falls to her death. The last frame of the film, shot from the ground below, captures a remote and tiny (i.e., diminished) Ruslan on the roof.

The Husband and Daughter of Tamara Aleksandrovna is often (and deservedly) identified as one of the darkest films of the period. What narratively motivates that darkness is the truncation of a family, specifically the reorientation of a father's parental role.[9] The first image of the film— the full, very Russian-looking face of the titular Tamara Aleksandrovna, singing softly to the camera—does not suggest the horror to follow and, indeed, evokes both universal ideals (female beauty, motherhood, abundance) and the value of the verbal (folk song), two phenomena attacked or eschewed in many films of the time. Soon, however, the song ends and the face becomes a mute, unsmiling mask. Tamara Aleksandrovna walks off, apparently disoriented, and is soon removed permanently from the narrative by being taken off to the hospital with peritonitis.

As the title suggests, the remainder of the film focuses on the other two-thirds of the family, Tamara Aleksandrovna's ex-husband and daughter. The family has already disintegrated by the time the narrative begins; the husband and wife are divorced but still live on different floors of the same apartment building.[10] The characters' descent into complete chaos and violence occupies virtually the entire narrative, and is foreshadowed in an exchange between father and daughter as they watch the ambulance pull away: the girl asks, "Dad, is she going to die?" ["Papa, ona ne umret?"], to which he replies, "Her? No" ["Ona? Net"], a cautious choice of words by the father, who seems careful not to predict that he himself and his daughter will be similarly spared. Verbal communication breaks down from this point on, a process that is highlighted by the film's score (a synthesized sampling of guttural vocal sounds, arranged in cacophonic melodies), as well as by the motif of pantomime:

the father and daughter play a pantomime game over the breakfast table, and later use pantomime to communicate with Tamara Aleksandrovna while standing on the street in front of the hospital. The verbal is almost entirely absent from the last ten minutes of the film, which are devoted to the spectacle of the father being savagely yet methodically beaten up by three teenage boys angry at the daughter for promising them sex and not following through. The increasing muteness of the film, along with the climactic violence perpetrated by the younger generation on a representative of the preceding generation, amounts to a demonstrative rejection of the possibility of productive intergenerational communication. The beating scene is followed by a final shot of the mutilated face of the father in the hospital, now separated from both daughter and wife, as he sings his own song (through broken teeth) to the accompaniment of his maniacal laughter. He is yet another infantilized father, isolated from his family and emblematic of perestroika cinema's dismemberment of the nuclear family as the last, smallest unit of collectivity. He is also the smallest unit of society, an individual consciousness, reduced to a near-primitive state and emblematic of just how comprehensive the breakdown of collectivity had become by the last few years of Soviet power. As the defenders of Soviet authority had done at the dawn of Soviet culture, perestroika-era filmmakers recognized and deployed the innate potency of familial relations on both thematic and metaphorical levels.

Utter pessimism such as Narutskaia's, combined with the anti-verbal impulse and the complete fragmentation of the familial paradigm, represented a rejection of the central (official) perestroika-era strategy, namely, presenting measured exposés of social problems together with clearly implied or openly identified causes of those problems. The refusal by some cultural producers to motivate clearly their use of such inflammatory imagery, verbally or otherwise, was one of cinema's main challenges to perestroika in the latter's capacity as an official sociopolitical policy, and in the articulation of that policy in the most prominent cultural genres associated with the period—journalistic *publitsistika*, documentary film, and the non-*chernukha*, mainstream "social problem" film. Criticized by many as an aesthetic dead end, perestroika-era cinema often unambiguously portrayed generational dead ends, thus playing a prominent role in the radical resignification of generational transition.[11]

Another, considerably more influential perestroika film foreground-
ing a father-daughter relationship is *Malen'kaia Vera*. The titular protagonist is a teenage girl living in a bleak, provincial port town on the Black
Sea. Between typical youthful pursuits such as going to nightclubs, chatting with her girlfriend about their love lives and family problems, and
having sex with her boyfriend, Vera must also frequently play a parental
role to her father. A working-class alcoholic, he is given to (verbally and
sometimes physically) violent outbursts directed at his wife, daughter,
son-in-law (whom he eventually stabs), and bathroom sink (which he
shatters in a rage). Like many cinematic drunks of the perestroika period, and like the titular husband in Narutskaia's film, Vera's father
becomes thoroughly infantilized: unable to walk unassisted, drooling,
his voice reduced to a throaty wail or a feeble cry; at the end of the film
he collapses alone in the tiny kitchen, presumably with a heart attack,
and barely has the strength to call out the names of his children, who
cannot hear him.

After the climactic (non-fatal) stabbing of Vera's new husband, Vera's parents browbeat the young couple into not pressing charges, and
the nuclear family (Sergei is still hospitalized) goes for a day at the beach,
intended as a restorative retreat. When a downpour interrupts their awkward picnic, Vera runs away and takes refuge under an overturned boat.
Her father follows her and—in the space of temporary intimacy created
by the deluge—reforges the bond with his daughter through what is visually marked as clearly paternal behavior.[12] That moment is pivotal for
Vera, who throughout the film searches for an adequate father figure—a
role for which potential pretenders are the physics teacher on whom she
has a crush and her brother, Viktor, a doctor working in Moscow who
comes home at his mother's request to talk some sense into Vera. But
ultimately he is merely a pharmacist—he can only offer her sleeping
pills, with which she attempts suicide. She (unlike Tornike in *Pokaianie*)
survives and even creates her own fledgling family unit by marrying her
boyfriend, but the film ends with a lonely death. That death, of Vera's
father, is metaphoric, for through his demise the film captures the "fate"
of the increasingly irrelevant and impotent Stalinist/Stagnation generation. The lonely death of Vera's father, however, is seemingly balanced
by the formation of the new family, one whose youth and distance from
the previous generation (and thus all Soviet generations) is marked not

only by its members' taut, tanned skin and 1980s fashions but also by their ironic dismissal of Soviet slogans and even Soviet-era non-political wisdom, such as the book on homemaking that Vera's mother gives her as a wedding gift. However, the ostensible evolution represented by Vera and Sergei's de-ideologized union is itself ironic, and is contradicted by the final shot of the couple, alone and miserable in the dark. Their rejection of even the semblance of faith in Soviet ideology is certainly an act of generational self-determination, but, as in so many other narratives of the perestroika period, equal or greater emphasis is placed on the utter lack of a new belief system to replace the discredited old one. The obsolescence of idealism is rendered even more tragic by the fact that Vera and Sergei are stuck in a social, psychological, and physical environment no different from that of their parents' generation, whose life trajectory they seem destined to reproduce. At the risk of overdramatizing the ending of the film, one could claim that the young protagonists are left with neither a past nor a future but only the toxic present moment.

Another film that tempers its sense of irrevocable loss with family-centered optimism is Mikhalkov's *Urga*, which depicts a happily functional nuclear family in the late-Soviet period. However, the happy family here is Mongolian. Gombo and his wife, Pagma, live with their three young children and Gombo's elderly mother in an isolated yurt in the vast Inner Mongolian steppe, a maximally open space that contrasts diametrically with the cramped quarters that dominate the mise-en-scene of *Malen'kaia Vera*. We are first introduced to the couple as they play a traditional sexual game on horseback in which the man chases the woman with a long herding lasso [*urga*] in order to catch and make love to her on the grassy plain. The *urga* is then stuck upright in the ground as a phallic "do not disturb" warning to others. In this opening scene, Gombo is unsuccessful: Pagma spurns his advances and rides off, establishing the central conflict of the film, which directly concerns fatherhood: Gombo wants to have a fourth child, but Pagma, raised in the city, is hesitant, especially since they have already exceeded the Chinese child-limit (for Mongolians) by one.

The opening minutes of the film also include tender scenes of father-son intimacy between Gombo and Bouin, which underscore not only their bond but also the transfer of cultural information (legends and tales about the Mongols and their glorious history of conquest) from one generation to the next.[13] Yet, as in the other films discussed above, when separated from the family, the father becomes infantilized: Gombo takes on the attributes and behavior of a boy his son's age when he leaves his family on his "mission" to the city—to purchase condoms (a task that emphasizes his isolation from his existent and potential progeny). He eats sweets, rides (and falls asleep on) an amusement-park roundabout, drinks a juice box, and tries out the bicycle he has bought for his children. The sequence is less an example of the "indigenous man's adventures in the big city" motif than a portrayal of a (temporarily) deracinated and "de-familied" father. The voiceover narrator at the end of *Urga*, who identifies himself as Gombo's fourth son (not yet conceived during the main action of the film) speaking from at least twenty years in the future, provides the familiar generational break: there is a smokestack at the former site of Gombo's *urga*, and a gas station on the site of the family's yurt.

The over-determinedly positive image of Gombo and his adoring son is the most explicit portrayal of paternal-filial relations in the film, but Sergei, the Russian, is also associated with such imagery, albeit more abstractly. His signature tune, which is so important to him that he has the music tattooed on his back, is "The Hills of Manchuria," a song about the thousands of Russian soldiers killed in the Battle of Mukden in the Russo-Japanese War of 1904–1905. Sergei sings the song, with its references to "sons of the Fatherland" [Otchizny rodnoi syny], immediately after a heated discussion with his friend, Nikolai, about how alienated Russian men are from their heritage, an alienation illustrated by both men's inability to recall the first names of their patrilineal great-grandfathers. The rupture in lines of heredity and memory, and Sergei's constant need to acknowledge, mourn, and repair that rupture, is symbolized by the road from Russia to China that both he and Nikolai are working to build.

The five emblematic films examined here are far from the only perestroika-era visual narratives to engage more or less directly the question of fathers and sons. Others of note include Vladimir Khotinenko's *Zerkalo dlia geroia* [*A Mirror for a Hero* 1988], a time-travel fantasy in which a man of the 1980s encounters his own father in the late-1940s; and Sergei Solov'ev's *Chuzhaia belaia i riaboi* [*The Wild Pigeon* 1986], which examines fatherlessness in the postwar period. In addition to these new productions, several prominent titles among the 1960s and 1970s films that were "de-shelved" by the perestroika-era Conflict Commission had

originally been censored in part precisely because of their politically in-
correct depiction of fathers, children, or the relationships between them.
Kira Muratova's *Dolgie provody* [*Long Goodbyes* 1971, released 1987], for
example, concerns a teenage boy living with his domineering divorced
mother, who tries repeatedly to interfere with the boy's long-distance
relationship with his father. Marlen Khutsiev's *Zastava Il'icha* [*Lenin's
Guard*], also known as *Mne dvadtsat' let* [*I Am Twenty* 1964, restored
1988], which Alexander Prokhorov discusses in his contribution to this
volume, was famously censored in part because of a scene in which a
man is visited by the ghost of his father, who died in the war but feels
incapable of giving his son any advice or words of wisdom. Aleksandr
Askol'dov's *Kommissar* [*The Commissar* 1967, released 1987] deals directly with the question of parenthood, and depicts the adoption of an
unmarried female Russian commissar's baby by a Jewish family.

The proliferation of fatherless sons and sonless fathers on the perestroika screen—once again, a motif that both reflected contemporary
social circumstances and symbolized the generational power dynamics
of a moment in Soviet history—suggests that many cultural producers
viewed the co-presence of more than one generation as a nonissue in the
1980s; that is, the question was not how to negotiate the latest generational
transition but how to represent a point in the country's history in which
transition itself (or at least positive, productive generational continuity)
was impossible, and which was marked by rupture on every level. Abel,
the impotent bureaucrat, has nothing to offer his son except a lethal dose
of vicarious, hereditary guilt, and he renounces his own father too late.
Pliumbum's ineffectual father cannot prevent his son from following
his misguided mania to a tragic conclusion (the death of Sonia). A final
example: Rolan Bykov's *Chuchelo* [*Scarecrow* 1984, released 1986] ends
with the representatives of family tradition and continuity, an elderly
art collector and his nonconformist granddaughter, who throughout
the film is persecuted by her classmates, exiling themselves from the
provincial town, a microcosm of a society in which the breakdown of
common cause and collectivity has made it impossible to live.

The co-presence of multiple male generations in a more or less restricted chronotope (a family residence or the symbolic and real power
institutions of a particular society) is a potential source of both conflict and continuity. As such, that co-presence lends itself to produc-

tive deployment in dramatic narratives, and is laden with metaphorical associations. During perestroika both the symbolic "national family" and the innumerable real families therein were subject to modification, truncation, or even mutilation by sociopolitical forces. Soviet film professionals, from both "inside" and "outside" the film canister, found myriad uses for the nascent, renascent, and discredited paradigms of paternal and filial kinship.

NOTES

1. The story of Pavlik Morozov, the fourteen-year-old boy who informed on his own father during the anti-*kulak* campaign of the 1930s, manifested this most personal of Soviet remythologized human categories in a concrete narrative form. As demonstrated by one of the films I analyze below, Vadim Abdrashitov's *Pliumbum, ili Opasnaia igra* [*Pliumbum, or a Dangerous Game* 1986], the Morozov myth was a Stalinist motif in the Soviet master narrative that was far from obsolete, even more than five decades after Pavlik's death at the hands of angry relatives.

2. For an application of Clark's notion of the Great Family to Soviet film, see Alexander Prokhorov's essay in this volume, chapter 1.

3. In Yeltsin-era Russia, which eschewed leader cultism, familial metaphors were sometimes displaced onto other symbols of the nation. Note, for example, the title of Vladimir Khotinenko's documentary film celebrating the 850th anniversary of the founding of Moscow, *My tvoi deti, Moskva* [*We Are Your Children, Moscow* 1997].

4. Although, in Brezhnev's case, the popular unconscious during the aptly named Stagnation period satirized his blindness to the notion of generational progress and succession, as evidenced by the following joke: "Brezhnev is playing with his grandson. He asks the boy: 'What do you want to be when you grow up?' 'General Secretary!' the boy responds without hesitation. Brezhnev is confused: 'What do we need two General Secretaries for?'"

5. Julie Christensen notes that the first reference to the film in the Soviet press was a simple statement that "Abuladze is completing a film about three generations of a Georgian family" (169).

6. Abuladze's desire to make a film that was at the same time universal and recognizably Georgian is reflected in the fact that, although the "city" of which Varlam was mayor is never named, a well-known Georgian Menshevik song is sung at his funeral (Woll and Turnbull 102). Also, Varlam's physical, verbal, and behavioral image, as many commentators have noted, is a composite of several notorious tyrants of the twentieth century: Stalin, Hitler, Beriia, Mussolini (Woll and Turnbull 24; Christensen 168) "and even Charlie Chaplin's 'great dictator'" (Christensen 168).

7. On the film's engagement with the question of Georgian history and identity, see Christensen passim; and Woll and Turnbull 99–103.

8. "A mozhet, tebe nravitsia vlast'? Smotri, eto opasno! Vchera v *Izvestiiakh* byla stat'ia, ia spetsial'no otlozhil, ty prochti. O tom, kakaia opasnaia shtuka vlast', kogda chelovek eshche ne sozrel moral'no. Ili ty schitaesh', chto ty sozrel? Mozhet, ty videl v zhizni stol'ko zla? No gde i otkuda, ia ne ponimaiu!"

9. On Narutskaia's film and its place among other representative texts employing the *chernukha* [dark naturalism] mode, see Horton and Brashinsky 164; Lawton 201; Plakhov 27, and Belopolskaya. For a more in-depth examination of the *chernukha* influence on Russian cinema, see Graham.

10. Belopolskaya's analysis of the film focuses on its use of the image of the apartment building staircase.

11. For critical evaluations of the *chernukha* trend in Russian culture, see Plakhov, Dobrotvorskii, and Zorin.

12. *Little Vera* is also a late-Soviet version of the archetypal beauty-and-the-beast narrative, which Bruno Bettelheim (for all his unreconstructed-Freudian dogmatism) has convincingly interpreted as symbolic of the difficulty a girl of marrying age has in transferring her love for her father to her husband (303–9).

13. Mikhalkov's 1993 documentary *Anna. Ot 6 do 18* [*Anna. From 6 to 18*], which follows the growth of the director's own daughter, Anna, and his 1994 drama *Utomlennoe solntsem* [*Burnt by the Sun*], starring Mikhalkov and his second daughter, Nadia, would depict both a similar type of father-child intimacy and cultural (this time Russo-Soviet) impartation of wisdom from one generation to the next.

REFERENCES

Belopolskaya, Viktoria. "Life on the Staircase." *Soviet Film* 10 (1989): 12–13.

Bettelheim, Bruno. *The Uses of Enchantment: The Meaning and Importance of Fairy Tales*. New York: Vintage, 1989.

Brashinsky, Michael, and Andrew Horton, eds. *Russian Critics on the Cinema of Glasnost'*. New York: Cambridge University Press, 1994.

Christensen, Julie. "Tengiz Abuladze's *Repentance* and the Georgian Nationalist Cause." *Slavic Review* 50, no. 1 (spring 1991): 163–75.

Clark, Katerina. *The Soviet Novel: History as Ritual*. 3rd ed. Bloomington: Indiana University Press, 2000.

Dobrotvorskii, Sergei. "Nasledniki po krivoi." *Iskusstvo kino* 7 (1991): 25–29.

Graham, Seth. "*Chernukha* and Russian Film." *Studies in Slavic Cultures* 1 (2000): 9–27.

Horton, Andrew, and Michael Brashinsky. *The Zero Hour: Glasnost and Soviet Cinema in Transition*. Princeton, N.J.: Princeton University Press, 1992.

Lawton, Anna. *Kinoglasnost: Soviet Cinema in Our Time*. New York: Cambridge University Press, 1992.

Mindadze, Aleksandr. *Vremia tantsora: Kinopovesti*. Moscow: AST-LTD, 1997.

Plakhov, Andrei. "'Chernukha' i chernaia dyra." *Sovetskii ekran* 12 (1990): 27.

Woll, Josephine, and Denise J. Youngblood. *Repentance*. Kinofile Companion 4. London: I. B. Tauris, 2001.

Zorin, Andrei. "Kruche, kruche, kruche . . . Istoriia pobedy: chernukha v kul'ture poslednikh let." *Znamia* 10 (1992): 198–204.

FILMOGRAPHY

Dolgie provody [*Long Goodbyes*]. Dir. Kira Muratova, 1971; released 1987. Odessa Film Studio.

Kommissar [*The Commissar*]. Dir. Aleksandr Askol'dov, 1967; released 1987. Gorky Film Studio.

Malen'kaia Vera [*Little Vera*]. Dir. Vasilii Pichul, 1988. Gorky Film Studio.

Mne dvadtsat' let (*Zastava Il'icha*) [I'm Twenty (Lenin's Guard)]. Dir Marlen Khutsiev, 1964; restored 1988. Gorky Film Studio.

My deti tvoi, Moskva [*We Are Your Children, Moscow*]. Dir. Vladimir Khotinenko, 1997. 12A.

Muzh i doch' Tamary Aleksandrovny [*The Husband and Daughter of Tamara Aleksandrovna*]. Dir. Ol'ga Narutskaia, 1988. Mosfilm.

Pliumbum, ili Opasnaia igra [*Pliumbum, or a Dangerous Game*]. Dir. Vadim Abdrashitov, 1986. Mosfilm.

Podranki [*Orphans*]. Dir Nikolai Gubenko, 1976. Mosfilm.

Pokaianie [*Repentance*]. Dir. Tengiz Abuladze, 1984; released 1986. Gruziia-Film.

Putevka v zhizn' [*Road to Life*]. Dir. Nikolai Ekk, 1931. Mezhrabpom film.

Serezha [*A Summer to Remember*]. Dir. Georgii Daneliia and Igor' Talankin, 1960. Mosfilm.

Sud'ba cheloveka [*Fate of a Man*]. Dir. Sergei Bondarchuk, 1959. Mosfilm.

Tragediia v stile rok [*Tragedy in the Style of Rock*]. Dir. Savva Kulish, 1988. Mosfilm.

Urga: Territoriia liubvi [*Urga: Territory of Love,* also known as *Close to Eden*]. Dir. Nikita Mikhalkov, 1991. Camera One, Hachette, Trite, Pyramid.

Utomlennoe solntsem [*Burnt by the Sun*]. Dir. Nikita Mikhalkov, 1994. Mosfilm.

PART TWO

War in the Post-Soviet
Dialogue with Paternity

FOUR

The Fathers' War through the Sons' Lens

TATIANA SMORODINSKAYA

VENERATING WORLD WAR II

Tengiz Abuladze's film *Pokaianie* [*Repentance* 1984] marked the beginning of perestroika and glasnost'. It suggested how society should deal with its criminal past for the sake of the future: acknowledge, repent, and renounce. The Son throwing the Father-tyrant's corpse off a cliff symbolized liberation from the repressive power of Soviet patriarchal ideology. It seemed inevitable during the perestroika years and the early 1990s that the collapse of the communist regime would also end numerous propagandistic myths of Soviet history. Various articles, TV programs, books, and documentary films revealed terrifying pages of the bloody history of the USSR, including some rather inglorious facts and hidden secrets about the major Soviet myth—the Great Patriotic War. In the early 2000s, however, owing to high oil prices and fast economic recovery, Russia started to revive its former superpower political ambitions, and demonstrated disturbing signs of a gradual restoration of patriarchal ideology, vividly illustrated by, for example, the Kremlin's control of the media. The new Russian masterminds do not try to restore communist ideals; rather, they strive to create a new unifying national idea, and they clearly realize the importance of the heroic past as a basis for a new patriotic doctrine.

The attempts to revisit World War II history critically, which were welcomed during the 1990s, now are perceived almost as a Russophobe heresy. Whereas virtually no films about World War II appeared for almost a decade after the Soviet Union disintegrated, the first six years of the new century have witnessed a deluge of war films, including mini- and multi-series TV productions. Some of them continue to explore, with integrity and openness, complex and painful truths about the war, at odds with Soviet mythology, but the majority of film directors use the history of World War II as a source of stories for action and adventure films. They include some exposé features for the purpose of extra plot complications, but make no effort to uncover historical truth, which appears to be uncalled for by both authorities and the general public. This essay examines contemporary cinema's treatment of World War II by the generation of "sons," and compares it with the Soviet screen depiction by the generation of "fathers" so as to identify the discrepancies, as well as intersections, between the two.

Passionate renunciation of the Soviet past after the fall of communism took place, unfortunately, against the backdrop of an economic crisis and painful market reforms. Rapid transition from the status of a "world superpower" to that of a Third World country caused social depression and political confusion among Russians. It became clear that Russia's disoriented society, deprived of its ideological foundations, needed to unite around some new idea(s) and reconcile with its past. Sons, who first rejected their Fathers, started to search for them in an effort to restore the interrupted succession of generations. The theme of fatherlessness taken up by countless films during the 1990s was impossible to ignore.[1] Often part of the plot was a desperate search for a lost father or an alternative paternal figure.[2] And if sons happened to find fathers, they accepted them regardless of past sins, faults, and mistakes. Taking into account the cultural, ideological, religious, and historical significance of the Father mythology in Russia's worldview, the desire to find a "lost" father and reconstruct the interrupted succession of generations became an increasingly important social and political task for a new Russian statehood. Sons realized the importance of the father's blessing, which Peter Blos, in his book *Son and Father: Before and beyond the Oedipus Complex*, calls "that protective magical spell" (12).

SONS IN SEARCH OF FATHERS: THE 1990S

Aleksei German's film *Khrustalev, mashinu!* [*Khrustalev, My Car!* 1998] is not only a gruesome portrayal of the atmosphere during the last days of Stalin's rule, but also shows a son's indirect homage to his father, a famous brain surgeon, general, and war veteran. Constructed as a phantasmagoric recollection of the past through the prism of a child's capricious memory, sporadic episodes and dialogues, and real and imagined scenes, it has at the center of that horrifying nightmare the son's admiration for his father. The teenage son is suppressed and ignored by his despotic father, whom he both worships and hates. At one point the son, struggling with love, fear, and embarrassment, is on the verge of reporting his father to the authorities. In an interview German stated that the father in the film is a brave man, though with his own flaws: "he started crying only one time, when he saw his son by the telephone [ready to report him—T.S.]" ["on zaplakal vsego odin raz, kogda uvidel syna riadom s telefonom"] (German). After the painful realization that both his son and his Father (Stalin), and his Fatherland, have betrayed him, the general, with a sinister smile, boards a train and disappears into the abysmal void of history. The narrator's (son's) final comment is: "I never saw my father again . . . He was neither among those arrested nor among those killed."

After decades of real-life father-son betrayals under Stalin, vividly illustrated by the mythology of Pavlik Morozov's Soviet martyrdom, the mass rejection of repressed fathers—"enemies of the people"—by their wives and children,[3] and complex love-hate relations between generations, perestroika finally witnessed a psychological and political yearning for reconciliation. One had to find in Soviet history an uncompromising event, a national heroic deed, whose valor all generations could proudly share. Such a glorious moment was unquestionably the Soviet victory over fascism. For all Russians (and former Soviets), Victory Day (May 9) is the only unchallenged Soviet holiday enthusiastically celebrated by people of all ages and political views. Heroism and the Soviet people's enormous human sacrifice are internationally admitted as crucial in the Nazis' defeat. Thus the only generation of fathers unconditionally acknowledged as worthy of sons' admiration is the generation of the Great Patriotic War veterans.

Soviet society always attributed the highest moral qualities to veterans, who presumably could never be corrupt or unfair, since they had endured a cleansing mortal ordeal and were part of a larger Soviet World War II mythology. The fallen soldiers were worshiped as saints and martyrs, and survivors were role models for the young. Aleksandr Shpagin, in his article "The Religion of War," provides an excellent definition of the World War II myth:

> The great myth brilliantly created some time ago according to an unspoken agreement in our society and suiting all strata of the population is a complex, profound myth, not at all old-fashioned and not like all the other Soviet myths. According to it, the War is the great exploit of the Soviet people; the War is a test of the durability of all human qualities; thanks to the War, we saved our country and the whole world from the "brown plague." The war is one of the best pages in our history. (5:57)[4]

The majority of films made in the 1990s, which focused on contemporary demoralization, criminalization, and deep spiritual crises, were labeled "*chernukha*."[5] Although World War II was not the focus of filmmakers' attention, elderly war veterans were frequently present on the screen and preserved their Soviet status as the ultimate moral authority in society. Indeed, they (or even their ghosts) were often the only source of spiritual strength and integrity in a confused post-Soviet milieu. For example, in *Voroshilovskii strelok* [*Voroshilov's Sniper*, Govorukhin 1996] a war veteran is the only one to defend his granddaughter's honor, and in *Vor* [*The Thief*, Chukhrai 1996] visions of a heroic father-soldier are the moral support for the little orphan San'ka until the criminal self-proclaimed stepfather replaces him.[6] In Sergei Ursuliak's film *Sochinenie ko dniu pobedy* [*A Composition Devoted to Victory Day* 1999], three war veterans reproached by their children and betrayed by the new state hijack an airplane and disappear into the "blue yonder." The metaphoric flight of the three father-veterans is obviously a bitter warning to their children[7] who are now on their own, unprotected and uprooted without the paternal "magic spell."

In response to the bleak screen portrayal of a society in freefall, in 1998 the journal *Iskusstvo kino* [*The Art of Cinema*] organized a roundtable discussion, "The End of the Century—the End of *Chernukha*?" ["Konets veka—konets chernukhi?"]. Film directors, critics, writers, and commentators on culture debated the exact meaning of the term and talked about the current state of film production. *Chernukha*'s dominance on the screen was explained by various factors, ranging from Russian masochism and artistic reaction to years of censorship to poor, untalented directing. In his opening remarks, Daniil Dondurei, the journal's chief editor, also mentioned a certain prejudice against producing uplifting patriotic films. He said that in the contemporary Russian cultural context it was considered shameful to think about the ideals and goals of personal and social existence, whereas in the West (for example, in the United States), goal-establishing mass ideology was approved and encouraged. That is why, Dondurei concluded, the Russian intelligentsia perceived President Yeltsin's call for the development of a national idea as funny and symptomatic of a national inferiority complex, or as a "belch" of the totalitarian regime.[8]

In the following few years discussion about *chernukha* and patriotism quickly became outdated. Rapid economic and financial recovery led Russia to pronounce itself "a sovereign democracy" and "an energy superpower," finally "up off its knees."[9] Patriotism was not only recognized as a fundamental prerequisite for uniting a nation, but it also became a well-financed imperative, issued by the state. The intelligentsia, including filmmakers, did not wait long to respond.

CELLULOID PATRIOTISM IN ACTION

The overwhelming majority of films produced by the new generation of Russian filmmakers fall into the category of "patriotic action" films. They achieve three goals: satisfy the urge for the reinstatement of national glory, make money at the box office, and, in most cases, do not radically deviate from the myth of the "holy war"; thus they do not hurt the feelings of veterans or the new Russian patriots.

The first film about World War II to appear after more than a decade was the cinematic adaptation of Emmanuil Kazakevich's novel *Zvezda* [*The Star* 2002],[10] a story of the heroic exploits and deaths of a group of Soviet scouts in 1944. The popularity of this film can be explained not only by its masterful cinematography, excellent acting, and a gripping plot but also by its patriotic pathos. Shortly after its release, the film critic Elena Stishova wrote: "Lebedev's *Zvezda* makes us understand what the collective soul was asking for. To put it very briefly—revenge. After long years of self-humiliation to recognize on the screen 'your own' and yourself so as to feel proud of yourself"] (17).[11] The "revenge" was both ideological and artistic. The young film director Nikolai Lebedev proved that a Russian movie can compete with Hollywood productions, be a tribute to fallen heroes and a patriotic boost for young Russians, as well as an action film providing quality entertainment.

An admirer of Alfred Hitchcock, Lebedev made *Zvezda* a suspense thriller. Into a post-Soviet heroic saga he incorporated dynamic action and the cinematic hyperrealism of contemporary Western war films, such as *Saving Private Ryan* (Spielberg 1998). *Zvezda* was a remake of Aleksandr Ivanov's 1949 movie, which was very popular in its time. By choosing to produce a remake, Lebedev obviously relied on the traditions of the Soviet war film, and Lebedev's Russian scouts (whom the Germans call "green spirits") are genuine superheroes precisely in the "fathers'" tradition. Brave, humane, and ready for self-sacrifice, they die with honor and pathos, just as in the 1949 version. Lebedev opted for much younger actors, however, which made the line preceding a heroic Russian character's inevitable valiant death more poignant and disturbing than in the earlier version: "And you have no wish to die. Right, Lieutenant?" ["A umirat'—to ne khochetsia, a leitenant?"]. Filming the remake in color added emotional power: lush, life-affirming summer settings that display the beauty of nature contrast with the gruesome, agonizing deaths of the handsome young characters. The soundtrack by Aleksei Rybnikov (composer of popular scores for the first Soviet musicals) intensifies the powerful catharsis of the final scene, where the burning house in which the heroes make their last stand recalls an eternal flame against the backdrop of the beautiful Russian landscape (Figure 4.1). In the epilogue the final frames of marching soldiers gradually are transformed from color into monochrome, bridging time, generation, and traditions, and paying tribute to those who fought in the war. In an interview Lebedev said: "At Mosfilm there actually exist a wonderful car park, lots of war equipment and machinery—moreover, in very good condition. It's impossible to make a film without props, and, thank God, there were people who'd preserved all those treasures, didn't squander them, and continue to keep them in good shape" (21–22).[12] The success of *Zvezda* was followed by a significant number of World War II films made by sons and grandsons, who mobilized not only preserved military equipment but also the strategic reserve of patriotism that the 2000s called for.

Zvezda (2002) also provided continuity with fathers' war films by casting Aleksei Kravchenko in one of the major parts. Seventeen years earlier Kravchenko had played a key role in the last Soviet World War II film, Elem Klinov's *Idi i smotri* [*Come and See* 1985], which presumably marked the end of the Soviet mythological film tradition. There, the distorted, almost insane face of the teenage guerilla fighter Flor (played by young Kravchenko) left no doubt that hatred, murder, and war can produce madness, moral degradation, and spiritual devastation, regardless of whether the war is "sacred and just." Klimov's film challenged the Soviet belief in a holy war as a cleansing moral experience, which brings out the best in people. As Shpagin notes: "On the surface the film preserved the usual antifascist features of Soviet war cinema, but internally it put an end to [that trend]. In reality Klimov didn't just put an end to it, but hammered a stake into the grave of the Soviet war myth, and so powerfully that for fifteen years after him nobody filmed anything about the war" (6:89).[13]

In her book, *Russian War Films*, Denise Youngblood divides post-Soviet World War II films into three groups: those that set the record straight, those that use World War II as entertainment, and those that transform the war into art. *Zvezda* obviously qualifies as entertainment, in the popular genre of catastrophe films, but with a timely patriotic overtone. In that respect it also observes traditions, for Soviet cinema likewise had produced World War II stories for entertainment, while never forgetting propaganda: in the 1970s, for example, there were plenty of war thrillers, war mysteries, and war adventures. Whereas in the 1990s directors of genre films favored the Chechen War as screen material, since 2000 the Great Patriotic War once again has become the primary military conflict for action-romance-adventure stories. Most post-Soviet World War II films following *Zvezda* prefer the adventures of saboteurs, spies, and snipers, partly for financial reasons perhaps (war epics require large-scale battle scenes and therefore demand a different level of financing not always available to Russian cinematographers), but also for the anticipated success of suspense plots at the box office. Unlike Soviet films, the new Russian World War II genre films often include enmities and episodes previously forbidden. These revelations not only expose some facts in the history of the war earlier passed over, but they also help complicate the plot and add spice to characters' development.[14] In such cases war merely serves as a basis for action or adventure plots. Such "costume war [films]" (in Aleksei German's words) often tell stories about imagined or mythologized fathers, without concern for historical accuracy. For example, in *Nesluzhebnoe zadanie* [*Unofficial Business*, Vitalii Vorob'ev, 2004], a regiment of Cossacks-*plastuns* [scouts] is anachronistically portrayed as a *spetsnaz* [special forces] reconnaissance unit, as indeed they were in the nineteenth century but not during World War II.

Screenplays purportedly based on memoirs likewise may revise the past and breed polemics. Aleksandr Atanesian's *Svolochi* [*Bastards* 2006], an exotic action film promoted as an exposé of one of the secret and brutal phases of World War II, provoked serious debates about the war's "truths" and myths. *Svolochi* is an adaptation of a chapter in Vladimir Kunin's autobiographical novel *Mika and Alfred*, in which the author claims that he had been trained in a Soviet secret camp for teenage saboteurs to be used for special missions at the enemy's rear. According to Kunin, the Soviet state recruited orphaned boys from among young prisoners sentenced to death for murder and armed robbery. Just before the film's release, the Federal Security Service (FSB; formerly the KGB) published an article claiming that such camps were established not by the Soviets but by the Germans.[15] Even if Kunin's account is false, the story seems to be consonant with actual Stalinist politics of the time. But verification is impossible, since access to KGB/FSB archives is still closed or limited. Atanesian's film has created a new—though this time, anti-Soviet—myth.

Svolochi is constructed according to the morphology of the traditional war film: training, assembling a team, flushing out the enemy, heroic exploits, death or happy rescue. That narrative structure was at the heart of countless Soviet war films, and has proved to be a success in post-Soviet Russia: in 2007 *Svolochi* won the "MTV Russia" best film award, which is based on popular vote. However, the renowned film director Vladimir Men'shov refused to present the award during the ceremony because, in his opinion, the film "disgraced his country" ["Ia ne sobiraius' vruchat' priz fil'mu, kotoryi pozorit moiu stranu"].[16] The chilling effect of *Svolochi*, which sets the film apart, is that teenage characters (unlike Ivan in Andrei Tarkovsky's *Ivan's Childhood* or other young avengers in Soviet War films) are not conscious heroes but are sentenced little criminals simply trying to survive. No patriotic rhetoric "elevates" the film, the young saboteurs have no love for their Motherland, and they make no attempt to atone for their guilt. At a point of no return, one of the boys regrets that he lied about his father's death at the front: "Maybe I should confess that my father is in a penal battalion"—in which case the boy cannot be considered an orphan and therefore cannot be recruited into a special saboteur unit.

As part of the fathers/sons screen dialogue, this comment likely alludes to a Soviet film, *Olen'ia okhota* [*Deer Hunt*, Iurii Boretskii 1981), which features sons unofficially enlisted in the fathers' military activities; fascists rely on children in a local orphanage in occupied territory to flush out a partisan unit led by an NKVD officer. The ploy proceeds from the German commander's belief that *chekisty* (NKVD personnel) traditionally nurtured warm feelings for war orphans—a belief based on Feliks Dzerzhinskii's supposed patronage of the schools-communes for homeless abandoned children. In the film Soviet partisans outsmart the Germans and save the boys from sacrificing themselves, though in real life neither the NKVD nor the Father of All Peoples, whose Criminal Code of 1935 held fourteen–year–olds as liable as adults for all activities, was particularly concerned about protecting and saving children.

WAR, UNCENSORED

Certainly films like *Svolochi* had no chance of being produced in the Soviet Union, which also held true for films about penal battalions, the Soviet counterintelligence agency SMERSH, the persecution of war veterans after the war, or the treatment of German prisoners.[17] Two recent highly rated TV mini-series, watched by millions, provide honest and shocking accounts of precisely those aspects of the war: *Poslednii boi maiora Pugacheva* [*The Last Battle of Major Pugachev*, Fat'ianov 2005][18] and *Shtrafbat* [*Penal Batallion*, Dostal' 2004]. The screenplays for both were written by Eduard Volodarskii, a member of the fathers' generation who authored more than fifty screenplays for Soviet films (including Aleksei German's *Moi drug Ivan Lapshin* [*My Friend Ivan Lapshin*] and *Proverka na dorogakh* [*The Trial on the Roads*]. His proposal to Filipp Ermash, the 1970s' minister of cinematography, to make a movie about penal battalions was rudely rebuffed (Volodarskii 32),[19] but the changed political climate twenty years later enabled him finally to realize his project. Volodarskii's case is rare, for ideas and proposals that had to be altered or abandoned by the older generation of Soviet cinematographers recently have found their way to the screen only thanks to the sons. As Petr Todorovskii, a war veteran and master of Soviet filmmaking, said: "Today war movies are filmed by young guys . . . they're free and can express everything they want to, they've plenty of information and technical capacities . . . as for us, we always censored ourselves" (Todorovskii 2005, 76).[20]

Back in 1965 Todorovskii made the film *Vernost'* [*Faithfulness*],[21] a sentimental story of first love, heartfelt friendship, and anticipation of the war's tragic ordeal. The lyrical, touching movie was typical of numerous Thaw films that paid attention to individual human destiny. Todorovskii coauthored the script, based on Todorovskii's personal experience as a trainee at a military school in 1943, with another war veteran, the poet Bulat Okudzhava. In addition to the obligatory optimism required of Soviet writers and directors, and ideological censorship, Thaw war films were characterized by the desire of middle-aged veterans to reenact the happy days of their youth, and to pay poetic tribute to the lost generation of their peers: the boys who, in Okudzhava's words, had "separation and smoke instead of weddings."[22] Many years later, in 2002, Todorovskii said in an interview: "[As a participant of the war] I saw a great many tragic and bloody episodes, a huge number of useless victims. A friend of mine died before my eyes. But many years later for some reason only happy reminiscences surface. That was life. There was love, passion. Humor. People remained people. And the first films I made were indeed happy" (Todorovskii 2002, 6).[23] In *Vernost'* concrete signs of war appear only at the film's end, seen by recruits from the train approaching the front, as a gloomy foreboding of their disastrous future, whereas the film itself presents the innocent, happy story of the awakening of sexual emotions. Nothing casts a cloud on student life at the military school: the instructors are fair and wise, friends are sincere and trustworthy, and the hardships of everyday life seem trivial and incidental.

Forty years later Petr Todorovskii's son, Valerii, produced a TV-miniseries titled *Kursanty* [*The Students*, Andrei Kavun 2004],[24] based on his father's autobiographical novel *Vspominai—ne vspominai* [*Recall—or Not*], which, according to the co-producer, Il'ia Neretin, Valerii virtually forced his father to write ("Kursanty").[25] As in his father's film four decades earlier, one of the major plot lines develops the story of first love.

Several main characters seem to originate in *Vernost'*, but *Kursanty* is far from poeticizing the happy days of young students' lives. Three months of rigorous and sometimes brutal training in a starving small town in the rear transform naïve romantic adolescents into mature, tough adults. Innocent kisses are replaced by passionate sexual experiences, military instructors range from traumatized war heroes to NKVD villains, and concepts of honor, friendship, and duty are fundamentally challenged. When a young officer and a student who try to help two starving women (with whom they are in love) by stealing grain from a warehouse, their efforts result in incarceration, a stint in the penal battalion, and broken lives for several people. *Kursanty* includes a set of conflicts genuinely representative of the wartime era (such as NKVD pressure, hunger and black market operations in the rear, unfair trials, false accusations, and repressions based on nationality) and carefully reconstructs the details of everyday life that militate against a "happy" picture. Whereas *Vernost'* leaves the fate of its characters unknown, a voiceover in *Kursanty* reports the tragic destiny of each character throughout the film. Todorovskii Sr. created a cinematic lyrical poem of love and innocence in anticipation of war's horrors, and his son produced a realistic film-novel that spotlights the brutal reality of experiences devoid of poetic ambiance.

Post-Soviet sons seem less concerned than the fathers with glorious victories on the battlefield and individual choices in the midst of a clear-cut opposition between right and wrong, enemy and "our own." The uncensored history of the war posed many unanswered questions and complicated previously unchallenged assumptions. The discrepancy in viewpoint and concept between the two generations of directors emerges starkly in the film *Svoi* [*Our Own* 2004], where a "father" adopts the "son's" stance. A collaboration between screenwriter Valentin Chernykh (b. 1935) and director Dmitrii Meskhiev (b. 1963), *Svoi* traces the life in the occupied territories and the fate of POWs. It demonstrates the unanimously acknowledged importance of "sorting things out" for the postwar generations of sons and grandsons. In an interview Chernykh admitted that the film drew on his childhood reminiscences (Kichin 7), and elsewhere he elaborated on what moved him to write about the occupation and POWs: "Maybe it's time to think about why we had so many POWs. . . . Why there were so many killed? . . . nobody's going to sort this out except for us" (Chernykh 85).[26]

Life in the occupied territories is probably the most controversial aspect of World War II history. To this day the very question of who was an occupant and who was a liberator in the territories annexed by the USSR in accordance with the Molotov-Ribbentrop Pact of 1939 (which included the Baltic republics, Western Belorussia, Western Ukraine, and Bessarabia) remains passionately debated. In his book *Okkupatsiia. Pravda i mify* [*Occupation. Truth, and Myths* 2002] the historian Boris Sokolov claims that people in the occupied territories experienced more losses and suffering than the rest of the Soviet population, especially if one considers the postwar persecution of those who were accused of collaborating with the Germans (Sokolov 329). The Soviet state condemned as treason any form of cooperation with the Germans, even for elementary survival, unless a person was on a special intelligence mission or belonged to an underground resistance organization. This perspective is so deeply rooted in public consciousness that any attempts to disclose historical facts contradicting the Soviet mythology are perceived as heresy.[27]

Whereas the distinction between "us" and "them" seemed apparent in the Soviet cinema of "fathers," Meskhiev's *Svoi* blurs that division, problematizing identity and identification for both the film's characters and its viewers. The village headmaster collaborating with the Germans (a former kulak persecuted by the Soviet authorities) provides shelter to three POWs, one of whom is his own son. Everybody wants to survive and has to make difficult choices about whether to trust, kill, or betray the others, and those choices, as Elena Prokhorova observes in her review, "are based on family allegiances and circumstances, not ideology" (Prokhorova). Unlike his Soviet predecessors, Meskhiev shows that communist ideas have not penetrated the everyday lives of Russian peasants, for whom clan, family bonds, and father-son relations are still more powerful than the class distinctions promulgated by the state. The film rehabilitates such national personae as the father of a biological family, lost in the artificial ideological constructs of Soviet paternal surrogates.

CHALLENGING THE WAR MYTH

Among many war myths, the myth of the people's heroic avengers waging a guerilla war in the occupied territories became the most powerful in Soviet war historiography. Numerous films glorifying the heroic struggle of partisan units produced at Belarusfilm studio bred the unofficial nickname "Partisanfilm" studio. In his *Stalin's Guerrillas: Soviet Partisans in World War II*, historian Kenneth Slepyan observes: "The movement became a critical part of the Soviet Union's official myth of the war that the regime used as a source of its own legitimacy. The partisans—or, rather, a sanitized version of them—became mythic heroes but only at the cost of the suppression of many of their actual experiences and memories" (Slepyan 278). Klimov's perestroika-era film, *Idi i smotri* (*Come and See* 1985), already challenged the depiction of valorous partisan heroes who represented the unanimous resistance of Soviet people led by the Communist Party. "They are definitely portrayed as jaded and amoral," maintains Denise Youngblood. "Everyone in *Come and See* seems to have lost the sense of right and wrong in the chaos of war" (Youngblood 1996, 93). However, the partisan mythology was so insistently promoted by Soviet films, literature, and official propaganda that revealing anything negative was blasphemy, and remains so to this day, particularly in Belarus. Previous attempts to de-consecrate the people's war in Soviet cinematography were always strictly blocked,[28] and the fate of a recent film confirms that this tradition still thrives in contemporary Belarus: The ground-breaking film-parable *Okkupatsiia. Misterii* [*Occupation. Mystery Plays* 2003], by the young Belarusian director Andrei Kudinenko, is banned from distribution on the grounds that it does not correspond to the "truth" of the war, can offend the feelings of war veterans, and may exert a negative influence on young generations.

Shot with a digital camera, Kudinenko's film is an independent project sponsored by the Hubert Bals Fund (Netherlands) at a cost of less than $50,000. Yet, this low-budget film marks the birth of national Belarusian cinema, and is a turning point in screen representations of partisan life during the occupation. It consists of three novellas: "Adam and Eve," "Mother," and "Father," each accompanied by an epigraph from the Holy Scriptures. Like medieval mystery plays, these segments and citations allude to biblical stories. Characters' actions are ruled by the basic instincts of survival and love, and have nothing to do with ideology. Fatal mistakes and wrong choices lead to death and destruction. As in ancient Greek tragedies, characters are torn between their private human desires and beliefs, on the one hand, and legitimate duties and obligations to the state—that is, to the more abstract world, on the other. *Okkupatsiia* is a cinematic homage not only to the memory of all Belarusians who survived the turmoil of occupation but also to the personal family histories of its authors: Kudinenko's grandfather perished in a penal battalion and the father of the film's screenwriter, Aleksandr Kochan, participated in the Belarusian underground, was incarcerated in a Soviet prison, and fought in a partisan unit.

The Belarusian filmmakers defined the genre of their film as existential drama with elements of a thriller. They considered the historical distance sufficient for them to take, finally, a detached and dispassionate look at the tragic events of what, as Kudinenko said in an interview, essentially was a civil war. The four partisans in the film are an NKVD officer, Rustam; a Russian partisan, Sergei; and two Belarusians. One of the Belarusians, Iakov, brags about being a "hereditary partisan," a grandson of the legendary Loiko, who fought "*moskali*" (Russians) back in the old days. He fights Germans because they killed his mother, but he also does not hesitate to kill Rustam when the latter cuts the throat of a collaborator's wife during a punishment operation (the commonplace execution of a collaborator): "My grandfather did not fight [the Russians] so that some Turks could slaughter our women."

In the first novella the young Belarusian orphan Adam is forced to join the partisans. When the Russian partisan, Sergei, wants him to kill a deserter from the unit who preferred peaceful life with a beautiful Polish girl, Eve, to fighting, Adam kills the Russian instead. The deserter meanwhile commits suicide, and Adam, bewitched by Eve's sexual appeal, stays with her, which makes him a new target for the partisans' revenge. The second novella, "Mother," is an existential poem about the invincible power of women's maternal instinct, and it radically revises Fridrikh Ermler's father-era *Ona zashchishchaet rodinu* [*She Defends Her Motherland* 1943] through humanization and de-ideologization. A mute woman loses her baby, which is run over by German motorcyclists, only to find one of the Germans later in the woods, wounded by partisans. Her first reaction is, predictably, the desire to kill him, but that impulse cedes to love, and the woman cares for the young German, breast-feeds him(!), and, when he recovers and leaves, she burns down her house and perishes in total madness and despair. The plot recalls a Soviet film by Leonid Golovnia, *Mater' chelovecheskaia* [*Mother of Hu-*

mankind 1975], based on Vitalii Zakrutkin's novel, in which a woman named Mariia, following the loss of her husband and son, unsuccessfully tries to save a fatally wounded German soldier. After he dies she rescues seven Russian orphans; taking care of them helps her to survive. The film's subtle religious allusions and its transformation of the enemy into a human being tested the limits of the Soviet myth, with its obligatory demonizing of the enemy. Rendering it acceptable was its life-asserting hymn to an epic Soviet womanhood, a symbol of humanism. Reflecting the "sons'" different, de-ideologized perspective, *Okkupatsiia. Misterii* does not privilege unconditional loyalty to state imperatives; instead, it shows natural instinct prevailing over reason, an absence of a heroic sense of duty, and fate's mercilessness over feeble humanity.

In similar fashion the third novella, "Father," suggests how easily one may be misled by pretenders. Iuzek, a little boy who lives with his mother and stepfather—a policeman collaborating with the fascists— longs to find his real flesh-and-blood biological father, who disappeared on Soviet territory before the war. His craving causes Iuzek to believe, all too readily, the partisan who pretends to be his father so as to penetrate the house of a traitor—a scenario paralleling that of Pavel Chukhrai's *Vor* [*The Thief* 1997]. After murdering Iuzek's parents (mother and step- father), the partisans take him with them, but on the way to the camp he gets lost, and in the final scene runs through a snowy forest calling for his illusionary father.

At least one reviewer has suggested that Iuzek's passionate desire to find his biological father symbolizes the quest for a national identity (Gusakovskaia). Indeed, reinstating Belarusians' national self is very important for Kudinenko, who views the Soviet past and the World War II occupation as the final blows to Belarusian identity. He opens the film with a mock-history (presented as narrative titles on the screen) of his people:

> Five hundred years ago they didn't know that they were Belarusians, but they had the largest state in Europe. With time they realized that the Belarusians no longer had a state, and they were considered either half-Russians or defective Poles. But they still existed. Finally, they were mixed with Soviet people. After the war and occupation only a few of them survived. Now Belarusians have a state, but they've discovered that they no longer exist.[29]

A radical cinematic reevaluation of World War II for Belarusians such as Kudinenko's requires a distanced, objective view of the past and a freedom from its emotional and mythological hold that, quite simply, were impossible for the fathers, who not only experienced the war firsthand but also were expected to share the official Soviet view of it. In contemporary Russian cinema only Aleksei German Jr., son of Aleksei Iurievich German, has managed to emancipate his artistic vision of war to that degree. War, in fact, constitutes one of the major links between three generations of creative males in the German family.

Aleksei Iurievich German, an uncompromising film director of integrity not much favored by authorities during Soviet times, paid homage to World War II in the films *Proverka na dorogakh* [*Trial on the Roads* 1971] and *Dvadtsat' dnei bez voiny* [*Twenty Days without War* 1976]. The latter, based on a story by Konstantin Simonov, and narrating a short span in the life of a war correspondent visiting the evacuation zone, fared quite well, whereas the former ran afoul of censorship and was shelved for fourteen years. *Proverka na dorogakh,* scripted by Eduard Volodarskii on the basis of stories by German's father, Iurii, was criticized for "de-heroicizing" the people's resistance during the war and for offering a sympathetic portrayal of a traitor. Indeed, the film challenges the official Soviet doctrine of no trust or forgiveness for former POWs and collaborators. The plot revolves around a Soviet POW, Lazarev, who agrees to serve in the Nazi police division in exchange for his life, but at the first opportunity joins a partisan unit, eager to atone for his guilt as a collaborator. Afforded that chance, he is "tested" in several saboteur operations and dies a heroic death. If showing an ex-collaborator's death in a heroic light was unorthodox, so, too, was the idea, expressed in the ongoing debate between Commissar Petushkov and the guerillas' commander, Lokotkov, that individual human life has considerable value. Such episodes as Lokotkov's refusal to blow up a railway bridge with a barge full of Soviet POWs floating under it was completely unacceptable to Stalinist ideology, which insisted that state goals be achieved at any price. German questioned one of the cornerstones of Soviet war mythology: Was the unprecedented Soviet human sacrifice[30] always justified and absolutely unavoidable? But German does not want to distance himself emotionally from the war, unlike his son, Aleksei German Jr., thirty years later in his debut film, *Poslednii poezd* [*The Last Train* 2003].

The father's film, *Proverka na dorogakh,* begins with a long shot of a Nazi transport moving through a snowy field, viewed through the binoculars of a partisan commander waiting to launch an ambush. The detailed close-up of the Nazis is accompanied by the commander's routine comments: that a handsome officer's winter boots which would fit someone in the partisan unit, and that "fascist bastards guzzle canned meat" and play chess with surprisingly tiny pieces. Unlike most Soviet war films, German's does not deliberately dehumanize the enemy; the film's close-ups show Nazi soldiers as ordinary people, tired and cold. The partisans' unemotional comments about the boots and looks of the people they are about to kill, in addition to the sounds of constant coughing and loud breathing, create the impression of a casual approach to the business of war, far from the official heroic pathos. Yet, despite these dissident elements in German's film, the depiction of war follows key aspects of the tradition: war is seen through the eyes of a Russian, the world unambiguously separates "us" from "them"/the enemy, and follows a logical chain of events and actions. In the words of a nurse in the Soviet classic *Oni srazhalis' za rodinu* [*They Fought for the Motherland,* Sergei Bondarchuk 1975): "War loves order" ["Voina poriadochek liubit"].

The son's *Poslednii poezd* deviates fundamentally from the World War II Soviet film tradition. German Jr.'s film implicitly polemicizes with his father's *Proverka na dorogakh,* for though stylistically it follows German Sr.'s distinct cinematographic manner, ideologically it breaks new ground. Whereas the "black and white" winter in *Proverka na dorogakh* is bright and appealing, winter in *Poslednii poezd* appears as a hostile blizzard, an animated landscape of disarray and total despair (Figure 4.2). *Proverka na dorogakh* traces a coherent storyline, with heroes and villains ("ours" and "theirs"), intelligible dialogue, and heroic exploits; *Poslednii poezd* dissolves into a nightmarish, distorted reality, similar to the portrayal of the Stalin era in his father's film *Krustalev, mashinu!* It is no accident that the soundtracks of both lack music, offering only scraps of conversation and random sounds, with the addition of gunshots, gusting winds, and constant coughing in *Poslednii poezd.* Most unorthodox is that the war in German Jr.'s film is seen through the eyes of the enemy, a fat, awkward German doctor, Doctor Fishbach, who has never used a gun and is unable to kill. He arrives on the last train to the front, just before the German army's hurried retreat. Instead of emphasizing Nazi brutality, the film shows how Doctor Fishbach and another German, a mailman, are lost and disoriented amid the chaos of moving frontlines and Russia's endless winter landscape as they struggle to survive and find the way out of the "existential dead end" that confronts them (Zubavina 36). While wandering in the woods, they unexpectedly encounter a group of terrified, abandoned Russian actresses and witness the partisans' composed murder of Nazi soldiers. The film's conclusion shows the hopeless doctor seated on a broken suitcase under a torn umbrella, holding a dying Russian actress's hand, unable to help or understand what she is saying. Despite his meticulous attention to hyperrealistic details, German Jr. attempted to look at the war from the maximum possible historical distance. What he achieved was a cinematic pacifist statement that removed the sacred halo from the myth of the "holy war"—an achievement psychologically and ideologically beyond the "fathers'" reach.

CONCLUSION

A perceptible tendency in contemporary world cinema is to depart from a conventional "heroes versus villains" portrayal of World War II, and to present a more objective, or at least more complicated, picture. The remoteness of the events helps to focus on the real issues, personalize war ordeals, and shed simplistic oppositions and ideological distortions. Every nation involved in World War II had its own tragic experience, and coming to terms with it requires the courage to acknowledge all aspects of one's actions, regardless of whether they were shameful or glorious. Paul Verhoeven's *Zwartboek* (2006) candidly deals with Holland's tragedy of collaboration. The taboo-breaking comedy *Mein Führer: The Truly Truest Truth about Adolf Hitler* (2006) by Swiss director Dani Levy ridicules the major villain of the epoch. Clint Eastwood's two films released in 2006 depict one of the bloodiest battles in the Pacific from the viewpoint not only of Americans (*Flags of Our Fathers*) but also of the Japanese (*Letters from Iwo Jima*), exemplifying the current interest in examining the war from all perspectives.

National strength is rooted at least partly in the ability to deal honestly with the collective past. Contemporary Russia, busy with the complex task of combining into a new national doctrine the legitimacies of both the Soviet Union and Imperial Russia, is struggling to part with its glorious myths. During this difficult process, various works on the small and large screen suggest that manipulating history once again has become a vehicle for mass propaganda. In the last few years Russian society has shown disturbing signs of historical amnesia. Numerous sociological polls indicate that the population does not care to know the truth about the past if it is painful and discomfiting. On television, films disclosing Soviet crimes coexist with such TV series as *Stalin. Live* (Grigorii Liubomirov 2006), anniversary films about Brezhnev (the mini-series *Brezhnev: Sumerki imperii* [*Brezhnev: Twilight of the Empire*, Sergei Snezhkin 2006], and such documentary mini-series as *I lichno Leonid Il'ich* [*And Personally Leonid Il'ich*, Leonid Parfenov 2006], all portraying Soviet leaders as "regular," unthreatening human beings. Numerous action films with KGB/FSB agents as superheroes alternate with film adaptations of works by Solzhenitsyn and Shalamov. Nostalgic talk of the "good old" Soviet past and of the need to reinstall the monument to Dzerzhinskii is no longer confined to the marginal urgings of old Communists. The abundance on television of old Soviet films, some of which are filled with Soviet propaganda and falsifications, suggests that mass historical ignorance has become quite welcome again.[31]

Perhaps the ever shrinking number of surviving war veterans should make cinema more responsible in keeping the record straight. "The photographic and celluloid images of World War II are so frequently used and reused that they have begun to supersede experience and memory. The power over such visual memory lies increasingly in the hands of those who create or manipulate such images. Indeed, producers of motion pictures and videos play a major role in the production and continuation of public memory of the war" (Chambers and Culbert 155). Without an active search for realities over myths, Russians will forget that the "fathers'" war experiences varied dramatically, as did family histories, which resulted in significant differences between families' lives during the war. Heritage as a unifying idea for a nation is a complex phenomenon. Balancing between the sensitivities of the populace's perception of World War II, on the one hand, and the desire to reveal the truth, on the other, while competing with numerous old Soviet films, today's Russian filmmakers face a difficult choice: to conform by fulfilling the state's and the public's demand for patriotic "light" war movies or take a stand and treat the war as a multifaceted human tragedy. This is the enormous challenge for cinema's "sons," and their "fathers'" lasting legacy depends on their decisions.

NOTES

1. *S.E.R.* (Sergei Bodrov 1989); *Brat* [*Brother*, Aleksei Balabanov 1997]; *Amerikanka* (Dmitrii Meskhiev 1998); *Kavkazskii plennik* [*Prisoner of the Mountains*, Sergei Bodrov 1996]; *Sirpota Kazanskaia* [*The Orphan of Kazan*, Vladimir Mashkov 1997]; *Voroshilovskii strelok* [*Voroshilov's Sniper*, Stanislav Govorukhin 1996]; *Strana glukhikh* [*The Country of the Deaf*, Valerii Todorovskii 1997]; *Lunnyi papa* [*Moon Daddy*, Bakhtyar Khudoinazarov 1999]; *P'esa dlia passazhira* [*A Play for a Passenger*, Vadim Abdrashitov 1995]; *Musul'manin* [*A Muslim*, Vladimir Khotinenko 1995]; *Vor* [*The Thief*, Pavel Chukhrai 1998]; *Mama* (Denis Evstigneev 1999); *Nebo v almazakh* [*The Sky Full of Diamonds*, Vasilii Pichul 1999]; *Kto, esli ne my* [*Who if Not Us*, Valerii Priemykhov 1999]; *Blokpost* [*Checkpoint*, Aleksandr Rogozhkin 1999]; *Mama, ne goriui* [*Mama, Do Not Be Sad*, Maksim Pezhemskii 1999]; *Khrustalev, mashinu!* [*Khrustalev, My Car!* Aleksei German 1998]; and many others.

2. In some films the absent father is replaced by a criminal, as in *Vor* [*The Thief*] and *P'esa dlia passazhira* [*A Play for a Passenger*], and in others by an older brother, as in *Brat* [*Brother*] and *Mama*, but in all cases the young characters search, often recklessly, for their biological fathers.

3. Common practice during Stalin's purges was a written rejection of the persecuted father or husband accused of being an enemy of the people, often followed by a change of surname, which sometimes helped to avoid being charged as a relative of an enemy of the people. A similar rationale of dissociation later prompted Jews to change or "russify" their (or their children's) surnames or patronymics to avoid discrimination. That phenomenon is evident in the film *Kholodnoe leto 53-go* [*The Cold Summer of 53*, A. Proshkin 1987].

4. "Velikii mif, kogda-to genial'no pridumannyi v sootvetstvii s neglasnym obshchestvennym dogovorom i ustraivavshii vse sloi naseleniia, mif slozhnyi, glubokii, otniud' ne kondovyi i ne pokhozhii na vse ostal'nye sovetskie mify glasil: voina est' velikii podvig sovetskogo naroda, voina est' proverka na prochnost' vsekh chelovecheskikh kachestv, blagodaria voine my spasli svoiu stranu i ves' mir ot korichnevoi chumy. Voina est' odna iz luchshikh stranits vsei nashei istorii."

5. For more on *chernukha*, see Seth Graham, "Chernukha and Russian Film," *Studies in Slavic Culture* 1 (2000): 9–27.

6. In the Russian version of the film the vision returns after the adult San'ka reconsiders the past.

7. A symbolic flight into the heavens could be a reference to Larisa Shepit'ko's *Kryl'ia* [*Wings* 1966]. But, unlike Shepit'ko's film, Ursuliak's is ironic and grotesque, devoid of pathos and tragic overtones, bitter and sarcastic, but at the same time comic and melodramatic. The final lines in the film are from a granddaughter's composition many years later: "Until now it remains a mystery, where did they [the veterans—T.S.] fly to. Their airplane immediately disappeared from the locator's screens. Search

groups looked for it all over the World, but it did not land anywhere." The film's closing titles appear to the sound of military march music against the backdrop of real
war veterans posing in front of the camera in their fully decorated uniforms.

8. "Seichas priniato izdevat'sia na temu presidentskogo zakaza na razrabotku tak
nazyvaemoi natsional'noi idei. Tvorcheskaia intelligentsia obozhaet kvalifitsirovat'
etu zadachu, vo-pervykh, kak neser'eznuiu, smeshnuiu, vo-vtorykh, kak kompleks
natsional'noi nepolnotsennosti I, v-tret'ikh, kak svoego roda otryzhku totalitarnogo
rezhima, kotoraia byla kharakterna dlia nepolnotsennykh obshchestv, takikh, ska-
zhem, kak Rossiia ili Germaniia v 30-e gody" (*Iskusstvo kino* 4 [1998]: 173).

9. In just five years alarming changes took place in Russia's social and political
life: the Kremlin came to exercise total control over TV channels, political opposition was discredited, and Russian nationalistic overtones started to appear on all
levels. Political criticism is now considered Russophobic, a revision of Soviet history,
lack of patriotism (known as "*ochernenie*"—lit., "painting black"). Alternative views
are expressed only through several newspapers and journals and one radio station.
Loyalty to the Kremlin, as during the Soviet era, ensures financial and administrative
privileges, thus encouraging officially commissioned products. Yet censorship, which
reigns on TV, does not affect book publications, internet sites, and film production.
The possible reason for that is the obvious assumption that the overwhelming majority of the population gets its information from central TV channels, which are state-
controlled. Therefore the potential "damage" done by several newspapers, the internet
(used by approximately 10% of the population), and films is considered minimal.

10. *V avguste 44-go* [*In August of 44*, Ptashuk 2001] was released a year earlier,
but technically it was a Belarussian film.

11. "*Zvezda* Lebedeva daet poniat', chego prosila kollektivnaia dusha. Esli ochen'
korotko—revansha. Posle dolgikh let samounichizheniia uznat' na ekrane svoe i
sebia, chtoby soboiu pogordit'sia."

12. "Na 'Mosfil'me' deistvitel'no sushchestvuet zamechatel'nyi avtopark, tekhnika voennykh vremen, prichem v ochen' khoroshem sostoianii. Bez rekvizita kino
sniat' nevozmozhno, i slava Bogu, chto nashlis' liudi, kotorye sokhranili eto bogat-
stvo, ne rastranzhirili i prodolzhaiut soderzhat' v ispravnosti."

13. "Vneshne fil'm sokhraniaet privychnye antifashistskie cherty sovetskogo voennogo kinematografa, a vnutrenne on stavit na nem krest. Klimov i v samom dele dazhe
ne krest postavil, a kol zabil v mogilu sovetskogo voennogo mifa, i nastol'ko moshch-
no, chto posle nego piatnadtsat' let voobshche nikto nichego o voine ne snimal."

14. In Aleksandr Rogozhkin's *Peregon* [*Transit* 2006] the action takes place in
Chukhotka's airport. It is one of the first feature films to touch upon the Land Lease
Program. The TV series *Eshelon* [*Echelon* 2005] by Nijole Adomenaite and Dmitrii
Dolinin depicts cases of looting and rape in occupied Germany, as well as a Soviet
officer's love affair with a German girl. Vasilii Chiginskii's *Pervyi posle boga* [*First
after God* 2005] is based on a story of the NKVD persecution of a famous submarine
captain. The TV mini-series *Diversant* [*The Saboteur*, Andrei Maliukov 2004] depicts
the rigorous training of young soldiers to transform them into professional saboteurs.
During one operation they realize that they are merely pawns in a big game, in which
it is not always clear who is the enemy and who is on "their side."

15. See the official statement on the FSB site at http://www.fsb.ru/smi/smifsb/
periodik/boyko.html (accessed 12 May 2007).

16. Available at http://www.lenta.ru/articles/2007/04/20/mtv/ (accessed 12 May 2007).

17. For example, Artem Antonov's 2005 film *Polumgla* [*Semidarkness*] examines the uneasy relations between German prisoners and local village women in Siberia, where prisoners are sent to build a radio tower. Initial hatred for the enemy is gradually replaced by mutual sympathy and collaboration for the sake of survival. Just when humanism seems to have overcome animosity, a firing squad arrives to execute the prisoners, who are no longer needed, thereby intensifying the hardships of the Russian women's lives.

18. A TV adaptation of V. Shalamov's stories.

19. "Eta ideia u menia rodilas' ochen' davno, kogda ia sdelal *Proverku na dorogakh* Gde-to v kontse 70-kh ia prines Ermashu zaiavku na fil'm o shtrafnom batal'one. On menia poslal na tri bukvy, skazal, chto ia soshel s uma, dopilsia do ruchki, esli ia ne ponimaiu, gde ia zhivu. Na etom razgovor zakonchilsia" (Volodarskii 32).

20. "Segodnia snimaiut fil'my o voine molodye rebiata . . . oni svobodny i mogut vyrazhat' vse, chto zadumali, u nikh more informatsii, tekhnika . . . My-to vsegda zanimalis' samoredaktirovaniem."

21. At the Twenty-sixth International Film Festival in Venice, in 1965, the film received the Opera-Prima Prize for the best directorial debut.

22. The line "Vmesto svadeb—razluki i dym" is from Bulat Okudzhava's poem "Akh, voina, chto ty, podlaia, sdelala" ["Ah, war, you miserable thing, what have you done"].

23. "Ia na voine videl ochen' mnogo tragicheskikh i krovavykh epizodov, ogromnoe kolichestvo bessmyslennykh zhertv. Na moikh glazakh pogib moi drug. No spustia mnogo let vsplyvaiut pochemu-to svetlye vospominaniia. Eto byla zhizn'. Byla liubov', strast'. Iumor. Liudi ostavalis' liud'mi. I pervye fil'my u menia deistvitel'no byli svetlye." Although war continues to be the subject of Todorovskii's films, it is cast in a different key from his first films: in 2003 he made *V sozvezdii byka* [*In the Taurus Constellation*], an emotional and tragic story of two teenage boys trying to survive in the Stalingrad region during World War II, which is partially based on his personal experience.

24. The movie was timed for the sixtieth Victory anniversary and was successfully broadcast on the TV channel "Russia." It was one of the first Russian films nominated for the Thirty-third International Emmy Award.

25. "Valera Todorovskii prosto zastavil svoego ottsa, Petra Efimovicha, sest' i napisat' vospominaniia pro to vremia, kotorye i legli v osnovu dannoi kartiny" ("Kursanty," *Rossia. Telekanal,* 12 March 2007; available at http://www.rutv.ru/tvpreg.html ?id=57076&cid=42&d=0 (accessed 12 May 2007).

26. "Mozhet uzhe i pora podumat': a pochemu u nas bylo tak mnogo plennykh? . . . Pochemu takoe kolichestvo pogibshikh? . . . krome nas nikto razbirat'sia ne budet."

27. For example, in 2006 the chief editor of the *Parliament Newspaper,* Petr Kotov, was forced to resign after publishing the article "Lokot'skaia al'ternativa" by Sergei Verevkin (*Parlamentskaia gazeta,* no. 19, 22 June 2006), which questioned the absence of alternatives for people in the occupied territories and described an economically successful case of collaboration in the town of Lokot' in the Briansk region.

28. For example, Valentin Vinogradov's film *Vostochnyi corridor* [*Eastern Corridor/Vostochnyi koridor*], made in 1966 by Belarusfilm, was excluded from the

All-Union film festival and accused of being non-artistic. The film questioned the established opposition of "ours" and "theirs," freedom and captivity, and various accepted stereotypes, violating the rigid structure of the myth. Shpagin calls the film's portrayal an "absurdist carnival," in which every action "twists into senselessness, into chaos" (Shpagin 6:80).

29. "Piat'sot let nazad oni ne znali, chto oni belorusy, no u nikh bylo samoe bol'shoe gosudarstvo v Evrope. So vremenem oni osoznali, chto u belorusov bol'she net gosudarstva, i ikh schitaiut polurusskimi ili defektivnymi poliakami. No oni vse eshche sushchestvovali. Nakonets, ikh smeshali s sovetskimi liud'mi. Posle okkupatsii i voiny utseleli tol'ko nekotorye iz nikh. Seichas u belorusov est' gosudarstvo, no oni obnaruzhili, chto oni bol'she ne sushchestvuiut."

30. The exact number is still unknown, ranging from twenty to thirty million people. The number publicly announced by Stalin was seven million.

31. This phenomenon corresponds to the Ministry of Education's recent approval and recommendation of a high school history textbook edited by Aleksandr Fillipov justifying Stalin's repressions as rational.

REFERENCES

Blos, Peter. *Son and Father: Before and Beyond the Oedipus Complex.* New York: Collier Macmillan, 1985.

Chambers, John Whiteclay, II, and David Culbert, eds. *World War II, Film, and History.* New York: Oxford University Press, 1996.

Chernykh, Valentin. "Esli rybka plyvet—skhvachu." *Iskusstvo kino* 5 (2005): 79–88.

German, Aleksei. "Izgoniaiushchii d'iavola." Interview in Paris, November 24 1998. *Iskusstvo kino* 6 (1999): 98–107.

Gusakovskaia, Nadezhda. "'Okkupatsiia. Misterii,' ili belorusov bol'she ne sushchestvuet." *Takaia* 6 (2007). Available at http://takaya.by/life/notice/okkup_misterium (2 August 2008).

Kichin, Valerii. "MMKF-2004: V avguste 41-go." *Rossiiskaia gazeta,* 24 June 2004, 7.

Konets veka—konets chernukhi? *Iskusstvo kino* 3 (1998): 158–67; 4 (1998): 166–75.

"Kursanty." *Rossiia. Telekanal.* 12 March 2007. Available at http://www.rutv.ru/tvpreg .html?id=57076&cid=42&d=0.

Lebedev, Nikolai. "Zritel' nas uslyshal" (interview with N. Sirivlia). *Iskusstvo kino* 8 (2002): 21–22.

Prokhorova, Elena. "*Svoi.*" *Kinokultura.* 1 June 2005. Available at http://www.kinokul tura.com/reviews/R1-05svoi.html.

Shpagin, Aleksandr. "Religiia voiny." *Iskusstvo kino* 5 (2005): 57–68; 6 (2005): 73–89.

Slepyan, Kenneth. *Stalin's Guerrillas: Soviet Partisans in World War II.* Lawrence: University Press of Kansas, 2006.

Sokolov, B. V. *Okkupatsiia. Pravda i mify.* Moscow: AST-PRESS, 2002.

Stishova, Elena. "Odinochestvo zvezdy." *Iskusstvo kino* 8 (2002): 17–21.

Todorovskii, Petr. "Kak Todorovskii sam sebia rezal. Interview with Marina Nevzorova." *Argumenty i fakty* 6 (448), 6 February 2002.

———. "V molodosti legko byt' schastlivym." *Iskusstvo kino* 5 (2005): 71–78.

Volodarskii, Eduard. Interview with Z. Vasil'eva. *Iskusstvo kino* 12 (2004): 27–33.

Youngblood, Denise. "Ivan's Childhood and Come and See: Post-Stalinist Cinema and the Myth of World War II." In *World War II, Film, and History,* ed. John Whiteclay Chambers II and David Culbert, 85–96. New York: Oxford University Press, 1996.

———. *Russian War Films: On the Cinema, 1914–2005.* Lawrence: University Press of Kansas, 2007.

Zubavina, Irina. "Shinel' ottsa. Poslednii poezd." *Iskusstvo kino* 12 (2003): 35–38.

FILMOGRAPHY

Dvadtsat' dnei bez voiny [Twenty Days without War]. Dir. Aleksei German. Lenfilm Studio, 1976.

Idi i smotri [Come and See]. Dir. Elem Klinov. Mosfilm Studio, 1985.

Ivanovo detstvo [Ivan's Childhood]. Dir. Andrei Tarkovsky. Mosfilm Studio, 1962.

Khrustalev, mashinu! [Khrustalev, My Car!] Dir. Aleksei German. Canal+, VGTRK "Rossiia," 1998.

Kursanty. [The Students]. Dir. Andrei Kavun. Prod. Valerii Todorovskii. VGTRK "Rossiia," 2004.

Mater' chelovecheskaia [Mother of Humankind]. Dir. Leonid Golovnia. Mosfilm Studio, 1975.

Nesluzhebnoe zadanie [Unofficial Business]. Dir. Vitalii Vorob'ev. Cinebridge, 2004.

Okkupatsiia. Misterii [Occupation. Mystery Plays]. Dir. Andrei Kudinenko. Studio Navigator, 2003.

Olen'ia okhota [Dear Hunt]. Dir. Iurii Boretskii. Gorky Film Studio, 1981.

Ona zashchishchaet rodinu [She Defends the Motherland]. Dir. Fridrikh Ermler. Alma Ata Studio, 1943.

Oni srazhalis' za rodinu [They Fought for the Motherland]. Dir. Sergei Bondarchuk. Mosfilm Studio, 1975.

Monanieba [Pokaianie] [Repentence]. Dir. Tengiz Abuladze. Qartuli Pilmi, 1984.

Poslednii boi maiora Pugacheva [The Last Battle of Major Pugachev]. Dir. Vladimir Fat'ianov. NTV, A-PRO Video, 2005.

Poslednii poezd [The Last Train]. Dir. Aleksei German Jr. Filmokom, 2003.

Proverka na dorogakh [The Trial on the Roads]. Dir. Aleksei German. Lenfilm Studio, 1971.

Shtrafbat [Penal Batallion]. Dir. Nikolai Dostal'. MakDos, 2004.

Svoi [Our Own]. Dir. Dmitrii Meskhiev. "Slovo," 2004.

Svolochi [Bastards]. Dir. Aleksandr Atanesian. Paradise Group, 2006.

Vernost' [Faithfulness]. Dir. Petr Todorovskii. Odessa Film Studio, 1965.

Zvezda [The Star]. Dir. Nikolai Lebedev. Mosfilm Studio, ARK-Film, 2002.

Figure 4.1. The fiery last stand as an eternal flame.

Figure 4.2. The desolation of the punishing winter.

FIVE

War as the Family Value: Failing Fathers and Monstrous Sons in *My Stepbrother Frankenstein*

MARK LIPOVETSKY

THE SYMBIOSIS OF MYTHS

The connection between the motif of war and the representation of fatherhood in Soviet and post-Soviet cultures is persistent yet not logically obvious. Since such films of the 1960s as *Sud'ba chelovka* [*Fate of a Man*, Sergei Bondarchuk 1959], *Kogda derev'ia byli bol'shimi* [*When the Trees Were Tall*, Lev Kulidzhanov 1961], *Mir vkhodiahshchemu* [*Peace to Him Who Enters*, Aleksandr Alov and Vladimir Naumov 1961], *Otets soldata* [*Father of a Soldier*, Rezo Chkheidze 1965], the understanding of the Great Patriotic War (the official Soviet term for World War II) as a means to sanctify the father figure is solidified in Soviet culture. All these and many other similar films and books appeared in the 1960s during the Thaw, which on the one hand, had removed the supreme patriarchal authority of Stalin and yet, on the other, had secured the victory in the war as the most important if not the sole legitimization of the Soviet regime. Invoking the war as the cornerstone of the father's authority, directors of the sixties strove to replace the collapsed and debunked father figure of Stalin with a less god-like image of the father, and thus simultaneously transformed the totalitarian mythology of war into a more democratic and humane mythology of the nation's collective suffering that was instigated by the war.

Although the war significantly depleted the male population and inevitably made women largely responsible for the well-being of families, war films of the sixties overwhelmingly failed to undermine, or at least to question, patriarchal authority and, moreover, rarely attempted to examine the connection between the war and women's changing social roles.[1] It is well known that the core of totalitarian culture was shaped by the affirmation of society's interests over the interests of the nuclear family, as well as by the mandatory defeat of individual values for the sake of collectivist ideologies. In contrast, the change of focus in the sixties from the social "fathers" to the private father-child relationships reflected the dramatic problematization of the entire system of Soviet values, a problematization that was generally indicative of Thaw culture. However, despite the anti-Stalinist ideology of the aforementioned films, the connection between the war and its culture of violence and suffering, with the symbolic capital of the father(ing), was a way of rewriting the totalitarian mythologies. As Alexander Prokhorov demonstrates, "Thaw culture has inherited from Stalinism the family trope—as a symbolic image of the Soviet society, and war—as the symbolic image of this society's main form of existence" (Prokhorov 152). In Thaw films the structure of the totalitarian Great Family was preserved in the realm of the nuclear family—it was domesticated and deprived of imperial grandeur, and yet it at least maintained and arguably increased its sacredness.

Thus the war theme shaped a unique discursive field in the culture of the 1960s to the 1980s, a field in which the official and liberal discourses frequently merged, or at least tolerated each other. The mythos of the war, invariably understood as the patriotic war in which the interests of the state were no different from the interests of an individual or a family, allowed the perpetuation of a balance, however fragile, between society and the individual of post-Stalinist Soviet culture. Moreover, the connection of the war themes with the father figure or, more precisely, with the idealization of patriarchal values and corresponding models of social order, constituted the very foundation of this balance.

The myth of the Great Patriotic War not only retained its symbolic value during the post-Soviet period but also has been significantly reinforced during the years of Vladimir Putin's presidency. The cultural historian and sociologist Lev Gudkov, while analyzing numerous polls of VTsIOM (All-Russia Center for the Studies of Public Opinion), argues that, since 1995 and up to the present, "an extremely structured social attitude towards the war is incarnated and consolidated in the main symbol that integrates the nation: victory in the war, victory in the

Great Patriotic War. In the opinion of Russia's inhabitants, this is the most important event in their history; it is the basic image of national consciousness. No other event compares with it" (Gudkov 4). Gudkov persuasively claims that the post-Soviet perception of the war, notwithstanding the newfound access to a wealth of previously banned historical information, still sustains all the main features of the Soviet myth of the Great Patriotic War:

- The virtual repression of all traumatic aspects of the war and postwar experience (i.e., the Holocaust, the coercive labor, the chronic hunger and poverty, ethnic repressions, etc.) combined with an emphasis on triumphant victory celebrations;
- Xenophobic overtones of the war myth: the victory of the war serves as proof of the superiority of Russia and of Russians over the entire world— "Russians are not willing to share their triumph with anyone else in the world. Sixty-seventy percent of those surveyed [in 2003—M.L.] believe that the USSR could have won the war even without the help of the Allies. Moreover, as Russian nationalism is intensifying and the war is receding further into the past, it has gradually begun to be integrated into the traditional idea of Russia's 'mission' and its 'rivalry with the West'" (Gudkov 7);
- "A number of unpleasant facts have been repressed from mass consciousness: the aggressive nature of the Soviet regime, Communist militarism and expansionism . . . the fact that World War II began with a joint attack of Hitler's Germany and the Soviet Union; the human, social, economic, and metaphysical cost of war . . ." (8);
- The war myth justifies an extremely low value placed on human life: "The idea that mass losses were inevitable and that millions of victims somehow 'are unavoidable' are a constituent element of the general semantic complex of national exploits and general heroism . . . Russians' mass consciousness is unable to imagine a war where the military leaders would aim to save the lives of their subordinates at any cost" (10).
- The war myth legitimates "people's view of themselves as victims of aggression" (9). "This was also expressed in a readiness to justify (but not to support!) any aggressive or repressive state policy against other countries or territories withstanding the USSR or Russia" (9) ranging from Hungary in 1956 and Czechoslovakia in 1968 to Afghanistan in 1979 and Chechnya in the 1990s and 2000s.

Bolstered by lavish anniversary celebrations of the victory in 2000 and particularly in 2005, and moreover fueled by the constant media bashing of Baltic countries and former Soviet satellites (especially Poland) that supposedly replace the memory of Soviet "liberators" with the glorification of the Nazis, the war myth in the twenty-first century, as Gudkov demonstrates, is the main foundation for negative self-identification ("us" vs. "them"), which, in turn, emerges as the formative impetus for the mainstream of post-Soviet culture: "This confidence [in being constantly victimized by "enemies"] was routinized in an extra-moral, socially primitive, archaic, almost tribal distinction between 'our people' and 'not our people' as a basis for social solidarity" (9). It naturally follows that today "the repression of the war [myth] keeps spawning state-sponsored aggression—the Chechen War and the restoration of the repressive regime" (11). Furthermore, the potency of the war myth elevates the wartime condition of normalized violence to "a norm of symbolic self-identity" (10): of contemporary Russians, 77 percent share the conviction that "Russians display their national character and mental qualities at the fullest in times of crisis, trial, and war . . . rather than in calm and happy times" (10). These phenomena certainly help to illuminate the connection between the war myth and the father figure as the symbolic manifestation of the "very principle of a 'vertical' construction of society, a mobilization, command-hierarchical model of social order" (11).

In this context, such cultural phenomena of contemporary Russia that problematize and deconstruct the mutually beneficial symbiosis between the war myth and the myth of the patriarchal authority acquire exceptional significance. *Moi svodnyi brat Frankenshtein* [*My Stepbrother Frankenstein*, Valerii Todorovskii (b. 1962) 2004][2] belongs to this rare species of contemporary films.[3] Todorovskii's film won three awards, including the Grand Prix at the Kinotavr film festival in Sochi (2004), was recognized as the best film of the Russian program at the Moscow Film Festival (2004), and received the FIPRESSI award in Karlovy Vary (2004), as well as several other prizes at various European film festivals (Rotterdam, Honfleur, and Lecce). The film's originality is especially conspicuous against the backdrop of reincarnations of the socialist-realist representation of the war, such as Nikolai Lebedev's *Zvezda* [*Star* 2000]. The film is also particularly striking in contrast to depictions of the war myth's justifications of nationalist and neo-imperialist ideologies, such as Aleksei Balabanov's *Voina* [*War* 2002] or Fedor Bondarchuk's *Deviataia rota* [*The Ninth Regiment* 2005]. Todorovskii's film, based on the original screenplay by Gennadii Ostrovskii (b.1960), tells the story of the invasion of a physically and emotionally maimed Chechen war veteran, Pavlik Zakharov (Daniil Spivakovskii) into the family of his alleged father, a former Muscovite physicist, Iulik Krymov (Leonid Iarmolnik, also the producer of the film), who previously had not known of his son's existence.

As it follows from the film's title and numerous textual signals, Todorovskii proposes a subversion of the Dr. Frankenstein story: first, it is not by accident that the 1931 classic *Frankenstein,* directed by James Whale, and with Boris Karloff as the monster, is directly quoted in Todorovskii's film; furthermore, *Moi svodnyi brat Frankenshtein* seems to place responsibility for the monstrosity of a paranoid, yet good-willed and forgiving son upon the father's shoulders and, in a broader sense, on the conscience of the contemporary liberal intelligentsia, who have safely separated themselves from the violence and terror of the post-Soviet period. According to Todorovskii's own description: "This is a story that has no way out. Everybody in it is right and guilty at the same time. This is a story about father and son, as well as about society, and the desperate situation, which we are all in. It's a story about the war. Not any particular war, but war in general. The war that's around us" (Khoroshilova).

However, despite the political angle, *Moi svodnyi brat Frankenshtein* cannot be defined as a political film, since it offers no clear answers to political questions and, moreover, avoids placing blame, whether it be upon the intelligentsia, the authorities, soldiers, officers, and so on. On the contrary, the film creates an atmosphere of permanent problematization, in which any assumption or interpretation that the viewer might take for granted is reversed in the next scene. This ambiance is created by the nervous music of Aleksei Aigi, as well as by the style of acting—psychologically precise, yet devoid of the melodramatic theatricality so typical of Russian actors. Furthermore, it can be argued that Todorovskii's film translates to the screen the multivoiced, meditative, and at the same time intellectually charged and historically explosive intonation of Iurii Trifonov's (1925–1981) prose. The most important intelligentsia writer of the so-called stagnation period of the 1970s and early 1980s, Trifonov in his novels relentlessly asked questions about the hidden underpinnings, and historical and moral *Unheimlich,* of the comfortable intelligentsia's life during the period of Stagnation. In *Moi svodnyi brat Frankenshtein,* Todorovskii does the same in the context of the present, post-Soviet stagnation, proudly presented by the authorities as "stabilization."

At a cozy Moscow home there appears, disturbingly, an abandoned son, dressed in poor clothing, his face disfigured by terrible scars and a black patch over his missing eye; he is the foreboding shadow of a war that the majority prefer to forget, at least as long as it does not affect their lives. Daniil Spivakovskii's stunning performance of this abandoned son, Pavlik Zakharov, is perhaps one of the best manifestations of post-Soviet *Unheimlich.*

It is the war or, in other words, normalized and routinized violence, that epitomizes the ultimate *Unheimlich* of contemporary Russia, and especially of Moscow's lifestyle. Pavlik's appearance in the life of the Krymovs tears down the barrier that normally keeps war at a distance from the comfortable "stabilization" of the twenty-first century. Naturally Pavlik brings destabilization and eventually death into his newly adopted family. In the film's finale Pavlik takes his newfound relatives hostage, sincerely believing that by doing so he is saving them from pervasive, invisible enemies; however, he is subsequently killed during the police "rescue" operation.

In Freud's interpretation, the "uncanny is in reality nothing new or alien, but something which is familiar and old-established in the mind and which has become alienated from it only through the process of repression" (Freud 241). When specifying the most typical meanings of the "repressed familiar," Freud mentions various manifestations of death (including motifs of the double, the automaton, and the mask), as well as fear of castration (frequently associated with images of animated severed limbs and heads). All these motifs are recognizable in the representation of Pavlik and, moreover, are augmented by the parallels with Mary Shelley's monster. Julia Kristeva argues that Freud's vision of the uncanny "teaches us to detect foreignness in ourselves": while it "creeps into the tranquility of reason itself and, without being restricted to madness, beauty, or faith anymore than to ethnicity or race, irrigates our very speaking being [. . .]. Henceforth, we know that we are foreigners to ourselves, and it is with the help of that sole support that we can attempt to live with others" (Kristeva 191, 170). Thus any representation of the uncanny inadvertently reflects the splits and doublings of cultural/societal identity, and therefore undermines the dominant societal/cultural mythology, usually promoting global and centripetal, rather than local and de-centering patterns for identity. The detection of the uncanny in the war-sanctioned father-son relationships defines the novelty of *Moi svodnyi brat Frankenshtein*, and not only indicates the split within the identity of the intelligentsia but also undermines both the patriarchal mythology and the resurrected social mythology of the war as "a norm of symbolic self-identity" (Gudkov 9).

WAR AND PEACE: THE MIMICRY OF OTHERING

Moi svodnyi brat Frankenshtein is reminiscent of numerous films, mostly American, that depict the post-traumatic stress syndrome suffered by many Vietnam veterans (for instance, films such as *The Deer Hunter* [Michael Cimino 1978] or even *Rambo: First Blood* [Ted Kotcheff 1982]). In Todorovskii's film it is easy to detect society's indifference to the needs of a physically and emotionally disfigured veteran; for example, an official from the Ministry of Defense utterly refuses to accept any responsibility for Pavlik's wounds, considering him to be "healthy" just as long as he does not wet his bed. Similarly, even the empathetic doc-tor at the military hospital says that she has a line of maimed veterans just like Pavlik that can easily stretch from the hospital to the Defense Ministry, and that only for $20,000 can she take care of Pavlik earlier than scheduled. The film's post-traumatic discourse is further made ap-parent by the immense gap between the Krymovs' peaceful middle-class lifestyle and Pavlik's horrific and agitated perception of reality through the prism of his nightmarish war experience.

As Iulik complains, "For him, everybody is the enemy," and Pav-lik's own actions legitimate this claim: he is on permanent alert, con-stantly making rounds, looking for "spooks," and not thinking twice before attacking "suspects." "They think that we are all dead, but there are three of us left," confesses Pavlik to his former army commander, Timur Kurbatovich (brilliantly played by Sergei Garmash). "They" are the "spooks," "*dukhi*" (ghosts, spirits)—the army argot first used in the Afghanistan campaign for "dushmans" or mudjaheds, which also refers to first-year recruits in the Russian army. The way Pavlik uses this "term" makes it obvious that he almost automatically suspects the ethnic Other to be the hidden enemy: in one scene he nervously and at length eyes a non-Slavic fruit seller; in another, he beats up a "black-assed" stranger so violently that the police arrests Pavlik, albeit only for a short while. Furthermore, Pavlik suspects the neighbor's boyfriend of being a spook, and is even suspicious of the Krymovs' best friends when they come to their dinner party ("They could have poisoned your drink!").[4]

It is possible to connect all these demented suspicions and paranoia to Pavlik's dream of obtaining a diamond eye to replace his missing one, which ultimately becomes a symbol for these distorted optics. Pavlik, however, believes his point of view to be far from distorted, and, in fact, superior if not transcendental. A definitive military etiology of this phantasm may be inferred from the fact that only his war commander can share this dream, while Iulik and his wife Rita (Elena Iakovleva) shrug in embarrassment.[5]

However, unlike the Vietnam veterans depicted in American films of the 1970s, Pavlik does not feel alienated. On the contrary, when he joins Egor to watch *Frankenstein*—the film Egor rented to make fun of his newly found stepbrother—Pavlik not only fails to recognize himself in the monster, who is "kind but unloved" but, moreover, does not notice the hint of compassion directed not only at the film's monster but also at him, Pavlik: "Who could love such a guy!" exclaims Pavlik with poise. Rather than feeling estranged and reviled, Pavlik firmly believes that once he has a diamond eye, all women will fall in love with him. Never feeling lost or disoriented, he acts confidently and calmly in the belief that he alone knows the truth and must therefore protect his newfound family members from the dangers they fail to notice.

Notably, several critics have detected in Todorovskii's film a polemical response to Aleksei Balabanov's depiction of another war veteran—the xenophobic and nationalist icon of the post-Soviet generation, Danila Bagrov (Sergei Bodrov Jr.), of the films *Brat* [*Brother* 1997] and especially *Brat 2* [*Brother 2* 2000]. "In my view, *Moi svodnyi brat Frankenshtein* can be adequately understood only as a conscious polemic with Aleksei Balabanov's film *Brat*, according to which the Chechen War generates its own heroes, who are invisible to the world, superfluous in it, but because of this no less real," argues Iurii Gladil'shchikov ("*Seansu otvechaiut . . . Moi svodnyi brat Frankenshtein*"). "In fact, *Moi svodnyi brat Franken-shtein* refurbishes the plot of *Brat*, and revamps its ideology," as Andrei

Plakhov claims, adding: "On the material of the war in the Caucasus Balabanov creates something like a tragic western with a lone hero. Todorovskii, on the contrary, transforms the patriotic myth of the country, of brothers and sisters, into a farce" ("*Seansu* otvechaiut . . ."). Balabanov presents his war veteran as the nation's defender from the insults and offenses of various Others, ranging from Chechens to Americans, and paints his hero as the prophet of "Russian truth" and the living proof of Russian (spiritual!) superiority over the world. Todorovskii's Pavlik, in contrast, appears not as a hero of our time but rather as its ultimate victim; and the film portrays his aggression against the universal Other not as a mission but as a symptom of clinical paranoia.

There is a method in Pavlik's madness, however: while perceiving the majority of humanity as aggressive and conspiratorial Others, Pavlik excludes from this circle of suspects those whom he designates as "his own." This category includes not only former comrades-in-arms such as Timur Kurbatovich or the emotionally disturbed lieutenant in the military mental institution, to whom Pavlik gives helpful advice based on their shared hallucinations, but also his new family members. Considering Pavlik's paranoia, it is surprising how readily Pavlik forgives his father, even after numerous betrayals: for instance, Iulik pretends not to recognize Pavlik at the train station; he does not invite him into his home until his wife, noticing that Pavlik has long been waiting by their door, forces Iulik to bring his son inside; he refuses to acknowledge their kinship; and finally, following Rita's demand that he get rid of the "monster," he drives Pavlik out into the middle of nowhere and abandons him like a stray dog. Arguably Pavlik perceives his father's various betrayals as tests of loyalty, or perhaps he subconsciously censors out the possibility of betrayal by his "kin." In the same vein, after Pavlik is attacked by Egor's friends at Egor's behest, he interprets the assault as a provocation coming from the Others, and not instigated by his brother: "They wanted to set me against you [menia na tebia razvesti khoteli]. But I'm not who they think I am . . . I'll cover for you."

The critic Viktor Matizen reminds us that the name of Todorovskii's protagonist is associated "not only with Saul/Paul but also with the three cult heroes of Soviet culture: Pavlik Morozov, Pavel Vlasov, and Pavel Korchagin" ("*Seansu* otvechaiut . . ."). The parallels with, or oppositions to, Pavlik Morozov and Pavel Korchagin are especially telling. For one,

Todorovskii's Pavlik stands in striking opposition to Pavlik Morozov, who garnered Soviet adulation for betraying his father for the sake of the "Great Family"; in contrast, Pavlik Zakharov from *Moi svodnyi brat* considers blood-based kinship an absolute value, and whatever he does is explicitly done for the safety of his father's family (as he understands it, of course). The parallels between Todorovskii's hero and Pavel Korchagin are not limited to the fact that the former lost his eye in the war and the latter was mutilated and became blind as a result of his dedicated service to the Revolution. The Soviet cult of Korchagin as a new martyr solidifying the self-sacrificial ethics of the Great Family laid the foundation for the Stalinist cultural concept of "chosen sons" who, because of their extraordinary service, are admitted to the "higher order of reality" (Clark 126–55). Thus, in a way, Pavlik tries to transform his kin into a Great Family, and attempts to restructure society into a circle of "proven [blood-related or war-tested] ours," thereby marrying the Soviet utopia with post-Soviet xenophobia.[6]

If war trauma is supposedly responsible for Pavlik's distorted worldview, then the essential question arises: Why do his reactions often and hauntingly mimic the lives of the so-called peaceful Muscovites? For instance, the cop who arrests Pavlik for assaulting a non-Russian cheerfully lets him go, claiming, despite the victim's protests, that no charges will be made against Pavlik: "Your son did right. Should fuckin' beat them. But by the book, right?" ["Syn u tebia molodets. Voobshche-to pizdit' ikh nado. No po zakonu"].

The mirroring effect between Pavlik and other characters in the film becomes especially obvious in the sequence beginning with the scene in which Pavlik intently stares at the "suspicious" fruit seller. Immediately following is the ambush on Pavlik organized by Egor and enacted by his friends, who, during the attack, quite literally mouth the same aggressive formulas—"Hey, freak! Get out of here! We're warning you: Don't you ever come here again! Move out of here!"—that are typically used against ethnic Others, such as the fruit seller in the preceding scene. At the same time, during Pavlik's fight, Spivakovskii in his body movements partly imitates Boris Karloff's performance as the monster, and Pavlik's hysterical feat, with strings of Pavlik's saliva dropping from his mouth onto the faces of the frightened and beaten attackers, makes the hero look really terrifying.

This sequence, as well as other scenes in *Moi svodnyi brat Fran-kenshtein*, suggests that, although the Krymov family and friends are appalled and alarmed by Pavlik and his actions, these representatives of the allegedly refined and liberal intelligentsia nonetheless follow the same principle of othering, thereby making the "prodigal son" a *true* monster. If anything, they are only differentiated from Pavlik by their lack of consistency.

Two firm, antithetical attitudes to Pavlik are embodied in the Kry-movs' children, Egor and Ania. Ania (Marianna Il'ina) immediately accepts Pavlik as her brother, and everything about him that others perceive as strange and forbidding she finds marvelous. Even Pavlik's phantom diamond eye finds a place in her wondertale narrative about a brother who never sleeps at night. She is not in the least afraid of Pavlik, as is evident in the scene at the railway station: searching for her and fearing where Pavlik has taken his new sister, their parents are frantic, but when they find Ania, she is cheerfully jumping around Pavlik, dis-cussing the comparative features of different prosthetic eyes. The con-trast between their panic and her playfulness is striking.

Egor (Artem Shalimov), on the other hand, immediately snubs Pav-lik as the Other. Following Dr. Astrov's principle that "everything in a man should be beautiful," which Egor ironically quotes during the film's opening scene, the fifteen-year-old boy detests his disfigured, provincial, and menacing stepbrother so much that he invites his friends to watch the Frankenstein movie in order to make fun of the monster's real-life double. Furthermore, he orders his father to "make Pavlik go away," and when his plea is ignored, he demands that Pavlik be beaten, thereby, ironically, materializing Pavlik's paranoid fears. Tellingly, the film's title embodies precisely Egor's perspective, which suggests that Egor's posi-tion is representative not just of this character but of the entire future generation as well (and, perhaps, the viewers, too).

The parents, Iulik and Rita, oscillate between these two opposing positions of rejection and acceptance. Iulik, at first striving to deny Pav-lik's presence, actually develops a sense of responsibility for his aban-doned son as the film progresses. The high point of his attachment to the boy occurs during the scene in the mental institution to which Iulik, prompted by Rita, attempts to admit Pavlik; he cannot bring himself to leave his son in such a "house of grief." Yet Iulik's sense of paternal responsibility and pity for Pavlik is indivisible from his simultaneous desire to separate his life permanently from his son's, which accounts for his repeated abandonment of Pavlik, most notably in the sequence on the isolated roadside, where, without explanation, he hands the bewildered youth a few rubles and drives off. Of course, Pavlik returns in no time, as the uncanny always does.

A reverse process marks Rita's response to Pavlik's "invasion." At the beginning, Rita shows Pavlik more compassion than does her husband. It is Rita who literally forces Iulik to allow Pavlik into their house and urges Iulik to care for him. She becomes "maternal," in a sense, but those maternal feelings are challenged when she confronts the danger to *her* biological children from a child who "belongs" to another woman and to whom she can only become a surrogate mother. Rita's shift from acceptance to fear is dramatically illuminated by her dream, in which she sees Pavlik tearing apart Egor's eye. When she realizes the depth of Pavlik's trauma, she herself develops a paranoid fear of him as the Other who can and will inevitably hurt her children.

Rita's change of heart toward Pavlik is noteworthy in several respects. First, despite the fact that the very organization of the Krymov family (in tune with the typical post-Soviet post-intelligentsia family) presents a stunning inversion of the patriarchal family's roles, Pavlik's appearance in the Krymov household invokes patriarchal stereotypes not only by "emasculating" Iulik but also by forcing Rita back into standard "maternal" and "domestic" roles: when Pavlik is around, Rita, first and foremost, cannot help but want to protect her children from the "invader"—a concern to which her real estate business plays second best.

Second, while performing these traditional gender roles, Rita nonetheless is forced to break with the supreme value of the patriarchal family—the wife's respect for, and subordination to, her husband. Her biological maternity (and blood is an issue in the film), however, masculinizes her, for a threat to her own children from Pavlik transforms her into the tough woman who insists that Iulik eject the threat from the household—again, a fascinating blend of "issuing orders" to the male while unable to act on them herself. In the scene after the party, Rira directly and aggressively (with physical and verbal violence) assaults Iulik's attachment to his newly found son. She undermines Iulik as a father ("You cannot protect your own family!") and exposes his professional failure (he cannot write even "a miserable article! Some great scholar!"). Iulik cannot defend himself rationally and utilizes the language of violence, by hitting and pushing Rita in response to her attack. Although in the next scene the couple is reconciled (apparently united by something more significant than patriarchal values), the importance of the scandalous scene remains. The scene makes clear that patriarchal gender roles, summoned by the "habitus" of war (epitomized, in turn, by Pavlik), cannot coexist with one another; the newborn "patriarchal family" with a strong father figure, on the one hand, and a maternal/domestic wife, on the other, can only internalize the discourse of war, thus demonstrating the incompatibility of patriarchal models with the actual complexity of the situation, which suggests that post-Soviet society is a "post-patriarchal" social family.

Third, Pavlik, as the (ironically treated) source of the patriarchal renaissance in the Krymov family, is at the same time the immediate reason for the sudden family feud. Related by blood only to Iulik and a complete stranger to Iulik's wife and children, Pavlik is simultaneously both *svoi* and *chuzhoi,* and yet not fully either. He cannot fit in anywhere, which is precisely what makes him a "monster." The oxymoronic nature of this situation is reflected in the fact that from the standpoint of patriarchal values, raised on war discourse, Pavlik is an *illegitimate* son. In reality this means that he is alien even within the value system that he, or rather the war discourse, presents as his own—the one he believes in and promotes as the universal and natural "order of things."

It is significant that the film's optics largely favor Iulik and his family's perception of Pavlik, rather than portraying Pavlik's vision of the world. From Pavlik's arrival at the railway station, he is consistently depicted as a monster—that is, the Other. His alienating image encourages us as viewers to feel solidarity either with Rita's hostility or, alternatively, with Iulik's hesitations. By this means, the film creates a powerful provocation. Since its logic reveals the mirroring of Pavlik's xenophobia in the Krymovs' perception of him as Other, the ultimate effect of the film is based on the viewers' recognition of the fact that we also desire to insulate ourselves from "my stepbrother Frankenstein," who also manifests *our* "uncanny."

In keeping with Kristeva's contention that the uncanny "teaches us to detect foreignness in ourselves," Pavlik's presence reveals xenophobic and paranoid attitudes toward the Other as the "foreignness" hidden deep within the mind-set of the polite and caring intelligentsia. Veiled and inconsistent at first, this foreignness increasingly grows vigorous, provoked by stressful conditions, until these othering attitudes ultimately encompass not only the Krymovs but also us, the film viewers.

WHAT IS TO BE DONE? THE INVERSION OF
FATHERING AND THE LANGUAGE OF VIOLENCE

"Pavlik says that he always knew that you'd find him," Rita tells Iulik. The irony of this statement is double-layered. To begin with, this is a direct quote from Mikhail Sholokhov's *Sud'ba cheloveka* [*Fate of a Man*] (and also from the film of the same title by Sergei Bondarchuk); in the original these words are spoken by the orphan Vaniushka when Andrei Sokolov, a war veteran who has lost his family, identifies him as his son. In Todorovskii's film, however, this phrase resurrects the entire father-war narrative only to subvert it: first, it is the son, not the father, who is deformed by war scars; second, Iulik never tried to find his son, as he was not even aware of his existence, and later argues that "according to the theory of probability," the chances of his being Pavlik's father are nil. This "turning inside-out" of the Soviet narrative reflects the actual inversion of father-son roles in the relationship between Pavlik and Iulik.[7] Tellingly, Iulik and Pavlik, father and son, are bonded through the echoing diminutive forms of their names, which suggests their similarity rather than the hierarchical relationships of an adult and a youngster.

From the outset Iulik is depicted as a weak father figure, or at least a drastically weakened one. Seemingly an authoritative and caring father, he, like many post-Soviet intelligentsia representatives, has irretrievably lost his social status during the last decade. A former physicist whose talent once promised a brilliant future, now he is virtually unemployed, writing articles about great scientists of the past for some popular magazines ("Or, for instance, Boyle Mariotte. Tell us about his life." "They're two different people." "See, that's already interesting!"). Rita, on the other hand, is a breadwinner, and the Krymovs' wealthy life entirely depends on her real-estate business. Though the patriarchal model of the father's authority is clearly subverted, both Iulik and Rita maintain the appearance of its preservation. As the film critic Elena Stishova notes concerning Rita: "She is the leader, the head, the bread-winner, but she remembers to demonstrate her woman's weakness, fragility, and fictitious dependence upon what He will say and how He will behave" (Stishova 78). Pavlik's unexpected arrival gives Iulik an opportunity to restore his authority. In Pavlik's view, Iulik's every word is sacred—the boy admires everything about him, including his silly poems and his fictitious scientific discoveries—simply because he is the Father.

However, despite his overemphasized respect for Iulik as the Father, it is Pavlik who fathers Iulik, only pretending to be an "obedient son," much as Rita pretends to be an "obedient wife" (the mirroring effect, once again). The true nature of the father-son relationship becomes obvious in the first conversation between the two, when Iulik tries to hide his fear of responsibility for this new addition to his family under quasi-scientific jargon, whereas Pavlik calmly dismisses Iulik's petty efforts with the simple reassurance, "Dad, don't think about it, okay? Don't worry. You have a lot of other things to deal with: your house, family, work. Everything's fine [Vse normal'no]." The image of Iulik napping on his son's shoulder while Pavlik is awake and "on guard" becomes a visual hieroglyphic of this inversion, and, tellingly, this very image was used for the film's poster (Figure 5.1).

Pavlik's fatherly authority stems from the war myth in which war experience stands for true, transcendental knowledge about life. Meanwhile Iulik, untouched by war, can only assume the role of a child who follows the veteran's wise leadership, gratefully accepting his protection. According to this paradigm, it is Major Timur Kurbatovich—the former battlefield superior whom Pavlik saved from death—who fathered Pavlik while in the army. He has greater war experience than the boy and not only can relate to Pavlik's traumas more effectively but also can serve as the youth's father figure, which is why Iulik and Rita place such high hopes upon the major's influence over Pavlik. But this "alternative father" utterly fails: not only does he accompany Pavlik during his watch along the external side of the building's wall in search of "spooks" in the neighboring fifth-floor apartment, but, as the film's finale reveals, it is Timur who gives the paranoid boy a pistol with two cartridges, despite having sensibly noted that the weapon is for war and not for "normal life."

The failure of this alternative, war-bound father figure as the magnified manifestation of Pavlik's fatherly role ultimately reflects the falsity of the war myth as the basis of symbolic authority, especially when applied to the Chechen War and its veterans. In the post-Soviet mindscape, this ongoing battle, unlike the mythologized Great Patriotic War, is not sanctified by victory, and its soldiers definitely do not fit the archetype of victims of imperialistic aggression. Moreover, the traumatization that is normally glossed over in the mythology of the Great Patriotic War is simply too tangible in the figures of Pavlik, Timur, or any other Chechen war veteran who appears in the film (such as the shell-shocked lieutenant in the mental institution). Deprived of these symbolic modifiers, the myth of war in *Moi svodnyi brat Frankenshtein* is reduced to the remaining fundamental elements (as outlined by Gudkov) of xenophobia and the language of violence.

Pavlik is truly versatile in the language of violence. "Can you bash somebody's mug in?" ["V mordu mozhesh' komu-nibud' dvinut'?"], Pavlik asks his stepbrother in a friendly tone during their first exchange. "What for?" Egor responds, obviously taken aback. "Just for kicks," explains Pavlik. "Whose face?" asks Egor, still confused. "Anyone's. Mine, for instance," encourages Pavlik. Especially indicative of the communication through violence is the scene in the public bathhouse, during which Iulik takes his son for a ritual of male bonding. At first they talk about boxing, and it turns out that Iulik used to be a champion of the sport, a talent Pavlik especially admires since his dislocated shoulder prevents him from participating in such an activity. Following this conversation, Iulik discovers that another man, who is tall and stout, has surreptitiously appropriated their birch-bunches [*veniki*]. Iulik tries verbally to make the thief acknowledge his crime, only to be condescendingly ignored. When Pavlik appears on the scene, he instantly resorts to action: grabbing a metal bowl, without hesitation he slams it down on the stranger's head until the man collapses. Pavlik's violence turns out to be more effective than Iulik's polite attempts at persuasion. Although embarrassed by his son's interference (they hurriedly escape the bathhouse), Iulik is undeniably impressed and influenced by Pavlik's language of violence, and this influence clearly manifests itself in the following scene: the party at the Krymovs.

This party scene is a central episode in Todorovskii's *Moi svodnyi brat Frankenshtein,* largly because during this party Pavlik, for the first and last time in the film, shares his war memories with those present:

> "Then they [spooks] ran into the village. Vasia and I chased them in the armored car. There were local folks there, running and shouting: don't kill us, please don't do this, what are you doing, we're your own folk [*my svoi*]. We wiped out the whole village [*My davai eto selo utizhit'*]." "Who? Civilians?" "Who can tell one from the other? It was dark and scary . . . We crushed about twenty of them with our vehicle [*Shtuk dvadtsat' tochno podavili*]. Vasia got a leave then . . . And I was washing the blood off the wheels for three days."

This recollection is so shocking that the Krymovs' guests—all their close friends—are speechless, despite the fact that just prior to this monologue they had greeted Pavlik with standard salutations and praises stereotypical for the war myth ("We respect you very, very much," "We are proud of you . . ."). Iulik himself attempts to use this rhetoric: when defending Pavlik from the attack of his friend Edik (Sergei Gazarov), Iulik argues, "[He] risked his life for you and me, for the children." Needless to say, this rhetoric is painfully inappropriate: stampeding and devastating an entire village with an armor vehicle hardly corresponds to the image of a defender, nor to the image of a victim of aggression. Yet Edik's definition of Pavlik as an "utter fascist" [*zakonchennyi fashist*] is no better; it belongs to the same mythological discourse of the Great Patriotic War, though the label is borrowed from its negative, rather than positive, rhetoric. Having failed to find adequate words to defend Pavlik and his war experience, Iulik begins a fight with his best friend ("I'll smash your light out!") and then with Rita, thereby putting into action what he has learned in the bathhouse. Furthermore, the next morning Iulik drives Pavlik away; the violence of this act is confirmed by Ania's reaction to news of it. She begins crying desperately when, after a safe "removal" of Pavlik, Iulik offers to buy her the puppy she has long dreamt about; Ania clearly recognizes a sinister meaning in this bribe and intuitively refuses this procedure of othering, which equates her brother with a pet that can be bought at the market and thrown out at will.

The problem, however, appears to be much deeper than Iulik's personal failure to communicate with Pavlik, his friends, or even the other members of his family without sacrificing one or the other side. Pavlik's monologue at the party describes an experience that does not fit any binary opposition, let alone the one suggested by the war myth. In fact, his words that one could not tell the difference between civilians and military tangibly erase binaries. Fear and panic fuse in Pavlik's discourse with blind hatred and indifference to human life, self-defense with blood-thirsty aggression, victimization with the position of a mass murderer—this complexity of feelings is the substance that generates the language of violence. What can Iulik or others utilize to challenge this language? The old and inadequate rhetoric of the Great Patriotic War? Or silence, quasi-communication as typified by Egor's or Rita's conversations with Pavel? It is no wonder that after failing to find any discursive counter-response to Pavlik's language of violence, Iulik unconsciously learns and takes verbal cues from his son—thus confirming Pavlik's role as father in their relationship. Especially noteworthy is the scene in the attic in which Iulik attempts to convince Pavlik that the "spooks" who he suspects lay hidden there are only figments of his sick imagination. In the attic, how-ever, Pavlik does indeed find and startle a man (who turns out to be just a bum), whom Iulik seizes; the fight begins, and Iulik starts beating the stranger so violently that Pavlik has to stop him: "Stop, Dad, stop. . . . You really got going, Dad" ["Vse, batia, vse. . . . Nu ty daesh', bat'"].

Pavlik's language of violence inevitably overcomes any discursive attempts at rebuttal, not only because it is stronger owing to its idoliza-tion of force but also because it is situated outside any discursive field. It is completely performative, and therefore immune to rhetorical in-terventions and oppositions. Revealingly, Pavlik's symbolic power, his fatherly role, becomes most obvious in the film's finale, during which he abducts Egor and Ania, and through this act establishes full control over Iulik and Rita as well. The orchestration of this hostage takeover and its outcome compellingly invoke media and cinematic representations of terrorism. By his actions, however, Pavlik demonstrates his unwavering care for his new family and his genuine desire to protect them from the dangers of the world (all crucial duties of the patriarchal father figure). But patriarchal authority based on war logic can be nothing but an act of terror. Furthermore, Pavlik's language of violence not only fails to protect "his own" but instead *produces* Others, creates enemies, and thereby transforms phantoms into very dangerous corporealities: almost immediately after locking himself and the Krymovs in their dacha, Pavlik finds himself surrounded by the police, whom he takes for "spooks." Spooks or no spooks, the attackers are determined to eliminate Pavlik as a hostage taker and can easily hurt the Krymovs; that is, they literally threaten Pavlik with his own nightmare. When Rita screams in desperation to the police: "Don't shoot! There are children here!" Pavlik responds, "Kids or no kids—they don't care [dlia nikh tut detei net], like I didn't back then. Period." This response is not as insane as it may seem, because Pavlik "back then" [i.e., in Chechnya] and the police "here" are both doing the same "job"—"fighting terrorism."

This deficiency of effective communication via the language of violence justified by the myth of war underlines a profound problem in contemporary Russian culture: the crises of the liberal intelligentsia who tried but ultimately failed to develop enlightened discourses of modernization that were opposed both to the Soviet rhetoric of power and to post-Soviet performances of violence. According to Boris Dubin, this failure derives from the post-Soviet intelligentsia's "distancing from the present, conservation of cultural models, and the adoption of xenophobia as a defense mechanism. . . . Today's Russian intelligentsia and its representatives, who pretend to leading positions, merely react to the situation, over which they have no control and [on which they have] no effect, as it were" (Dubin 338). Being isolated and out of touch with the present, in Dubin's opinion, is responsible for the purely negative identification of the post-Soviet intelligentsia with the times: not unlike other social groups, the intelligentsia "identifies itself through negation and becomes consolidated around 'the image of the enemy.' . . . [The intelligentsia's] own incapacity for self-realization, its suspiciousness and aggressiveness are projected onto the interpretation of the enemy and extrapolated to its imaginary constructed figure" (339).

It is this sociocultural collapse of the intelligentsia that is exposed by Iulik's failure as a father figure: he is symbolically bankrupt, and Pavlik and his war-sanctioned language of violence only make this bankruptcy painfully transparent. From this perspective, it becomes clear why Todorovskii's film does not really encourage the parallel between Iulik and Dr. Frankenstein, who, of course, in Shelley's novel, is responsible for the *purposeful* and *knowing* creation of the monster. Paradoxically, Iulik is responsible precisely because he *does not know* and, furthermore, *does not want to know* about Pavlik's existence, and therefore tries to insulate himself and his family from Pavlik's violent and demented world. In doing so, Iulik transfers onto Pavlik the same procedures of othering and producing enemies that normally appall him as well as other liberal post-Soviet intellectuals similar to him.

After the Krymovs escape from the surrounded house, Pavlik essentially disappears; although it is implied that the police kill him, we do not see him die, nor is his body presented to the viewers. The anticlimactic nature of the film's finale is further underlined by the complete lack of dialogue between the surviving family members, and between them and the police. The silence, or the covering of discourse by white noise, signifies a repeated circle of repression of the uncanny, which will be forgotten in the same way as the traumas that have produced it. The film ends with a distant high-angle shot that shows the members of the police force congratulating themselves, and then Iulik embracing his family. This conclusion is a visual expression of yet another repression of *Unheimlich*. If one recalls Kristeva's notion that the *Unheimlich* brings awareness "that we are foreigners to ourselves, and it is with the help of that sole support that we can attempt to live with others" (170), then this seemingly tender, peace-restoring embrace acquires precisely the opposite significance, namely, the revealed and repressed knowledge of the nuclear family members' mutual foreignness. By extension this image can be interpreted as a powerful metaphor for the "social family" of post-Soviet society, which, in desperately trying to deny its own unconscious/otherness, chooses repression over any forms of negotiations. During this scene only the distant sound of military drums is detectable in the background, and this beat provides a powerful indication of the *Unheimlich* that has just revealed its perversely "familiar mug," only to be once again forced into the darkness of non-recognition.

The Soviet myth of war adopted by the post-Soviet rhetoric of national identity exemplifies the repression of the historical experience of terror as the source of societal uncanny. However, it must be underscored that the son (a representative of the future generation, albeit in the paternal role), and not the father (normally representative of the past), embodies the uncanny in Todorovskii's film. This inversion suggests that not only the past but also the present and, moreover, the future are persistently repressed in the contemporary Russian mindscape. The failure of the father figure to establish a meaningful connection between the past, present, and future is inevitable in this dead-end condition, which *Moi svodnyi brat Frankenshtein* uncovered behind the façade of the social "stabilization" of the 2000s.

NOTES

1. Symptomatically, the texts that demonstrate how the war undermined and problematized the father's role in the family and society—for instance, Andrei Platonov's magnificent short story "Vozvrashchenie" ["The Return" 1946]—were consistently marginalized. Among these marginalized exceptions one should also mention the film *Kryl'ia* [*Wings,* Larisa Shepit'ko 1966; and *Dikii med* [*Wild Honey,* Vladimir Chebotarev 1966 (based on the eponymous novel by Leonid Pervomaiskii)].

2. Produced by Prior-Film and Rekun TV: producer, Leonid Iarmolnik; director of photography, Sergei Mikhalchuk; production designer, Vladimir Gudlin; and music by Aleksei Aigi.

3. Another important example is *Svoi* [*Our Own* 2004], directed by Dmitri Meskhiev and written for the screen by Valentin Chernykh. In this film, which is situated in the first months of the war, the opposition between "us" and "them" emerges as constantly floating and problematic. In *Svoi* the complex relationships between the newcomers and their host, a father figure, reveal the dialectics of the kinship and war-like hostility between the members of the "social" family. The father in Meskhiev's film manages to save his family and create the social solidarity between those who are "ours" by subverting the very foundations of the stereotypical Soviet requirements to "our man": the father turns out to be a former *kulak,* who supposedly illegally returned to his native village from exile, and is the German-appointed *starosta* [elder] of the village. However, the film does not entirely deconstruct the Soviet myth of the "war father"; rather, *Svoi* releases it from the Soviet stereotypes while preserving the mechanism of the elevation of the "vertical," patriarchal authority in the war setting. The father, while embodying the antipode of the Soviet father figure, preserves a similar authority to distinguish between right and wrong, to define who is "ours" and who is the "enemy," although his worldview has nothing to do with Soviet ideological or even nationalist systems. If *Svoi* inverts the Soviet myth of the "father vis-à-vis war," Todorovskii's film presents a radical deconstruction of this foundational archetype.

4. The "post-traumatic" interpretation is supported by sophisticated viewers of the film such as the critic and film director Oleg Kovalov and the writer Tatyana Tolstaya:

> Not raising his voice and rendering a somewhat 'private' story, Todorovskii demonstrates how the hypocritical and indifferent society betrays its children—at first transforming them into physical and moral freaks, and then contemptuously turning away from them [. . .] This film is akin to Polish films of "moral anxiety," which are usually based on the seemingly impassive depiction of "family chronicles." The most conscientious and courageous socially engaged statement in the cinema of recent years. (Kovalov, "*Seansu* otvechaiut . . .")

Neither a good and decent Moscow bourgeois family, their circle, nor even society wants to take responsibility for boys whom they themselves send every year to learn how to kill—for our security, for what else? You are the warrior, sonny, be proud of it. You are all covered in blood, freak, don't dare to approach us. The elder son [Pavlik] is a top graduate of this school, an inhabitant of the world of shadows, who has elevated to the state of absurdity a natural archaic logic of any society: ours are good, aliens are bad. Defend your own kind until your last breath; kill the others before they kill you. A defender crazed in his defense. (Tolstaia, "*Seansu* otvechaiut . . .")

5. This motif can also be interpreted as an indirect reference to the monster from James Whale's *Frankenstein* (1931). As Rick Worland mentions in his analysis of the film: "a drawing of the monster's eyes radiating beams of light as clawlike hands stretch toward the viewer dissolves into a field of slowly circling eyes, suggesting at once the monster's menace as well as its own terror of the existence it beholds" (162).

6. It is significant that Pavlik includes in his Great Family his war buddy Vasia Tobolkin, for whom he patiently waits at the railway station, having repressed the friend's martyr-like death before his own eyes. This detail demonstrates that Pavlik's utopia can be built only in proximity to the land of death, since it necessitates a war with the entire world of Others. It is quite logical, then, that Pavlik approaches the materialization of his utopia in the film's finale, his master plan finds its ultimate fulfillment in the abduction of his newly found brother and sister, which, in turn, leads to a hostage situation ending with Pavlik's own death.

7. The same is true for some other films—such as *Ivanovo detstvo* [*Ivan's Childhood*, Andrei Tarkovsky 1962] or *Koktebel'* [*Koktebel*, Boris Khlebnikov and Aleksei Popogrebskii 2003], in which the son is marked/aged by traumatic experience and therefore assumes the paternal function by default, for the father qua father is essentially missing.

REFERENCES

Clark, Katerina. *Soviet Novel: History as Ritual.* 2nd ed. Bloomington: Indiana University Press, 2000.

Dubin, Boris. "Rossiiskaia intelligentsiia mezhdu klassikoi i massovoi kul'turoi." In idem, *Slovo-pis'mo-literatura: Ocherki po sotsiologii sovremennoi kul'tury,* 329–40. Moscow: Novoe literaturnoe obozrenie, 2001. Available in English at http://www.stanford.edu/group/Russia20/volumepdf/dubin.pdf (accessed 12 March 2004).

Freud, Sigmund. *An Infantile Neurosis and Other Works.* In *The Standard Edition,* trans. James Strachey, in collaboration with Anna Freud, Vol. 17 (1917–19). London: Hogarth Press and the Institute of Psycho-Analysis, 1955.

Gudkov, Lev. "The Fetters of Victory: How the War Provides Russia with Its Identity" Translated by Mischa Gabowitch. *Eurozine,* May 2, 2005. Available at http://www.eurozine.com/articles/2005-05-03-gudkov-en.html (accessed 3 May 2007). Original Russian version: "Pobeda v voine: k sotsiologii odnogo natsional'nogo simvola," in Lev Gudkov, *Negativnaia identochnost': Stat'i 1997–2002 godov,* 20–58. Moscow: Novoe literaturnoe obozrenie, 2002.

Khoroshilova, Tatiana. "Frankenshtein—nash syn i brat," *Rossiiskaia nedelia,* June 25, 2004. Available at http://www.rg.ru/2004/06/25/frankenstein.html.

Kristeva, Julia. *Strangers to Ourselves.* Translated by Leon S. Roudiez. New York: Columbia University Press, 1991.

Prokhorov, Aleksandr. *Unasledovannyi diskurs: paradigmy stalinskoi kul'tury v literature i kinematografe "ottepeli."* St. Petersburg: Akademicheskii proekt, DNK 2007.

"*Seansu* otvechaiut . . . *Moi svodnyi brat Frankenshtein.*" *Seans* 21/22 (2005). Available at http://seance.ru/category/n/21-22/films2004/frankenshtein/mnenia (accessed 3 May 2007).

Stishova, Elena. "Semeinaia khronika vremen neob"iavlennoi voiny." *Iskusstvo kino* 7 (2004): 77–82.

Worland, Rick. *The Horror Film: An Introduction.* London: Blackwell, 2007.

FILMOGRAPHY

Moi svodnyi brat Frankenshtein [*My Stepbrother Frankenstein*]. Dir. Valerii Todorovskii. Mosfil'm, 2004.

Figure 5.1. Pavlik and Iulik at the railway station. The inversion of fatherhood.

SIX

A Surplus of Surrogates: Mashkov's Fathers

HELENA GOSCILO

I cannot think of any need in childhood as strong
as the need for a father's protection.

SIGMUND FREUD, *CIVILIZATION AND ITS DISCONTENTS*

SENTIMENTAL VERSUS SOBERING PATERNITY

Frequently touted as Russia's matinee idol and answer to Antonio Banderas,[1] Vladimir Mashkov has enjoyed a long and successful career on stage and screen,[2] assuming a wide variety of cinematic roles, most famously those of Tolian, the eponymous protagonist in *Vor* [*The Thief* 1997] and of the corrupt, flamboyant entrepreneur Makovskii in Pavel Lungin's *Oligarkh* [*Tycoon* 2000].[3] In recent years he also has tested his abilities behind the camera. Such seeming versatility discourages a perception of Mashkov as an actor typecast or overly invested in roles steeped in glamour or monochromatic machismo. Yet a curious aspect of his professional trajectory during approximately the last decade, and one that meshes with general tendencies in contemporary Russian cinema, is his preoccupation as both actor and director with fatherhood, evidenced in *Amerikanskaia doch'* [*American Daughter,* Karen Shakhnazarov 1995], *Sirota kazanskaia* [*Sympathy Seeker,* Vladimir Mashkov 1997], *Vor* [*The Thief,* Pavel Chukhrai 1997], and *Papa* [Vladimir Mashkov 2004].[4]

The plots of the first two revolve around father-daughter relationships, draw on fairy-tale formulas transplanted to a contemporary setting, and ultimately subsume the theme of paternity in other issues the directors apparently deem more pressing or promising. Combining comic melodrama with cardboard characters and liberally borrowing from Western road movies such as Peter Bogdanovich's *Paper Moon* (1973), Shakhnazarov's *Amerikanskaia doch'* struggles to demonstrate Russia's moral superiority to the United States through its fantasy figure of a sensitive, caring Russian father, enacted rather diffidently by Mashkov. *Sirota kazanskaia*, which marked Mashkov's directorial debut, is an innocuous, sentimental comedy belonging to the category of the New Year's film—in orientation, approximately the equivalent of the Western Christmas story.[5] Indeed, many of the frames resemble animated New Year's greeting cards for children (Figure 6.1). The blend of slapstick routines and the utterly predictable outcome of the individual, sequential efforts by three middle-aged men (Valentin Gaft, Lev Durov, and Oleg Tabakov) to be recognized as the father of a young schoolteacher (Elena Shevchenko)[6] living in the provinces provides what undiscriminating viewers typically laud as "heartwarming entertainment" (Figure 6.2). Though the film raises such issues as loneliness, self-interest, and the (pre-DNA) difficulty of definitively establishing paternity, the lightweight comedy ultimately showcases Russians' probity and their big-hearted capacity to bond over food and drink under even the unlikeliest circumstances (Figure 6.3). Dedicated to "all dads and moms" ("vsem papam i mamam posviashchaetsia"), *Sirota kazanskaia* oozes the logic-defying "feel-good" sentiment that one associates with Hallmark productions and an era when Father Knew Best.[7] Notable for outstanding performances by children, both this film and *Amerikanskaia doch'* unwittingly suggest that females' relationships to fathers lend themselves to frothy treatment and reside in the interstices of more significant phenomena.[8]

These breezy screen flirtations with paternal themes could hardly contrast more with Chukhrai's *Vor* and Mashkov's *Papa*, which embed the problems of fathers and sons in the historical context of Stalinism and abjure humor for tragedy-tinged melodrama. Though radically divergent in their aesthetics and their perspective on fatherhood, *Vor* and *Papa* make paternity the conceptual node of the narrative, borrow selectively from the genre of the *Bildungsroman,* extend the plot into multiple temporalities, rely on the chronotope of the train to convey historical and psychological dislocation, and conjure fantastic visions of the ideal father.

STALINIST MACHISMO: HOMELESSNESS, OR STEALING OUR HAPPY CHILDHOOD

The generation that is ruling Russia now [. . . was] raised in a cult of violence, where militarism was the value of the day.

PAVEL CHUKHRAI, "VLADIMIR'S DIRECTORS," 2003

Both the powerful effect and box-office success of *Vor* owe a great deal to the actors' performances in the three major roles[9] and to Chukhrai's skill in sustaining two intersecting levels of signification via the father figure: the historical/national and the psychological/universal theorized by Freud and Lacan. Accompanied throughout by a retrospective voiceover of the now adult "son," the film starts with his birth and ends with his surrogate father's death: in 1946 the solitary, pregnant war widow Katia (Ekaterina Rednikova), carrying a battered suitcase along a depopulated country road, suddenly experiences violent contractions, and without any assistance delivers a baby on the spot (offscreen). Six years later, traveling across the country on a crowded train, she and her son, Sania (Misha Filipchuk),[10] encounter the uniformed, self-confident Captain Tolian (Mashkov), who with slick rapidity overwhelms her sexually in a quick bout of furtive, "stand-up" intercourse on the platform between cars. Forming a pseudo-family, the trio moves into a communal apartment, where Tolian lies, charms, and manipulates his way out of awkward situations (Figure 6.4). After winning the other occupants' trust, Tolian "treats" them to a night at the circus so as to steal their portable possessions in their absence. Though horrified to discover that Tolian is not an officer but a common thief, the sexually besotted Katia remains with him,[11] and the pattern of deception and robbery continues as the threesome travels from town to town so as to elude detection. When Katia finally decides to leave Tolian, the police catch up with him just as she and Sania prepare to board yet another train. Following Tolian's imprisonment and deportation, Katia dies from a botched abortion, and Sania finds himself in an orphanage. In the version released abroad, the film concludes with the adolescent Sania's (Dima Shigarev) chance encounter outside a tavern with a dissipated, seedy, hard-drinking Tolian, whom the disillusioned Sania shoots—and presumably kills—before fleeing back to the orphanage, with the words, "After that there was nothing."

In the original, longer version shown in Russia, however, the final meeting between "father" and "son" occurs in Chechnya, where Sania, now a colonel in his late forties (Iurii Beliaev), recognizes Tolian in the broken-down old drunk who grovels before the Russian soldiers, begging for a drink, only to expire in Sania's arms. The last glimpse of Sania conflates the adult man and child: lying on a bunk in the train departing Chechnya, Sania, his back to the camera, grasps his head in his hands, while the camera zooms in on the leopard tattooed above his shoulder blades before cutting to Sania as a child staring through the train window—to glimpse his "real" father in uniform standing on the flatcar of a passing freight train moving in the opposite direction. Tellingly, "authentic" paternity here appears but intermittently, solely as a perpetually receding phantom. And the middle-aged Sania literally and figuratively bears the mark of the only father he ever knew in an era of pretenders to the paternal throne.[12]

Chukhrai deftly conveys the atmosphere of post–World War II Soviet Russia—numerous war widows and orphans, incessant everyday hardships, ugly communal apartments, and tacky belongings—as the populace struggles to recover from the devastating trauma that decimated the nation's male population and left entire sections of cities in ruins.[13] Omnipresent trains convey the deracination and dislocation of the era, in which loss, absence, and irreparable psychological, as well as physical, damage constitute a harrowing norm. Tolian may be the thief of the film's title, but the more significant and far-reaching robbery is perpetrated by Stalin's paranoid policies and by the war, which steals countless lives and reduces daily existence to shambles. *Vor* focuses on the travails of recovery from devastation, over which the iconic figure of Stalin as the ultimate Father presides.

Unlike other post-Soviet revisitations of the Stalinist epoch, such as Sergei Livnev's *Serp i molot* [*Hammer and Sickle* 1994], Chukhrai's film conveys Stalin's mythological status indirectly, through several modes of visual and verbal representation.[14] As the Generalissimo exaggeratedly credited with Germany's defeat and deified as the savior and Father of All Peoples, Stalin functions as the nation's secular patron saint: he dominates living space visually through his ubiquitous iconic portraits, mirrored in the profile tattooed on Tolian's chest. Stalin is also verbally invoked in the thief's toasts and his claim of being Stalin's son—the mendacious "secret" Tolian confides to the credulous Sania, but, more significant, an apposite metaphor for part of his own double identity. Tolian adopts in degraded and domesticated form the macho militarism of Stalinism and the latter's insistence on collective celebration, captured in the Leader's enunciative slogan "zhit' stalo luchshe, zhit' stalo veselee" ["life's become better, life's become happier"]; Tolian also benefits from the trust automatically elicited by his fraudulently donned officer's uniform, which mimics Stalin's calculatedly chosen habitual garb even in peacetime. Tolian's "escape clause" when challenged is his impassioned cry of having sacrificed and suffered for the sake of the country.[15] Maintaining, à la Stalin, that instilling fear in others paves the route to power, he invariably deploys attack as the best form of defense[16] and orchestrates festivities with near-strangers so as to camouflage his intentions to rob them (just as guests at Stalin's evening dinner parties routinely were imprisoned or executed shortly afterward). Stalin's cult of personality reached its apogee after the war, when all cultural forms genuflected before the omniscience of the Infallible Father, transforming dread into reverent awe in airbrushed photographs, gigantic sculptures, flattering portraits, sycophantic songs, and hagiographic screen and literary narratives. As a reduced Stalin who understands the significance of violence and fear as vital components of military/psychological power, Tolian inspires a kindred awestruck terror in his "adopted" son, causing the child (and later, the adolescent) to urinate involuntarily in his presence, dreading any and all punishment for undefined wrongdoings. With time, Sania comes to idolize his rough, "absolute" pseudo-father, just as the Soviet population worshiped Stalin, turning a blind eye to his policy of iron-fisted control and the murder of millions.

Ambiguous images and identifications play a pivotal role in the film, not only in Stalin's elevation to mythical status (too well known to necessitate elaboration in the film's diegesis) but also in Tolian's reliance on Stalin as an authoritative and authoritarian source. As Father, Stalin provides the successful model of male power disseminated through his assiduously monitored public image, which camouflaged a dramatically different private self.[17] The two "selves" imprinted on Tolian's flesh parallel in miniature the king's—and Stalin's—two bodies, both susceptible to readings on two different levels of sophistication.[18] Anyone versed in the criminal world of Stalinist camps instantly understands that the tattoo of Stalin's profile above Tolian's heart, far from inscribing his blood relationship to the Generalissimo, functions as an I.D. certifying time served not in the army but in prison. Tattoos of Lenin and Stalin on the bodies of Russian inmates served as sui generis bullet-proof vests, based on prisoners' certainty that prison guards would not dare to shoot at the sacrosanct images of the Soviet leaders—leaders whom the inmates vilified in their sweeping rejection of all authorities outside the criminals' own code of laws (just as Tolian dismisses all official authority but uses its conventions for his own purposes). Sania's innocence and his desperate desire for a father worthy of hero-worship by definition predispose him to read any "paternal text" superficially, trustingly. Trapped between the ever elusive, receding ideal of the heroic father killed in combat and the physically present, self-confident paternal surrogate prepared to impart the lessons of manhood, Sania gradually surrenders to the ambiguous allure of the latter.

In similar fashion the tattoo of a leopard on Tolian's upper back evokes those traits associated with the animal—strength and physical power—which Tolian advocates as masculine desiderata, though his own behavior reveals a predilection for bluffing, cunning, and retreat. Yet, in a narrower sense, this second tattoo also provides pertinent information about Tolian, since for the zoologist, the leopard, an opportunistic predator of extraordinary adaptability, is infamous for its stealth and ability to go undetected.[19] Tolian's tattoos, then—one politico-historical, the other social-zoological—are complex signs that neither Katia nor Sania (unlike the viewer) can interpret correctly. Though accurate in their analogical significance, the signs preposterously aggrandize the dimensions of their sphere of signification. Ultimately Tolian as scheming and intimidating imposter is a diminished double of Stalin as mythological object of universal, terrified veneration. The thief as officer approximates Stalinist tactics on a petty micro-scale: like Stalin, he betrays everyone's trust and "robs" not only his country(wo)men of what is justly theirs but also his "son" of a normal childhood and adolescence, just as Stalin castrated the younger generation, who during the Thaw emerged as ineffectual dreamers and, later, as the passive, disoriented amnesiacs of early Stagnation.

Without slipping into bona fide allegory or parable,[20] the film easily lends itself to a historical reading in which Tolian as the self-proclaimed husband of Katia/Russia evokes Stalin as the surrogate, self-nominated father to the Soviet populace. The object of an idolatry founded on naïve perceptions and illusions proves a devious criminal and, though discredited, leaves behind an indelible legacy of fear, violence, and existential uncertainty as well as implacable strength. This is the military paradigm analyzed by Mark Lipovetsky in his essay in this volume on Valerii Todorovskii's *Moi svodnyi brat Frankenshtein* [*My Stepbrother Frankenstein* 2004] (chapter 5). In Todorovskii's film the war in Chechnya (the sphere of the adult Sania's activity in *Vor*) produces its updated versions of Stalinist-era traumas and illustrates the nation's inability to move beyond its inherited militaristic mentality, which in post-Soviet Russia overlaps with that of the criminal world, as is made clear in Brian Baer's examination of redeemed patriarchy in Aleksei Sidorov's immensely popular TV series *Brigada* (2002–2004) (chapter 9).

What enriches *Vor* is Chukhrai's deftness in inextricably interweaving the historical with the personal/timeless/universal issue of paternity and filiation. The film leaves no doubts about the father's essential role in ritual initiations into full-fledged masculinity, and, as both Janet Maslin and Susan Larsen have noted, this is precisely the significance of Tolian in Sania's life (Larsen 661). The trajectory of the male relationship in the film offers a textbook illustration of the Oedipal paradigm. Initially Sania's jealous resentment of Tolian's free access to Katia manifests itself in his attempt, quite literally, to replace Tolian in his mother's bed, his futile efforts to interrupt their sexual intercourse by loudly kicking at the door of the room from which he has been locked out,[21] and, later, when Tolian hits Katia, his threat to kill him with Tolian's own gun—the classic symbol of potent masculinity. As his mother subsequently observes, it is Sania's rebelliousness at the train they are about to board that ultimately leads to Tolian's arrest and imprisonment; only at the decisive moment of Tolian's deportation along with the other convicted prisoners does Sania, for the first and last time in the film, cry out "Papka, papka rodnen'kii! Ne pokidai nas!"/"Daddy, daddy, dear! Don't leave us!" as he futilely races after the vehicle that removes Tolian from his life. That scene is pivotal, for it shows "loss of the father" as a precondition for Sania's acknowledgment of Tolian as such—a scenario to be repeated in A. Zviagintsev's *Vozvrashchenie* [*The Return* 2003], examined by Yana Hashamova (chapter 7). Moreover, in finally accepting Tolian as father, Sania simultaneously loses his capacity to experience visions of his biological father, who was killed in the war before Sania's birth, but who in the early parts of the film periodically "appears" to the boy in the compensatory image of a hazily idealized soldier. Thus Sania symbolically kills both fathers, and thereafter, in keeping with Freud's scenario, increasingly yearns for Tolian's return (*Totem and Taboo* 10).

As in the Oedipal family drama, the insertion of "the third" into the intimate mother-son dyad effects the transition to a model-identification with the father that both Freud and Lacan deem a prerequisite for the attainment of maturity/access to the Symbolic Order. That process and its significance are made clear in two segments that confirm Tolian's fulfillment of the paternal function. After boys in the courtyard outside the communal apartment attack Sania, Tolian teaches him the "correct" manly response—violence—and lends psychological support through his tough, truculent presence when Sania repays the boys in kind. Whereas that brutal episode ultimately qualifies as a mini-lesson in the aggressive tactics inhering in the masculine ethos, a later exchange that shows genuine bonding between an insecure Sania and a briefly compassionate Tolian focuses on the inestimable value of male self-confidence. Tellingly this rapprochement takes place in the *bania,* where the duo's literal nakedness tropes their psychological shedding of all pretence. Sania's sudden, nervous realization that the size of his genitalia does not compare with those of the adult males milling around them prompts Tolian's unexpectedly kind reassurance that maturation and boldness will eliminate the discrepancy ("budesh' smelyi, u tebia vyrastit" ["if you're bold, it'll grow to full size"]). Characteristically Tolian supplements his encouragement with a brief reference to his own manly stoicism when five booted men beat and kicked him in the kidneys, causing him to pass urine with blood for three days, presumably in prison. In short, Tolian educates Sania into the traditional set of traits that constitute machismo ("smotri, kak ia" ["look at how I do things"]), and the scene in the *bania* clarifies how the literal male penis provides access to the symbolic phallus and its prerogatives.

Chukhrai buttresses that "revelation" with a trope he cleverly elaborates in the last third of the film—the gun as the classic symbol of virility, which the military context naturalizes. Indeed, the gun/rifle/knife as emblem simultaneously of masculine potency and violence that fathers hand over to sons recurs systematically in films of patrilinear filiation (see chapters 3, 4, 5, and 7 in this volume). After Tolian's exit from Sania's life, the gun/baton, which Tolian passes on to his "son" (along with a small portrait of Stalin, the epitome of violent paternity, and a watch, which tracks historical progression), becomes the adolescent's prized symbolic possession at the orphanage as he waits expectantly for Tolian to rescue him.[22] It is the weapon Sania uses to shoot Tolian after the latter disavows his paternity by dismissing the boy—emasculated and regressing into a urinating child—when they unexpectedly meet outside a local tavern.[23] Whereas the version of the film distributed abroad provides a death-knell closure, ending with Sania's tossing the gun away and returning to the orphanage, with the words "After that there was nothing," the original Russian version concludes on a more complex note. It omits the short scene in the orphanage, instead cutting to a crucial sequence that complicates the viewer's understanding of Tolian's role in Sania's life: decades later, the middle-aged Sania, now a military colonel en route to Chechnya, recalls his first shot and his conviction that it was necessary to kill Tolian ("Ia dolzhen byl eto sdelat'" ["I had to do it"])—a self-reassurance he repeats whenever he pulls the trigger in combat. In other words, he has embraced the mode of masculinity learned from and advocated by Tolian. Upon discovering that the old, alcoholic Tolian has retained his tattoo of Stalin and yet removed that of the leopard, he reacts revealingly with the laconic remark, "Priznalsia!" ["He's admitted it"]—presumably referencing Tolian's final admission that he is nothing more than a predatory thief and not Stalin's biological son.[24]

In her article "Mama vykhodit zamuzh" ["Mama Gets Married"] Tat'iana Moskvina states,

> I marvel at Pavel Chukhrai's insight, which with literal precision/accuracy reflects [. . .] the metahistorical incident in the concrete historial tonality of the post-war period. His film *The Thief* narrates the mother's

tragic delusion/error and the substitution for the father with an evil thief, a predatory shameless animal. What's sad is that both mother and son could never jettison their love for him, [could never] come to hate him and [thus] break free. (Moskvina 223)[25]

Here Moskvina seems to miss the film's major point, namely, that fathers may find sons expendable but the son's identity formation requires a father, however inflexible, merciless, or abusive.[26] Tolian is the only father Sania knows, and the leopard tattoo on Sania's back at film's end symbolically demonstrates that the son, despite the privations and torments of his maimed childhood, has adopted the misread "better side" of his surrogate father—empirically evidenced by his conduct as a "manly," authoritative representative of the country's military power structure. Ignoring his subordinates' disapproval, he orders that the women and children being evacuated from Chechnya be transported in his train car. And when one of the women peremptorily demands vodka from him, he obligingly pours some for her—only to see her use the alcohol as a compress for her ailing son, in a reminiscent image[27] that prepares us for the film's final frame. This last frame returns to Sania as a six-year-old semi-orphan longingly gazing through the window at the phantom vision of his father traveling in the opposite direction, paralleling the shot of Tolian's wounded body moving off on the freight train when Sania shot him and ran away.

Shuttled between the remote model of his father's phantom image and the harsh reality of Tolian's immediate presence,[28] Sania ultimately matures into manhood by drawing on both: although his tattoo duplicates Tolian's, his "military service to his country" parallels his father's participation in World War II. Lacking a genuine father, Sania, paradoxically, has three pseudo-fathers: the imagined, unknown biological father, Tolian, and the Father of All Fathers, Stalin, who all play defining roles in his identity. Iconic (Stalin), phantom (biological), and surrogate (Tolian) fathers together fulfill the paternal function theorized by Lacan, enabling Sania to enter the Symbolic order and embrace full-fledged social masculinity.

Admiring the film as "brilliant," Stephen Hunter in his review perceptively remarked that Chukhrai's "stroke of genius is to comprehend the attraction of Stalin, not merely the evil." That attraction, copiously documented in memoirs and films, obtains not only on the level of nation but also on that of the individual family, in which the strong or tyrannical father provides both a buffer (Freud's "protection") and a blueprint for masculinity that enable the son to effect the rocky transition to adulthood. With poignancy and a profound understanding of psychological subtleties, Chukhrai's film dramatizes the dilemma of the son who dreams of an ideal father to be worshiped and emulated in a world that equates masculinity with authority, strength, and independence, but who may fall victim to paternal authority congealed into tyranny, strength degenerated into arbitrary violence, and independence reduced to indifference. It is from this environment of degraded values that such a son must salvage elements that will cohere into an acceptable self, battling his loyalty, a priori guilt, and gratitude for those brief interludes of authentic closeness with the Father, who, after all, represents the Law.

THE FAMILY ROMANCE AND THE TRIUMPH
OF THE FATHER'S GHOST

Unfortunately, paternal love has not yet been praised enough. [. . .] My father loved me very much, but I think that I didn't manage to give him enough love as his son. That's why *Daddy* [*Papa*] is my return of that debt.

VLADIMIR MASHKOV, "DADDY IS MY DEBT TO MY PARENTS"

The paternal image in *Vor* could hardly contrast more with that in *Papa*, which likewise teems with fathers. Both star and director of *Papa*, which received the award for the audience's favorite film at the Moscow International Film Festival in 2004, Mashkov dedicated the work to "our dads" ["nashim papam posviashchaetsia"] in a spirit of sentimentality that suffuses the entire film.[29] "Based on motifs" from a 1956 play by Aleksandr Galich, *Matrosskaia tishina* [*Sailors' Rest*], whose title references the notorious remand prison in Moscow,[30] the film allowed Mashkov to transfer to the screen the role of the Jewish father, Abram Il'ich Shvarts, which he had played not only in Oleg Tabakov's theater ("Tabakerka") for more than a decade but also in countless productions abroad. Perhaps his repeated enactment of Shvarts on the stage, which by definition requires a certain exaggeration in the absence of close-ups, accounts for Mashkov's performance on screen, so overblown as to intermittently verge on parody.[31] According to several interviews, Mashkov undertook the film version of Galich's play partly to compensate for his inadequate appreciation of his father during the latter's lifetime. Thus *Papa* may be viewed as a mini-monument to paternity.

The film's simple plot spans fifteen years in the life of David (Andrei Rozendent, then Egor Beroev), the musically gifted son of Abram Shvarts (Mashkov), a widowed Jewish storekeeper [*zavkhoz*] who surreptitiously manipulates accounts with the aid of his assistant, Mitia Zhuchkov (Sergei Ugriumov). Starting with David's boyhood in a Ukrainian shtetl in 1929, the narrative shifts to his success at the Moscow Conservatory in the midst of Stalin's purges (May Day, 1939), and concludes with his experiences as a Red Army officer in World War II during the Germans' retreat westward in 1944.[32] Omitting the final act of Galich's play, which emanates the optimistic atmosphere of the Thaw (May 1955—David has not survived, but his son continues the Shvarts line),[33] *Papa* ends inconclusively, with a severely injured, feverish David calling out "Papa!" on the medical evacuation train carrying doctors, nurses, and wounded Russian soldiers from the front to a safer location.

Fathers proliferate in *Papa*'s concentrated focus on father-son relations. As the pivotal character whose maturation supplies the narrative momentum of this celluloid *Bildungsroman*, David interacts with three paternal figures: his biological father, a despotic alcoholic who beats him when provoked, holds him hostage to incessant violin practice, and generally keeps him on a tight leash, yet dreams solely of securing the boy's future success and happiness; the spiritual, philosophical pseudo-father, Meyer Wolf/Meier Vol'f (Sergei Dontsov), who, understanding Abram's weaknesses and David's frustration, comforts both through his attentive calm and empathy; and Ivan Kuzmich Chernyshev (Anatolii Vasil'ev), the ideological father at the Moscow Conservatory, who favors David as the virtuoso prodigy, but toes the party line and brooks no criticism of official Soviet policy, which sanctions the vilification and extermination of Jews. By remaining unquestioningly faithful to the dictates of the ultimate False Father (Stalin), the politically orthodox Ivan Kuzmich compromises his paternal function. That the outwardly repellent and maladroit Abram fulfills his, despite overwhelming historical odds, may be deduced from the film's title, the validation of

Abram in the final sequence, and the last word in the film—"Papa," pronounced four times.

A variation on the "crime and punishment" plot, the film locates its emotional peaks and valleys in David's attitude toward his father, which finds articulation in discursive and symbolic patricide, eventually atoned for by belated remorse. While still in Tul'chin, the boy passionately blurts out to Meyer Wolf his intention of killing Abram after the latter, infuriated at his son's theft of his postcards and denial of culpability, subjects him to intemperate, violent blows disproportionate to the misdemeanor. At the Moscow Conservatory, basking in his popularity and eager to advance professionally, David cleaves to his politically obedient paternal mentor and severs contact with his past ("Ne khochu pomnit' nikakogo Tul'china! [. . .] U nas ne bylo proshlogo" ["I don't want to remember Tulchin at all! [. . .] We had no past"], including his provincial father, whom he erases and replaces with a mythical father—a musical conductor, of whom he need not be ashamed in front of his new, influential surrogate, Ivan Kuzmich. And when Abram arrives at the Conservatory dormitory with garlic, money, and embarrassingly provincial manners so as to reestablish contact with his son, David drives him away, expressing the patricidal wish absent from Galich's play, "Chtob ty sdokh!" ["May you croak!"].

Editing contrives to endow the angry shout with the weight of a fatal curse, thereby intensifying the egregiousness of the son's crime. Almost immediately afterward, David's voiceover reports Abram's execution, along with Tul'chin's entire Jewish population, by the Nazis. The enemy enacts David's tabooed desire, which, contrary to Freud's psychoanalytical paradigm of Oedipal relations (*Totem and Taboo*), in this instance springs not from hatred of the father as a sexual rival for the desired mother (mothers and incestuous congress have no place in the film) but from the fantasy that Freud explicated as the "family romance." Indeed, Mashkov's emphasis on nurturing, vulnerability, and supplicating tenderness in the dormitory sequence sooner transforms Abram into a maternal figure, so that in a sense he incarnates both mother and father in the family unit. According to Freud's theory of the family romance, pubertal children who feel slighted or injured by their parents frequently engage in daydreams that relegate current, unsatisfactory parents to the status of replacements for the imagined genuine parents, to whom the fantasy assigns a more exalted social rank (Freud, "Family Romances" 41–45). This scenario maps David's disavowal of his far from imposing Jewish father and his ready adoption of Ivan Kuzmich as the "authentic" life-guide, whose position, authoritative demeanor, and ties with the political center create the illusion of power. The painful scene at the dormitory marks the turning point in David's betrayal of his real father for the sake of an illegitimate surrogate in accord with the compensatory illusions of the family romance (Figure 6.5).

All too pointedly the film offers a counter-model of filiation, juxtaposing David's callous ingratitude toward Abram, whom he scorns, with his friend Slava Lebedev's respectful love and admiration for *his* father. When the latter is imprisoned as an "enemy of the people," later to be packed into a freight train bound for one of Stalin's concentration camps, Slava unhesitatingly opts to be expelled from the Conservatory rather than renounce him. Slava's declaration of filial love affirms the father as ideal model and underscores precisely what is lacking in David's attitude toward Abram: "Ved' otets . . . Ia ne prosto ego liubil. Ia im vsegda gordilsia. Ia smotrel na nego, kak na sebia samogo, tol'ko vsroslym" ["You know, my father . . . I didn't simply love him. I was always proud of him. I looked at him as at myself, only adult"]. Whereas David repudiates his father for the sake of his own career, Slava honors his by adhering to their shared principles and relinquishing his own prospects for future fame. The misguided egotist desires his father's death, and the man of integrity sacrifices his professional life "in the name of the father."

A film explicitly intended to glorify paternity requires that David learn the iterated moral precept at its core—the sacredness of fathers who "make" their sons. And sentiment dictates that he realize the error of his ways too late, after Germans have razed Tul'chin to the ground and killed its Jewish inhabitants, including Abram. Boozy, bossy, unprepossessing and unlikable, Abram nonetheless ultimately emerges as the mouthpiece and the incarnation of the film's simple message: a father invests his love and energy in his son for the sake of generational continuity, thereby doing God's work. As director, co-scriptwriter, and actor, Mashkov seems unaware of, and leaves unresolved, the psychological complexities inherent in a vampiric paternal "self-sacrifice" that not only places a crushing burden on the son in terms of expectations but also credits not the son for his achievements but the father as the Source. In the film's concept of generations, the son's life imperative is obedience to his father's will ("Thy will be done").[34] Hence the note of triumph in Abram's disturbing speech to his son, which the film validates:

> You'll grow up, stand on the beautiful stage of the Large Concert Hall of the conservatory, and after finishing your magnificent violin performance, glowing with a youthful smile, after long and wild applause by the smartly dressed Muscovites, you'll say: "*It's all my dad!* He was an incredible drunk and swindler, but *he made of me what I am!*"[35] (emphasis added—H.G.)

Part of that self-aggrandizing, lachrymose prophecy resurfaces in Abram's final, reassuring words to David about David's son, who will become a great violinist and after a performance will announce to the audience, "Eto moi papa sdelal iz menia, to chto ia est'" ["It's my father who made of me what I am"]. As his son's "maker," the father parallels God, who "made" man in His own image and dictated the terms of His son's life (and death).

Like *Vor,* but in more radical and unexamined terms, *Papa* propounds the primacy of the father in male identity formation. Having had no communication with his son after David's uncompromising rejection of him five years earlier in Moscow, at film's end Abram makes his final appearance as a ghost on the evacuation train so as to teach his wounded offspring the lesson of paternal devotion and the value of historical/familial memory (Figure 6.6).[36] Unlike the regularly scheduled train from Tul'chin to Moscow, which provides David access to professional advancement, this train—a carrier of suffering and death but also of love and compassion—affords him the opportunity to recover his humanity and reconcile with his father's spirit. Here the train symbolizes not horizontal (and eventually upward) mobility but an epiphanic journey "within."

Throughout, the railroad functions as a key metaphor, variously connoting instability and teleology,[37] while also serving as a spatial and temporal marker. For transitions between decades Mashkov relies on the effective device of synthesizing visual image and sound: the camera focuses on traversed railroad tracks as the soundtrack mimics progression in a musical score (the movement along parallel lines naturalizing this complicity). A shot of railroad tracks and the plangent notes of Tchaikovsky's Violin Concerto are collapsed into convincing temporal transitions that otherwise would seem abrupt and wholly arbitrary. The two neatly dovetail when David's musical gift puts him on the train to Moscow.

Mashkov intertwines journeys (usually via train) with the film's major themes of identity, connection, and belonging. *Papa* ultimately suggests that "home," however problematic, constitutes life's meaning. Despite its ambitions, in other words, the film demonstrates its own provincialism, which probably accounts for Alena Solntseva's assessment of *Papa* as "narodnoe kino," devoid of subtleties (Solntseva). Whereas the "cosmopolitan," solitary Meyer Wolf travels to Israel so as to see firsthand the sacred Wailing Wall, his sedentary friend Abram mentally visits cities around the world through his huge collection of postcards, but he remains in Tul'chin, where, presumably, he has spent his entire life. Disappointed in Israel's Wailing Wall, Meyer eventually feels the need to return "home," only to perish along with Tul'chin's residents. And David, who in the first and second segments of the film wishes to forget the existence of both Tul'chin and his father, realizes Meyer's prophecy when he ultimately understands that the shtetl has its own Wailing Wall—the site of his boyhood games and one of the shtetl's few structures to survive the devastation of World War II. That discovery occurs only when he returns to Tul'chin in the capacity of an army officer fighting to preserve his "home" and homeland. In a sense David's father, for better and worse, *is* Tul'chin, which is why Abram briefly leaves the "familial" environment only once, when he boards the train for Moscow, weighed down by the provisions he brings for his urbanized son. Whereas Tul'chin's younger generation (David, Hannah, and Tania) succumbs to the irresistible pull of the center, with the "underground paradise" of its dazzling metro,[38] Abram as the quintessential father not only feels out of place in the capital, but, grasping the significance of roots, family, and belonging, remains where, as he points out, he knows practically everyone.[39] Tul'chin is his personally experienced center— one that enables him to provide for his son's "happiness."

In that respect Abram is the modern Soviet version of Balzac's eponymous father in *Père Goriot* (1834): both men stiflingly embrace their offspring's happiness as life's ultimate telos. Like Galich's play, *Papa* finds absolute value in the continuity of generations and "home"—thereby allying itself with those nineteenth-century novels that structurally overlap with the *Bildungsroman* and locate individual fulfillment within familial traditions (e.g., Pushkin's *Kapitanskaia dochka* [*The Captain's Daughter*], Goncharov's *Obyknovennaia istoriia* [*An Ordinary Story*], Turgenev's *Ottsy i deti* [*Fathers and Sons*], and Tolstoi's *Voina i mir* [*War and Peace*]). In a political reading of the film, of course, obsession with continuity suggests the crucial importance of peaceful succession by the nation's leaders.

Unlike *Vor*, which garnered unanimous praise, *Papa* elicited critics' reservations, inter alia, for slighting the uniqueness of the Jewish experience by universalizing its moral dilemmas (Felperin, Gurevich).[40] The deportation of Slava's father, Ivan Kuzmich's speech about the infallible justice and rationality of the party, and the truck labeled Bread [*Khleb*], which any reader of Solzhenitsyn would recognize as transport for those condemned to the camps, all allude to the Stalinist stranglehold on people's daily lives. Yet, during the late 1930s, these phenomena were hardly Jewish-specific. Indeed, the film attempts to make a "big statement" by elevating its issues to the level of myth, chiefly through the device of trebling, associated exclusively with David and, as Erich Neumann convincingly argues, reflecting "the threefold articulation underlying all created things, [including . . .] the three temporal stages of all growth (beginning-middle-end, birth-life-death, past-present-future)" (Neumann 228). Constellated around David are not only three fathers but also the three women in love with him—Tania, whom he marries; Hannah, whose avowal of love remains unrequited; and Liudmila Shutova, the organizational whiz at the Conservatory, who, as chief nurse on the medical train, soothes him with comforting lies. Matrosskaia tishina likewise has triple meanings: conceived by David's imagination as a peaceful graveyard and harbor for old ships and sailors, it is, in fact, a Moscow street (where Hannah and her uprooted family reside) and a detention prison. The film also develops three notions of play, and David engages in all of them—music (on the violin), sports (football by Tul'chin's Wailing Wall), and life and death (the dangerous game he plays with other Tul'chin boys on the railroad tracks as they face oncoming trains to test their daring). Above all, the concluding segment of the film evokes the religious trinity of the Father, Son, and Holy Ghost through Abram's sudden apparition on the train, preceded by the camera's protracted focus on a glowing lamp, which creates the impression of a "holy light" announcing Abram's coming.[41] The farewell between the dead father as "spirit" and the son almost at death's door intimates a miracle, a religious vision.

In his efforts to rationalize why he wept while watching the film, the critic Grigorii Zaslavskii wondered whether the explanation might reside in the immemorial moral analogy between the biological father and the divine Father, before Whom all are to varying degrees guilty: "In general, relations with parents aren't simple, and in this sense they seem to repeat here, on earth, the complex relations that connect each of us with God, whom we call Father."[42] By elevating Abram to the status of wise messenger from the next world, Galich and Mashkov underscore that parallel. Thus David as repentant son receives forgiveness for his sins against Abram from the Heavenly Father through the earthly father qua God's emissary.

If Chukhrai's Vor benefits from the director's complex, restrained exploration of paternity, Mashkov's Papa tugs at audiences' heartstrings through a bathetic, unambiguous assertion of "fathers' rights" and righteousness, sanctioned by "love." Without glamorizing Stalin, Chukhrai directly conveys his enigmatic aura and the lasting hold of his militaristic machismo on the collective imagination through the specific instance of Tolian as Sania's surrogate paternal figure. In dramatizing how Stalin indelibly marked the generation whose biological fathers perished in the "Fatherland War" [Otechestvennaia voina], the film recalls such earlier cinematic works as Tofik Shakhverdiev's documentary, Stalin s nami? [Is Stalin with Us? 1989], which likewise gives the paradoxes of the Stalin cult their due. Mashkov shuts down the problems raised by Stalin as an ostensibly loving but demonstrably tyrannical father by transforming his individualized, partial analogue, Abram, in the second and third sections of the film into a tender-hearted, feminized nurturer—and a casualty not of Stalinist pogroms but of the invading Nazis. World War II, in fact, is the director's (and Galich's) deus ex machina, for, without it, engineering the reconciliation between father and son, during which the father equates son with rod/ina, would have been extraordinarily difficult. Both conceptually and structurally Papa suffers from the inconsistencies in Abram's functions within the film: as a Jew, he is a victim of Stalin's policies (a scenario defanged and swiftly displaced onto Slava's father), while as a "loving" father-dictator, he resorts to the Stalinist tactics of rigid control, physical force, and an absolutist imposition of his own teleology on the "loved one." Whereas *Vor* strives for balance in its examination of the highly contradictory internal enemy as revered icon, *Papa* abandons domestic/national conflicts so as to introduce, in highly emotional terms, the struggle against an external enemy that remains the single uncompromised event in Soviet history uniting Russians to this day.

Their substantial differences notwithstanding, both films show paternal masculinity diminishing over time, even as sons' physical and psychological power increases, thereby setting the stage for a role reversal. Though temporary in *Papa* and truncated in *Vor*, that reversal registers the rhythms of generational succession. In acknowledging the effects of temporality/succession, both films ineluctably evoke the myth of the Greek Titan Kronos [Κρονος],[43] who castrated and deposed his father, Ouranos [Ουρανός], and, to forestall an identical fate, swallowed his children, only to be overthrown by his saved, youngest offspring, Zeus [Ζευς]. The pagan Greeks' grim perception of father/son rivalry among the primordial and Olympian deities could hardly be more remote from the Old and New Testaments' monotheistic image of paternal omnipotence, in which the Law of the Father is absolute and eternal—beyond time. In that regard, Stalinist culture and its Father/Leader sooner echo the Bible than the ancient Greek myths, which may explain at least in part the post-Soviet era's inability to extricate itself from the shadow of its most powerful Father.

NOTES

My thanks to Michelle Kuhn for her thoughtful response to this chapter, and mega-gratitude to Alexander Prokhorov for his many invaluable, eye-opening suggestions.

1. Janet Maslin's review of *Vor* describes Mashkov as "a popular Russian leading man with a glowering machismo [*sic*] and a resemblance to Antonio Banderas"—a comparison Mashkov himself likes to mention. In similarly overblown terms, Stephen Hunter refers to Mashkov's portrayal of Tolian as "beaming with dark radiance." See also the interview conducted by Nataliia Khliustova (2003).

2. A graduate of MKhAT and the protégé of Oleg Tabakov, Mashkov made his film debut in late perestroika (1989) and has directed several plays as well as two movies. In 1997 he received the Chaika Award for his 1996 version of *The Threepenny Opera* at the Satyricon.

3. All but one of Mashkov's many film awards are Russian, the majority of them for his early starring role in *Limita* (1994).

4. Such is the case only in his Russian films, not in the Hollywood movies where he appears, such as *The Quickie* (2001) and *Behind Enemy Lines* (2001), which do not dwell on family ties.

5. The best-known example of the genre in Soviet cinema remains El'dar Riazanov's *Ironiia sud'by, ili S legkim parom* [*Irony of Fate* 1975], shown on Soviet/Russian television every New Year's Eve. On the genre in general, see Alyssa DeBlasio's (2008) intelligent article, which maps out its constitutive features and adduces copious examples.

6. Shevchenko is Mashkov's first ex-wife and the mother of his daughter, Mariia Mashkova.

7. For a review of *Sirota kazanskaia* and other "New Year" films, see L. Maslova, "O prazdnichnom torte, denezhnom krugovorte i russkom Gollivude," *Iskusstvo kino* 4 (1998): 88–94.

8. As even Russian critics acknowledged, Allison Whitbeck's beguiling performance as the "American daughter" trumped all other aspects of the film, while the two brief segments in *Sirota kazanskaia* featuring the extraordinary Misha Filipchuk, who would return as the son in *Vor*—to rave reviews—likewise steal the show, although Oleg Tabakov acquits himself admirably in the thankless role of the expert cook who is one of the paternal claimants.

9. *Vor* garnered many prizes, and Mashkov's performance won the Nika, and the Kinoshok and Sozvezdie Awards.

10. Critics unanimously lauded the beguiling performance of Misha Filipchuk, one critic calling him "a terrific child actor with eyes bigger than Bambi's [*sic*]" (Leah Rozen, *People* 50/2 [28 July 1998]: 35).

11. According to Lev Anninskii, Katia thereby exemplifies the paradigm of True Russian Womanhood (20).

12. For other films dramatizing the post–World War II "adoption" of orphaned boys by ex-military men, see Marlen Khutsiev's *Dva Fedora* [*Two Fyodors* 1958] and Sergei Bondarchuk's *Sud'ba cheloveka* [*Fate of a Man* 1959].

13. Stanley Kauffmann commends Chukhrai for evoking "a sense of national restlessness in postwar Russia" (24). In a meandering review, Anninskii contends that the reproduction of the era is so faithful that the film should have been shot in black and white (20).

14. On other films depicting the Stalin era, such as Ivan Dykhovichnyi's *Prorva* [*Moscow Parade* 1992] and Petr Todorovskii's *Ankor, eshche ankor* [*Encore, Again, Encore!* 1992], see Larsen.

15. Soviet citizens genuinely believed that Stalin worked tirelessly through the night in the interests of the people. For instance, V. Govorkov's famous poster of 1940, "O kazhdom iz nas zabotitsia Stalin v Kremle" ["In the Kremlin Stalin Looks after Each of Us"], shows Stalin writing at his desk by lamplight, a red star visible in the darkness through the open window behind him. See the Stalinka Web site at http://images.library.pitt.edu/cgi-bin/i/image/image-idx?c=stalinka, visual no. 113.

16. During the early phase of World War II, the Soviet army fared disastrously owing to Stalin's order that troops stand against the enemy at all costs. Once troops adopted the strategy of "the fighting retreat," the tide turned. On a personal/ad-

ministrative level, Stalin eliminated many of the old Bolsheviks and former allies in anticipation of their challenge to his monopoly on authority.

17. For instance, on the basic level of physiology, Stalin ensured that airbrushed photographs, paintings, and posters, as well as carefully orchestrated appearances in public downplayed or disguised his pockmarked skin, crippled arm, and short height.

18. Kantorowicz identifies those two entities as the sublime, immaterial body of the Leader's symbolic function (the icon) and the empirical, perishable flesh and bones of his everyday self (the man). See Ernst H. Kantorowicz, *The Kings's Two Bodies: A Study in Medieval Political Theology* (Princeton, N.J.: Princeton University Press, 1957).

19. According to Alix Lambert, a predator's tattoo on the chest usually signals a sentence for a serious crime, such as robbery, which in the Soviet era earned a long prison sentence (128).

20. Gerald Kaufman, however, criticizes the film precisely for its "pretentious" attempt at "a political allegory" (Kaufman 43), whereas Stephen Hunter refers to it as a parable stopping just short of allegory (Hunter D.01). Stanley Kauffmann bluntly calls it a political allegory, and (crudely and inaccurately, in my view) equates Sania with "the new generation that rids its country of Stalin" (24).

21. The film evokes femininity through the traditional trope of fluids: the inaccessibility of his mother leads Sania to flood the communal apartment; Tolian's hyper-masculinity triggers the boy's "feminine" incontinence in the two scenes of his involuntary urination, and it is telling that Sania is able to shoot Tolian because the latter pauses to urinate at the train that enables him to escape. The sole fluid permitted masculinity is vodka, identified throughout with Tolian, who raises toasts to his icon, Stalin, eventually transforms Katia into a drinker, and dies begging for vodka.

22. A motif built into the image of the father as protector, expectation of rescue by the symbolic or biological father repeats itself throughout post-Soviet films. See, for instance, the statement in *Moi svodnyi brat Frankenshtein* cited by Mark Lipovetsky in chapter 5: "Pavlik says that he always knew that you'd find him."

23. Immediately before scrambling onto the train, Tolian pauses to urinate beside the tracks, and it remains unclear whether the contrast between his pseudo-father relieving his bladder when he chooses to do so and his own reflex of involuntary urination is what finally pushes Sania to shoot Tolian. The comparison of father/son urination recalls the scene in chapter 17 ("Ithaca") of James Joyce's *Ulysses* (1999), where Stephen Dedalus and his ideological father, Leopold Bloom, engage in a "pissing contest" of sorts. In *Vor* the motif is inseparable from the penis/phallus and issues of masculinity. Astoundingly, Robert Meister's study *fathers* [sic], comprising interviews with fathers and their offspring, records just such a father-and-son urinating episode (101).

24. Yana Hashamova argues for the ambiguity of the conclusion, whereby it is uncertain whether the old alcoholic is Tolian (personal communication). My disagreement rests on the simple fact that the words he shouts to the soldiers repeat *verbatim* those Tolian uses earlier to avoid arrest for passing himself off as a military officer.

25. "Divlius' pronitsatel'nosti Pavla Chukhraia, s bukval'noi tochnost'iu otrazivshego [. . .] metaistoricheskoe proisshestvie v konkretnoi istoricheskoi tonal'nosti

poslevoennogo vremeni. Ego kartina *Vor* rasskazyvaet o tragicheskom zabluzhdenii mamy i podmene ottsa na zlogo vora, khishchnoe besstyzhee zhivotnoe. Pechal' v tom, chto ni mama, ni syn tak i ne smogli okonchatel'no izbavit'sia ot liubvi k nemu, voznenavidet' ego i osvobodit'sia."

26. As Larsen accurately observes, "Fil'm uchit, chto zhit' bez ottsa—pust' dazhe takogo cherstvogo i beschestnogo, kak Tolian—nevozmozhno" ["The film teaches that it's impossible to do without a father—even such a callous and dishonorable one as Tolian"]. Her contention that the conclusion of the film's original version demonstrates the impossibility of extirpating "the complex legacy of the Stalinist past from the post-Soviet present" strikes me as indisputable (Larsen 662–63). More broadly, like Henrik Ibsen's *Ghosts* (1881), *Vor* affirms the Freudian insight that individuals carry psychological baggage inherited from parents, mostly acquired during their formative childhood years.

27. The mother with a small boy echoes the early sequence of Katia and Sania on the train early in the film.

28. According to John Simon, Tolian "becomes a hard but efficacious paterfamilias" (49).

29. One Western critic dubbed the film "a four-hankie tearjerker that preaches to the choir" (Gurevich), and another referred to the film's "hammy histrionics, button-pushing sentimentality" (Felperin). Russian commentators also noted the lachrymose sentimentality of the melodrama; see Fadeev ("udivitel'no nezhnyi i sentimental'nyi" ["amazingly tender and sentimental"]), Kichin, Solntseva ("fil'm prostoi, naivnyi, iskrennii, i vyzyvaet potoki slez" ["the film is simple, naïve, sincere, and elicits copious tears"]), and Zaslavskii ("fil'm [. . .] tonet v slezakh" ["the film drowns in tears"]). According to both Kichin and Zaslavskii, Russian audiences wept.

30. When the oligarch Mikhail Khodorkovskii was arrested in 2003, he spent his detention at Matrosskaia tishina before being sentenced.

31. Grigorii Zaslavskii, criticizing the film's theatricality, also ascribes the exaggerated nature of Mashkov's performance to its overly direct transfer from the stage.

32. Despite Mashkov's efforts to "capture" the historical era, commentators were troubled by the sloppiness of having Ukrainian Jews speak Muscovite Russian in a film manifestly committed to re-creating the specifics of time and place during various decades in the Soviet Union. See, for example, "Vat Is in an Accent."

33. Labeling his play a "dramatic chronicle in four acts" ["dramaticheskaia khronika v chetyrekh deistviiakh"], Galich provided specific dates for all four acts: August 1929; May 1937; October 1944; and 9 May 1955, the tenth anniversary of Germany's defeat—Victory Day. According to a review in the *Moscow Times,* Mashkov claimed that the final act resulted from pressure applied to Galich by the Soviets (Birchenough).

34. Here again I disagree with Yana Hashamova, who interprets the camerawork at one juncture as evidence that "David's desire is the desire of the father or David materializes his father's dreams." Specifically, after David resentfully responds to Abram's insistence that he play the Chaikovsky Violin Concerto, the camera "cuts to an aerial shot of the house, then to a sunflower-field with boys running, which dissolves into a shot of the sky with birds flying off electric wires dissolving yet again into David's playing hands" (personal communication). I find the cut to the

sunflowers, followed by a pan of the sky, a pathetic tribute to "the eternal power" of Chaikovsky's music, invoked throughout the film for various purposes, which does not erase Abram's alienating projection of his own ambitions onto his son. Moreover, surely an extended shot of the heavens sooner implies divine omnipotence than generational consensus? Michelle Kuhn has suggested that the film gradually moves from the specifics of Jewish Tul'chin to an abstract religious sphere that fully emerges in the last sequence on the train (personal communication), and the aerial shot may be intended to adumbrate that "expansion."

35. "Vot podrastesh', budesh' stoiat' na krasivoi stsene Bol'shogo zala konservatorii i, okonchiv svoe velikolepnoe vystuplenie na skripke, ozarish'sia iunosheskoi ulybkoi, a posle dolgikh i burnykh applodismentov nariadnykh moskvichei, skazhesh': 'Eto vse moi papa! On byl redkii p'ianitsa i zhulik, no *on sdelal iz menia, chto ia est'*'" (emphasis added—H.G.).

36. The sequence in which the father's ghost reveals truths to the son evokes Shakespeare's *Hamlet* and Marlen Khutsiev's *Zastava Il'icha [Il'ich's Guard]*. For an analysis of the latter, see chapter 1 in this volume.

37. In the fourth act of Galich's play, omitted in the film, stage directions in the form of commentary note, "Moskva zhivet vokzalami" ["Moscow lives through railroad stations"] (302).

38. Tellingly Abram experiences difficulties negotiating this more modern means of transportation/mobility.

39. An episode toward film's end similarly affirms the sanctity of home, when one of the fatally wounded soldiers on the medical train obsessively repeats the name of his native village, Sosnovka, begging to be let off there.

40. That generalizing tendency results, in part, from having Ukrainian Jews speak Muscovite Russian in a film that strives to recreate the specifics of a given time and place. That "inauthenticity" troubled several reviewers, although Zaslavskii decried not the film's inaccuracies in the details but the performances of Mashkov (overly theatrical) and Egor Boroev, whose blandness in the role of David rendered the character utterly uninteresting.

41. In a work about father-son relations, Abram is a name (chosen by Galich) that cannot avoid recalling the story of Abra[ha]m and Isaac in Genesis (22:1–19). Galich's stage directions leave no doubts that the light accompanying Abram's Visitation functions as a halo (Galich 294).

42. "S roditeliami voobshche otnosheniia ne byvaiut prostymi, i v etom smysle oni kak by povtoriaiut zdes', na zemle, te neprostye otnosheniia, sviazyvaiushchie kazhdogo iz nas s Bogom, kotorogo nazyvaiut Ottsom."

43. Kronos, significantly, was frequently confused with Khronos [Χρονος], the god of time, perhaps because as both son and father Kronos demonstrates the symbolic violence of generational succession.

REFERENCES

Anninskii, Lev. "Dostoianie obvorovannykh." *Iskusstvo kino* 1 (1998): 19–22.
Berardinelli, James. "*The Thief (Vor)*." Available at http://www.reelviews.net/movies/t/thief.html (accessed 26 February 2007).

Birchenough, Tom. "His Father's Son." *Moscow Times* (3 September 2004). Available at http://context.themoscowtimes.com/story/135941 (accessed 28 February 2005).

Blos, Peter. *Father and Son: Before and Beyond the Oedipus Complex.* New York: Free Press, 1985.

DeBlasio, Alyssa. "The New-Year Film as a Genre of Post-War Russian Cinema." *Studies in Russian and Soviet Cinema* 2, no. 1 (2008): 43–61.

Fadeev, Mikhail. "*Papa.*" *World Art* (15 September 2004). Available at http://www.world -art.ru/cinema/cinema.php?id+167 (accessed 5 January 2007).

Felperin, Leslie. Available at http://www.entertainment-news.org/breaking/721/papa .html (accessed 28 February 2005).

Freud, Sigmund. "Family Romances (1908)." In Sigmund Freud, *The Sexual Enlightenment of Children,* ed. Philip Rieff, 41–45. New York: Collier Books, 1966.

———. *Totem and Taboo.* In Sigmund Freud, *The Basic Writings of Sigmund Freud,* trans. and ed. A. A. Brill, 807–930. New York: Modern Library, 1938.

Galich, Aleksandr. *Matrosskaia tishina.* In "*. . . Ia vernus' . . .: Kinopovesti. P'esy. Avtobiograficheskaia povest',*" 251–318. Moscow: Iskusstvo, 1993.

Gurevich, David. "Russian Film Week in New York." Available at http://www.images journal.com/2004/features/russia/text.htm (accessed January 30, 2005).

Hunter, Stephen. "*The Thief* Steals the Show." *Washington Post,* 4 December 1998, D.01.

Joyner, Will. "Through the Eyes of a Child." *New York Times* (12 July 1998): 2.

Kauffmann, Stanley. "A Felon, A Fellini." *New Republic,* 10 August 1998, 24.

Kaufman, Gerald. "Searching for the Past." *New Statesman* 4934 (17 July 1998): 43.

Khliustova, Nataliia. "Chto podelat', esli ia pokozh na Banderasa?" *Gazeta.* Available at http://www.gzt.ru/headline_text.gzt?id=51550000000006381 (accessed 27 November 2003).

Kichin, Valerii. "Vzdokh o proshlom." *Rossiiskaia gazeta* (28 June 2004). Available at http://www.rg.ru/printable/2004/06/28/vzdox.html (accessed 17 February 2007).

Kuhn, Michelle. *Papa* [review]. *KinoKultura,* no. 7, January 2005.

Lacan, Jacques. *ÉCRITS: A Selection.* Translated by Alan Sheridan. New York: W. W. Norton, 1977.

Lambert, Alix. *Russian Prison Tattoos.* Atglen, Pa.: Schiffer, 2003.

Larsen, Siuzan [Susan]. "Melodrama, muzhestvennost' i natsional'nost'." In *O Muzhe(n)-stvennosti. Sbornik statei,* ed. S. Ushakin, 630–63. Moscow: Novoe literaturnoe obozrenie, 2002.

Mashkov, Vladimir. "*Daddy* Is My Debt to My Parents." *Moldova Online.* Available at http://www.welcome-moldova.com/articles/vladimir-mashkov.shtml (accessed 17 February 2007). Interview with Ludmila Mamaliga.

Maslin, Janet. "Stealing Love and Loyalty, among Some Other Things." *New York Times,* 17 July 1998, E1.

Meister, Robert. *fathers.* New York: Richard Marek, 1981.

Moskvina, Tat'iana. "Mama vykhodit zamuzh." In *Pokhvala plokhomu shokoladu,* 217–33. Moscow: Limbus, 2002.

Neumann, Erich. *The Great Mother.* Translated by Ralph Manheim. 2nd ed. Princeton, N.J.: Princeton University Press, 1963 [1955].

O'Flynn, Kevin. "Father Figure." *Moscow Times,* 18 June 2004. Available at http://context .themoscowtimes.com/print/php?aid=133962 (accessed 12 January 2007).

Simon, John. "Thieves of Hearts." *National Review*, 1 September 1998, 49–50.
Solntseva, Alena. "On Shuberta navershival, kak chistyi brilliant." *Vremia novostei* 163 (9 September 2004). Available at http://www.vremya.ru/2004/163/10/107130.html (accessed 27 February 2005).
"Vat Is in an Accent." Available at http://theshredder.com/russstuff/papa.htm (accessed 28 February 2005).
"Vladimir's directors." Available at http://www.vladimirmashkov.webcentral.com.au/films/directors.htm (accessed 11 February 2003).
Zaslavskii, Grigorii. "Papa, papa, bednyi papa . . ." *Iskusstvo kino* 9 (2004). Available at http://www.kinoart.ru/magazine/09-2004/repertoire/zaslavski0408 (accessed 10 March 2005).

FILMOGRAPHY

Amerikanskaia doch' [*American Daughter*]. Dir. Karen Shakhnazarov. Kur'er, Mosfil'm, 1995.
Papa. Dir. Vladimir Mashkov. "TransMashHolding," NTV-PROFIT, 2004.
Sirota kazanskaia [*Sympathy Seeker*]. Dir. Vladimir Mashkov. NTV-PROFIT, 1997.
Vor [*The Thief*]. Dir. Pavel Chukhrai. NTV-Profit, Productions Le Pont, Roissy Films, 1997.

Figure 6.1. The kiosk resembling children's New Year greeting cards.

Figure 6.2. Phony father and infantilized daughter *cum* toy.

Figure 6.3. Three pseudo-fathers celebrating.

Figure 6.4. Faux-family portrait.

Figure 6.5. Supplicating father and suffocated son.

Figure 6.6. Papa, posthumously illuminated, enlightens his son.

PART THREE

Reconceiving Filial Bonds

SEVEN

Resurrected Fathers and Resuscitated Sons: Homosocial Fantasies in *The Return* and *Koktebel*

YANA HASHAMOVA

MASCULINITIES: THERE ARE FATHERS
AND THEN THERE ARE FATHERS

At the turn of the millennium, gender studies exhibited an increased interest in and concern about contemporary masculinity, an anxiety that mainly stems from the perception of "manhood in an awkward predicament." Recurrent fears of "man in crisis" produced a body of scholarship shifting the focus from singular masculinity to masculinities and from viewing woman as a social construct to a persistent belief that man is the socially constructed gender. Social scientists and psychiatrists alike dwell on the difficulties men experience in negotiating their roles as fathers, husbands, lovers, and workers (Coward 95, Clare 1). Rather brazenly Guy Corneau proclaims: "Woman is, Man is made," basing his pronouncement on the biological realities of sexual difference that mark woman with menstruation and leave man vulnerable and in need of acquiring his identity (14). Much in the same fashion, Francis Fukuyama claims that masculinity and fatherhood are the socially constructed identities, in effect reversing Simone de Beauvoir's seminal feminist truism. Stella Bruzzi's monograph (2005) on fatherhood and masculinity as represented in Hollywood cinema of the 1990s argues that these "crisis" books within gender studies promoted the sensitive and caring father as a male archetype, which "in turn cemented the importance of the need for male role models, a move that reflects a fundamental ambivalence within the men's movement: men were radicalized to the extent that they were more in touch with their feelings, but they were also regressing into essentialism" (157–58). Masculinity was understood as a role model to be passed from father to son.

On the other side of the Berlin Wall and after the disintegration of the Soviet system and its social organization, both men and women experienced difficulties identifying their places and roles in the new society. Men found themselves threatened by the instability of the new Symbolic order, which, unlike the Soviet system, required that they locate their niche within society instead of vouchsafing them a secure place within a stable hierarchy. Consequently men felt that they had to find new ways of empowering their positions and restoring their machismo, which some, paradoxically, perceived as having been damaged during the Soviet period by women's emancipation. Viktor Erofeev, a contemporary Russian writer, claims that the Soviet system ruined Russian men because it liberated women socially and sexually, and women's demands threatened and weakened Russian men (51–56; 112–17). Feminist scholars of Soviet society, such as Lynne Attwood, also elaborate on this paradox, observing that men seemingly became weaker and less resourceful because they perceived that women no longer needed their "protection" (1990; 1993, 65–88). These brief observations of men's identification anxieties in Russia today resemble Western scholars' discussion registered in the body of "man in crisis" books.

Of particular importance to Russian culture, however, and to this discussion is the function of the father in individual, family, and social identifications. Russia's centuries-long history of tsarism reveals a particular conversion of the tsar's figure into the "father of the nation." The Russian collective imagination knows the mythic preeminence of the "batiushka tsar" and his much-revered authoritarian status. In the history of twentieth-century Russian totalitarianism, the father symbol positioned the leader (Lenin and Stalin) as a paternal god who reigned above all (Schoeberlein). Later in the twentieth century, however, this paternal function of the leader weakened and the first secretaries of the Communist Party morphed from ideal fathers into government functionaries. Thus one can argue that the nostalgia for the return of the paternal figure in Russian culture, evident in most recent films, although similar to Western gender anxieties, also results from the long and successful political tradition of upholding the figure of the leader as the father of the nation, a tradition that faded away in the last quarter of the twentieth century. It is no surprise that Vladimir Putin's image has slowly but firmly undergone reverse alteration, from a party functionary to authoritative leader (and perhaps father) of the nation.[1] Such concerns (more social than political) about the destabilized father function, however, are not uniquely Russian and are also registered in America: David Blankenhorn's influential *Fatherless America* contends that the absence of fathers has become America's most pressing social dilemma. Recently emotions around fathers and fathering have become heightened and convoluted both in America and in Russia, evident in an array of films that explore various aspects of paternity.

In the 1990s Hollywood cinema created a wide range of father images in various genres. Viewers saw traditional (white) fathers (*A Few Good Men* 1992, *A River Runs Through It* 1992) and black fathers (*Boyz n the Hood* 1991 and *Jungle Fever* 1991); fathers in romances (*Sleepless in Seattle* 1993, *The American President* 1995, and *One Fine Day* 1996) and fathers in comedies (*Father of the Bride 2* 1995, *Mrs. Doubtfire* 1993, *Father's Day* 1997, and *The Birdcage* 1996); courageous (loving) fathers (*Backdraft* 1991 and *Gladiator* 2000) and indecisive (destructive) fathers (*Happiness* 1998, *American Beauty* 1999, and *Magnolia* 1999).[2] Even though Russian cinema of the same period also offered a range of father roles (most of them discussed in this collection), two prominent 2003 films reveal a remarkably similar perception of the father's role in family and society: Andrei Zviagintsev's debut film, *Vozvrashchenie* [*The Return*], and Aleksei Popogrebskii and Boris Khlebnikov's *Koktebel'* [*Koktebel*], both premiering in 2003. Certainly the portrayals of the actual fathers in these two films diverge, but the desire for the Symbolic function of the father manifested in the two cinematic narratives overlaps.

This chapter examines the representations of fathers, their roles in the family, and their relationships with their sons, as well as the overall Symbolic perception of the father in Russian society, reflected in these films. Intriguingly, these films present a diverse picture of paternal characters, but the overall desire that lurks through the cinematic narratives nostalgically fancies the return of paternal authority, which can restore law and order and promise a positive future.

My analysis distinguishes the presentation of actual fathers in films from the father's role as paternal metaphor and organizational principle. Sigmund Freud's *Moses and Monotheism* maps out the myth of the primal father as follows: once there was a primal father in total possession of all females, who was murdered by rebellious sons. His death, surprisingly, resulted in the establishment of matriarchy. With time, the fraternal clan reintroduced the father figure and created the cult of the father, and thus established patriarchal power.[3] Here I follow more closely Jacques Lacan's interpretation of Freud's myth as a metaphor for paternal power and organizational principle (Lacan 1977, 179–225). According to Lacan, the father figure (or its Symbolic role: *"nom du père"*) interferes with the mother-child imaginary identification/connection in order to secure the child's maturation and individual development. Contrary to common belief, the responsibility of the father is not to forbid desire but to make the desire of the child possible, namely, to introduce the child to the Law and Symbolic castration, thereby securing his independent mature growth. Either the lack or the excess of this paternal function can possibly result in a series of psychological imbalances. Faithful to his beliefs about the crucial function of the Symbolic father in society, Lacan reacts to Fedor Dostoevsky's religious concerns expressed in *Brothers Karamazov*:

> *If God doesn't exist,* the father [Karamazov] says, *then everything is permitted.* Quite evidently, a naïve notion, for we analysts know full well that if God doesn't exist, then nothing at all is permitted any longer. (Lacan 128)

Although this passage reveals Dostoevsky's fear of godlessness, Lacan uses it to call attention to the special power he (Lacan) grants the Symbolic (the Law) in his revisions of the superego. Lacan contends that, far from being hostile to *jouissance,* the superego, in its opposition to the ego, is the very thing that makes *jouissance* possible.

OMNIPOTENT VERSUS INEPT FATHERS

The single largest Russian cinematic surprise of 2003 was the international acclaim of Zviagintsev's debut film, *The Return,* a work intensely preoccupied with the father-son relationship and the paternal metaphor. The story, a father's journey with his sons, unfolds in modern times somewhere in Russia and resembles the genre of the road movie. A father returns home to visit his boys (aged twelve and fifteen) after years of absence. The father's history is unclear; viewers do not learn where he has been or what he does; even the sons need to look at a photograph hidden in the attic to reassure themselves that he is their father. After a few days of painful initiation into manhood, when the father teaches them how to pay in a restaurant, to put up a tent in the forest, and to navigate a boat in a storm, the tension and conflicts between the three escalate and culminate in the father's death. He dies falling off a tower, which the younger son, Ivan, has climbed in an attempt to escape from him (Figure 7.1).

A more modest project, Popogrebskii and Khlebnikov's *Koktebel* is also a road movie, structured around a father-son trip from Moscow to Koktebel, Crimea, where a relative of theirs lives. The director presents a string of episodes and encounters with strangers as the two make their way south, occasionally traveling by train but mostly walking. The father finds an odd job repairing the roof of a lonely pensioner, who accuses them of stealing and shoots at the father. Protective and possessive, the son finds a female doctor and, after she saves the wounded father's life, the man quietly shares his life story with her, noting that when he took to drink after his wife's death, his son grew up on his own. Jealous of the two adults' growing relationship, the frustrated boy sets out alone for Koketebel, only to discover upon his arrival that his aunt no longer resides there.

The two films construct their cinematic narratives around the developing and bumpy relations between father and son(s), which change as the sons gradually mature and begin to acquire increasing control in the relationships and consequently the narratives. The films, however, portray the actual fathers differently. In *The Return* the father is the omnipotent figure of authority, untroubled by doubts about his parenting skills, whereas the father in *Koktebel* is an uncertain and insecure parent.

The narrative of *The Return* unfolds in seven days, from Sunday to Saturday, akin to the biblical story of Creation, as the father oversees his sons' rites of passage—from adolescence to manhood. Since he is presented as the ideal archetypal father figure (or the despotic divinity of the Old Testament), omniscient and impervious to questions and challenges, his image, paired with the seven-day narrative, blurs the boundary between real and Symbolic paternity. Matters concerning the biblical allusions in his image are highly complex. The film's references to fishing (the father takes his sons on a fishing trip) evoke the Christian Ichthus (Jesus fish), interpreted by St. Augustine as "Christ, God's son, savior." The associations of the father with Christ are further implied by an early mise-en-scène of the sleeping father in the morning after his arrival. Positioned at the door and facing the feet of the sleeping father (covered with silky sheets), the camera lingers on his stretched body, capturing his length with a slightly high angle. The mise-en-scène and the angle recall Andrea Mantegna's painting *Lamentation over the Dead Christ* (1490), the camera angle allowing the spectator to gaze at the sleeping father as if observing Mantegna's work. Evoking different cultural tropes, this fusion of the Old and the New Testaments' symbols in the image of the father deepens and complicates the perception of his functions in the film.

The mystery surrounding his personal biography only reinforces this complexity. Viewers know nothing about the father's profession or his recent past; they see only a man who, after years of absence, reenters the life of his family (wife, sons, and mother-in-law) and assumes his roles, which are immediately and unhesitatingly granted to him, as father, husband, and head of the family. A symmetrical frame that positions the father in the center of a frontal shot, situated between his wife and mother-in-law, their backs toward the viewer, cinematically establishes his indispensable place in the family.

By contrast, the image of the father in *Koktebel* is rather uncomplicated: he is indecisive, shy, and alcoholic (a vice that he fights during the road trip). In a monologue he confesses that he was a bad husband and father, and the audience witnesses his struggle to become an adequate parent. When repairing the tin roof of a loner in return for room and board, the father appears caring and sensitive but at the same time somewhat alienated from his son. That alienation continues when the father, attracted to the female doctor, noticeably prefers her company to his son's. Ultimately both fathers fulfill their paternal roles but in dissimilar ways, a paradox that will become clearer later in this chapter (Figure 7.2).

The Return opens with Ivan on a high diving tower, afraid to jump in the water. If he climbs down, his friends will laugh at him, and he chooses to stay on top, crying, until his mother comes to the rescue.

The tower invites phallic associations, and in one of the last scenes the father's fall off an observation tower and his death similarly imply his emasculation. The tower that leads to his father's death empowers Ivan, who has overcome his fear of height, presumably owing to his experience with his father.

Whereas the older boy, Andrei, instantly likes his father and submits to his authority, obeying all of his (often odd) requests, Ivan has doubts and resists accepting a man he is seeing for the first time in his life. Ivan often confronts his father and questions his authority. Notably, the image of the father is a dual fantasy of the two sons: a trustworthy and protective figure for Andrei, the father strikes Ivan as an imposter and abuser. While Andrei accepts the father's orders, behavior V. Mikhalkovich calls "po zhenski poslushen" ["obedient like a woman"], Ivan rebels and often suffers verbal and physical abuse as a consequence: in an episode in which Ivan refuses to drink the shot of vodka the father offers, the latter harshly pulls Ivan's face toward the shot, commanding, "Drink." Despite his general tendency to obey his father, Andrei is also punished for returning late from fishing; the father slaps him several times, for, as the older brother, he is held responsible for the boys' tardiness. Yet, unlike Ivan, Andrei accepts and identifies with his father. Highlighting the discrepancy between the actual father figure and his Symbolic function, this dual fantasy marks the complex subjectivity and pronouncedly unconscious desire that surround the Symbolic meaning of the father, in both family and society (Figure 7.3).

Predictably, Andrei, as the older son obedient and committed to the fantasy of his father as a protector, assumes the leadership position after the father's death. Ironically, the rebellious Ivan—nurturing the opposite fantasy, that of the abusive father—recognizes his father only after his death (a move faithful to the Lacanian understanding of the father's role). Prompted by Andrei's scream of "Papa!" as the two watch the sinking boat with the father's dead body, Ivan echoes the emotional shout ("Papa!"), running toward the boat. For the first time (and perhaps burdened by guilt) he sincerely utters the word that recognizes his father as such, or, in Lacanian terms, he invokes the Name-of-the-Father. "The true function of the Father . . . is fundamentally to unite (and not to set in opposition) a desire and the Law" (Lacan 321). Further, Lacan asks: "What is a Father?" and (following Freud) replies, "It is the dead Father" or, rather, the Name-of-the-Father. Full of contradictions (and complexities), this scene intends to convey Ivan's acceptance of his father and his own maturation, but the pathos of missed opportunities and awareness of the father's failings lurk behind Ivan's accelerated transition to manhood. On the one hand, the death of his father secures Ivan's maturation and passage into manhood; on the other, the traumatic event ultimately exposes the son's essential displacement in the Symbolic. After uttering "Papa," Ivan faces Symbolic castration and achieves access to the Symbolic, but at the same time he also discovers the void (the sinking boat with his father's body) as a distinctive mark of this Symbolic. The paradox here is that the discourse of the master is unexpectedly and prematurely curtailed. That discourse is supposed to expose the inherent strains and cracks in the Symbolic, perhaps the lurking of the Real, which complicates the sons' efficient (though rocky) passage to adulthood. In other words, the father's death opens up a wound that it professes to heal. Such complexity and ambiguity naturally lead to various, often contradictory, interpretations of the film.[4]

Similar contradictions, concealed in the function of the father, as well as the gradual blurring of the boundary between the biological and the Symbolic father, occur in *Koktebel,* where, despite the father's inadequacies, the son matures and acquires independence. While the film shows a comfortable bond between father and son, reinforced by their shared adventures, and suggests the father's leadership (e.g., he teaches his son about birds and planes), in the middle of the narrative the son appears to appropriate the leading and more decisive role in the relationship. Several episodes that focus on the son (the scenes in which he protects his father and locates the doctor, his escape, and his handling of a seagull at the end) reaffirm the boy's independence, decisiveness, and maturation. As in *The Return,* the narrative shifts attention from the father to the son.

Despite the fathers' contrasting modes of parenting, two particular episodes approximately in the middle of the films' narratives signify their effective influence on the maturation of their sons, which is subsequently cemented by the endings of the films. In *The Return,* after the boys return late from fishing and the father punishes Andrei, Ivan interferes in the conflict to defend his brother: he grabs a knife and threatens his father, crying out, "Why are you torturing us? You're nobody. Nobody." This denouncement of the father is followed by a chase in which several dolly shots track Ivan's flight from his father through a forest, with the father following. The shots are almost blurred and the motion is emphasized through deceleration and a flow of music. This visual representation of the chase (manipulating the viewer's perceptions) is Symbolic in its treatment of relative space: the twelve-year-old Ivan suddenly is shown outstripping his father, who seems unable to catch up by reducing or eliminating the distance between them. Effectively escaping his father, Ivan climbs an observation tower, an ascent presented through point-of-view shots that alternate between Ivan's and the father's perspectives until the father, who tries to reach Ivan, falls to his death—a scene recorded through Ivan's eyes. The whole episode visually grants Ivan ascendancy, buttressed by the father's change in emotional attitude to his son, from brutality to tenderness: in the tower-scene the man who just moments earlier abused both boys begs Ivan to stop and listen to him, using a diminutive form for "son" (*synok*). Viewers simultaneously witness not only Ivan's maturation and empowerment, but also the father's moment of limitation and loss of power.

A parallel episode reversing father-son roles appears in *Koktebel*. In mid-narrative the father is threatened with a gun and wounded by the solitary pensioner whose roof he has been repairing. Realizing the danger, the son reacts quickly and sensibly, drawing his father away and urging escape. Though the duo's flight through the forest shows the son following his father and the scene is shot realistically (without the poetic movement in the corresponding scene in *The Return*), the sequence likewise marks a turning point in the relationship of father and son. Popogrebskii and Khlebnikov end the next scene, in which the son tries to bind up the wound while the father angrily snaps at him, not with the slow movement that Zviagintsev uses to signal a profound change, but with a fade-to-black, which serves essentially the same function of destabilizing the field of vision. Thus the cinematic properties of this episode elevate the father's wound into his Symbolic incapacitation. Subsequently viewers see the son taking matters into his own hands: in the middle of the night he locates a doctor and, his distrust of his father increasing, soon leaves him in the doctor's house so as to pursue his own dream of reaching Koktebel.[5] The turning point in both *The Return* and *Koktebel* is conveyed through visual means that register a decisive psychological transition that hints at the Symbolic death of the father. The disruption of visual rhythm in these scenes suggests something beyond what the gaze can immediately grasp—the sons' rite of passage into manhood (Figure 7.4).

In *Koktebel* the son's independence is further suggested by the film's various references to flight, connected to both father and son early in the film, but in the second half of the narrative mainly to the son. On the way to Koktebel the boy stops at a monument—dedicated to aviation—erected on a small hill and tries to let a piece of paper fly away in the air. This scene, however, does not eliminate complexities, for the monument is in ruins and the paper does not ascend vertically but is swept along by the wind horizontally.[6] The disruption of the paper's vertical flight, captured here, additionally emphasizes the boy's disconnection from the father.

Apart from these pivotal moments, other sequences in both films reinforce the perception of the sons' transformations. Early in *Koktebel*, Popogrebskii and Khlebnikov offer a long, claustrophobic take of the son sitting in the enclosed space of a cargo train: from a full shot of the boy the camera zooms in to a close-up of his profile and lingers. The film concludes with a parallel shot of the boy in profile but now seated on the edge of a quay, looking at the vast open space before him. The Symbolic spatialization measures the expansion of possibilities at his disposal accompanying his maturation and independence. That maturation, however, comes at a cost, as implied in the following, rather unnerving scene: when a seagull lands next to the boy and pulls his sleeve with its beak, he grabs the bird by the throat and after squeezing it, tosses it in the air. At the same time the cruelty does not diminish the significance of the choice the son makes: the bird is not killed but freed, and it rises high in the air (quite differently from the horizontal movement of the piece of paper). Like Ivan, who overcomes his fear and climbs the tower, the son at the end of *Koktebel* manifests growth and decisiveness. The camera then cuts to a bird's-eye shot of the sad, lonely boy on the quay, who is shortly joined by his missing father. The sadness speaks directly to the cost of this maturation but also hints at the son's acceptance of the Symbolic, with all its gaping holes.[7]

In *The Return*, after the father's death, the film ends with a series of black-and-white photographs conveying the boys' happiness and enjoyment during the trip. Viewers never see the sons as happy as they appear in the photos, thus exposing the latent Symbolic function of the father. Although the father is absent from most of the photos, his presence and influence are felt through the setting and details of the pictures, which capture moments from the boys' trip—in the car, holding fishing rods, on the beach, and so forth—and portray the way they related to each other. The last photograph, from an earlier period, shows the father with one of his sons as a baby, thereby confirming what throughout the film has been under question: whether he genuinely is the biological father. Although the film invites various interpretations, *The Return*'s ending evokes the return of the father. The black-and-white images of happiness appear not only as a defense mechanism compensating for his frightening death but, more important, as a confirmation of his function: though authoritarian and abusive, the father secured the sons' rite of passage. As already pointed out, however, his early death exposes the cracks of the Symbolic: as the sons gain access to the Symbolic they simultaneously encounter the trauma of the Real.

In addition to mythological associations (the journey across water and the river Styx, for example) and numerous visual references to Andrei Tarkovsky, the film offers a modern (re)vision of Freud's myth about the primal Father and especially its development by Lacan.[8] These myths are familiar to Russians, as much from Freud or Sophocles as from Dostoevsky's complex execution of the filiation theme. Perhaps because of the film's profound and multidimensional preoccupation with the theme of paternity, questions about authority, leadership, and guidance seemingly come across as ambiguous. The scenes of the genuinely concerned father running after his distressed younger son and Ivan's emotional acceptance of his dead father appear controversial to some critics. Aleksandr Sekatskii criticizes the credibility of the story, arguing that the problem emerges from the impatient and hasty attempts of the "prodigal father" to correct in a few days his long absence from his sons' life (203). Surikova expresses a similar disbelief in the ending, asking whether it is possible for regular boys to look at the photos after the traumatic experience. Again, these incongruities, apparent on the level of the cinematic narrative, vanish when one reads the film through Lacan's understanding of the Symbolic function of the father.

The last shot of *Koktebel* incorporates both father and son in a frontal medium frame, the father's mysterious appearance next to his son at the end of the film coming across as illogical and not very credible in the immediate logic of the narrative. Bykov writes, "The wandering ends nowhere, and a finale in which father and son touchingly find each other will hardly deceive anyone."[9] Just like *The Return*'s black-and-white photographs conveying happiness, the deus ex machina reunion of father and son testifies to the crucial Symbolic function of the father, despite the controversial and problematic behavior of actual (biological) fathers, but also to a collective desire for the return of the father. The presentation of the actual fathers differs significantly in the two films, but by and large they both insist on the resurrected father, even if this contradicts the logic of the narratives and the characters. These inconsistencies prompt critics such as Sekatskii, Surikova, and Bykov to expose flaws in the narratives, but on a Symbolic level these endings resurrect the Father only to reaffirm Lacan's insistence: "If God doesn't exist, nothing is possible."

THE RETURN OF THE SYMBOLIC FATHER

Unlike such Western father-son films as *The Full Monty* (Peter Cattaneo 1997), in which the father feels guilty and inadequate because he cannot afford to take his son to an expensive football game and therefore cannot bond with him in a traditional homosocial ritual, the father in *The Return* feels no guilt or doubts about his position and his power, despite his absence during his sons' childhood. Elena Stishova contends that "Zviagintsev accumulates the new existential experience [. . .] of the deconstruction of the patriarchal world in which Russia existed and still exists" (Stishova 2004).[10] Although Stishova confirms the patriarchal discourse of the film, she also suggests its decline. I support her argument only if the decay that she perceives results from the problematic roles of actual fathers.

According to Lacan, lack or excess of the paternal function leads to psychological disturbances and problematic individual development. The sons' dual fantasy of the father in *The Return,* paired with the portrayal of an inadequate father in *Koktebel,* creates an impression of conflicting father images. Despite the inconsistency that these images project, however, they evoke persistent desire for a cohesive and single father function that produces mature and independent sons. The two films open a space for imagining strong sons in the absence (or surplus) of mighty fathers or, in other words, for imagining effective fathering that results from a multiplicity of paternal roles.[11]

This cinematic desire for the return of the father extended to Russian society and culture coincides with a stabilization of the Russian economy and a rather rapid consolidation of President Putin's power. After the chaotic and lawless 1990s, the Kremlin took control over most media and proceeded with the re-nationalization of the oil industry under the pretext of persecuting illegal tax evasions of powerful and successful oil and gas companies. The president decided to appoint regional governors, who previously had been elected by the people. Journalists critical of the Kremlin have been threatened and killed. These facts, however, have not diminished Putin's popularity, which consistently remains at approximately 70 percent.[12]

In accordance with these social sentiments, the two films end on a reassuring note, confirming the boys' maturity and independence while ignoring the problems that the absent or controversial paternal figure can generate for their emotional development. Mike Van Diem's *Character* (1997), for instance, also concludes with a portrayal of a professionally successful son despite his father's abuse, but addresses the emotional side of this success by constructing an image of a son who is unable to find emotional warmth and happiness in his life. In a similar manner *The Return* and *Koktebel* choose to end affirmatively, with the sons' maturation and forgiveness. Both films, however, introduce a deeper and a more complex meaning to the father-son relationship. The rite of passage is accomplished and the desire for the resurrection of the Father is apparent, but all this comes at a cost: Ivan's emotional cry, "Papa!" and the son's loneliness and sadness at the end of *Koktebel* expose the incompleteness and inherent lack within the Symbolic and perhaps intimate the presence of the Real, which reminds the young sons of life's limitations.

ABSENT MOTHERS VERSUS ENDURING FEMININITY

Whereas the son in *Character* develops his personality through constant relational swings between mother and father, the Russian father-son films eliminate the mother figure, to focus on homosocial bonds and relationships. The mother sets the narrative of *The Return* into motion, but she disappears from the film, only to (re)appear briefly in the black-and-white photographs. The photos tend to emphasize the father's bond with his sons, and the few that include the mother portray her as isolated and alone. In *Koktebel* the female doctor appears only in the middle of the narrative, and the father is eager to abandon the trip and remain in the comfort of her hospitality and affection: she fulfills the traditional dual function of caretaker and homebody. It is the son who insists on pursuing his plans; jealous of his father's heterosexual relationship, he is not easily distracted by a fantasy of family happiness. Anxieties about paternal vulnerability and absence are displaced into homosocial bonds that exclude mothers.

The two fathers in these films experience no visible difficulties in performing their roles as lovers or partners. Yet, though both quickly and easily establish sexual relations upon their meetings with women, they appear little invested in these relations and leave the women to pursue interaction with their sons. To evoke Lacan again, the father normally functions as the third term, interrupting the bond mothers form with their children. The father of *The Return* arrives at home to separate the boys from their mother, thus introducing them to the Law. A scene in the film complicates this logic, however. After abandoning Ivan on the road for several hours, the father drives back for him. Having waited in pouring rain, soaked and angry, Ivan confronts his father with the questions, "Why did you come for us? We were doing fine just with mother. Why did you come? To tease and torture us?" Surprisingly, his father replies, "Your mother asked me to come and spend some time with you." Although the mother asks for the father's return, he is the one who takes the boys on a trip away from their mother.

The mother in *Koktebel* is absent, and the only woman in the narrative is rejected by the son. It appears that the Imaginary bond here is between father (as caretaker) and son, with the female doctor functioning almost as the third term, which introduces the son to the Symbolic. The son leaves on his own, but he is driven away by the woman's intimacy with his father.

The complicated nature of the parent-child relations and identifications in these cinematic narratives makes possible several interpretations of the fathers' function in the lives of their sons. The dominant male presence and the absence of mother figures, however, remain unquestionable. In general, patriarchalism manifests itself in two aspects: the paternal (father/son) and the masculine (husband/wife). Although the two films present fathers who easily perform their roles of lovers, the latter aspect of patriarchalism is absent from the films, which, one can therefore argue, advance not only homosocial bonds but also a patriarchal Symbolic structure, both excluding women. These fathers do not procreate but create their sons as if alone. This is why these films revise (rather that duplicate) Freud's myth of the parricide, in which the brothers' motive is not so much to become independent and free but to *gain access to women.* That goal appears irrelevant for the sons in the Russian films, since women and mothers barely figure in the narratives.

To complicate matters further, the two films employ the metaphor of water, which lends itself to various and often clashing interpretations. Pertinent to the films is the symbol for water (graphically illustrated as Δ), which combines the grace of heaven and the womb to suggest female divinity.[13] The image of water dominates *The Return,* which opens with a shot of water that fills the whole frame and continues with a lengthy underwater shot focusing on sunken objects, particularly a sunken boat. The father and sons' seven-day trip revolves entirely around water: they arrive at rivers and lakes, where they fish, and twice they experience rainstorms. At film's end, when the father's body is submerged in water, the camera shifts from a bird's-eye view of the father sinking to an underwater shot capturing the rope of the boat. Uncannily this view resembles the opening scenes, but, more important, the rope, one can argue, alludes to a severed umbilical cord. Thus water, fluidity, and arguably femininity metaphorically frame the experience of father and sons in *The Return* but remain latent and denied in the plot.[14]

The image of water, though not as prevalent in *Koktebel,* is nonetheless present in the film, above all as the father and son's final destination. After leaving his father, the son hitchhikes, and his conversation with the truck driver makes it clear that the boy is seeking the sea rather than just Koktebel. Upon arriving in the sea-city, instead of looking for his aunt, he finds himself at the beach, staring at the water. The last several shots present the son sitting on the quay, thus framed by water.

How can one interpret or reconcile this contradiction, namely, that on the level of content the two films deny women presence, whereas on the level of the visual, femininity marks the experience of fathers and sons? Karl Marx's vital insight rests in his argument that the essence of commodity can be found in its exchange-value, rather than in its use-value. In other words, the latent quality of commodity resides in its form, not in its content. This Marxist intervention in the analysis of the two films, and especially in the interpretation of the feminine presence in them, further exposes the latent contradictory desire buried in the cinematic narratives. Although the woman's role is denied in the immediate content of the films, its importance lurks veiled in the aesthetic choices, thus suggesting the futile (although commanding) social yearning for resurrected homosocial experience.

VOLATILITY VERSUS STABILITY

To return to the gender concerns addressed at the beginning of this essay, namely, the insistence on the plurality of masculinities and on the socially constructed male gender, I again cite Bruzzi, who concludes her study of paternal representations in American cinema with the following passage:

> The most recent period has offered a pluralisation of the father's image within American cinema, but there remains a fundamental ambivalence towards what to do with the authoritarian, traditional father. Much of 1990s' Hollywood dispenses with him, but ultimately it seems to protest. that the traditional father is what we want. Contemporary American cinema acknowledges the validity of alternative paternal models, nevertheless it still feels—often quite urgently—the lack of a strong, conventional father. (191)

A kindred ambivalence—the multiplicity of paternal representations coexisting with the latent desire for the traditional father—but resulting from different historical and cultural conditions can be detected in Russian cinema of the 1990s and the early twenty-first century. Films such as *Vor* [*The Thief,* Pavel Chukhrai 1997], *Otets i syn* [*Father and Son,* Aleksandr Sokurov 2003], *Moi svodnyi brat Frankenshtein* [*My Stepbrother Frankenstein,* Valerii Todorovskii 2004], and *Papa* [Vladimir Mashkov 2004] limn a wide range of paternal characters and their relationships with their sons, and dwell on preserving continuity.

An analysis of *The Return* and *Koktebel* shows that these Russian films also promote the volatility of paternal (male) positions. I contend that despite this volatility, the final and overall presentation of the father figure is surprisingly unified. This paradox testifies to Russia's latent desire for the resurrection of paternal authority, a desire more pronounced than the hesitant Western dreams of the conventional father. In *The Return* and *Koktebel* the anxieties of decentralized male roles produce nothing but nostalgia for the return of the father. Also significant is the rejection of women, whose presence, however metaphorical, pushes through the aesthetic positions of the films. Culturally projecting these cinematic conclusions onto Russian society at the turn of the century, one can argue that anxiety over confused political, economic, and social structures of the 1990s is displaced onto a more stable present and future. Apprehensions about gender challenges are displaced into homosocial bonds that marginalize or exclude women, a displacement that a Marxist twist in the analysis of the two films proves fruitless.

In addition to reaffirming Lacan's insistence on the vital function of the father figure, these disarticulations and paradoxes evoke Marx's grasp of the contradiction of capitalism: instead of deflating the circulation of capital, deterritorialization facilitates its universalization. Or, as Deleuze and Guattari put it, the late capitalist universal regime relies on disassembling fixed identities, which at the same time are reassembled in one global capitalist system (257). To apply this thought to the topic of paternity as interpreted in the two films is to connect it to Stishova's detection of the decline of patriarchy in Russia even as the country embraces it. In other words, the deconstruction of patriarchy projected in the volatility of male positions only produces one unified desire for the (return of the) father. Early-twenty-first-century patriarchal discourse in Russia attempts to discard the multiplicities of male roles and reassembles them in one sturdy patriarchal system. The more male positions are perceived as challenged (the more social and political reality is unstable), the stronger the desire to resurrect the father (leader).

NOTES

1. Brian James Baer, in his essay in this volume, also emphasizes the significance of the father figure for Russia's political history (see chapter 9).

2. For more on the Hollywood post-World War II tradition and fatherhood, see Bruzzi.

3. For more on the myth, see Freud (1953, 23:80–84, 130–32).

4. On the one hand, see V. Makhalkovich, who argues that this film remains in a feminine discourse and is "anti-Zerkalo" ["anti-Mirror"], contrasting it with the male bonding of father and son in Tarkovsky's *Mirror*. Similarly, at the end of her article, O. Surikova points out the film's "anti-machismo" as a possible appeal to Western viewers. On the other hand, E. Stishova claims that the film reinforces Russia's patriarchal world, although in decline.

5. For a connection between the name of the town, Koktebel, and its subsequent renaming into Planerskoye, and their meaning for the father and son journey, see Vladimir Padunov, at http://kinokultura.com/reviews/R103koktebel.html (accessed 24 April 2004).

6. The vertical axis represents patriarchy and the authority of the father, and the horizontal expresses equality and brotherhood. For more detailed discussion on these relationships, see Baer in this collection (chapter 9). Dmitrii Bykov also comments on the importance of this scene in the film.

7. My argument here counters Evgenii Gusiatinskii's belief that the boy does not become a prodigal son, because the father finds him before the son returns on his own. The appearance of the father, quite unconvincing in the overall logic of the narrative, marks only the Symbolic function of the father.

8. Trakovsky's influence is most noticeable in the following scenes: the boys' looking through a book, similar to a scene in *Mirror;* the beach scene at the end, a reminder of the last scene in *Ivan's Childhood;* and the camera's inquisitive voyeuristic movement in the cabin on the island, a replica of the camera movements in several scenes from *Mirror*. For more, see Goscilo's article on Tarkovsky in this collection (chapter 10).

9. "Stranstvie konchaetsia nichem, a final, v kotorom otets i syn trogatel'no nakhodiat drug druga, vriad li kogo obmanet" (Bykov).

10. "Andrei Zviagintsev akkumuliroval v svoem fil'me novyi ekzistentsial'nyi opyt, dolgoe vremia ne imevshii vykhoda,—opyt raspada patriarkhal' nogo mira, v kotorom zhila i prodolzhaet zhit' Rossiia" (Stishova).

11. Basing his analysis of *The Return* on Aleksandr Etkind's internal colonization theory, Mark Lipovetsky offers a similar interpretation. Comparing *The Return* to *Cuckoo* (Aleksandr Rogozhkin 2002) and especially the role of mediation in both, Lipovetsky writes: "Zhestkaia 'muzhskaia' vlast', ne priznaiushchaia mediatsii, osnovannaia na patriarkhal'nom/ imperskom dominirovanii, ottorgaetsia, khotia i stanovitsia ob"ektom posleduiushchei nostal'gii po transtsendental'nomu avtoritetu" ["Brutal manly power, which does not accept mediation, and which is based on patriarchal/imperial domination, pulls away, although it becomes an object of subsequent nostalgia for a transcendental authority"].

12. For more on these changes, see Tatiana Smorodinskaya's article in this volume, chapter 4.

13. In addition, and in a more psychoanalytic manner, Luce Irigaray explores fluid mechanics/fluid forms as a signifier of feminine identity, which she develops as a critique of Freud's phallocentric concept of individual identity, based on the phallus as the only (first) term of identification (106–19). Objecting to the assumption that the phallus is at the center of identity formation, Iragaray juxtaposes solids and fluids, arguing that female identity should be viewed autonomously, independent of male identity. She does not imply a regressive retreat to the anatomical but extends her argument into a broader (Lacanian) discourse of ideology and language, which are both

marked by phallocentrism. In such a discourse, "by virtue of her 'fluid' character," woman is deprived "of all possibility of identity" (107).

14. V. Mikhalkovich notes the female presence in connection with the metaphor of water. "Itak, *Vosvrashchenie* vvelo 'nash' pattern v glub' 'zhenskoi' stikhii" ["So, *The Return* injected 'our' paternity into the depths of the 'feminine' elements"].

REFERENCES

Attwood, Lynne. "Sex and the Cinema." In *Sex and Russian Society,* ed. Igor Kon and James Riordan, 65–88. Bloomington: Indiana University Press, 1993.

———. *The New Soviet Man and Woman: Sex Role Socialization in the USSR.* Bloomington: Indiana University Press, 1990.

Blankenhorn, David. *Fatherless America: Confronting Our Most Urgent Social Problem.* New York: HarperCollins, 1996.

Bruzzi, Stella. *Bringing up Daddy: Fatherhood and Masculinity in Post-War Hollywood.* London: British Film Institute, 2005.

Bykov, Dmitrii. "Koktebel off lain." *Iskusstvo kino* 10 (2003). Available at http://www.kinoart.ru/magazine/10-2003/repertoire/bykovo310/ accessed 24 April 2004).

Clare, Anthony. *On Men: Masculinity in Crisis.* London: Chatto and Windus, 2000.

Corneau, Guy. *Absent Fathers, Lost Sons: The Search for Masculine Identity.* Translated by Larry Shouldice. Boston: Shambhala, 1991.

Coward, Rosalind. *Sacred Cows: Is Feminism Relevant to the New Millennium?* London: HarperCollins, 1999.

Deleuze, G., and F. Guattari. *Anti-Oedipus: Capitalism and Schizophrenia.* Minneapolis: University of Minnesota Press, 1983.

Erofeev, Viktor. *Muzhchiny.* Moscow: ZebraE. 2002.

Freud, Sigmund. *The Standard Edition of the Complete Psychological Works.* Edited by J. Strachey. London: Hogarth, 1953.

Fukuyama, Francis. *The Great Disruption: Human Nature and the Reconstruction of Social Order.* London: Profile Books, 1999.

Gusiatinskii, Evgenii. "Ni poezdov, ni samoletov." Available at http://kinoart.ru/magazine/10-2003/repertoire/guso310/.

Irigaray, Luce. *This Sex Which Is Not One.* Translated by Catherine Porter, with Carolyn Burke. Ithaca, N.Y.: Cornell University Press, 1977.

Lacan, Jacques. *The Seminar of Jacques Lacan, Book 2: The Ego in Freud's Theory and in the Technique of Psychoanalysis.* Edited by Jacques-Alain Miller. Translated by Sylvana Tomaselli. New York: W. W. Norton, 1988.

———. *Ecrits. A Selection.* New York: W. W. Norton, 1977.

Lipovetsky, Mark. "V gnezde kukushki." *Iskusstvo kino* (2006): 72–77.

Mikhalkovich, V. "Kuda poklazhi tianut voz?" *Iskusstvo kino* 4 (2004). Available at http://www.kinoart.ru/magazine/07-2004/review/mikhalkovicho407/.

Padunov, Vladimir. "*Koktebel*': Review." Available at http://kinokultura.com/reviews/R103koktebel.html.

Schoeberlein, John S. "Doubtful Dead Fathers and Musical Corpses: What to Do with the Dead Stalin, Lenin, and Tsar Nicholas?" In *Death of the Father: An Anthro-*

pology of the End in Political Authority, ed. John Borneman, 201–20. New York: Berghahn Books, 2004.

Sekatskii, Aleksandr. "Otsepriimstvo." *SEANS* 21/22 (2005): 198–206.

Stishova, Elena. "Na glubine." *Iskusstvo kino* 1 (2004). Available at http://kinoart.ru/magazine/01-2004/repertoire/homewardbound0104/.

Surikova, O. "Ostrov neizvestnykh sokrovishch." *Iskusstvo kino* 1 (2004). Available at http://kinoart.ru/magazine/01-2004/repertoire/surikova0401/.

FILMOGRAPHY

American Beauty. Dir. Sam Mendes. USA, 1999. DreamWorks SKG.

The American President. Dir. Rob Reiner. USA, 1995. Castle Rock Entertainment.

Backdraft. Dir. Ron Howard. USA, 1991. Imagine Films Entertainment.

The Birdcage. Dir. Mike Nichols. USA, 1996. Nichols.

Boyz n the Hood. Dir. John Singleton. USA, 1991. Columbia Pictures.

Character. Dir. Mike Van Diem. Netherlands/Belgium, 1997. First Floor Features.

Cuckoo [Kukushka]. Dir. Aleksandr Rogozhkin. Russia, 2002. Kinokompaniia CTB.

Father and Son [Otets i sin]. Dir. Aleksandr Sokurov. Russia/German/Italy/Netherlands, 2003. Isabella Films B.V.

Father of the Bride 2. Dir. Charles Shyer. USA, 1995. Sanddollar Productions.

Father's Day. Dir. Ivan Reitman. USA, 1997. Northern Lights Entertainment.

A Few Good Men. Dir. Rob Reiner. USA, 1992. Castle Rock Entertainment.

The Full Monty. Dir. Peter Cattaneo. UK, 1997. Redwave Films.

Gladiator. Dir. Ridley Scott. UK/USA, 2000. DreamWorks SKG.

Happiness. Dir. Todd Solondz. USA, 1998. Good Machine.

Jungle Fever. Dir. Spike Lee. USA, 1991. AO Acres & A Mule Filmworks.

Koktebel [Koktebel']. Dir. Aleksei Popogrebskii and Boris Khlebnikov. Russia, 2003. PBOUL Borisevich R.U.

Magnolia. Dir. Paul Thomas Anderson. USA, 1999. Ghoulardi Film Company.

Mrs. Doubtfire. Dir. Chris Columbus. USA, 1993. Blue Wolf.

My Stepbrother Frankenstein [Moi svodnyi brat Frankentshtein]. Dir. Valerii Todorovskii. Russia, 2004. Mosfilm.

One Fine Day. Dir. Michael Hoffman. USA, 1996. Fox 2000 Pictures.

Papa. Dir. Vladimir Mashkov. Russia, 2004. NTV-Profit.

The Return [Vozvrashchenie]. Dir. Andrei Zviagintsev. Russia, 2003. Ren Film.

A River Runs Through It. Dir. Robert Redford. USA, 1992. Allied Film Makers.

Sleepless in Seattle. Dir. Nora Ephron. USA, 1993. TriStar Pictures.

The Thief [Vor]. Dir. Pavel Chukhrai. Russia/France, 1997. NTV-Profit, Productions Le Pont, Roissy Films.

Figure 7.1. The (authoritarian) Father in *The Return*.

Figure 7.2. Andrei after the death of the father (*The Return*).

Figure 7.3. Father and son on the road (*Koktebel*).

Figure 7.4. The son protecting his father (*Koktebel*).

EIGHT

The Forces of Kinship: Timur Bekmambetov's *Night Watch* Cinematic Trilogy

VLAD STRUKOV

In Timur Bekmambetov's *Night Watch* and *Day Watch* the father and son are divided by their loyalties to the opposing forces of Light and Darkness, and each of them finds this separation excruciatingly painful. The director chooses the realm of the family, with a special focus on parent-child relations, to explore the social phenomenon of authority. He constructs a myth that accounts for Russia's contemporary social structure, a myth that serves as a source of morality and generally as the origin of civilization. Prompted by the structure of the films, I analyze the father-son relationship as a set of cultural oppositions and choices that culminate in the concept of the secret workings of fate. The underlying structure of the myth illuminates Bekmambetov's assertion that, unless the Oedipus complex is resolved, a person's identity is incomplete, and therefore a sociocultural transition is not possible. My discussion addresses the issue of familial and social disengagement propagated by the films, and authority as a guarantee of father-son and, ultimately, national unity.

THE FIGURE OF OEDIPUS AND THE WORKINGS OF FATE

Night Watch [*Nochnoi Dozor* 2004] and *Day Watch* [*Dnevnoi Dozor* 2005][1] are the first two installments in a planned sci-fi/fantasy/horror/vampire trilogy based on a series of hugely popular fantasy novels by Sergei Luk'ianenko. Though *Night Watch* and *Day Watch* develop the same narrative, the former lays the foundation for the second part of the series.

The events of the films relate to three major time periods: 2004, 1992, and the distant past. From the first film we learn that there is a new type of social order whereby "Others" [inye], who possess supernatural powers, live among normal humans. The Others fall into two groups—the Dark ones, who gain their power by feeding on the blood of humans, and the Light ones, who are supposed to protect people from their Dark opponents. Although being one of the Others is biologically predetermined, a human being can be "initiated" and become a vampire if she or he falls prey to another vampire. The division into Light and Dark Others results from an ancient conflict brought about by a curse imposed on a virgin who once lived in Byzantium. The conflict culminated in the Middle Ages, when the armies of Light and Dark forces, under the leaders Geser (Vladimir Men'shov) and Zavulon (Viktor Verzhbitskii), respectively, met in battle on an ancient arched bridge. When it became clear that the Dark and Light forces possessed equal powers and the clash was doomed to finish in mutual extermination, Geser halted the fight; the forces of Light and Dark signed a truce to end the devastating battle. Since then the forces of Light govern the days, and the nights belong to their Dark opponents, and each side establishes a Watch to ensure peace.

Bekmambetov domesticates the members of the Day and Night Watch: in modern Moscow the former roam the night as vampires, and the latter operate under the cover of Moscow's electric utility repair crew [Gorsvet]. The director also transplants the metaphysical conflict of good and evil into the private realm of the family and the individual, whereby a person's experience is also a paradigm of destiny. Bekmambetov connects the two spheres, the private and the public, the real and the fantastic, the actual and the allegorical, through the myth of Oedipus as dramatized in Sophocles' tragedy Oedipus Rex.[2] The events of the myth become a defining element of the films' thematics and stylistics, as well as an engine for the father-son dynamic.

The first film's prologue is staged in a manner recalling the visit of Laius, the ruler of Thebes, to an oracle who tells him that his son will supplant him. With the agreement of Laius's wife, Jocasta, the baby is left on a mountain to be eaten by wild animals. In Night Watch, in 1992 Moscow, Anton (Konstantin Khabenskii) seeks help from a sorceress, Dar'ia (Rimma Markova), in order to regain his unfaithful wife, Irina (Mariia Mironova), only to learn that his wife carries another man's child—

information that subsequently proves inaccurate. The comparison with the myth reveals the nature and the dynamic of the conflict: Anton's suspicions of Irina's infidelity and his desire to avenge his wife prompt him to ask the sorceress to terminate Irina's pregnancy. Bekmambetov shows the origin of the conflict in the destruction of the family rather than in the conspiracy of the husband and wife to maintain their power.

Anton's first encounter with his son, Egor (Dmitrii Martynov), occurs twelve years later on a train on the Moscow metro. Having drunk some pig blood in order to catch a vampire, Larissa (Anna Dubrovskaia), who attacks innocent victims in Moscow, Anton is lured to his son, but luckily a cursed woman, Svetlana (Mariia Poroshina), distracts him from engaging in a vampiric act. The scene relates to the part of the Greek myth in which Oedipus, on his way to Thebes, meets an old man—Laius—who is rude and aggressive, and therefore falls victim to Oedipus's uncontrollable fury. The association with the myth defines the scene on the Moscow metro as that of attempted murder and identifies Anton's symbolic function no longer as that of Laius (the victim of filicide) but rather as that of Oedipus (the perpetrator of filicide). Indeed, both Anton and Oedipus find it hard to control their instincts (the latter is blinded by his rage, the former is under the influence of the intoxicating drink); both act aggressively toward a member of their blood family because they are unaware of their true identity and believe they are dealing with complete strangers. Thus the switch in Anton's symbolic function (Laius → Oedipus) suggests that *Night/Day Watch* presents a case of a *reversed* Oedipus complex, to be analyzed later in the chapter.

The viewer is not confused by the transformation of Anton's role thanks to a temporal discontinuity: via non-diegetic means, Bekmambetov uses a title to signal that twelve years elapse between Anton's visit to the sorceress and his first encounter with Egor. From the point of view of diegesis, the director allows twelve minutes before the characters' first meeting. To achieve his purpose, Bekmambetov borrows the principle of a temporal gap from *Oedipus Rex*. Sophocles uses the delay of twelve years to signify his hero's maturation and his inauguration as the King of Thebes and Jocasta's husband, thus focusing on the figure of Oedipus and his self-discovery (Sophocles 49–51). In *Night Watch* the time discontinuity enables the director to shift some of the myth's events to the plane of the contemporary and thus to signal his interest in constructing the myth in the present rather than uncovering the events of the past. In other words, Bekmambetov sees the original father-son conflict as unfolding in its actuality and defining the future rather than the current situation. Bekmambetov underscores his point by allowing virtually zero historical distance between the time of the making of *Night Watch* and the events the film presents: although the events of the myth relate to the mythical past, *Night Watch* constructs the mythical present as the story unfolds. The director enhances the simultaneity of historical processes of the real and universal qualities of the magical worlds by appropriating motifs and narrative tools from the ancient myth. For example, the future of the child (Oedipus; Egor) is defined not only by his parents' ambitions but also by the interference of other subjects—or, metaphorically speaking, by fate. Shepherds take pity on the baby and, instead of leaving it to die, present the boy to the childless King of Corinth, Polybus, who brings him up as his own, giving him the name "Oedipus"[3] (Sophocles 54–57). Similarly, the Night Watch intervenes and prevents the murder of the unborn child in the process of being aborted by the sorceress. Bekmambetov interprets this interference as a point of entry into the magical world ruled by fate rather than reason. Anton therefore begins to function as a mediator between the seen and the unseen, between the real and the imaginary, and between good and evil.

Another important parallelism[4] between the myth and the film is their use of oracles and messengers as tools that propel the narrative. In the myth, Oedipus learns from the oracle of Apollo that he will kill his father and marry his mother. In *Night Watch*, in 2004 Moscow, Anton-Oedipus receives his second prophecy in the form of a telephone call. An unidentified caller commands Anton to capture Larissa, who is pursuing Egor. The analogy between the two texts reveals that Larissa and Egor form a male/female relation whose bond is suggested by the anticipated vampiric intercourse; Anton therefore functions as their symbolic child whose purpose is to prevent their congress. Another important instance of comparison is between the scene in the myth in which the Corinthian messenger arrives to tell Oedipus that Polybus is dead and that he was Oedipus's adoptive father, and thus Oedipus is the murderer of Laius (Sophocles 92), and the scene in *Night Watch,* in which Anton accesses secret files on Night Watch's intranet to learn that his own clan categorizes and uses him as a murderer. The correlation demonstrates Anton's own role in discovering the truth about himself and his past: like Oedipus, he becomes a tool of his own fate as he brings his investigation to a conclusion to proclaim himself guilty of his murderous attempts.

Bekmambetov utilizes the matrix of the myth in order to concatenate the otherwise disjunctive structure of the film. With the help of implicit allusions he rebuilds a complete chronology of events and renders the ancient myth's thematics. For example, Bekmambetov retains the metaphor of the road where the father and the son meet for the first time, to convey the workings of fate as well as to suggest that his characters' search for identity is not accomplished. Both Anton and Egor are nomads whose space has not yet been determined. Like Oedipus, who may not remain in Corinth and is twice exiled from Thebes, they remain on the road, or in the Gloom[5]—the in-between space of individual and cultural identification—thus maintaining their free status. In *Night Watch,* with the help of digital imagery, Bekmambetov demonstrates what is known as Oedipus "road rage," a sudden attack of anger when he "sees red" and is unable to control his temper. The director allows Anton's vampiric gaze to penetrate Egor's skin; the father sees—and so does the viewer—the pulsation of blood in the arteries in the son's head. The image of Egor's circulation system is accessible to Anton and the viewer only, and not to Anton's fellow train passengers. Thus the viewer is invited to participate in the scene and in Anton's—male—gaze. This means that the events of the first film are presented from Anton's point of view, and the director wishes his audiences to associate with the figure of the father in the father-son conflict, a perspective that is doomed to be reversed in the second installment of the trilogy.

Another example of how the Greek myth influences the visual paradigm of the film is the scene of the liberation of Ol'ga (Galina Tiunina). Geser presents Anton with a stuffed owl; in his kitchen Anton accidentally guesses the spell and releases Ol'ga from the body of the bird in which she has been trapped for sixty years. The scene, of course, relates to the story of the Sphinx, a hybrid creature with the body of a lioness, the head of a woman, and wings, and a monster who terrorizes Thebes (Sophocles 50–52). In the film the scene is visually orchestrated in the manner reminiscent of the two most famous Greek representations of Oedipus solving the riddle of the Sphinx (Figure 8.1). The owl is poised on a kitchen table facing Anton; as he pronounces the spell, the owl transforms into a woman; she asks Anton to turn away and continues to occupy her pedestal until the metamorphosis is complete. In *Night Watch* Ol'ga accompanies Anton, and together they form a symbolic parental relation with Egor as their child. In the scene of recognition, when Anton identifies Egor as his son, they all come together in a typically domestic setting with Anton watching television and Ol'ga sewing up Egor's shirt and chatting with the boy.

The myth's notion of contamination (Thebes succumbs to a vile plague, which kills children and animals, and is caused by pollution or by the sin of the unpunished murder) is rendered in the film thanks to the character of Svetlana. Her mother has a fatal renal disease and requires a kidney transplant but categorically refuses Svetlana's offer of her kidney, prompting her daughter to a moral assessment of her motivations. Kidneys remove waste products and excess fluids from the body via the urine, thereby maintaining a critical balance of salt, potassium, and acid; symbolically a kidney is an organ of purification, and a kidney problem suggests contamination or aberration. Svetlana's motive is thus impure, and, having realized it, she puts a curse on herself. Her curse is so powerful that it threatens to destroy the city of Moscow.[6] Svetlana's masked wish for her mother's death inverts Anton's explicit desire for the elimination of his son. As Svetlana and Anton eventually form a couple, Bekmambetov accentuates the connection between contamination and incomprehension, or guilt and fate (Anton, like Oedipus, is completely unaware of the nature of his own deeds). Anton's blindness[7] is rendered with the help of digital imagery that transforms his eyes into those of a vampire. In addition, he constantly wears dark glasses that obstruct his vision (i.e., blinded vision versus blinded language); and, finally, he wanders in the Gloom, or permanent darkness, which ultimately suggests impurity, ignorance, and displacement. The characters of *Night Watch* strive to overcome contamination by embracing either their parental (Anton) or filial (Svetlana) duty. Unlike in the myth, in the film the crime per se never occurs, since on three occasions Anton has the opportunity to murder his child, but, luckily, each time he fails to do so. Thus the film's emphasis falls on the motivation and morality rather than the consequences, whereas ancient Greeks perceived Oedipus guilty of his father's death, since, in accordance with their law, the act itself rather than the motive defined a crime.

Like Sophocles' play, *Night Watch* demonstrates that a man's character is his fate, for it is in fulfilling his personal characteristics—his relentless pursuit of knowledge, his perseverance and confidence in himself, and his proneness to anger—that Oedipus meets his destiny, unwittingly realizing the prophecies (Sophocles 96–99). *Night Watch* invokes the concept of fate and fatalistic visions of experience that are shown to create, guide, reward, and afflict the characters. Picturing fatal forces, the film, like the myth, introduces the entire concept of divinity, or superhuman personalities who control the rules and the events of our lives according to their own principles, which generally remain unintelligible. These are not only the figures of Geser and Zavulon (substitute fathers—empowered men who issue orders) but also of Anton, Svetlana, and Egor, a divine family. Critically, in the film's most poignant scene, which should be identified as a rite of passage,[8] Egor enters the pantheon of "the chosen ones" in the presence of his blood father and Ol'ga, who, just like Svetlana, functions as Egor's substitute mother.[9] Ol'ga accounts for Egor's otherness as follows: "An 'Other' has superhuman abilities because throughout his life he has met superhuman challenges and he has had to put forth superhuman efforts." This—as with many other scenes in the films—is perceived as an imaginative act, as it permits characters and subsequently the viewer to understand the situation and establish a relationship with the controlling forces of existence. Such a relationship takes the form of communal practice, since Egor enters the Symbolic order at the same time that he joins his clan. In the fatalistic universe, a character who confronts fate becomes a hero; in *Night Watch*, the conflict is personalized, as the father and son challenge each other, and it may not be resolved—as it is not resolved in *Day Watch*—until a secession of power is established. The role of the hero in a Greek tragedy is to explore the roots of his society's beliefs; here the hero questions the clan's policies. Egor freely articulates what his father only suspects, that is, the arbitrariness of the divide between the Dark and Light forces. In *Night Watch* Egor, unlike Anton, is shown to be able to make decisions in response to a crisis and to step forward and take risks in the face of fate. It is this personal quality of will and determination that separates

Oedipus from the chorus in *Oedipus Rex,* and Egor from Anton in *Night Watch,* as the chorus and Anton both acknowledge their timidity, bewilderment, or anxiety in the face of the crisis (Sophocles 55–65), Thus, in *Night Watch,* Anton is portrayed as a follower who subsequently will require his son to become the leader.

THE FAMILY AND THE CONSTRUCTION OF THE EGO

In Freudian interpretation and in Bekmambetov's appropriation, the Oedipus complex is the decisive crisis from which arises, by virtue of the mechanism of identification, each individual's structure as a personal ego. The films explore the ways in which unconscious desire is limited, organized, and structured through the activities of the social world. The myth is used to symbolize how the unconscious is socialized. The Oedipus complex describes the triangular configuration constituted by the child, the child's natural object (mother), and the bearer of the law (father) (Freud 1952, 18–75). Therefore, it is the prime site for observing the operation of internalizing and identification (or "taking in" that which is outside, and here, the regulations on sexuality imposed by the father or, more generally, by the social order) and making it central to the psyche (Freud 1957, 26–38).

The narrative structure of *Night Watch* utilizes a temporal discontinuity to account for Egor's present age—twelve years old—which undoubtedly suggests that he occupies the fifth stage of psychosexual development (six–twelve years) (Freud 1957, 113–17). According to Freud, the latency stage has its origins in the resolution of the Oedipus complex and the start of the child's identification with the same-sex parent (Egor → Anton) (Freud 1957, 113–17). However, because of Anton's absence, Egor's solution of the Oedipus complex has been delayed and has therefore resulted in problems such as adjusting to a group (Egor is never shown in the company of his peers; instead, as the final scene of Satan's banquet demonstrates, he chooses to associate with a more mature club, the Day Watch); phobias (Egor's initial fear of vampires later turns into his uninhibited exploitation of his vampiric inclinations); and other juvenile delinquencies. He requires his father's intervention to progress to his final—genital—stage of development. When Anton fails him, Egor chooses Zavulon as his father figure and achieves maturity. The difference between the roles of Anton and Zavulon is visually marked: in the final scene of *Night Watch*, when Anton and Zavulon clash in a brutal fight on top of an apartment block, Anton defends himself with an electrical light pole (i.e., he needs to appropriate his phallus from outside), whereas Zavulon extracts his spinal cord and turns it into a magic sword (i.e., he produces and governs his own weapon).

Although Egor chooses Zavulon as his mentor, he inherits his blood father's relentless pursuit of knowledge, which, in Freudian terms, is defined as the epistemological drive. The origin of the drive lies in the curiosity of the child confronted by the enigma of sexuality or, as presented in the films, by the enigma of the Day/Night Watch opposition, whereby the first is conveyed as a form of vampirism, in itself a form of sexuality. It is possible to claim that Egor's vampirism is, in fact, a sublimated sexual drive (*Day Watch* shows that the victims of his bloodsucking are women),[10] or a movement from the luring relationship with his father to a new Symbolic order, by means of his phobia and its transformations. When in the final scene of *Night Watch* Egor chooses the Dark side, his father appears in his life as the figure that interferes with the satisfaction that the child is trying to obtain, and thus it is not surprising that the son denies his biological father as well as the law of civilization that the father introduces.[11] To Egor, the Day Watch constitutes the pleasure principle (ironically manifested in the realm of the everyday as a lavish lifestyle) (Freud 1957, 120–21). Anton, and with him the Night Watch, opposes it with the reality principle that carries the burden of the imperatives of culture.

In *Totem and Taboo* Freud tried to give the Oedipus complex a historical foundation and constructed a myth: one day the sons killed the primal father and ate him, and there followed a new social organization founded on guilt (Freud 1952, 1–17). Likewise, Bekmambetov constructs a creational myth that involves the Dark and Light forces invisible to the human eye but accountable for the existing social and cultural organization. Bekmambetov, like Freud, mythologizes fictional events to reveal the hidden truth of the language, as words may mean the opposite of what they say. The truth that language conveys shifts from what is said and what is known to the unspeakable—the taboo or the truce. In Freudian terms, the contents of the unconscious, which are contained in the oracle, can no longer be suppressed and break forth into the light.

To Oedipus-Anton, truth comes only through struggle and with painful reluctance (Freud 1957, 87).

Since Anton's own Oedipus complex has not yet been resolved (his blood father is never portrayed or even mentioned in the films), he needs his son to undo his own past to determine the present. Oedipus first must suppress all the embodiments of the empirical father that gave him a false certainty, for only through the murder and the recognition of it can he experience the father not as a mere absence but as a presence that marks him forever. This explains Anton's persistent desire to eliminate Egor. His first attempt is disguised as a sorceress's act: he is frustrated because his wife has rebuffed him and he wants revenge. He acts on the grounds of false knowledge, as he is made to believe that the child is not his. In other words, the male child's desire for the mother is contradicted by paternal authority backed by the father's real and imagined power to harm him, which Freud conceptualizes as the boy's fear of the threat of castration.

Anton's second encounter with the son takes place on the Moscow metro while Anton is still unaware that Egor is his son. Now the murder is disguised as an act of vampirism, which suggests an incestuous intercourse but also "common blood"—that of filiation. In a later scene Anton, still unaware of Egor's identity, enters his flat and thus performs a symbolic penetration. Prior to this encounter, Egor is enveloped in the fantasy of a narcissistic link to the mother. Anton's intrusion transfers Egor from his dyadic state—he is never shown in a domestic setting again—into the triadic structure in which he needs to obey the demands and regulations of reality. The boy's development is based on the assumed dichotomy between the father and mother whereby the former symbolizes reality and maturity, and the latter, fantasy and narcissism.

Finally, in the scene on top of the building, where the murder is disguised as a fight between Anton and Zavulon, and Anton—this time perfectly aware of Egor's identity—acts on the basis of fabricated knowledge, Bekmambetov reveals some deeply internalized "aggressivity" (Lacan 2001, 9). It is derived from both the boy's hostility toward the father and his fantasy that the father is murderously hostile to him. The latter is illustrated in a straightforward manner: Anton threatens to kill his son with a knife. According to Freud, this threat not only forces the repression of sexual desire but institutes a new structure within the mind, the superego, the source of an unconscious but continuing scrutiny of a person's wishes (Freud 1957, 141). In *Night Watch* this shift takes place in a new way: Egor never conforms to his biological father's authority;[12] on the contrary, he takes the side of the Dark force and chooses Zavulon as his authority figure. Egor thus undermines the authority of his blood father, and identification with the real father never occurs. If, according to Freud, the father embodies the constraining force of society, then Egor rejects one set of laws (Night Watch) in favor of another (Day Watch) (Freud 1957, 87).

From Anton's perspective, the construction of the ego follows the pattern of (1) unrecognizability of the father; (2) transgression of the father; and (3) fabrication of the Father (described above as false knowledge, lack of knowledge, and fabricated knowledge). This pattern reaffirms Lacan's idea that the Oedipus complex is a portal into a different order of experience, the Symbolic order of language and culture, which, as the "Law of the Father," structures all interactions, even the early, extraordinary intimate ones between mother and infant (Lacan 2001, 139–46). For the same reason that Freud saw the Oedipal father as defining reality for the child (by placing a limit on narcissistic fantasy), Lacan claims that these structures derive from the "No" of the father because they depend on the recognition that complete possession of the other, complete wholeness, is impossible and that something exists outside the mother-infant bond (Lacan 2001, 152–53).

While Anton undergoes a linear development, the films themselves are structured as a symbolic loop in terms of time, space, and progression. At the end of the second film, in 2004, Anton returns to Dar'ia's apartment and on the wall writes "No" with "the chalk of fate," thus negating his previous act (agreement to exterminate his unborn child). In other words, he subjugates himself to the "law" and resolves his own Oedipus complex. Bekmambetov demonstrates Anton's advancement by allowing him to return to the past and relive the events of the day back in 1992: on his way to Dar'ia's apartment he meets Svetlana, and the film encourages viewers to assume that he follows her and never reaches the sorceress's apartment. In *The Seminar*, Book XI, Lacan writes: "The real is that which always comes back to the same place" (Lacan 1992, 49). Indeed, Anton returns and embraces the Real. The Real should not be understood in the Freudian sense, which distinguishes the world external to the human mind from one's own imaginings. Rather, in Lacan's terms, the Real is the endless daunting power that supersedes the power of the Symbolic (Lacan 1992, 49). While *Night Watch* strives to convince the viewer of the presence of transcendental powers within the mundane, the ending of *Day Watch* disavows those powers. The confrontation between Geser and Zavulon is reduced to a chess game, and the great magicians are portrayed as typical Russian retirees enjoying their afternoon in a park (Figure 8.2).

THE DIALECTICS OF PARENTHOOD

According to Freud, paternity becomes identified through death (Freud 1952, 3–6). The films present maternity as empirically verifiable (in fact, the status of Egor's mother or of Galina Rogova [Irina Yakovleva], the murdered vampire, is never questioned), whereas paternity constitutes uncertainty, fiction, or speculation. Fatherhood always remains an abstract notion or a shadow, as when Anton literally turns into a ghost when he enters Egor's apartment through the Gloom. Eventually the narrative reverses Freud's observation, for the father returns in material form but loses his abstract authority. In other words, the films rely on the mythology of parenthood, whereby, according to Freud's notions of the taboo that regulates the circulation of women in a tribe, the father is dismembered to be re/membered in the abstract (Freud 1952, 1–18). Indeed, the father looms far larger in death, for by virtue of no longer being bodily accessible, he has become ubiquitous, institutionalized in the law that the son attempts to transcend. With this celebration of cerebration, *Night/Day Watch* presents the familiar landscape of the matter/mind dualism, with its networks of gendered alliances: form/substance, body/soul, nature/culture, and private/public.

Duality is the main structural component of the films. Characters are divided regarding their psyche, social affiliation, and moral stance. The divide also cuts across families by the types of parenthood already aggregated in the myth of Oedipus, and categorizes family members regardless of their gender, class, and other social categories. Egor is constantly torn between two models of paternity, incarnated in Anton and Zavulon—that is, between his biological father and his adoptive/substitute father,[13] who tries to replace the missing father and compensate for the deficiencies in the child's education. Further, the two major father figures in the films—Geser and Zavulon—function as spiritual fathers/mentors for Anton and Egor, respectively. Inevitably the child (Egor) is fascinated with his teacher (Zavulon) and convinces himself that the mentor loves him in return, yet as a son he fails to realize that the object of his affections is not his mentor but, rather, his own biological father (Anton). In fact, Egor is attracted to Anton (in *Night Watch*, in the scene in Egor's apartment, where Anton appears as trustworthy, strong, and affectionate) until he discovers Anton's real identity and past actions. The father's sudden return therefore marks the separation between father and son.

The Anton/Egor dual dynamic slots into a broad series of child/parent conflicts. While Anton makes an arduous effort to regain his son, the father (Valerii Zolotukhin) of Kostia (Aleksei Chadov) becomes obsessively protective over his child, trying to ensure that Kostia does not indulge his thirst for blood. The fears of Zolotukhin's character spring from guilt, since he initiated his son into vampirism during the boy's childhood—that is, he interrupted his normal progression toward identity formation. In contrast to Anton, Kostia's father is portrayed as a loving parent, tender and caring, who, in the absence of the mother, fulfills the maternal functions; for example, he does his son's laundry. In keeping with the films' scrambling of gender roles, he actualizes his parental instinct through traditional paradigms of femininity (Figure 8.3).

Secondary characters are also organized in child/parent groupings: Svetlana and her mother; Svetlana's neighbor and his mother; Galina's daughter and mother; Dar'ia and her daughter, and so forth. In these groupings, characters struggle to maintain uneasy relationships: Svetlana's mother is fatally ill; the neighbor's mother dies under the influence of an evil spell; Galina is murdered; Dar'ia daughter, Mashen'ka, is permanently trapped in the body of a rubber spider-like doll. Other—predominantly male—characters, such as Semion, Ignat, and Tolik, have neither children nor permanent partners. In short, the personae in the fictional universe of *Night/Day Watch* are either unable to form a traditional nuclear family or are engaged in unstable or inadequate relationships.

The secondary characters and the conflicts they introduce into the narrative illuminate the condition of the main character. In *Night Watch* the character of Anton displays the tragedy of an individual: he fails in his relationship with Egor as well as in the prospect of (re)marriage. After his wife's departure and his unsuccessful contract with Dar'ia, Anton abstains from relationships with women in self-imposed penitence. He drops out of his social milieu, begins to drink, and learns how to be aloof and disdainful. His search for his own identity (he is dubious about his involvement with the Night Watch) is also a search for the concept of a father's role and thus is symptomatic of the impending split between the social order of Soviet and post-Soviet Russia. His desire for change inevitably carries within it the anticipation of failure and loss.

THE CURSE OF THE VAMPIRE

Anton validates his parenthood not only through attempted filicide but also through symbolically incestuous assault. In *Night Watch,* having drunk blood in order to adopt temporarily the identity of a vampire, Anton is lured to drink his son's blood. The scene conjures up disquieting notions of an indissoluble union—a kind of marriage between human and vampire—as well as a symbolic incestuous union between parent and child.[14] On the Moscow underground an old lady, oblivious of Anton's state, calls him by the common Russian blasphemy that literally means "bloodsucker" [*krovopiets*]. Thus, on one level, *Night/Day Watch* exploits the classic interpretation of possession by ingestion, whereby the vampire's lust for blood is more than a reflection of the human or animal appetite for food and drink. On another level, "bloodsucking" is a metaphor for human parasitism and exploitation in general. Finally, in Freudian terms, Anton's vampiric inclination represents the return of the masculine repressed[15] (Freud 1957, 92). Sexual repression means that the human characters must be presented as celibate: Anton abstains from sex for twelve years (as does Svetlana, who—before she learns that she is an Other—is unable to enter a sexual relationship despite her strong sexual desire).

The films are full of the imagery of blood, which denotes not only violence and aggression but also filial relations. As *Night Watch* opens, Anton consumes a mixture of his own blood and alcohol, prepared by the sorceress in order to exterminate his child. *Day Watch* concludes with a banquet scene, in which, while Egor contends with Svetlana,

Dar'ia feeds Anton with *vinaigrette,* a popular Russian vegetable dish whose ingredients include beetroot; it looks like a salad made of human flesh. In both instances Anton consumes what symbolically should be interpreted as the body of his son, and thus the films evoke a creational myth of Kronos, chief of the Greek gods in the first generation, who, when told that one of his children will supplant him, devours them one by one. The use of the Greek myth in the films encodes resignation to the passing of time (Kronos—chronology), the overtaking of age by the young, and the necessarily step-like character of the genealogical ladder through time.

Thanks to Anton's vampiric experience he warms to his son, because he is able to understand his son's drive emotionally as he builds his sympathetic identification with Egor. The other identificatory experience that brings Anton closer to his son results from his psyche's entry into a female body: in *Day Watch,* in an act of supernatural invasion of a human personality, Geser exchanges the bodies of Anton and Ol'ga in order to hide him from persecution by the Day Watch, who accuse Anton of murdering the vampire Galina Rogova. As Anton embraces the symbolic female, he is able to carry out his nurturing and protecting instinct. Growing increasingly concerned with his son's life, he is ready to sacrifice his professional standing and ultimately his own life for the sake of Egor's well-being. Anton risks everything when he breaks into the storeroom where the Night Watch keeps material evidence of the Day Watch's nasty deeds and steals the hat Egor lost at the crime scene when caught sucking a victim's blood. Thus Anton is presented as a self-sacrificing father; however, he remains a criminal because he has broken the laws of parenthood and the policies of the Night Watch.

The crimes of the father allow Bekmambetov to render the idea of the child's victimization. For that purpose, the director constructs an image of a sympathetic vampire, an unwilling victim of circumstances/ fate and a complex mix of rage, retaliation, and redemption. The vampire body of Alisa, Kostia's inamorata (Zhanna Friske, ex-diva of the Russian pop group Blestiashche), is filled with melodramatic significance. She is forced to wear the ring of Zavulon (the head of her clan), which suggests her sexual and emotional subjugation to him (Figure 8.4). The possession of the ring signifies lost innocence and victimhood. Kostia's refusal to drink human blood is also a sign of sacrifice, which, in melodramatic terms, is crucial to the establishment of virtue. The signs of virtue are made visible (in a Freudian gesture, Alisa cuts off her finger) and powerful (Alisa's acts initiate the destruction of Moscow) to render the idea of the struggle for children's innocence to be acknowledged and their virtue to be recognized. The Alisa-Kostia-Zavulon dynamic strives to assert the cultural aspect of the Oedipus complex—namely, that civilization develops at the expense of sexual instincts—by showing how Alisa's sexual drive almost annihilates the civilization it has built.

Bekmambetov utilizes sets of father-son relations—Kostia-Zavulon, Egor-Anton—to call the viewer's attention to the idea that children are victims of their parents' actions. Galina Rogova's daughter loses her mother and remains in her grandmother's care. Egor is victimized in a number of ways: he is used as bait by the Night Watch; he falls prey to Andrei and his girlfriend; he is the "prize" to be won in Geser and Zavulon's games of power; and he experiences direct threats on his life, pain (high blood pressure and nose bleeding caused by the vampire's lure, and loss of consciousness upon entering the Gloom), fear, and moral pressure when he is forced to choose between the Light and Dark forces. In the first film his vulnerability is shown through near-nakedness—in trunks at the swimming pool, shirtless at home. Though the most powerful Other, he is portrayed as defenseless, disoriented, and perplexed.

Another child-character for whom the director creates empathy is Kostia, who, like Egor, is victimized by his blood father. A victim of fatal circumstances (his father "initiated" him into vampirism when he was a child), Kostia experiences a guilt that equates with original sin—that is, the sin of the father rather than the sin of the child. Kostia symbolizes the moral conscience that Zavulon, the head of his group, lacks. Alienated from his clan and unable to connect with Alisa because she is controlled by Zavulon, according to the affirmation-denial dynamic, Kostia rises up against the parent—not his loving father but the tyrannical father figure of Zavulon. Consequently it is not his blood parent but rather an adoptive father who performs his sacrificial murder in order to retain his control over the female member of the clan (Alisa). The scene of Kostia's death is orchestrated in an extremely dramatic manner and thus evokes the passions of Greek tragedy and the aura of metaphysical crisis. When Zavulon is in the banqueting room of the Kosmos hotel celebrating Egor's birthday, Kostia bursts in clutching a bone (a phallic symbol), with which he threatens to kill the leader of Day Watch. Zavulon, by his magic, makes the bone rise in the air; he holds Kostia, and together they dance a macabre tango. The bone drops between them; Zavulon presses Kostia fiercely to him, and the bone pierces Kostia's body, killing him. Zavulon continues to hold Kostia in his devilish embrace, moves out of the room by breaking the window, and keeps on moving in the air. Hovering high above the ground Zavulon finally releases Kostia's corpse. Kostia's death sequence does not finish here: released by Zavulon, Kostia's body is supposed to fall on the ground, but the camera shows that only his hat reaches the snow.

Thus Zavulon manifests his power over his adoptive son through the latter's corporeal, symbolic, and metaphysical deaths. The metaphysical pathos of the scene lies in its inversion of Jesus Christ's temptations of signs: "Then the devil took Him into the holy city and had him stand on the pinnacle of the temple, and said to Him, 'If you are the Son of God, throw yourself down'" (Matthew, 4:5–6). Satan attempts to force Christ to prove God's power through command and might rather than through suffering and pain.

Kostia's story is the prime example of how, in *Night/Day Watch*, both parental and filial figures experience guilt and are symbolically punished or sacrificed. Their execution takes the form of murder or disappearance. The example of the latter is the destiny of Kostia's father. In *Day Watch* he begins to show signs of an uneasy conscience about having introduced his own son to vampirism, and he collaborates with Zavulon in the hope that the latter will mollify his demands on Kostia. He agrees to murder the vampire, Galina Rogova, so that Zavulon can accuse Anton of the homicide and violation of the truce. At the end of *Day Watch* their conspiracy is revealed, and Kostia's father is eliminated, removed from the narrative by the Great Inquisitors. The figure of Kostia's father demonstrates how guilt transforms into moral corruption and degradation, signaled in the film by the character's profession of butcher as he frequently appears among dismembered animal carcasses. By eliminating both Kostia and his father, Bekmambetov shows that the whole family is contaminated by impurity, symbolically represented as vampirism: the bloodline transmits not only vitality but also defilement.

PATRIARCHY AND HISTORY

In *Night/Day Watch* the sense of history is created by the depiction of three clearly demarcated generations:[16] the older adults—Geser, Semion, Ol'ga,[17] Zavulon, Dar'ia, and Kostia's father; the younger—Anton, Svetlana, Alisa, Kostia, and Galina; and children—Egor and Galina's daughter. The films accentuate the generations' biological, psychological, and social differences. The older generation appears knowing, seasoned, and emotionally stable; indirect references are made to the tragedies and painful experiences the older adults endured in their social and private lives, and overcame. This is particularly true regarding the Night Watch: for example, Geser and Ol'ga wear Soviet World War II military uniforms in a photograph shown in *Day Watch;* in *Night Watch* Semion recalls how he suffered shell shock after stepping on a mine in 1941. In contemporary Moscow the actions of their generation are concerted and decisive; the characters represent responsibility and capacity for sacrifice. For instance, in *Day Watch,* Semion dies in a car crash but, in the process, saves his team. Most important, they never question the Truce. Powerful figures of complete authority for their groups, they have earned that authority through previous experience and knowledge of life.

The older generation of the Night Watch noticeably differs from the younger one in relation to new technologies brought about by the modern age. Semion is an extremely skillful driver of his old-fashioned yellow truck, but he does not know how to use computers. Geser rarely comes in direct contact with new technologies; he is a representative of an old school of Soviet managers who relies on orally reproduced instructions and commands. So Egor finds understanding outside the Night Watch: he turns to Zavulon because he is the most technically savvy person of the older generation: in the first film, for example, he plays a computer game[18]—a skill that appeals to Egor's generation, enabling them to speak a common language.

The characters' generational membership overlaps with their historical associations. Geser and Zavulon, as well as other characters in their age group, are "Soviet people" in the sense that they have lived for most of their lives under the communist regime. Egor—born in 1992—symbolizes the post-Soviet generation, and Anton's contemporaries belong to the transitional generation of perestroika. They are portrayed as non-conformists—Others—who question the Truce and its implications—that is, the old social order and the laws governing it. For example, Alisa overthrows Zavulon's power; Kostia argues with his father about the evils of vampirism. However, these characters representing "transition" remain unsuccessful or only partly successful challengers: Alisa escapes Zavulon's bonds but fails to keep Kostia, who dies because of his father; Anton manages to strike a favorable moral balance but is incapable of reestablishing parental relations with his son. Anton commits treason not only against his father's generation but also against his own son. It is apparent that Bekmambetov disparages the perestroika generation; at the same time he redeems it, however, by entrusting its representatives with the magical "chalk of fate" and subsequently granting them a chance to rewrite/reconcile with the past and determine the future.

CONCLUSION

Anton's return to the past, which defies historical/chronological progression, is possible and accountable because the notion of reversible transformation governs the narrative and symbolism of the two films. The plot of *Night/Day Watch* is based on retributive tactics that Dark and Light forces adopt against each other, whereby vengeance is paralleled by a strong sense of equality and justice. Alisa attempts to take revenge on the murderer of her best friend, Galina; Larissa retaliates against the Night Watch for misleading and unfairly inculpating her; Egor carries out a harsh reprisal against his father, and so forth. Equally vampirism is used as a narrative device that blurs the edges of the landscape (through digital imagery), characterization, moral dispositions, and mood shifts so as to enhance the interplay of the real and the fantastic that produces mystery, hesitancy, and doubt. Moreover, characters constantly change into animals and birds (Ol'ga →an owl, Dar'ia →a frog, Il'ia →a bear, etc.); Ol'ga and Anton exchange bodies; Zavulon's spinal column turns into a sword; Egor's destructive yo-yo flies back; and so on. Finally, computer-generated imagery suggests plasticity of matter and the possibility of infinite modifications. This narrative mode and cinematic style present the generational conflict and father-son confrontation not as irreparable but instead as reversible, not as fixed but fluid, not as one dominated by predestination but rather by the logic and pragmatics of the day.

The dual conflict of the film, and thus the seemingly stable structure of the narrative, is undermined by the triangular—and therefore unstable—paradigms of characterization and imagery, which swirl around the Freudian concepts of the id, ego, and superego, as well as Lacan's Symbolic, Imaginary, and Real. The triad is rich in symbolism (for example, the three roads: hell—purgatory—paradise), and it overrides the dichotomy of the Night versus Day Watch by introducing a new element (for example, the films' social structure—the Night Watch versus the Day Watch—is destabilized by the presence of people who do not belong to either group). Moreover, the characters function in three historical periods and in three types of space: place = presence, non-place = absence, and the Gloom. The spatial triad may alternatively be interpreted as the underground, the surface, and the space above ground because these places are where Anton's attempts at killing Egor take place: on the metro, in the apartment, and on the roof of the house. The films also present three different generations, three forms of existence (life, death, and being in a body of another subject). The poetics of both films challenges their philosophy of the ancient divide and the truce, and incorporates transformation and change to signify progression from one generation to another. Thus *Night/Day Watch* presents a two-fold conflict: one involving Anton's relationship with women, particularly his ex-wife and Svetlana, the other involving his son Egor. Alternatively the conflict may be viewed as a combination of Oedipal triads: in *Night Watch* the son rejects his father because the former has already established a stable relationship with his mother; in *Day Watch* Egor rejects Svetlana as his surrogate mother and desires to bring Anton into the realm of his own family.

The films focus on male maturation, which they connect with vampirism, while generally presenting monstrosity as a male attribute. The initiation of the vampire is symbolic of sexual initiation: for example, Egor begins to drink human blood at the age of twelve, namely, at puberty; Andrei (Il'ia Lagutenko, the leader of an extremely popular musical band, *Mummii Trol'*) seduces Larissa and substitutes a vampiric bond for their sexual relationship; and Kostia's father first initiated his wife into vampirism and, upon her death, turned to his son, transforming his sexuality into vampiric desire. The film series represents a male tragedy, for *Night Watch* stresses Anton's flaws as father, and *Day Watch* shows his incapacity as husband. The tragedy is grounded in the notion of error that overwhelms a man: Anton finds himself in the world of tragic appearance that contains and conditions his—and generally—the human condition from the beginning, including a man's nature and aims, and his role as husband, father, and member of a social group (the Night Watch). The conflict between child and parent assumes the form of a power struggle: in *Night Watch* Anton and Egor clash over the validity of the past; in *Day Watch* the control over time shifts into the future, as Egor and Svetlana contend for the love of father/lover, respectively. On the metaphysical level, the collision between Egor and Svetlana, the most powerful magicians ever born, results from the eternal conflict of Dark and Light forces, with Anton as their mediator: he is a communicator between the past and the present; between male and female; and between the Soviet and post-Soviet generations. Thus the director shows how the radical political and social changes of the 1990s undermined parental authority, especially that of the father. The crisis of the father systematically coincides with the crisis of masculinity. The director enables his protagonist to overcome both these crises in the realm of the fantastic through the process of identification based on the Oedipus complex.

Thus the films are simultaneously concerned with verification (Anton is paranoid about establishing his paternity, which creates a sense of historical perspective) and veracity (Geser consistently provides an alternative account of historical events). Both notions signify cultural systems that aim to mediate the world by introducing meaning. The films teach us that causality—father-son affiliation—is just another form of historical representation; history itself depends on conventions of narrative, language, and ideology,[19] which are presented as a divide between those who are able to stand aside from the conventional account of the past—Others—and those who are not. Bekmambetov presents a link between the two through the figure of Anton and his relations with his son, whose personal conflict also constitutes a generational conflict. The latter takes the form of a continuous battle between the Dark and Light forces, to which Bekmambetov gives a Freudian slant and Oedipal structure. The director demonstrates an unholy combination of filicide and cannibalism/vampirism as a divine patriarchal prerogative. Accordingly the films emphasize the role of paternity and the importance of the son as heir and perpetuator of the lineage. *Night/Day Watch* raises the questions of biological determinism and cultural potency: the films portray Anton as an impotent father, as someone incapable of fathering children and maintaining parental relations with them daily. In broad terms, the historical period of the 1990s is under the influence of Anton's generation and is defined as that of enervation, incapacity, and affliction. When Anton meets Svetlana in 2004 (*Day Watch*), after twelve years of sexual abstinence, his sexual desire normalizes, enabling reclamation of paternal potency. Eventually he reestablishes his parental authority (on the personal level) and reconstructs the social and cosmic order by maintaining the balance instituted by the truce. The latter signals the possibility of historical and cultural reconciliation and a national unity that charts the symbolic progression from paternity to patronage. To reiterate, this advancement becomes possible because Anton reconnects with the Soviet past through the figure of his adoptive father, Geser, and simultaneously establishes a link with the post-Soviet generation through his blood child, Egor, and, by so doing, determines the nation's future.

NOTES

1. Produced by Pervyi kanal, Kinokompaniia Tabbak, Bazelevs-Prodakshn; leading producers: Aleksei Kublitskii and Varvara Avdiushko; producers: Anatolii Maksimov and Konstantin Ernst; screenplay: Sergei Luk'ianenko and Timur Bekmambetov; photography: Sergei Trofimov; and music: Iurii Poteenko.

2. The exact date of production is unknown, possibly around 425 BC.

3. Here I analyze only the most striking similarities. Secondary themes and details of representation are not necessarily void of interest. For example, the name of Oedipus—swollen foot—suggests his unbridled sexuality (erect penis) and tracks its origin to his brutal parents. In the play, his name and the actual foot deformity are used as *evidence* in support of his origin. In *Night Watch*, the director has to provide convincing *evidence* for Anton as well: when the Night Watch intervenes, they file a report against Dar'ia that is later used against Anton to convince Egor of his father's murderous intentions. Ironically, the Night Watch appears in disguise—as a lioness and a bear (i.e., as wild animals that may have eaten Oedipus); and so forth.

4. Another example of parallelism between the film and the myth is the portrayal of the real mother and her function in the narrative. Jocasta is shown as a knowing mother: from the moment of her conspiracy with her husband till the final scene when, having momentarily realized that Oedipus is her son, she rushes out and later hangs herself by her hair, Jocasta is presented as an agent of her own destiny. In *Night Watch*, the director saves Egor's mother, Irina, from the ordeals of guilty

motherhood: she abandons her flat and the film's narrative altogether just before the father, Anton, arrives. His arrival precedes the crucial scene of recognition that changes the course of father-son relations: Anton notices a photograph of Irina and Egor and realizes that Egor is his son.

5. Gloom offers the experience of synaesthesia and the paradoxes of perception with the fallacy of sense and speech. Bekmambetov demonstrates the overdetermination of false sensory perception, and verbal error sets off the special nature of a knowledge that can be spoken only through the distorting mechanisms of language, the processes of condensation, displacement, splitting, and doubling that Freud studies intensively in his *Interpretation of Dreams*.

6. In the process of visualization the curse takes the form of a funnel—in Russian, *voronka*—which is a Freudian symbol relating to female desire and concepts of maternity. The funnel is made of ravens—in Russian, *vorona* or *voronka*—whereby the raven symbolizes an evil omen. Thus, in construction of visual paradigms, Bekmambetov utilizes the method of free associations. In psychoanalysis, this method is used to undermine authority. Therefore, if Anton is a model of self-divided, sublimating authority who is unable to properly emulate himself, then the director undermines his authority as the hero of civilization.

7. In the myth, having learned the whole truth, Oedipus rushes to Jocasta but finds her dead, so he takes the brooches from her dress and uses them to gouge his eyes. He thus attacks the eyes that are known for seeing through reality's confusion to the truth. Later he administers his own punishment: he exiles himself.

8. Anton participates in Egor's entry into the symbolic realm: the father spills his blood to save his son who has lost consciousness. In this way the director visualises the *blood* relation between these two characters.

9. To clarify, Irina, Ol'ga, and Svetlana are three mother figures similar to the female triad of the Oedipus complex: the woman he assumes to be his "real" mother, Merope; the unknown mother of his fears, with whom he is fated to commit incest; and Jocasta.

10. The women Egor assaults include Svetlana (i.e., his adoptive mother). Thus Bekmambetov reveals the dynamics of the Oedipus complex as Egor desires his mother and achieves his purpose symbolically through an act of vampirism.

11. In Lacan's view, the father introduces the principle of law, particularly the law of the language system. When this law breaks down or if it has never been acquired, as in Egor's case, then the subject may suffer from psychosis.

12. Ironically, his name suggests "ego" as a manifestation of his fixed identity.

13. *Day Watch* also explores the paradigm of the substitute mother. Alisa performs this function with regard to Kostia, the young vampire. She not only is his object of desire but is also a maternal figure. To achieve her goal, Alisa undergoes symbolic castration (she chops off one of her fingers) and thus is able to embrace his youth.

14. For vampires, blood is the equivalent of semen.

15. The fear of the vampire or, rather, the fear of becoming a vampire stems from a combination of love, hate, and guilt, which, according to Freud, results from a child's incestuous love for the mother and hatred for the father (Freud 1952, 1–18).

16. To reiterate, in the fictional world of *Night/Day Watch*, the bloodline exists only between Anton and Egor—between the perestroika and post-Soviet generation—

thus signifying a break from the Soviet culture that is eventually bridged by Anton's symbolic association with his adoptive father, Geser.

17. Ol'ga appears quite young for her generation, because she spent sixty years as an owl and, apparently, this slowed down the aging process.

18. The computer game shows a fight between two avatars who resemble Anton and Zavulon. The game precedes the actual fight, and thus Bekmambetov introduces the idea of predestination and reveals Zavulon's desire to kill Anton.

19. In her *A Poetics of Postmodernism,* Linda Hutcheon writes, "Historiographic metafiction [...] refuses the view that only history has a truth claim, both by questioning the ground of the claim in historiography and by asserting that both history and fiction are discourses, human constructs, signifying systems, and both derive their claim to truth from that identity" (93).

REFERENCES

Freud, Sigmund. *Introductory Lectures on Psychoanalysis.* Translated by W. J. H. Sprott. London: Hogarth, 1957.

———. *Totem and Taboo.* Translated by James Strachey. New York: W. W. Norton, 1952.

Hutcheon, Linda. *A Poetics of Postmodernism: History, Theory, Fiction.* New York: Routledge, 1988.

Lacan, Jacques. *Ecrits: A Selection.* Translated by Alan Sheridan with a foreword by Malcolm Bowie. New York: Routledge, 2001.

———. *The Seminars.* Edited by Jacques-Alain Miller. Translated and with notes by Dennis Porter. New York: W. W. Norton, 1992.

Sophocles. *Antigone, Oedipus, Electra.* Translated by H. D. F. Kitto. Edited by Edith Hall. New York: Oxford University Press, 1994.

FILMOGRAPHY

Dnevnoi dozor [Day Watch]. Dir. Timur Bekmambetov. Pervyi kanal, Kinokompaniia Tabbak, Bazelevs-Prodakshn, 2005.

Nochnoi dozor [Night Watch]. Dir. Timur Bekmambetov. Pervyi kanal, Kinokompaniia Tabbak, Bazelevs-Prodakshn, 2004.

Figure 8.1. *Oedipus solving the riddle.* Author unknown.

Figure 8.2. Geser and Zavulon watch Svetlana and Anton pass by
(*Day Watch*).

Figure 8.3. Kostia and his father attend to domestic chores (*Day Watch*).

Figure 8.4. Zavulon speaks to Alisa before the final ball (*Day Watch*).

NINE

Fathers, Sons, and Brothers: Redeeming Patriarchal Authority in *The Brigade*

BRIAN JAMES BAER

No one could or was allowed to attain the father's perfection of power, which was the thing they had all sought. Thus the bitter feeling against the father which had incited to the deed could subside in the course of time, while the longing for him grew, and an ideal could arise having as a content the fullness of power and the freedom from restriction of the conquered primal father, as well as the willingness to subject themselves to him. The original democratic equality of each member of the tribe could no longer be retained on account of the interference of cultural changes; in consequence of which there arose a tendency to revive the old father ideal in the creation of gods through the veneration of those individuals who had distinguished themselves above the rest.

SIGMUND FREUD, *TOTEM AND TABOO*

FATHERS OR BROTHERS

In *Totem and Taboo* Sigmund Freud offered a psychologized interpretation of the very origins of human society. After studying the myths and religious practices of "primitive" peoples, Freud reconstructed the foundation of human society in the narrative of an all-powerful primal father who restricts his sons' access to the tribe's women. Coming together as a "band of brothers," the sons murder the father and assume leadership of the tribe. However, they cannot simply replace the father/autocrat; as a collective they now represent a different mode of social organization, or governance. As Freud comments: "Though the brothers had joined forces in order to overcome the father, each was the other's rival among the women. Each one wanted to have them all to himself like the father, and in the fight of each against the other the new organization would have perished. For there was no longer any one stronger than all the rest who could have successfully assumed the role of the father" (917). While an individual son may aspire to the father's absolute power, this band of brothers was forced to share governance and therefore to forge a new concept of rule, marked, in Freud's phrase, by a "democratic equality" (921).

Political theorists, too, contrast fraternity and patriarchy as "two opposing political orders" (Anderson 1999, 86). As Benedict Anderson put it in *Imagined Communities,* traditional empires and kingdoms are organized vertically in relation to a "high center," and "its legitimacy derives from divinity, not from populations, who, after all, are subjects, not citizens" (19). On the other hand, the modern nation-state, regardless of its actual governmental structure, "is always conceived as a deep horizontal comradeship" (7). In other words, although many modern nation-states, such as those that describe themselves as "national socialist," are not organized on the basis of truly democratic institutions, they all imagine themselves through a rhetoric of equality and comradeship.

The tension between the horizontal bonds of brotherhood and the vertical ties of patriarchal authority has always been especially acute in Russian society. On the one hand, Russian nationalists since the early nineteenth century have attempted to define Russia's uniqueness in a natural fraternity, represented by, among other things, the peasant *mir,* or commune, and the Orthodox concept of *sobornost',* or shared leadership, a rejection of the supreme authority of the Holy Father in Rome. Though such "attempts to find in the 'Russian soul' an innate striving toward communality . . . may often represent little more than romantic flights from present reality," James Billington notes that the harshness of Russia's geography and climate made communal action a real "practical necessity" for much of Russia's history (1966, 19). On the other hand, Russian society—from the level of the peasant family to that of government rule—has been characterized for centuries by vertical partriarchal hierarchies in which absolute authority is centralized very often in a single male authority figure. The coexistence of these horizontal and vertical models of masculine authority reached a level of absurd incoherence during the Stalinist period, when the absolute authority of "Comrade Stalin" made a grotesque mockery of the Soviet rhetoric of equality among citizens in a classless society, and the Russian chauvinism of the Soviet state belied the official rhetoric of the brotherhood of Soviet peoples.

The collapse of the vertical authority of the Soviet system and its rhetoric of fraternity initiated a profound rethinking of the relationship between the vertical and horizontal bonds structuring Russian society, represented by fathers and sons, and bands of brothers, respectively. Although that foreign import, democracy, promised to invigorate and strengthen fraternity, privatization produced a generation of powerful capitalists—the oligarchs—who came to represent a new vertical hierarchy based on the accumulation of capital. Moreover, the erratic behavior and buffoonery of post-Soviet Russia's first president, Boris Yelstin, inspired in many Russians nostalgia for the strong and sober patriarchs of old. By the end of the 1990s the democratic rhetoric of fraternal equality, now associated with social chaos and economic hardship, seemed to many Russians no less hollow than the now defunct Soviet rhetoric of comradeship.

Within this context the Russian mini-series *The Brigade* (*Brigada*) burst onto the Russian cultural scene. The enormously popular Russian television series, which ran from 2002 to 2004 and was directed by Aleksei Sidorov, traces the lives of four friends against the backdrop of the fall of the Soviet Union and the emergence of a chaotic democratic Russia, with particular attention paid to Sasha Belov (Sergei Bezrukov), a fatherless veteran of the Afghan War, who emerges as the de facto leader of the group. Narrative tension is created through the complex interweaving of the two mutually exclusive and traditionally Russian conceptions of political authority—that of the collective and that of the strong leader, with Sasha in the increasingly difficult situation of remaining true to his "brothers" while establishing his rightful claim to a patriarchal authority that he ultimately redeems. In reconciling the exercise of vertical authority with horizontal loyalties, the character of Sasha Belov suggests the possibility of there being a strong leader who is not a tyrant, a father who stays true to his brothers, a message that can easily be read as an apologia for the centralization of powers and the "verticalization of government" carried out by then Russian president Vladimir Putin.[1]

The series consciously aligns itself with the Putin era in two rather obvious ways. The subtitle of the series, *Once upon a Time in Russia,* which, of course, alludes to Sergio Leone's critically acclaimed gangster saga *Once upon a Time in America* (1984), creates some distance between the time the series was broadcast (2003–2004) and the historical period covered in the narrative (1989–2000).[2] In other words, it offers a Putin-era perspective on the immediate pre-Putin past. Second, the series represented a level of technical sophistication that also tacitly distinguished the period of production from the period of the action and, also through its subtitle, suggested a challenge to Western supremacy in the field. Broadcast on the Rossiia channel, *The Brigade* was shot on cinema-grade film and was the most expensive television series to date, with an average episode budget of $200,000, a cast of more than 100, and over 350 shooting locations.

THE RUSSIAN *SOPRANOS*

While the subtitle alludes to Leone's classic gangster film and many scenes make reference to Francis Ford Coppola's Godfather trilogy, particularly *The Godfather* (1972) and *The Godfather Part II* (1974), critics and viewers repeatedly describe *The Brigade* as the "Russian *Sopranos*," referring to the popular and acclaimed HBO series. True, both series deal with the personal and professional life of an organized crime boss, but from its very first episode *The Sopranos* presents the patriarchal values of the traditional Italian mafia family in crisis. The capo, Tony Soprano, self-conscious about his position and the authority he wields, experiences debilitating panic attacks, which eventually lead him to seek the help of a psychiatrist, a woman, no less—he chooses an Italian woman psychiatrist over a Jewish man. Tony, it turns out, is surrounded by a number of strong and demanding women, in addition to his psychiatrist, including his wife, his daughter, his sister, and, of course, his horrible castrating mother. His patriarchal authority is also challenged by his father's brother, who bears the (oxy)moronic name of Uncle Junior, underscoring his impossible predicament of being structurally positioned as both senior and junior to Tony, which echoes Tony's own psychological predicament as a son who has become a father (and capo) before feeling fully empowered to assume the role. That tension, never resolved, animates the series throughout its run.[3]

In *The Brigade,* by contrast, the crisis of masculine authority that is posed at the outset of the series is never interiorized by Sasha Belov. All the threats to Sasha's assumption of patriarchal power come from the outside. Sasha almost never doubts himself. That absolute confidence and lack of interiorization are reflected in his criminal sobriquet—Sania Belyi—which sounds like the name of a hero from a medieval Russian *bylina.* In other words, the crisis of masculinity in *The Brigade* is not presented in psychological terms, as in *The Sopranos,* but, rather, in absolute moral terms as a spiritual problem. Sasha's epic task is not so much to reestablish patriarchal power as to redeem it. Moreover, unlike Tony Soprano, Sasha is aware of the epic nature of the task before him; he has his eye on history. This is underscored in the second episode, when, hiding out from the police at a dacha outside Moscow, he reads a history of ancient Rome. And when he visits the dacha with his wife in episode 13, that history is still there, lying on the desk, just where Sasha left it. Sasha also takes to referring to his partners in crime as his *oprichniki,* the name for the separate estate of Janissaries created by Ivan the Terrible.

Furthermore, Sasha Belov's story is given a clearly allegorical dimension absent from *The Sopranos.* The great events in Sasha's personal life parallel—and symbolically represent—great events in the life of the Russian nation. For example, like the hero of Aleksei Balabanov's 1997 film, *Brother* [Brat], Sasha is twenty-one at the beginning of the series, on the very threshold of adulthood. Sasha marries during the coup attempt of 1991 and his son is born during the siege of the Russian Parliament building in 1993, conflating Sasha's personal or private life with the death of the Soviet Union and the troubled birth of a democratic Russia. The latter connection is further emphasized by the fact that Sasha's wife undergoes a very difficult labor. Finally, Sasha is elected to the State Duma in 2000, the same year Putin is elected president and, in the eyes of many Russians, begins the task of restoring order to Russian society (Figure 9.2).

ABSENT FATHERS AND MOTHER RUSSIA

In the opening episode of *The Brigade* Sasha, who is fatherless—his father died when he was very young and he "almost doesn't remember him"—appears as a soldier in Afghanistan. The loss of the war in Afghanistan, of course, exposed the weaknesses of the Soviet military and spelled the beginning of the end of Soviet power. When Sasha returns to civilian life, he finds that his girlfriend, Lena (Elena Panova), to whom he had remained true, has become a prostitute, and the Russian society that he knew when he went to war has changed for the worse. Sasha beats up his girlfriend's pimp, Mukha (Sergei Aprel'skii), in hand to hand combat, after which Mukha is murdered and Sasha is framed for the crime; he must now seek protection outside the law. As his friend Kosmos remarks, "Someone out there clearly doesn't like you."

Sasha's "descent" into criminality, therefore, does not betray an inner corruption or the presence of negative qualities such as greed and ambition. Although he works outside the law, Sasha's virtues are repeatedly praised throughout the series by a host of different characters. In the first episode his mother states: "Sasha was always so just [*takoi spravedlivyi*]." His wife, a concert violinist, describes her husband during his election campaign as "the most hard-working person" she knows. And an official police report gives the following assessment of Sasha's character: "Extraordinary willpower. Emotionally stable. Motivated as a leader." Nonetheless Sasha feels guilty about his criminal past and at one point vows to his wife that their son will not end up like him—he'll be a human being [*chelovek*]. Olga (Ekaterina Guseva) offers him absolution, telling him, "You've got to stop blaming yourself."

Sasha is innocent to the extent that he is forced to go outside the law by the corruption and failure of Russia's "fathers" and the disloyalty of Russia's women, and to seek protection and opportunity within a criminal brotherhood, or *bratstvo,* organized around a traditional masculine code of honor. The corruption of specifically masculine ideals of honor and justice is suggested when crooked government officials use a video of the film *Rambo: First Blood* (1982) to transfer bribe money. The film, which portrays the heroic and violent stand of one man against the unjust treatment of Vietnam War veterans, is a favorite of Afghan War vet Sasha and his band of brothers.

The references to Rambo are in fact crucial in establishing the moral parameters of Sasha's world. Whereas the mafia films discussed above trade in the profound moral ambiguity of a *pater familias* who is also a cold-blooded murderer, *Rambo. First Blood* offers a narrative that attenuates Rambo's guilt, painting a moral universe in the stark black-

and-white colors of melodrama. When the film opens, Rambo (Sylvester Stallone) is walking down a country road in an idyllic American landscape outside the town of Hope: mountains rise up in the background, and a lake, glistening in the sun, opens up before him. A Vietnam War veteran, John Rambo, took part in what Susan Faludi refers to as "the central masculine crisis of his generation" (296). Now a civilian, he is looking for one of his war buddies, Delmar Barry, the only other one of their tight-knit group of friends to survive the war. That Delmar is black underscores the utopian nature of this brotherhood—it transcends race. However, Rambo discovers from Delmar's embittered wife, who now lives in a run-down shack, that his buddy has died from cancer caused by Agent Orange, the first indication of the film's central theme that these American heroes have been betrayed by their own country—not by any weakness in themselves. Dejected, Rambo walks toward the local town where the sheriff, Wilfred Teasle (Brian Dennehy), begins to harass him as a vagrant, chasing him out of town. When Rambo returns, looking for some place to eat, the sheriff arrests him. In the town's jail, he is continuously insulted and brutally treated by the police officers, which he endures in silence. But eventually Rambo snaps when he has a flashback to the brutal treatment he received at the hands of the North Vietnamese. He overpowers several policemen, forcing his way out of the jailhouse, and now, clothed in buckskin, he takes refuge in the forest.

While pursuing Rambo, the sheriff learns that this dirty vagabond is, in fact, a former green beret who was a recipient of the Congressional Medal of Honor for his service in Vietnam. His former commanding officer, Colonel Sam Trautman (Richard Crenna), explains to the sheriff that he's lucky Rambo killed only one of the policemen who chased him in the woods: he could have killed them all. At the end of the film, he spares the sheriff's life. Rambo's exercise of restraint in the face of humiliating injustice is crucial to attenuating his guilt as is the fact that he was provoked: "They drew first blood," he tells Trautman. And when a sadistic police officer falls out of a helicopter as he tries—against orders—to shoot Rambo, Rambo cries out: "It's not my fault." If Rambo is presented as a victim of unprovoked hostility, a kind of "warrior-saint" (Faludi 364), the sheriff is presented as an archetypal villain. He becomes obsessed with capturing Rambo, abandoning any professional objectivity and putting his men in unnecessary danger. Moreover, the film presents this melodramatic confrontation of good and evil, innocence and corruption, in generational terms—Rambo is continually referred to both by the sheriff and by Colonel Trautman as "boy" and "kid"—making this a story of betrayal of heroic sons by corrupted (Teasle) or absent (Trautman) fathers.[4]

The moral logic of *The Brigade* derives clearly from *Rambo. First Blood,* not from the gangster film. Sasha Belov, in part by virtue of his moral character and in part thanks to the narrative itself, is able to preserve, largely untainted, his basic moral values and his absolute loyalty to his friends, his family, and his country. At the same time the series makes clear that it is not Russia that has betrayed Sasha, but rather, as Kosmos puts it, "someone" with a personal vendetta against him.[5] That "someone" turns out to be Vladimir Evgenievich Kaverin, or Volodia (Andrei Panin), a corrupt police officer who becomes a government operative and Sasha's arch-nemesis, pursuing him through every episode until finally Sasha defeats him—fair and square—in elections to a seat in the Russian Duma.[6] Volodia is the one who plants the gun used to kill Mukha on Sasha to frame him for the murder, forcing Sasha into the criminal underworld. Like Teasle in *Rambo. First Blood,* Kaverin is obsessed with revenge and prepared to do anything to exact it.[7] His moral corruption is manifested physically in the prosthesis that replaces the hand he lost in Chechnya, fighting as a mercenary for the "other side." After losing the election to Sasha, Kaverin removes the glove covering his mechanical steel hand and makes a fist as he contemplates his revenge, resembling a villain from a James Bond film. The rather surprising "moral clarity" of this gangster series suggests we are in the presence of a "melodramatic masculinity" as described by Susan Larsen in her analysis of post-Soviet depictions of the Stalinist past (89). But whereas the films Larsen analyzes tend to "identify heroic Russian masculinity as the principal victim of Stalinist evil" (89), *The Brigade* identifies the major threat to heroic Russian masculinity in the moral chaos and rampant materialism of post-Soviet culture itself. And so, to redeem Russian masculinity, Sasha Belov as hero must make his way through the spiritual wasteland of post-Soviet culture uncorrupted.

The brotherhood, or *bratstvo,* that Sasha forms with his three closest childhood friends—Kosmos (Dmitrii Diuzhev), Pchela (Pavel Markov), and Fil (Vladimir Vdovichenkov)—is a reaction to the disloyalty he encounters on all sides in late-perestroika Russia. Modeled in many ways on Sasha's experience in the military, this *bratstvo*, like Rambo's, is marked by the total loyalty of the brothers to one another. For example, Farkhad (Farkhad Makhmudov), a Tadjik who served in the army with Sasha, ends up in a competing criminal gang, but the strong bond he and Sasha forged in Afghanistan prompt them to form a criminal alliance. In fact, Sasha often questions would-be associates on their service in Afghanistan: "Where did you serve? What colonel did you serve under?" ["Gde ty sluzhil? Ty pod kakim polkovnikom sluzhil?"]—which may in fact be a direct reference to Rambo's Colonel Trautman. Those who pass the test and prove that they had indeed served, earn the epithet *"brat"* and a place in Sasha's alternative masculine collective. Sasha's respect for his fellow soldiers suggests that the war was lost not by the soldiers who served but rather by the older generation of military and political leaders owing to their incompetence and corruption, echoing Rambo's anguished cry: "I did what I had to do to win. But somebody didn't let us win."

Unlike Rambo, however, who never mentions his country, Sasha shows unwavering loyalty not only to his brothers but also, and perhaps more importantly, to Mother Russia. Two decisions in particular reflect Sasha's uncorrupted sense of right and his loyalty to his homeland above all else: his refusal to sell drugs inside Russia or weapons to Chechen rebels. Sasha's allegiance to Mother Russia is further underscored when he allows his firstborn son to be baptized in a Russian Orthodox Church, and when he establishes a Restoration Fund (Fond Restavratsii) to restore old buildings and churches. On the level of metonymy, Sasha preserves the honor of Mother Russia when he intervenes as his henchmen threaten to sexually assault the blond Russian secretary of the Jewish businessman Artur Veniaminovich Lapshin, protecting her from violation.

The issue of selling drugs harks back to *The Godfather II,* in which Michael Corleone must decide whether to modernize the "family business" by taking it into the drug trade. The risk, his advisers warn, is that the sale of drugs will necessitate contact with the dregs of the criminal underworld and that the availability of drugs will have a corrupting influence on the organization. Sasha Belov faces a different problem. It is not *whether* to sell drugs but *where.* Sasha makes the decision—against the urging of his greedy "brothers"—never to sell drugs inside Russia. At the same time Sasha's own refusal to use drugs distinguishes him from his Tadjik friend Farkhad, on the one hand, and from his friend and brother Kosmos, on the other. When Farkhad offers Sasha cocaine and Sasha refuses, Farkhad comments: "That means I'm stupid and you're a genius." The outcome of the series would seem to support Farkhad's assessment.[8]

Sasha's unquestioned loyalty to Mother Russia will eventually destroy his friendship with Farkhad when the Tadjik gangster's elders ask him to betray the agreement he has made with his "brother" not to sell drugs in Russia. Farkhad initially resists but ultimately understands that he cannot go against the wishes of his elders. Farkhad is, nevertheless, allowed to travel to Moscow to speak with Sasha in the hope of reaching some kind of compromise, but Sasha remains firm. While gang warfare looms, Sasha is conveniently relieved of the task of killing his Tadjik "brother" when a third criminal group murders Farkhad. This is the first of several times when the series relies on a deus ex machina to obviate the need for Sasha to descend into some moral gray area, in this case, having to dispose of one of his brothers.[9]

The incident with Farkhad drives home the distinctly nationalist coloration of Sasha's *bratstvo*, defined by unwavering loyalty to Mother Russia. Farkhad's ethnicity is made meaningful in two ways. First, unlike Sasha, who has a strong love for his *Rodina* (Motherland), Farkhad never expresses any attachment to his country. His loyalty is to his clan. Second, the series characterizes his traditional Tadjik culture as an uncompromising patriarchal authority that refuses to recognize Farkhad's brotherly obligations to Sasha, whom he calls his "blood brother."[10] Farkhad's absolute allegiance to his elders forces him to betray his agreement with his wartime brother. In contrast, Sasha owes nothing to his superiors, who are for the most part physically destroyed or morally corrupted or both.

Sasha's brotherhood is defined against two contrasting social categories: the traditional patriarchy of Farkhad's clan, on the one hand, and, on the other, modern, self-sufficient masculinity, represented in the series by another non-Russian, the Jewish businessman Artur Veniaminovich. Whereas Farkhad demonstrates great dignity and courage, Artur Veniaminovich is one of the series' most negatively portrayed characters. An emotional and despotic boss, he lacks a family and visible roots, and, moreover, is variously associated with the West. For instance, the large mug in which he is served his tea features his face above the words "Big Boss" written in English letters. In fact, when Sasha and his band take over his company, Artur Veniaminovich not only flees to "filthy America" [pogannaia Amerika], as Sasha's puts it, but also before boarding the plane curses Russia: "Poshel ty v zhopu s tvoei voniuchei rodinoi!" ["You can stick your lousy homeland up your ass!"].[11]

In a nice structural symmetry, Artur Veniaminovich is a middleman in the trade of Tadjik aluminum, and his insistence that his assistant make the contract with the Tadjiks as tough as possible reveals his heartless approach to business. Moreover, in sharp contrast to Sasha and his brothers, Artur Veniaminovich is chubby, sweaty, and often hysterical. Moreover, he is shown repeatedly wearing a bright red blazer in marked contrast to the predominantly black attire of Sasha and his men, thus associating him with the new Russians of the Yeltsin era, while the men of the brigade would seem to foreshadow the more restrained tastes of the Putin-era businessman. At one point, in an attempt to avoid Sasha and his henchmen, he locks himself in his office bathroom, sits on the floor and gets drunk, all the while mumbling incoherently. This negative portrayal, which marshals a number of traditional anti-Semitic tropes, works to counter any pity Russian viewers might feel for him when Sasha and his gang take over—without provocation—the company he has built over many years to use it as a front for their criminal activities. Furthermore, Artur Veniaminovich's Russian secretary remains at the company after he is forced out and becomes a loyal supporter of Sasha and his gang. In fact, Kosmos proposes marriage to her just before he is murdered.

Defined against traditional vertical patriarchy, represented by Farkhad and his clan, and against modern (Western?) masculinity, represented by the successful New Russian businessman Artur Veniaminovich, Sasha's Russian brotherhood appears as a kind of golden mean. A communal male organization, it is less restrictive than traditional patriarchy, which demands total loyalty to one's elders, and also less selfish than modern masculine identity, which demands loyalty to nothing outside oneself.[12] The portrayal of the two non-Russians, Farkhad and Artur Veniaminovich, outlines a symbolic geography, in which Russia is situated between the less economically developed but resource-rich Tadjiks and the more economically successful but exploitative West.[13] In the final episode of the series, after Sasha has faked his own death, the despicable Kaverin and Artur Veniaminovich, now business partners, are touring an enormous mall they are building. With Artur Veniaminovich beaming at his side, Kaverin declares with a hint of sarcasm: "We have given our people the happiness of consumption. More money, more goods, a happier, more beautiful life" ["My podarili narodu schast'e potrebleniia. Bol'she deneg, bol'she tovarov, bol'she schastlivoi, krasivoi zhizni"], thus placing the series's two most unattractive characters firmly on the side of Western consumer culture.

LONGING FOR PATRIARCHY

Brotherhood or fraternity as a solution to the collapse of patriarchal authority, however, eventually presents problems for the group. In other words, it becomes evident that this alternative structure is not a permanent solution to the collapse of patriarchal authority. Like Sasha's sojourn through the wilderness of criminality, brotherhood appears a necessary transition from patriarchy corrupted to patriarchy redeemed, but only a transition.

Perhaps the most fundamental problem with brotherhood as a political or organizational structure is that it presumes a certain degree of democracy or shared rule, of which, of course, there is little or no tradition in Russia. Sasha expresses his own ambivalence toward the concept when, returning from a business trip to Miami, he is met at the airport by Kosmos and Fil, two of his closest brothers, who present him with a glass of champagne. Yeltsin's siege of the White House is under way and Fil raises his glass "to the victory of democracy" ["za pobedu demokratii"], to which Sasha replies, "What are you doing?" ["Nu, ty chto?"]. It is unclear whether Sasha is questioning the siege as a "victory" or as having anything to do with "democracy." In any case, he refuses to toast.

The series presents two fundamental problems with fraternal governance. The first is competition among the brothers for more control. As Fil puts it in the eleventh episode: "Everyone wants to be the boss" ["Vse khotiat byt'nachal'nikom"]. However, not all the brothers are portrayed as equally responsible and equally equipped to share leadership. For example, Kosmos develops a serious drug addiction, and Pchela sells arms to Chechen rebels against Sasha's orders and, in general, seeks greater "independence from Sasha Belov" ["nezavisimost' ot Sashy Belova"]; and Fil is often presented as someone of limited intelligence. As Sasha's brothers begin to misbehave and become themselves corrupted, the need for a strong, responsible leader becomes more obvious, and the increasing disarray within the brigade reflects the chaos of Russian society (Figure 9.2).

The second problem with fraternal governance involves succession. How does a *bratstvo* continue into the next generation? Sasha's destiny to assume leadership is underscored by the fact that he is the first one in the group to marry and to father a male child. This change in status makes Sasha a complex figure—he is now both brother and father—and guarantees a line of (masculine) succession. When Sasha refuses to toast to the victory of democracy in Russia, Kosmos jumps in with an alternative toast: "Let's drink instead to your future son" ["Luchshe pit' za tvoego budushchego syna"], to which Sasha replies: "God forbid it's a girl" ["Ne dai bog esli doch'"]. But Sasha is lucky—something repeatedly pointed out in the series—and his first child is a son, which leads Sasha back to the Orthodox Church. In fact, when he receives news of his son's birth, he crosses himself, and he later agrees to have his son baptized. The baptism of little Van'ka is another of many references to Coppola's *Godfather* films. It is also an opportunity for Sasha to assert his role as father. When, after the service, his friend Fil says, "Now I'm a father," Sasha immediately sets him straight: "No, you're the godfather. I'm the father." In a nod to a classic mafia film motif, Olga resists having her son brought up like his father, but when she hears Sasha is running for political office she drops all those concerns and begins to flirt with her estranged husband with the goal of winning him back.

And while Sasha's son represents a kind of temporal bridge between Russia's chaotic present and a more stable—and legitimate—future, Sasha's increasing involvement with cultural restoration projects, and, in particular, the restoration of churches, underscores his concern for healing Russia's troubled relationship with its own past. In fact, the poster for Sasha's political campaign features Sasha with his son in his lap and a Russian Orthodox church in the background. The slogan reads:

"Our future is in our hands." Of course, that Sasha's son is in the poster with him produces a certain ambiguity of reference. Is the possessive pronoun a democratic gesture, referring to the Russian people, or is it a patriarchal boast: the future is in the hands of Sasha and his heir.

Intertwined with this intensifying critique of brotherhood as a solution to the collapse of patriarchal authority is the expression—mostly on Sasha's part—of a profound nostalgia for that authority. Like the hero of the popular film *Brat,* Sasha is at the very threshold of manhood and plans to pursue a conventional career path: he wants to enter the geological institute, motivated, he says, by a love of volcanoes, a not so subtle symbol of the virility for which Sasha will find no legal outlet in late-perestroika Russia. Later, in the second episode, he buys a dog, a mastiff, whom he names Volcano. And while still in the breeder's home, Sasha notices an enormous portrait of another mastiff, whom Sasha takes to be Volcano's father. He holds the dog up to the portrait and coos: "Your dad's got authority. A cool dad" ["Tvoi papa avtoritetnyi. Krutoi papa"].[14] Fil seems to share this nostalgic desire for a strong authoritarian father figure. When working as an extra in a film about World War II, Fil plays the part of a German soldier. During a break in shooting, he comments, "There's chaos everywhere" ["Vezde bardak"], and then picks up a copy of Hitler's *Mein Kampf* that he is in the middle of reading. The scene intimates that the lack of order in Russian society may give rise to a dictator.

The dog breeder will turn out to be a spiritual mentor for Sasha, teaching him martial arts and, through that, Eastern religious concepts of self-discipline and transcendence. In general, Sasha displays great respect for his male elders, despite the fact that he is continually betrayed by them, confirming once again Sasha's concern for succession: he seems to understand at some level that he must preserve and protect the structural position of the father in order eventually to assume the position for himself. In other words, he respects the "office" of father. One of his role models is Viktor Petrovich, "a highly placed government official who is teaching Sasha to play tennis." A good student, Sasha remarks that he will become a fine player if he continues to play with Viktor Petrovich. And while Sasha acquires an appreciation for the trappings of an upper-class lifestyle from him, he never loses his ability to connect with the "common people."

REDEEMING PATRIARCHY

Ultimately the series shows Sasha's rise to power not as a restoration but as a redemption of patriarchal authority. This is accomplished in two ways: first, Sasha's criminality is portrayed as an inevitable consequence of the corruption of Russian society; and second, he manages to resist being corrupted by his time spent in the criminal underworld. Presenting Sasha as the victim of historical circumstances attenuates his personal responsibility for his criminal activities, if not absolving him of that responsibility. In fact, the fourth episode presents that very line of reasoning when Sasha sings one of his favorite childhood songs: "I was born in a godforsaken place, I'm not guilty of anything, not guilty of anything . . . And I'm your brother, I'm a human being" ["Ia ni v chem, ni v chem ne vinovat . . . A ia vash brat, ia chelovek"]. In the following scene, he explains to his wife: "I don't do evil. I just live" ["Ia ne delaiu zla, ia zhivu"]. Later, toward the end of the series, during his political campaign, he again invokes the chaos of Russian society to justify his actions: "If the state is corrupt, and if it can't meet its responsibilities, then ultimately there'll be chaos in the country. And so I, as a candidate, consider it my primary duty to stop this chaos" ["Esli vlast' prodazhna, esli ona ne mozhet otvechat' za svoi slova, to v kontse kontsov v strane nachinaetsia khaos. Tak vot ia, kak kandidat, schitaiu svoei osnovnoi zadachei etot khaos prekratit'"].

What enables Sasha to redeem patriarchal authority is not only the presentation of his criminal activities as justified by the state of post-Soviet society but also Sasha's resistance to irrevocable corruption during his time spent in the criminal underworld. In fact, although Sasha is guilt-ridden over his criminal activities and always strives to "go legal," we rarely see him commit any horrible acts or even fire his gun. In the initial episode he fights the pimp Mukha in hand-to-hand combat before being shot. Although bloody and almost unconscious, he vows loyalty to his friends. Toward the end of the series, during a television debate with his political—and moral—opponent, Volodia, he speaks out of turn, explaining that although he may have been forced to act outside the law, "everybody says that I have always kept my promise. I never acted unjustly and I always answered for my words" ["[Ia] nikogda ne

postupal protiv spravedlivosti i vsegda otvechal za svoi slova"]. When
he concludes, the audience and the moderator of the debate break into
enthusiastic and extended applause. After winning the election, Sasha
savors his victory, shooting flares into the night sky; Olga comes out and
he says to her: "Guess this riddle: whether winter or summer, it's the very
same color." "I know, I know," she responds, "It's Sasha Belyi." As he implies with this riddle, he has not changed, and, as his surname suggests
(Belyi means "white"), he has not been corrupted.[15] Sasha appears as the
male counterpart of Sonia in Dostoevsky's *Crime and Punishment:* he
is a gangster with a heart of gold. Sergei Bezrukov, the actor who played
Sasha Belov in the series, compared his character to Robin Hood.

Sasha's stint in the criminal underworld has not corrupted him; in
fact, it has taught him a number of important spiritual lessons. The first
is that of humility. He must learn to exercise his growing power not for
selfish reasons but for the good of others and of society as a whole. This
spiritual challenge is narrativized throughout the series in a number
of ways. For example, Sasha never expresses ambition. He never gives
voice to a desire for more money or power for himself. Sasha is the only
husband and father in the group throughout much of the series—Fil
will later marry and have children, but his family plays only a small role
in the series—and seems to be motivated chiefly by a desire to provide
a better life for his wife and son. Moreover, the immediate impetus for
Sasha to assume power is that his mafia brothers seem incapable of the
selfless discipline necessary to bring order to the organization and to
Russian society. As discussed above, Sasha refuses to betray Russia for
personal gain. When he is finally forced to send arms to Chechnya, he
arranges to have the shipment blown up upon arrival, and though Pchela
is infuriated by the enormous loss of money, Sasha is jubilant. He willingly sacrifices profits to save Russian lives (Figure 9.3).

To underscore Sasha's selflessness, the writers of the series go to
great lengths to present his rise to power as inevitable, less a question of
personal ambition than of fate. For example, when he forces Artur Veniaminovich to play backgammon with him and keeps winning, after he
exacts the concessions he wanted out of Artur, he tosses the dice onto his
desk and rolls double sixes. Ostensible coincidence also seems to confirm
Sasha's destiny to lead. For instance, before meeting his future wife, Olga,
Sasha finds her telephone number and calls her. When he finishes recit-

ing Alexander Pushkin's poem "Ia pomniu chudnoe mgnovenie," Olga asks his name: "Is it Alexander?" she jokes. Of course, it is. Subsequently he inscribes himself in the tradition of other such historic Alexanders as Alexander Nevsky, Alexander the Great, and the tsars Alexander I, II, and III. When Sasha is forced to go underground to evade the law, Kosmos draws a parallel between Sasha's fate and that of Vladimir Il'ich Lenin, who spent years underground before becoming the leader of the Soviet state. Later, when Sasha is forced to leave Moscow, he spends time in the Urals, another parallel with Lenin's biography, foreshadowing his eventual—and inevitable—rise to "legitimate" power. It is no coincidence, then, that when Farkhad gives Sasha a horse, Sasha names it "Znak sud'by" ["Sign of Fate"], and gallops on it bareback through the fields.

Closely related to the role of fate in Sasha's rise to power is the concept of charisma. Sasha's natural ability to relate to others makes him a born leader. For example, when he goes to pick up his dog, Volcano, at the breeder's, someone else has already claimed him. The breeder—subsequently Sasha's spiritual guide—decides to let the dog choose his own master. He chooses Sasha. The treatment of animals, in fact, plays an important role in indexing the spiritual state of the various characters.[16] For example, in episode 8, while Sasha is estranged from his wife Olia, someone gives him a bird in a cage as a gift. Sasha declares: "I feel sorry for the bird . . . Let's let it go" ["Mne zhalko ptichku . . . Dai otpustim"]. And they release it. While this scene clearly suggests a metaphor to describe Sasha's predicament—his criminal lifestyle is like a golden cage— it also demonstrates Sasha's ability to empathize with the weak and helpless. Kosmos, on the other hand, in his descent into cocaine addiction, takes out a gun and shoots at a stray kitten, shouting, "I'm going to wipe creatures like you off the face of the earth" ["Ia osvobozhdaiu mir ot takikh tvorei kak ty"]. Later Volodia, now thoroughly corrupted and consumed by thoughts of vengeance, runs against Sasha for a seat in the Duma. He receives a stuffed alligator as a gift and, thoroughly satisfied with himself, puts his feet up on his desk, next to the alligator, revealing that he is wearing alligator shoes.

Although Sasha appears to be driven by fate rather than personal ambition, the great temptation that confronts him—and anyone who rises above the collective—is the sin of pride. For example, when Sasha asks his nemesis, Volodia, why he framed him for the murder of Mukha,

Volodia explains, "Because you're a pushy [*naglyi*] son of a bitch who thinks he's the smartest guy and who doesn't care about anyone." In this case the charge carries little weight, coming as it does from the corrupt and emotionally damaged Volodia. Sasha simply retorts: "No, Volodia, it's you who's the son of a bitch. Now I understand why they sacked you from the police force." The accusation, however, does hit home in a scene from the eighth episode, when Sasha, who has now become the group's de facto leader, tells Fil: "Listen to your daddy" ["Poslushai papu"]. This comment enrages Fil, who then strikes Sasha in the face and tells him: "Ever since you've risen higher, your head has become full of shit." Contrary to all the conventions of the gangster genre and, for that matter, to traditional masculine codes of honor, Sasha does not strike Fil back. In a display of spiritual maturity and humility [*smirenie*], he simply wipes the blood from his lower lip and asks forgiveness: "Okay, brother. Forgive me. I was wrong" ["Ladno, brat. Prosti. Ia byl ne prav"].

Despite his new-found wealth, power, and the trappings of an upper-class lifestyle, Sasha does not allow himself to acquire an inflated sense of his own superiority. This is demonstrated in the thirteenth episode when Sasha encounters the police officer who discovered him hiding out in a dacha in episode 2. An honest man, he refused the money that Sasha's group offered him and, after losing his job because of the incident, was forced to live on bread and water. He eventually goes to Serbia to fight, to which Sasha exclaims: "You're kidding? For which side?" "For our side," the officer responds, underscoring the fact that although the two men may be on opposite sides of the law, they, too, are brothers, sharing a loyalty to their country and to their country's Orthodox allies. In any case, the officer harbors no resentment against Sasha, and the two go for a ride together, drink vodka, and sing songs. Sasha then asks the officer for forgiveness: "Sorry, brother. Because of me your life is ruined. Forgive me." And later, when Sasha departs, he tells the officer: "I'm sorry your life is ruined. Call me any time."

Another aspect of pride that Sasha must overcome is the desire to be wholly self-sufficient, to rely on no one outside oneself. For example, when he is at his lowest point emotionally, living away from his wife and son, he spends time in a casino and gets very drunk. The next day he says to his lover, Ania, "It sucks to depend on someone, right, An'? I'm ashamed," to which Ania responds, "You always depend on someone."

Later, when Viktor Petrovich scolds Sasha for having destroyed the shipment of arms to Chechnya, calling him a "pushy guy [*naglets*]," Sasha's response, "You always depend on someone," demonstrates that he has fully interiorized the spiritual lesson Ania imparted. Furthermore, when Fil is shot and lying in a coma, Sasha goes to Viktor Petrovich for help. To Viktor Petrovich's question, "Is there anything you need from me?" Sasha replies, "Moral support" ["Moral'naia podderzhka"]. He has learned to ask for help. Along the same lines, when he breaks off his affair with Ania, he reconciles with his wife, telling her: "I can't live without you" ["Zhit' bez tebia ne mogu'] (Figure 9.4).

In fact, Sasha increasingly trades in spiritual and emotional truths. For example, when Kosmos is suffering from a full-blown addiction to cocaine, Sasha tells him that he will get him out of it. Kosmos queries: "Literally?" And Sasha responds: "Morally" ["Moral'no"]. Similarly, when doctors recommend that Fil, lying in a coma, be allowed to die, Sasha declares, "We'll pray to God that Fil will come to and he'll come to." Later, when his belongings, including his Orthodox cross, are stolen, Sasha fearlessly confronts the police officer responsible for the raid and demands the return of his "cross." "What kind of cross," the officer asks. "An Orthodox cross [*provoslavnyi*]," Sasha explains. At this point the camera shoots a close up of an icon on the police officer's wall and then moves back to Sasha, who walks out of the office with his cross in hand.

The religious references only increase as the series progresses. During Sasha's political campaign, for instance, Viktor Evgenievich tries to smear him, bringing up his criminal past and going so far as to bring Artur Veniaminovich back from America. He even has a poster made that portrays Sasha as a criminal. As a sign of his spiritual and emotional discipline, Sasha calmly hangs the poster on the wall of his office above a quotation from the New Testament, "Speak tersely. Ask little. Leave quickly" (I Peter). In a television advertisement, an average Russian explains why he supports Sasha: "He's a good man. He helps people. He builds churches." Kosmos later describes Sasha as an innocent victim of a government smear campaign: "Formally, they're clean and you're the sacrificial lamb. If you become a politician, their plan fails." And when Sasha is shot, Fil carries him in his arms, telling him: "Bear it. Bear it. God bore it, too" ["Terpi. Terpi. Bog terpel tozhe"]. The religious or spiritual significance of this suffering is brought out later in the series when Sasha is lying in bed with his wife and she is shown fingering the scar from the bullet wound.

FROM HERO TO TOTEM

An everyman, Sasha Belov's story up until episode fourteen is a kind of fairy tale, as suggested by his sobriquet Sania Belyi. As a fairy-tale hero, Sasha endures a series of moral tests as he makes his way through the spiritual desert of post-Soviet Russia. Having retained a certain purity of soul, he is given the mantle of legitimate leader when he is elected to the State Duma. Wielding patriarchal power with justice while remaining loyal to his brothers, Sasha represents the ideal union of father and brother, embodying a resolution to the conflict in Russian culture between repressive vertical authority and the horizontal bonds of fraternity.

It is no coincidence, perhaps, that this fairy tale ending coincides with the election of Vladimir Putin as president of Russia. Although Putin is never mentioned by name in the series, the parallels between Sasha Belov and the Russian president are difficult to ignore. Both men study martial arts and are characterized by personal discipline. Sasha's time as a criminal boss parallels Putin's time in the Soviet KGB, and both men were elected to the Russian government in the national elections of 2000. And, of course, there is the obvious physical similarity: both men are of modest height. Moreover, the increasing popularity among Russian politicians of words and phrases from the camp/criminal jargon makes this parallel all the more plausible.[17] So, despite critiques from government officials that the series glamorizes criminality and lawlessness, the narrative of *The Brigade*, which traces the restoration and redemption of patriarchal authority in the most positive terms, may easily be read as offering tacit support for the consolidation of presidential power in the "authoritarian democracy" of Vladimir Putin. Indeed, although Sasha is elected in a democratic process, he vows rather ominously to his future constituents to "do everything to stop the chaos."

However, the series does not end with the fourteenth episode and, in typical Russian fashion, it eschews a happy ending. In episode 15, Sasha decides he must avenge the murder of his brothers. He does so execution-style, becoming a sort of killing machine or avenging angel.[18] This ending abruptly interrupts the fairy-tale narrative that features Sasha as an idealized hero, a conciliatory figure, uniting paternal power and fraternal loyalty. Sasha now becomes a profoundly ambivalent figure, akin to the totem described in Freud's myth of society's origins, which serves as a ritual substitute for the all-powerful primal father. That its ritual sacrifice incites both celebration and mourning attests, Freud argues, to the deeply contradictory emotions we hold for the primal father and his absolute power (915).

In executing those who killed his brothers, Sasha assumes absolute authority, the power over life and death, which once belonged to the primal father. However, the path of vengeance, the series makes clear, is also a path of self-sacrifice, for in following this path Sasha gives up everything he worked his entire adult life to obtain. He sends his wife and son off to America and abandons any hope of a legitimate career. He is utterly alone at the end. Clearly, by taking the law into his own hands in this way, Sasha is also submitting to the law, that is, to the code of masculine honor which demands that he avenge the murder of his brothers. This makes him a representation, in Freudian terms, not of the primal father himself but of the totem, for he embodies both the desire for the father's power and guilt over seizing it. And whereas the conciliatory figure of Sasha as deputy offers a narrative of historical resolution, which might have served as an apologia for Putin's authoritarian democracy, the figure of Sasha as totem—that is, both sacrificial lamb and avenging angel—presents a far more ambivalent commentary on the future of absolute authority. That Viktor Petrovich and Igor'Leonidovich, the highly placed government officials who act as puppet masters throughout the series, survive suggests that Sasha's execution of Kaverin and Lapshin has not fundamentally altered the nature of absolute power in Russia. It simply promises further bloodshed between fathers and sons, inscribing contemporary Russian history within the timeless complexes of the human psyche while offering Russian viewers the opportunity to celebrate/mourn their president's inexorable consolidation of political power.

NOTES

1. *"Vertikal' vlasti"* is a term used to designate the top-down nature of government (Visson 2006, 18).

2. Leone's film is, in fact, noted for the use of flashbacks, which create a complex multiple frame. The plot moves along three different, historically charged temporal

planes: 1921, representing the period of postwar prosperity; 1933, in the midst of the Great Depression; and 1968, a year marked by enormous social and political unrest. This film, as the title suggests, has rather lofty pretensions, narrating not only the lives of four gangster friends, but the history of twentieth-century America.

3. Another significant difference vis-à-vis *The Sopranos* is that women in *The Brigade* play only a very small role, and their psychology is often simplistic or underdeveloped. In fact, it is a mystery as to why Olia, a violinist at the conservatory, remains with Sasha after discovering that he is wanted by the police and then witnessing the orgy that takes place at the dacha where Sasha is hiding out. The only motivation is provided in a much later episode, when Olia tells Sasha: "I like the way you solve problems," after he has beaten up a former classmate of hers who was making unwanted advances. The only female to play a major role in the series is Mother Russia.

4. Rambo's personal responsibility for the death and destruction he has unleashed is further attenuated in an alternative ending shot for the film, in which Rambo puts a pistol in Colonel Trautman's hand, pointing it at his own stomach and declaring: "You made me. You kill me." When Trautman tries to lower the pistol, Rambo grabs his hand and pushes the trigger, causing Colonel Trautman to shoot and kill him.

5. This clearly echoes Rambo's anguished declaration in *Rambo. First Blood* that while serving in Vietnam he "did what [he] had to do to win. But somebody didn't let us win."

6. Also like Teasle, which rhymes with "weasel," Panin's surname has a distinctly unheroic ring. It is derived from the word *kaverna*, meaning a cavity in both a medical and geographical sense, which would make him the antithesis of the volcano, the object of Sasha's intellectual passion. In that sense, it would also suggest a gendered symbolism. Of course, it may also suggest the word *kaverznyi*, which carries the pejorative meaning "to play dirty tricks."

7. The "abnormal" nature of Kaverin's obsession with Sasha Belov is further underscored in a scene with Kaverin's girlfriend when she returns to him after having had an affair. "You can't forgive me, can you? But you must have had women over all those years?" she asks. "No," Kaverin responds, "Only a man." She immediately understands and tells him, "Forget about Belov already."

8. Incidentally Sasha will later try cocaine, but the drug, he insists, has absolutely no effect on him. He is, it would appear, immune—another indication of his physical (or mental?) self-control.

9. At the end of the series, after Sasha has won his seat in the Duma, all his brothers in crime are conveniently killed off by a rival gang, once again obviating the need on Sasha's part of distancing himself—or destroying—his brothers. This is another example of how the moral universe of *The Brigade* differs from that of gangster films such as *The Godfather II*, in which Michael Corleone orders the killing of his brother Fredo.

10. Although the two men have a strong bond as war veterans, it should be noted that they are not entirely equals: Sasha was a sergeant in the army, Farkhad only a private.

11. Later during Sasha's campaign for a seat in the State Duma, Artur Veniaminovich returns to Russia and accuses Sasha of having "stolen his motherland from him"—but the claim rings hollow after he has cursed Russia as "your lousy homeland."

12. The masculinity of Sasha's brotherhood is also increasingly defined against homosexuals. In the first episode, for example, Kosmos admits to being a Michael Jackson fan, to which Pchela retorts: "He's a gay black man" ["On—goluboi negr"]. Later, when Sasha and Olga are shopping for a carriage for their newborn son, Sasha refuses to consider a blue one—light blue [*goluboi*] being slang for gay.

13. A similar symbolic geography emerges at the beginning of the tenth episode—which takes place in 1995—in which Sasha hears of a terrorist attack in Chechnya. Enraged, he throws all the plates off the kitchen table. In the next scene Kosmos, Pchela, and Fil are at the firing range. Fil shoots at the target and then exclaims: "That's what we'll do to all the Americans." The juxtaposition of the two scenes positions Russia between two threats, one coming from an underdeveloped East and the other from an overdeveloped West: Chechen terrorists and America.

14. It should be noted here that the Russian word *avtoritet* can mean "authority," but today the term commonly refers to the head of a criminal organization (Visson 2006, 19).

15. Although Sasha shows ingenuity and perseverance, the "gods" play a huge hand in his fate and it is these events that occur outside Sasha's control, not any inner epiphany or self-awareness, that drive the narrative. This also corresponds to the idea of *sud'ba*, or "fate" among Russians, expressed in "the feeling that human beings are not in control of their lives and that their control over events is limited; a tendency to fatalism, resignation, submissiveness; a lack of emphasis on the individual as an autonomous agent, achiever, and controller of events" (Wierzbicka 1996, 395). The role of fate in the series is crucial if Sasha is to remain fully Russian and avoid the sin of excessive ambition and the charge of being a selfish careerist.

16. The topos of the treatment of animals as an indication of one's spiritual state was developed most thoroughly in the works of Fyodor Dostoevsky, particularly in his novel *Crime and Punishment*. As a boy, the hero, Raskolnikov, witnesses the beating of an old, decrepit horse. The brutal scene leaves an indelible impression on the boy and helps shape his conception of evil in the world. The beating of the horse is associated structurally in the novel with other acts of cruelty against the innocent and helpless, such as Svidrigailov's violation of a young girl and Raskolnikov's own murder of the pawnbroker's sister, Lizaveta.

17. For more on the use of camp/criminal jargon by Russian politicians, see Visson 2006, 13–15.

18. When Sasha executes Kaverin, he pushes his body into the foundation pit of the mall, a not so subtle commentary on capitalist greed.

REFERENCES

Anderson, Benedict. *Imagined Communities*. London: Verso, 1991.
Bakhtin, Mikhail. "Forms of Time and of the Chronotope in the Novel." In *The Dialogic Imagination. Four Essays*, ed. Michael Holquist, trans. Carol Emerson and Michael Holquist, 84–258. Austin: University of Texas Press, 1981.
Billington, James H. *The Icon and the Axe: An Interpretive History of Russian Culture*. New York: Vintage Books, 1970.
Faludi, Susan. *Stiffed. The Betrayal of the American Man*. New York: William Morrow, 1999.

Freud, Sigmund. *Totem and Taboo*. In *The Basic Writings of Sigmund Freud*, ed. A. A. Brill, 807–930. New York: Random House, 1966.

Larsen, Susan. "Melodramatic Masculinity, National Identity, and the Stalinist Past in Postsoviet Cinema." *Studies in Twentieth Century Literature* 24, no. 1 (winter 2000): 85–119.

Visson, Lynn. "Terminology and Ideology: Translating Russian Political Language." In *Translating Russia: From Theory to Practice,* ed. Brian James Baer, 8:7–22. Columbus: Ohio Slavic Papers, 2006.

Wierzbicka, Anna. *Semantics, Culture, and Cognition: Universal Human Concepts in Culture-Specific Configurations*. New York: Oxford University Press, 1992.

FILMOGRAPHY

Brigada [*The Brigade*]. Dir. Aleksei Sidorov. Moscow, Avatar-Fil'm/Telekanal "Rossiia," 2002.

Rambo. First Blood. Dir. Ted Kotcheff. Lions Gate Films, 1982.

Figure 9.1. Sasha Belov in the midst of his transition from "brother" to mafia boss.

Figure 9.2. A drug-addled Kosmos, wielding a gun.

Figure 9.3. Kosmos and Pchela give themselves up to reveling while Sasha looks on.

Figure 9.4. An armed Sasha standing next to a graffitied version of his wife's nickname, Olia, contrasting his two roles, as mafia boss and loving family man.

PART FOUR

Auteurs and the Psychological/Philosophical

TEN

Fraught Filiation: Andrei Tarkovsky's Transformations of Personal Trauma

HELENA GOSCILO

I don't like his [Tarkovsky's] missionary manner and his meditations on sacrifice, predestination: "Oh, how I am suffering. None of you knows how to suffer as I do."

KIRA MURATOVA, INTERVIEW

Our clientele is all humanity. From earliest childhood. Little boys get patricidol popsicles—throttlepops—to vent their hostilities. The father, you realize, is the source of society's frustrations. And with the help of a freudo or two, Oedipus complexes are speedily resolved!

STANISLAW LEM, *THE FUTUROLOGICAL CONGRESS*

No truly sincere person will ever express his feelings openly, true feeling always has some kind of veil.

ANDREI TARKOVSKY, *TIME WITHIN TIME*

CINE-KENOSIS AS AUTEUR AURA

Unanimously acclaimed Soviet Russia's premier cinematic *auteur,* Andrei Tarkovsky (1932–1986) declared himself incapable of distinguishing between (his) art and (his) life, and ceaselessly explored his personal obsessions on celluloid. Adulatory assessments of his works enshrined those obsessions as an uncompromising, heroic commitment to such metaphysical and philosophical categories as spirituality, conscience, time, and memory in a repressive state declaratively inimical to metaphysics. An arrogant and categorical perfectionist,[1] Tarkovsky perceived and presented himself as a martyr-genius, his pronouncements invariably projecting his allegedly unique, God-given talent against a background of comprehensive mediocrity. Anything that was not in some way "his," in fact, Tarkovsky consigned to the dubious or second-rate. That exceptionalist self-conception emerged in interviews, conversations, correspondence, and diaries: "You have to be above it. I am Tarkovsky, after all. And there is only one Tarkovsky, unlike the Gerasimovs of this world, whose name is legion" (Tarkovsky, *Time within Time* 67). The admiring Aleksandr Sokurov recalls Tarkovsky's advising him to follow his example ("Berite primer s menia") and announcing, "Ia velikii chelovek" ["I am a great man"] (Sokurov 101). Not unlike Anna Akhmatova, who deftly orchestrated all aspects of her alluring myth, Tarkovsky erected a reputation-monument to himself that others proceeded to extend, refine, and enhance.[2]

While dismissing as "abysmal" and "pathetic" a university debate about his film *Andrei Rublev,* Tarkovsky singled out a math professor's remark—that "some artists [. . .] make us feel the true measure of things. It is *a burden which they carry throughout their lives, and we must be thankful to them"*—as the sole redeeming statement that made it "worth sitting through two hours of rubbish" (Tarkovsky, *Time within Time* 8–9, emphasis added). The motif of Tarkovsky's cine-kenosis persists to this day in such publications as Nikolai Boldryrev's recent biography cum commentary, revealingly titled *Andrei Tarkovsky's sacrifice [zhertvoprinoshenie Andreia Tarkovskogo* 2004]—the lowercase intended to forestall readers' misperception of "sacrifice" as merely a reference to the director's 1986 film instead of his entire career.[3] Tarkovsky laid the foundation for this mythology not only by his demeanor but also by the initial title he selected, in a spirit of pretentious self-pity, for both *Zerkalo* and his diaries—*Martirolog*—and his request of Ernst Neizvestnyi that the sculptor create "The Crucifixion" for his headstone.[4] Both the Soviet system of censorship and the intelligentsia abetted this image of the inspired martyr, the former through persistent prohibitions and obstacles,

the latter by speaking of Tarkovsky's vision in hushed tones and ratio-
nalizing his prickly, intractable behavior as an excusable reaction to the
harsh constraints meted out to him by the Soviet establishment.[5]

Those constraints were, indeed, formidable, as copiously attested by
scholars, coworkers, relatives, and friends, though mild by comparison
with the restrictions and sanctions imposed on the flamboyant and certainly no less gifted Sergei Paradzhanov—one of Tarkovsky's favorite directors (Volkova 64). Official representatives in cinema administration,
such as Filipp Ermash, who took over Goskino in 1972, and the director/
actor Sergei Bondarchuk (Surkova, *S Tarkovskim i o Tarkovskom*, 383–84)
ensured frustrating conditions for Tarkovsky's work: insufficient Kodak
film stock for multiple takes;[6] demands for changes in, and deletions of,
scenes in virtually all his films; limited circulation of his works—moreover, in secondary domestic theaters; irregular reviews; and so forth.[7] Yet
the state apparatus did not ban Tarkovsky's films and even at the peak of
its xenophobia permitted him to travel and work abroad—partly reacting
to the West's interventions on his behalf, while also wishing to display
a "Soviet" director to the foreign intellectuals who admired him. During the Soviet era Kira Muratova, who, like Paradzhanov, encountered
incomparably greater hurdles (shelved films, lack of financial support,
etc.), did not automatically interpret official strictures as testimony to
her sublime uniqueness,[8] perhaps because on principle she disavows the
supremely Russo-Soviet notion of the film director as an extraordinary
being of infinite wisdom, and of art as a displaced version of religion:
"Art in general shouldn't dress itself in the mantle of 'prophet, teacher
of life'" (quoted in Taubman 106). As Ol'ga Surkova notes, "Tarkovsky's
fate was dramatic but not tragic, as he deemed it then, and we did too"
(*S Tarkovskim i o Tarkovskom* 399).[9] In fact, as Robert Bird emphasizes,
"Tarkovsky remained *within* the mechanisms of the Soviet system and
the world of the Soviet imaginary" (29). The etiology of Tarkovsky's self-
conception as a singular, persecuted genius—a cine-Christ—therefore
should be sought elsewhere.[10]

Eulogistic collusion with the director's self-presentation in a *sociopolitical* context has discreetly sidestepped or downplayed what was arguably the central event in Tarkovsky's *personal* life: At the age of four,[11] he
experienced the "loss" of his poet-father, Arsenii Tarkovsky, when the
latter deserted the family for another woman. Evidence suggests that

his departure and the breakup of the family proved traumatic for the son. Contacts were infrequent, relations strained, and the son's sense of abandonment persisted well into adulthood. In interviews he tirelessly pointed out that he had been raised in an exclusively female environment (grandmother, mother, and sister [Boldyrev 22]), which may explain why in adulthood he especially esteemed and was drawn to men. According to Natal'ia Bondarchuk, the female lead in Tarkovsky's free adaptation of Stanisław Lem's *Solaris*, during the shooting of the film Tarkovsky asked her how old she had been when her parents divorced, and, noting that he had been even younger, he followed up with an eloquent non sequitur, "Probably children suffer more than their parents who divorce. [. . .] I also love my father very much, tenderly and faithfully" (*About Tarkovsky* 131–32). The scriptwriter Aleksandr Misharin, who coauthored Tarkovsky's supremely autobiographical *Zerkalo* [*Mirror*], recollects that Tarkovsky "had been hurt very much when his father left the family" (*About Andrei Tarkovsky* 53). Aleksandr Sokurov concurs (Sokurov 102). A diary entry of September 1970 by Tarkovsky records the following revealing sentiments of the twenty-eight-year-old director:

> I haven't seen my father for ages. The longer I don't see him the more depressing and alarming [*sic*] it becomes to go to him. *It's patently clear that I have a complex about my parents.* I don't feel adult when I'm with them. And I don't think they consider me adult either. Our relations are somehow tortured, complicated, unspoken. [. . .] I love them dearly, but I've never felt at ease with them, or their equal. (Tarkovsky, *Time within Time* 19; emphasis added)

That complex, I argue, finds fulsome articulation in Tarkovsky's oeuvre[12] and overrides all social and political issues.[13]

Though reports indicate that in conversations with his parents Tarkovsky's filial anguish remained unexpressed,[14] it found several other, inevitably mediated outlets. Attempts to "reclaim" his father assumed multiple forms: choosing the career of a "poetic" director (cf. Maya Turovskaya's *Cinema as Poetry* 1989);[15] subsuming and simultaneously reconnecting with his father through citation of his verses in *Zerkalo* (1974), *Stalker* (1979), and *Nostalghia* (1983);[16] emulating him in private life (leaving *his* first wife and son for another woman);[17] and, in a letter from Italy (1983), justifying and painstakingly explaining to his disapproving parent his decision to remain abroad—that is, to "abandon" his "home/land."[18] Abandonment and psychological distance, rooted in his relations with his father, reticulate throughout Tarkovsky's oeuvre as a wound that never healed.[19]

THE PROBLEMATIC SECOND SEX AND THE SENSITIVE MAN

Within his rigidly hierarchical scheme of things, Tarkovsky elevated his view of gender to a self-evident principle of life, whereby "women are nature, and men are spirit" ["Zhenshchiny u Tarkovskogo—eto priroda, muzhchina—dukh"] (Boldyrev 88), and he readily admitted that he never gave women's inner life a thought ("Ia ob etom nikogda ne dumal—o vnutrennem mire zhenshchiny," Bodlyrev 59), for they have no independent existence as agents and creators. Various recent studies have cited his notorious, iterated conviction that women, by definition, are born to support and serve men: "What is a woman's essence [*sush-chnost*']? Subordination and self-denial out of love"; "I think that a woman's true significance [*smysl*] is self-abnegation [*samootdacha*]" (Boldyrev 58–59).[20] The journalist Irena Brezna recalls his apodictic pronouncement, "A woman doesn't have her own inner world, and she should not have it. Her inner world must be absolutely dissolved in the inner world of a man. A man must keep his inner world for himself" (*About Andrei Tarkovsky* 350). Whereas during the Soviet era, and especially Stalinism, such a convenient perspective held sway among the homosocial male collective of self-proclaimed geniuses,[21] post-Soviet Russia has moved beyond the fantasies of misogynistic intellectual provincialism, which Tarkovsky, naïvely confusing his personal dilemmas with universal "truths," embraced while priding himself on a universalist intellectual openness. At least one Western study has adverted in passing to his ambivalent sexual orientation,[22] but speculation about Tarkovsky's sexual preferences seems redundant in light of the copious evidence that in life and on celluloid his most profound engagement was with male figures and their strivings and dilemmas. In the immediate domestic milieu during Tarkovsky's formative years, the adult male represented the unknown, the lack, the absence, and therefore inevitably became the object of desire and fetishization.[23] In fact, Tarkovsky's biography as lived and projected on screen resembles an enacted gloss on the Lacanian model of the Imaginary and the Symbolic: "raised by women," Tarkovsky indefatigably proselytized love and Home (Imaginary), and to the very end struggled against the Law of the Father (Symbolic),[24] while the absence of his own father created the single weightiest and psychologically most incapacitating trauma in his life.

Nowhere do Tarkovsky's denigration of women and his yearning for a loving father surface more nakedly than in his diploma film, *Katok i skripka* (*The Steamroller and the Violin* 1960).[25] This Sovietly sentimental love story between two sensitive males—the violin-playing seven-year-old Sasha and the operator of a steamroller, Sergei—shows their intimacy thwarted by the interference of two crass women.[26] From their first encounter, Sergei adopts the role of ideal surrogate father: he rescues Sasha from courtyard bullies, invites the boy to drive the steamroller with him (Figure 10.1), protectively covers him with his own jacket during a thunderstorm and lifts him over a huge puddle, treats him to lunch, talks "man to man" with him, fixes his violin case, and agrees to a movie date at the Zaria Theater to see *Chapaev* (1934)—another male-produced narrative about homosociality in the quasi-paternal vein of socialist-realist maturation scenarios. In the space of several hours Sergei, whose affection for Sasha manifestly exceeds that of the boy's mother, manages to teach the love-hungry Sasha responsibility and courage while winning his admiring trust (Figure 10.2). Sergei and Sasha's bonding, in fact, rehearses along highly personal lines the metaphorical Chapaev filiation paradigm, whereby wise paternal figures teach, and harness the talents and passions of, their biological or surrogate sons, both despite and independent of women, who *by (biological) definition* are unequal to the weighty task of securing the nation's well-being.

The film, as Boldyrev acknowledges, reduces women to "a sea of women, straightforwardly demanding, almost cruel in their narrow zeal, eager to serve the social order, to do everything 'according to the rules.' The world of Poesy is outside women's realm of competence. [. . .] And in general women in the film prove to be the element that keeps the two men, the 'son' and 'father,' apart" (89).[27] The relentless criticism by Sasha's arid, metronomic music teacher, which every few seconds interrupts his impassioned violin playing, culminates in the crushing verdict that he suffers from "too much imagination." A kindred disciplinarian, his mother, preoccupied solely with cleanliness and propriety, ignores his feelings and punitively controls her fatherless son instead of sympathizing with him. Tarkovsky cleverly conveys the uncommunicativeness of the mother-son exchange through the mediation of a mirror in which she is reflected throughout the conversation (Figure 10.3). Unlike in the street scene earlier in the film, where refraction through mirrors serves to multiply and enrich visual images of the city that delight the artistic boy, here the mirror merely distances and dehumanizes. Ultimately bloodlines and class differences wilt under the powerful impact of what throughout Tarkovsky's career constituted the omnipotent, elevating force of Male Bonding liberated from womanhood.[28]

Though less flagrantly coercive, younger females likewise prove circumscribed beings: Sergei's nameless female coworker, all too obviously harboring romantic notions about him, engages in flirtatious teasing and waylays him at film's end so as to accompany the distraught Sergei to the movie theater. Even younger but cut from the same gender-cloth, the little girl waiting with Sasha for her music lesson coquettishly strains for his attention and, in an overly symbolic sequence, consumes the apple he denies himself so as to generously leave for her. In short, with the fugitive exception of the gentle mother who comforts her tearful son after *his* violin lesson, females (whatever their age) are insensitive or manipulative or both, dwelling on an appreciably lower plane. In fact, they are the steamrollers, whereas the two central males incarnate the finesse and aesthetics symbolized by the violin, as attested by Sergei's request that Sasha play for him, and his tenderly meditative demeanor during the performance—to the accompaniment of water, Tarkovsky's perennial trope for a sacramental moment.[29] As the film's concluding shot demonstrates, only the imaginative "corrective" of desire can bring together the boy and the surrogate father bound by a spiritual affinity: escaping his mother's confining space, Sasha runs out onto a huge, completely depopulated square, where Sergei and his steamroller await him. The "happy ending" reunites son and surrogate figure in a compensatory fantasy of "alone together at last," their union sanctified by the flock of pigeons/doves that alight on the square as the reunited duo drives off into the distance.

As Boldyrev remarks, the autobiographical nature of Tarkovsky's first screen effort could hardly be more blatant (89). Whatever Tarkovsky's hagiographical praise for his mother, whose richly documented penchant for masochistic self-sacrifice accords with the director's notions of "women's 'natural' role," her constant availability and support merely certified her readiness to fulfill the purportedly quintessential duties of her gender and rendered her an overly prosaic figure that could be taken for granted and ultimately dismissed. If she was the all-too-familiar/familial Rock of Gibraltar, Arsenii Tarkovsky was Mont Blanc—inaccessible, remote, and therefore all the more beguiling to a son who prized the unattainable while espousing appreciation of the everyday.

An examination of four full-length films by Tarkovsky reveals the shifting strategies he assayed to come to terms with his formative childhood experience of abandonment and with his complicated feelings for his poet father. Boldyrev contends: "In general he fundamentally reproduced his childhood in his films [. . .] his father's leaving the family was a cosmogonic [sic] catastrophe for the child [. . .], the consequences of which he unconsciously strived to set right, to eliminate in his adulthood—that is, to restore his inner primordial harmony" (19, 22).[30] Biographical evidence confirms the futility of these efforts, while Tarkovsky's oeuvre testifies to their tenaciousness, for problematic paternity and filiation in myriad formulations stamped his films from the early beginnings at VGIK to his final *Zhertvoprinoshenie,* shot abroad shortly before his death.

COMPETING SURROGATE FATHERS IN THE MIDST OF WAR

Tellingly, Tarkovsky's first full-length feature, *Ivanovo detstvo [Ivan's Childhood* 1962], dramatizes the exploits during World War II of, once again, a fatherless boy.[31] Based on Vladimir Bogomolov's novella *Ivan* (1957), Tarkovsky's prize-winning debut departs stylistically from the spare, restrained narrative of the literary text so as to highlight mood and psychology. Both film and novella abound in homosocial bonding and apotheosize the dauntless, Nazi-hating boy whose ability to reconnoiter unobtrusively behind enemy lines renders him an invaluable scout in the Soviet resistance. But whereas the reader of Bogomolov's text learns about Ivan's family situation obliquely from a brief statement by Kholin (Ivan's father, a frontier guard, perished on the first day of the war, his baby sister was killed in the boy's arms during the retreat [36], and the whereabouts of his mother are unknown), Tarkovsky dwells on the family drama. Similarly, whereas in the novella Ivan merely asks

Gal'tsev whether he talked in his sleep (18)—a sleep presumably haunted by tormented dreams about his family's fate—Tarkovsky's intensely psychological approach shows not only the boy's nightmares through periodic flashbacks but also images of his equally anguished waking obsessions.

Though the bulk of *Ivanovo detstvo* depicts the devastations of war, Tarkovsky frames the diegesis in two near-wordless sequences conveying the joys of carefree boyhood during peacetime, concretized as nature, sun, water, and geographic expanse.[32] Both sequences feature Ivan's mother as a loving nurturer without even hinting at a father's presence. Before the credits roll, the film opens to the iterated, beguiling sounds of a cuckoo, leading to an ambiguous shot that proves to be a dream-turned-nightmare: a smiling, half-naked Ivan standing beside a tree gazes directly at the viewer before ambling through a sun-washed, tree-dotted meadow that would evoke the happy innocence of Eden if not for the spider web that partially screens Ivan's face and, in retrospect, ominously qualifies the Edenic setting (Figure 10.4).[33] The monitory significance of the web becomes clear when Ivan stoops to drink water brought by his smiling mother, whose upper body suddenly tilts grotesquely as a shot resounds.[34] The final sequence of the film, which follows the revelation that Ivan was captured, interrogated, and hanged by the Nazis,[35] combines family motifs from the boy's various dreams: Ivan drinking water, his mother smiling as she waves farewell to him, and his playful sister (never named, but his companion in an earlier dream), running along the beach, chased by a carefree Ivan, who overtakes her. The radiant, open-form shot of Ivan laughing in the sun-kissed water that seems to have no end point projects the unrecoverable ideal of Paradise Lost. His headlong flight into "the beyond" poignantly presents the possibility of a "happy end," one that could not contrast more starkly with his violent execution. Thus his escape into infinity materializes fantasy[36] instead of reflecting reality; it conveys what might have been. As much is confirmed when the dead tree beneath which Ivan pauses—recalling the Stygian swamp he fords to shuttle between the Nazis and the Russian camps—expands into an all-encompassing blackness that fills the screen at film's end. The regularly juxtaposed antitheses of horror and doom, on the one hand, and lighthearted pleasure in the natural world and close human relations, on the other, index the tragic discrepancy between Ivan's aberrant, maimed childhood as experienced during the war and the pastoral, simple delights of his prewar existence, terminated by his family's extinction.[37]

Recollections of that life constitute the content and atmosphere of the only completely happy dream (perhaps because Kholin awakens Ivan before the shocking disruption when a Nazi bullet shatters the dream's blissful tranquility)—of Ivan and a girl who presumably is his sister[38] perched on the back of a truck loaded with apples. Ivan lovingly handles the fruit, which he holds up to the rain in rapture and offers to his sister. Halting at a beach, the truck spills some of the apples, which horses slowly begin munching, in an atmosphere that conveys the fullness of an untroubled childhood amid benign surroundings and thus vividly accentuates the traumatic cost of the war for Ivan.[39] Though the mother does not appear in this dream, all other retrospective scenes feature her warm intimacy with her son. For instance, in his second dream, the two discuss stars as the mother draws water from a well, until again the crack of a shot terminates the magic moment, capped by an image of her dead body, splashed by water, beside the well (Figures 10.5 and 10.6). In perhaps the most psychologically revealing, if disturbing, sequence in the film, which comprises Ivan's enactment of his vengeful pursuit of Nazis in the church/bunker when left alone, his mother's role acquires an additional dimension. This series of chaotic impressions, with shouts in German, explosions in the background, sobs, and jagged, rapid cuts, accords with the aura and aesthetic of Ivan's nightmares (Figure 10.7). Partly to imply the continuity between Ivan's nightmares, memories, thoughts, and immediate experiences, it interweaves images of his surroundings with his tortured visions—most notably a quick glimpse of his mother's face, quickly followed by a tilted icon of the Madonna and child, then a cross (a symbol associated with Ivan throughout). Together with the iterated pairing of Ivan and his mother, this juxtaposition begs for their identification with the illuminated holy image, which adverts, of course, to a narrative of salvation that excludes the biological father and sanctifies mother and son.

Strikingly, the film, which repeatedly "resurrects" mother and sister through dream visions, sweepingly makes on-screen memory of the father taboo. Moreover, Ivan's sole reference to fatherhood takes the form of negation: when, in an episode absent from Bogomolov's text,

Griaznev prevents Ivan's flight from the prospect of enrollment in a military school, the boy's bitter riposte to Griaznev's solicitous rebuke fleetingly confronts his bleak status as solitary orphan: "I haven't anyone [any family] . . . Are you my father or what? [. . .]. Why should you decide [for me]?" ["Net u menia nikogo . . . Da, chto vy mne, otets, chto-li? Reshat'!"].[40] Indeed, Ivan ultimately rejects or distances himself from all self-appointed paternal surrogates in the personae of Griaznov, Kholin, Gal'tsev, and Katasonych—who all wish to adopt him. An "adult" boy, prematurely aged through his grueling war ordeals, Ivan in unexpected ways exemplifies what William Wordsworth called "the child [who] is father of the man."[41] Fully aware of his value for the Soviet army, Ivan commands information denied even senior officers; peremptorily issues orders to adult personnel, such as Gal'tsev; not only reproves Kholin for smoking[42] but self-confidently spurns his help in negotiating the Stygian river to the "other side" (of Nazis and death); and so on. He is that ambulatory paradox—a child war veteran, forced by abnormal circumstances to "play" the father rather than be the son. In that sense, Ivan fits neatly into the cultural paradigm of the "*puer senex*" discussed in José Alaniz's essay (chapter 11) on Aleksandr Sokurov's *Otets i syn* (2003).[43]

Through the figure of Ivan, then, Tarkovsky recasts his afflictive loss of father not only as an opportunity to acquire and reject eager surrogate paternal caretakers but also as the onset of premature but empowered adulthood in martyrdom—a martyrdom verbally underscored by Kholin's remark to Gal'tsev that the boy has suffered beyond description (36), and visually signaled by the icon of the Madonna and child as well as sundry crosses that dot the ravaged landscape of Ivan's Christ-like "stages" en route to death. On the one hand, Ivan surmounts the absence of the father; on the other, as a solitary, unprotected boy, he perishes. Thus the film synthesizes a defiant indifference to paternal absence with a tragic sense of the consequences that such an absence entails.

THE PRODIGAL SON IN OUTER SPACE

This denial or erasure of the father contrasts radically with Tarkovsky's unexpected wish-fulfillment introduction of a wise and caring paternal figure ten years later (1972) in his ultra-subjective, award-winning adaptation of Stanisław Lem's *Solaris*—a novel devoid of such an ideal and of the perennial Tarkovskian preoccupation with the sovereignty of Home and love.[44] Tarkovsky domesticates Lem's philosophical novel, which speculates about the nature of knowledge, as well as the uncertain status of humankind, and its putatively praiseworthy values, in the universe. Lem disliked the film, famously objecting that Tarkovsky had not adapted his novel but had made *Crime and Punishment*. A second adaptation, by Steven Soderbergh in 2002, likewise bemused Lem, who confided in an interview "Indeed, in *Solaris* I attempted to present the problem of an encounter in Space with a form of being that is neither human nor humanoid." With characteristic irony he repudiated the pertinence of love, and especially romance, to his novel: "To my best knowledge, the book was *not* dedicated to erotic problems of people in outer space [. . .] This is why the book was entitled *Solaris* and not *Love in Outer Space*" (Orlinski). Substituting his personal dilemmas of family and love for Lem's coolly intellectual investigation of man's encounter with alterity in the cosmic order, Tarkovsky subordinates the philosophical implications of that confrontation to Kris Kelvin's domestic relations—ostensibly with his dead wife, who appears as one of the space station's neutrino-based Phi-creatures, but in reality with his parents.

In fact, Tarkovsky supplements Lem's plot with three episodes/relationships to underline the father/son theme, which could hardly be more remote from the Polish author's concerns. Lem relegates the pilot Berton,[45] who reports on his search for Fechner, "the ocean's first victim" (40; English trans.), to the background as a hearsay character; he belongs to an earlier phase of Solaristics. By contrast, Tarkovsky's film transforms him into a long-standing friend of Kelvin's father who arrives *with his son* at the dacha to show his videotape of the official hearings on Fechner's disappearance. Significantly, Burton initially intends to leave the boy at the dacha, but, offended by Kris Kelvin's skeptical dismissal not only of the videotape but also of Burton's insistence that "knowledge is truthful only if it's based on morality," he changes his mind. While Burton is unexpectedly elevated to the role of a "good father," Fechner, whom the eloquently named Dr. Messenger in Lem's novel diagnoses as probably having suffered a childhood trauma, metamorphoses in the film into a father who abandoned his son. Not Fechner as a child, but *his child* (whom Burton reportedly later sees in person when he visits Fechner's widow) floats as a Phi-creature on the Ocean's surface. Thus, according to Tarkovsky, Fechner's death presumably serves as condign punishment for his paternal betrayal: "Okazalos', chto on [Fechner] ostavil sirotoi syna! Ushel iz sem'i" ["It turns out that he [Fechner] left his son an orphan. He abandoned the family"]. These two secondary relationships, which occupy relatively little screen time, mark the two antipodes of fatherhood, thereby amplifying and establishing a measure of sorts for Kelvin's (and Tarkovsky's) relations with his father, which psychologically occupy center stage in the film.

As in *Ivanovo detstvo*, Tarkovsky's deviations from the literary source include the provision of a frame—one that adapts the biblical story of the prodigal son, and therefore begins and ends with Home.[46] In showing the son, not the father, electing to leave the familial nest, the filmic narrative inverts Tarkovsky's personal biography and transfers control over events to the son. Lem's novel, which casts Kelvin as a solitary, independent agent, starts with his flight to the Solaris space station and in its eleventh chapter adverts in passing to Kelvin's father in the context of space exploration: Kelvin visualizes the face of Giese, "the father of Solarist studies and of Solarists," as engraved on the title page of his book, where his head stands out—"so like my father's, that head, not in its features but in its expression of old-fashioned wisdom and honesty" (161–62; English trans.). Merely a hearsay character in Lem, identified with moral integrity by analogy with the scientists Giese and Gibarian, who in the novel seem to matter incomparably more to Kelvin, the father, as always, is crucial for Tarkovsky. In his *Solaris,* the father represents origins, Home, responsibility, and, ultimately, forgiveness of a son whose alienation Tarkovsky imparts through various devices in the prolonged introductory section that lasts almost an hour.

As he prepares to leave for Solaris, Kelvin roams the huge, inviting grounds of his parental home—lush, sunlit, with an enormous lake, a free-running horse, and the family dog. In two symbolic acts he washes his hands à la Pilate in the lake and burns the photograph of Hari, his dead wife,[47] whom throughout the film Tarkovsky collapses into Kelvin's mother (as noted above, Tarkovsky's first wife struck acquaintances as a "double" of his mother). These gestures of disengagement acquire further significance when the father tells Burton that he forces his son to walk an hour every day: otherwise Kelvin would have no contact with "the earth."

The dacha and the grounds are yet another Tarkovskian Eden, one rooted in family tradition. The father confesses, "I don't like innovation," and, in the spirit of Nikolai Fedorov, preserves continuity with his familial predecessors through Home: when building the dacha he intentionally duplicated his grandfather's house. Moreover, in one of the film's many parallel contrasts between father and son, he keeps the photograph of his late spouse (presumably dead or shed) prominently displayed. Whereas the father obviously values human connections through time and is associated with organic life, the son privileges isolation and space and allies himself with the rational and mechanical. Tarkovsky visually signals the impassable divide between the two men by an extended shot of them on opposite sides of a window, with Kris Kelvin "on the outside," under the rain, looking in, and the father indoors, amid the books, domesticated bird, photographs, and other objects grounded in a history of the past. In one of the numerous doublings in the film, Kelvin's estrangement from father and Home before his departure mirrors his distanced attitude toward his wife, Hari, who after his departure from their shared apartment many years ago committed suicide.

Buttressing the visual dimension, sparse, almost Chekhovian pseudo-dialogue captures the lack of authentic communication between the two Kelvins, corroborating the father's remark, "We talk so rarely together." In fact, the only genuine conversation takes place between the father and Burton—hence the loaded, Freud-evocative question the father poses to his son: "Are you jealous that he [Burton], and not you, will bury me?" Kelvin's inability to make contact—ironically the goal of the Solaris space project, yet one that Kelvin, a psychologist (!), cannot achieve even on earth—prompts his father to declare, "It's dangerous to send men like you into space." Presumably Kelvin lacks the ability to love or express emotion ("morality"), for his father confides to Burton, "He reminds me of an accountant preparing an annual report," a judgment Burton endorses when Kelvin refuses even to entertain the possibility of the Ocean's capacity to penetrate the human psyche: "He's a bookkeeper, not a scientist. You were right."

Kelvin's flight in space tropes his journey in time, "forward into the past." Forced into self-confrontation on Solaris, he succumbs to dreams and visions of an earlier self primarily involving not his father, who appears in only one sequence on a videotape, but his mother and wife. The video captures Kelvin as a child who literally "follows in his father's footsteps" in the snow on the family grounds, while his mother watches, holding on a leash the dog familiar to the viewer from the introductory segment as part of Home. A spring/summer shot of an older Kris, again with his mother in the background, leads into an image of Hari, and the camera quickly shifts between Hari and the mother, the two women wearing an identical shawl and eventually becoming indistinguishable in one striking shot that merges their two faces and in another sequence during Kelvin's fever, where Hari twice transforms into his mother. Indeed, it is the two-women-in-one who enable Kelvin's anagnorisis: Hari as Phi-creature through her suicide, and the mother in the black-and-white dream sequence contemporaneous with Hari's act of self-elimination.[48] Against a background with a clock that has stopped and then resumes ticking (Kelvin's life, suspended in disabling detachment, now may move forward), a melancholy Kelvin informs his mother that he does not recognize her face and that he feels lonely;[49] in other words, he breaks his customary reticence to acknowledge his lamentable lack of genuine contact with Hari/the mother and, presumably, with people in general. The mother's response as she bites into an apple is, "Why do you hurt us?[50] [. . .] Why didn't you call? You live a strange life. Unkempt . . . dirty." In a ritual evoking the cleansing act of baptism, she washes his arm, then kisses the back of his head, whereupon he sobs, "Mama!"[51] This birth into a new self enables Kelvin *psychologically* to accept Snaut's announcement, "It's time for you to return to earth," and the Ocean materializes Kelvin's desire to revisit his primary relationship—with his father, at the dacha. Unlike in *Katok i skripka,* here women play what Tarkovsky considered their "predestined" role, that of facilitators for the male.

Once again strolling through the family grounds, Kelvin as returned prodigal son finally approaches the same window in the dacha through which he peered before setting out for Solaris. This time, however, the rain is pouring indoors onto his father, who notices his son and emerges from the house, symmetrically reversing their roles at film's beginning.[52] Kelvin falls on his knees, embracing his father's legs, and, in a pose duplicating Rembrandt's *Return of the Prodigal Son* (c. 1668), the father rests his hands on Kelvin's shoulders, the Home dog at their side (Figure 10.8). In other words, the imagined "positive ending," which recalls *Katok i skripka* and *Ivanovo detstvo,* comprises an emanation orchestrated by the mysterious Ocean, whose capacity to tap into humans' profoundest yearnings leaves protagonist and father, once again, "alone together at last." Though achieved only "virtually," the filial cathexis marks the attainment of a long desired yet repressed reconciliation with the father.

Certainly Tarkovsky's desire is paramount at film's end: his father's shattering abandonment is not only displaced onto the son but is also rectified through the penitent return and silent but apparently loving reunion. The Ocean functions perfectly as the vehicle for this revision of the past, inasmuch as it projects unarticulated but obsessive yearnings. The now self-aware prodigal son's *psychological* return to the father and Home is, Tarkovsky maintained in an interview, "a return to the cradle, to his source, which cannot ever be forgotten" (*Time within Time* 364). Symptomatically the cradle is patrilinear—not the mother, but the father, who designs his "cradle" according to *his* forebear's specifications, dominates Kelvin's psychic underground—the repressed early years. Tarkovsky's dream scenario of compensation transgenders Home and the Imaginary so as to incorporate the Lost Father into the formative paradigm of Family—a scenario here openly acknowledged as located in the sphere of desire.

REPLICATION ACROSS GENERATIONS: MY FATHER, MYSELF

In numerous ways *Solaris,* with its filiation, family, home, doubles, and mirrors, functioned as a covert rehearsal for *Zerkalo,* unanimously regarded as Tarkovsky's most explicitly autobiographical film and frankly conceded by him as such.[53] Johnson and Petrie aptly characterize *Zerkalo* as "a family affair, with Tarkovsky's mother playing the mother as an old woman, his father reading his own poetry, his second wife, Larissa, in a telling cameo role as a shallow, well-to-do doctor's wife, and his stepdaughter as the wartime love interest of the teenage hero" (115). Only colleagues' sage advice dissuaded Tarakovsky from assuming the role of the adult protagonist. Not just the "behind the scenes" arrangements but also the transparently autobiographical onscreen specifics of *Zerkalo* render analysis of its father-son relations virtually superfluous, for *Zerkalo* unambiguously exposes the extent to which Tarkovsky's celluloid explorations originate in his profound personal dilemmas.

Reportedly Arsenii Tarkovsky remarked that in *Zerkalo* the director "settled accounts" with his parents.

Although it is inconceivable that Tarkovsky, with his conviction of divinely ordained uniqueness, would regard himself in any way representative, the second half of the film incorporates newsreels spanning three decades (1930s–1950s) to generalize his familial drama onto several generations of Soviet citizens in a framework of domestic and international events, presented synecdochically and from a nationalistic perspective. As in *Ivanovo detstvo,* children's miseries and losses as a result of war receive special emphasis in narrative scenes intercut with newsreels. Both categories illustrate how history literally and figuratively maims not only soldiers but also innocent children, whose war-related psychic hardships include paternal disappearance or abandonment. One adult Spaniard, for instance, remembers how painful it was, in his boyhood, to part from his father during the Spanish Civil War—a conflict that resulted in a large influx of refugees into the Soviet Union. Ultimately, however, these sections sketch a socio-historical context for the individual drama of the Tarkovsky family, which spans approximately forty years—from the politically landmined Stalinist thirties to the Stagnation seventies—served up in fragments, dreams, and images that are often stunning but occasionally sag under the weight of portentous significance.

The film confirms, yet again, Tarkovsky's unresolved psychological problems with his father, his Oedipal "confusion" of mother and wife—here embarrassingly materialized in Margarita Terekhova's assumption of both roles (Mariia and Natal'ia)—and his wishful identification with his father: Ignat Danil'tsev plays not only Aleksei as a boy[54] but also the son, Ignat. Together with the title, this heavy-handed casting reduces successive generations to the replication denoted in the title, which the many mirrors in the mise-en-scène rather clumsily emphasize. Indissolubly bound to paternal identity, the son seems condemned to mimic the father as an aloof loner in a family defined by tension and scant emotional warmth. This scenario of (self-exculpatory?) bio-psychological determinism along Freudian/Skinnerian lines is startling in a director with a reputation for complexity. Perhaps more insistent than complex, the film begs less for stylistic than for psychological analysis along Freudian lines, which posit not only the Oedipal complex but also the adolescent transfer of cathexis to the father as the norm of male identity formation. One could argue that Tarkovsky's/Aleksei's choice of wife who is a mother-duplicate actually enacts the Oedipal complex, but this "tabooed possession" stems not from rivalry with the father but from the desire to possess *him* through sameness. In other words, the Freudian trajectory is thwarted or at the very least modified by the father's perennial absence, hence his status not as resented rival but as ever inaccessible object of desire—for both mother/wife and son.[55]

Intriguingly, the verbal superimpositions in the film are psychologically no less revealing than the diegesis. For clarification and coherence Tarkovsky relies on the voiceover of a first-person narrator—Innokentii Smoktunovskii, whose voice Soviet audiences, if not Western viewers, would have no difficulty recognizing and associating with his arguably most famous role: that of Hamlet, likewise a father-idolizing son with "incompatible" parents and an onerous psychological inheritance.[56] The narrator's prosaic commentary regularly cedes to extracts from Arsenii Tarkovsky's poems, recited by the poet himself as pointers or conceptual nodes in those portions of the film that convey not only *his* biography but also his director-son's, further collapsing the two into a single synthetic image of talented creativity/remote paternity. The dominant tone and import of these lyrics is exultant; they celebrate nature, young love, and immortality, and in doing so unwittingly underscore the discrepancy between words and experience as depicted on screen: repeatedly what starts as love degenerates into irritation, resentment, and futile quibbling; the idyllic environment has its ominous side; and if art and memory constitute immortality, then the latter hardly conduces to the happiness or enlightenment of those who remember—at least according to the terms of the film. Childhood has its magical moments (portrayed in often breathtaking shots) but also pain and loneliness, conveyed in images of separation and solitude.

Tarkovsky and critics have bluntly called *Zerkalo* an act of exorcism, but they have circumnavigated the question of which strategies deployed for this purported pseudo-abreaction proved effective. To assume that mere reenactment on screen suffices to heal the trauma of paternal abandonment is surely too primitive and, moreover, contestable in light of Tarkovsky's subsequent films. Yet *Zerkalo*'s introductory sequence, in which a psychologist helps an adolescent overcome his stammer by a purely mental "liberation," codes Tarkovsky's expectation of his own recovery from his decades-long trauma through this self-referential revisitation on screen—an expectation that, according to him, he fulfilled.[57] Though the mother in *Zerkalo* frames the film visually—a device intended to establish her decisive role in the family melodrama—the voices of the father (Arsenii Tarkovsky) and son (Tarkovsky via Smoktunovskii) ultimately control the narrative in an authoritative blend of poetry and prose that unites the two, in this instance through their complementary creativity and their behavioral sameness.

Though *Zerkalo* may impress many viewers as the last word in cinematic retrospection and insularity, Tarkovsky in a public appearance in April 1975 improbably declared, "The purpose of *Mirror,* its inspiration, is that of a homily: look, learn, use the life shown here as an example." An example of what, he did not specify. His coy announcement that the film "is no more than a straightforward, simple story" devoid of symbolism (*Time within Time* 367),[58] however, inclines one to approach his self-commentary with skepticism. As a reader of Tarkovsky's lectures perceptively noted, Tarkovsky's statements contradicted his films, sometimes dramatically so.[59] In the case of *Zerkalo,* personal therapy veiled in aestheticization indisputably outweighs homily. And Tarkovsky's last film indicates that in *Zerkalo* he did not lay the troubling theme of father-son relations to rest.

PATERNAL LOVE AS THE PYRE

Made in Sweden while Andrei, the son from his second marriage, was refused an exit visa and therefore remained in the USSR without his parents, Tarkovsky's final work, *Sacrifice* (*Zhertvoprinoshenie; Offret* 1986), plays a valedictory variation on the kenotic scenario familiar from Tarkovsky's earlier works. As Boldyrev correctly notes, for a change, the protagonist is not the son striving to come to terms with his past but instead the father—the erudite, troubled Alexander (Erland Josephson), who "sacrifices himself" so as to save the world, and above all his son, Malysh/Little Man, from imminent nuclear disaster (Boldyrev 218). Whether the apocalyptic threat is genuine or a product of Alexander's imagination remains uncertain, for nothing in the film confirms the phenomenological status of his horrific vision of devastation, shot in the black and white Tarkovsky usually reserved for dreams and fantasies.[60] What matters for Tarkovsky is not the objective reality, however, but Alexander's readiness to sacrifice himself for the sake of a better world and his beloved offspring in it. Whereas self-sacrifice, according to Tarkovsky, defines women's essence,[61] in this strained and lugubrious narrative it is embraced by the middle-aged melancholic who, trapped in an unhappy marriage to the domineering and self-assertive Adelaide, volubly (if sometimes incoherently) decries the violence, fear, power, and materialism of modern existence. His alienation is comprehensive, embracing politics, society, and domestic life, in which all seem coercive and misguided, propelled by forces devoid of a spiritual dimension.

Weak in structure and glutted with dogmatic philosophizing, the confused film nonetheless is clear on one point: the love between father and son. Though the son rarely appears on screen, his presence at the beginning and end (in Tarkovsky's signature device of the structural frame) helps establish the film's governing concept of self-sacrifice in overtly religious terms.[62] As the father, aided by the son, plants a sickly tree, he relates a parable about the capacity of faith and steadfastness to effect miracles: long ago, an old Orthodox monk, Pamve, planted a withered tree on a mountainside and instructed the young novice Ioann Kolov to water it daily at precisely the same time. After three years of rigorous adherence to these directions, the obedient Ioann suddenly saw the tree restored to life and laden with blossoms. This transparent lesson about the powers of faith translated into ritualistic devotion posits its universality at the film's conclusion: a panoramic shot shows the ambulance carrying Alexander away after his act of arson speed past the tree, while the camera gradually zooms in for a close-up of Malysh standing beside it. After pouring water on the base of the once dead but now "resurrected" tree, he reclines under it and, gazing at the sky/heavens, muses about his father's illuminating tale and the significance of the biblical passage he quoted in the film's opening sequence (John I. 1), "'In the beginning was the Word.' Why is that, Papa?" The precedence of word over deed is a source of chronic distress for Alexander, though (or because?) his various professions of actor, scholar, and journalist by definition rely on the medium of words, whereas the divine Word *is* Deed.[63] That distress finds relief in Alexander's existential deed of destroying all his possessions through fire, so as to ensure a New Beginning. Here, as in *Ivanovo detstvo,* the tree is central and obviously must be understood as the Tree of Life, which the Bible references in both Genesis (2:9, 3:22, 3:24) and Revelation (2:7, 22:2, 22:14), or the hiero-cosmic symbol of the Cosmic Tree or Pillar of Life as manifestations of the Sacred, so richly explicated by Mircea Eliade (27–59). The Tree symbolizing immortality,[64] advice about its maintenance, and his own self-elimination are Alexander's salvific gift to his son.[65]

Boldyrev interprets the destruction of the family dwelling, quite reasonably, as Tarkovsky's final, symbolic farewell to his personal myth of Home (Boldyrev 218), which he finally recognized as untenable. Most remarkable about the symbolic closing scene, however, is that for the first time in the film Malysh, who has been mute throughout, suddenly gains the power of speech. In the initial twenty minutes or so of the film Alexander speaks *at* Malysh, who remains silent as his father relates not only the parable to him but also the "story of origins"—an explanation of how he and Adelaide chose to live in that particular location, where Malysh was also born. Immersed in his monologic recollections, Alexander loses sight of his son. When the child suddenly and playfully leaps upon him from behind, Alexander instinctively reacts with violence, his blow causing Malysh's nosebleed. The scene not only evokes the paradigm of the father wreaking physical violence upon the son, which extends at least as far back as the biblical narratives of Abraham's sacrifice of Isaac and God's sacrifice of Jesus, but also symbolizes the psychological impositions forced upon the boy, who cannot "speak for himself." That unexpected, bloody manifestation of "paternal power" prepares the viewer for Alexander's final redemptive act, which recalls Freud's claim that "self-sacrifice points to a blood-guilt" (Freud 925): Alexander eliminates both paternal tradition (Home) and himself as paternal presence, thereby liberating the son into selfhood and language.

Tarkovsky's last onscreen configuration of father-son relations ends with the promise of rebirth and independence for the son, but at the cost of the father's self-inflicted withdrawal from the son's life. Here, then, the paternal absence is rationalized, springing not from desire for another woman or for escape from the family, but from self-abnegating love for the son, in a scenario that, arguably, belongs to the realm of fantasy. Freud maintains that in the son's patricidal competition with the father, the latter's "removal [. . .] contained an element which in the course of time must have brought about an extraordinary increase of longing for the father" and that the son's violence against the father was "animated by the wish to become like the father," a wish expressed in "incorporating parts of the substitute for him in the totem feast" (Freud 10). Tarkovsky's films and writings broadly follow this pattern but with a significant adjustment: while the father's voluntary departure—and not death at the son's hands—unquestionably bred a sense of desolation and chronic "longing" for him, and the son's efforts to become "like him" are amply documented, Tarkovsky desired to possess not the mother but the unavailable father. The choice of his first wife, a "double" of his mother, was dictated by his yearning to "inhabit" his father, to unite with him through mimicry. Unlike other directors of the Soviet and post-Soviet era, such as Marlen Khutsiev, Sergei Bondarchuk, Andrei Smirnov, Aleksei German, Aleksei Sidorov, and Timur Bekmambetov, who rely on the trope of filiation to articulate their concept of Soviet/ Russian history, Tarkovsky struggled to come to terms above all with his personal experience of paternal abandonment, attempting to reconcile his psychological trauma with his philosophical convictions in films that creatively revised not history, but his story.

NOTES

As always, I render loving gratitude to Bożenna Goscilo, my chief, mercilessly helpful critic of several decades.

The first epigraph is from A. Plakhov, "Kira Murtova: Mne nuzhna lozhka deg-tia." *Kommersant* (4 November 1998): 10; cited in Taubman 10. Andrei Mikhalkov-Konchalovsky states, "Tarkovsky's childlike traits were his extremely naïve belief in the absolute power of art, and hence in his extraordinary messianic role" [*About Andrei Tarkovsky* 191]; the second is from Stanislaw Lem, *The Futurological Congress*, trans. Michael Kandel (New York: Harcourt Brace, 1985 [1979]), 103; and the third is from Andrey Tarkovsky, *Time within Time: The Diaries, 1970–1986*, trans. Kitty Hunter-Blair (Calcutta: Seagull Books, 1991), 384.

1. The actor and film director Nikolai Burliaev remembers a visit with the cameraman Vadim Iusov to Tarkovsky shortly before the latter went abroad to film *Nostalghia*, during which Tarkovsky informed both colleagues that they "could only be truly creative in his films" (*About Andrei Tarkovsky* 87). See Paola Volkova's unapologetic summary of various recollections, "Postoianno i mnogo vspominaiut, chto u Tarkovskogo byl, miagko govoria, trudnyi kharakter" ["People regularly and copiously recall that Tarkovsky had, to put it mildly, a difficult character"] (Volkova 30).

2. Tarkovsky's ambitions declared themselves in a notation in his diary of 1976: "I must learn to use a cine-camera, and do some filming here. It is possible to attain immortality" (*Time within Time* 131). A typical example of a cued cult worshiper is Leila Alexander, his Swedish interpreter during work on *Zhertvoprinoshenie*. In

reminiscences titled "Secrets and Sacraments [sic] of Andrei Tarkovsky," she writes, "Andrei [. . .] was obsessed and God-inspired in making films. And he offered his sacred gift as a sacrifice to his viewers. I had the good fortune of being next to the Great Artist, the Great Spirit. My eternal gratitude and love goes to the Great Master Andrei Tarkovsky" (*About Andrei Tarkovsky* 315).

3. Ol'ga Surkova's *Tarkovsky i ia* (2005) counters this homiletic tradition through its "exposé" of Tarkovsky's purportedly nasty traits (failure to keep his word and honor a contract, refusal to pay promised fees, etc.) and an annihilating portrait of his second wife, Larisa. In a blurb on the book's cover, Surikova cites the question posed in Pushkin's little tragedy *Mozart and Salieri* regarding the compatibility of genius with evil [*zlodeistvo*], and answers in the affirmative with regard to Tarkovsky. In their bilious resentment, these recollections could hardly differ more from Surkova's volume, *S Tarkovskim i o Tarkovskom* [*With Tarkovsky and On Tarkovsky*] (2005), published the same year. A recent article by Igor' Mantsov offers a scathing evaluation of Tarkovsky's oeuvre on both aesthetic and philosophical grounds.

4. See *Time within Time* 69. According to P. D. Volkova, Tarkovsky's widow refused such a headstone after his death (P. D. Volkova 89). Irma Raush, Tarkovsky's first abandoned but worshipful wife, cites his Christ-quoting note, "Moe sobstvennoe budushchee—*eto chasha, kotoraia ne minuet menia*, sledovatel'no, ee nado ispit'" ["My own future is *a cup that will not pass me by*; therefore I must drain it"] (Volkova 355; emphasis added).

5. As Nina Anosova puts it, "Today, there are some who compare Tarkovsky's life, both personal and artistic, to a classical tragedy" ("Flashbacks," in *About Andrei Tarkovsky* 49; translation adjusted for correct punctuation). See also Natal'ia Baranskaia's view that "Andrei Tarkovsky's life [. . .] was shortened by fierce struggle [sic] for the right to speak in his own voice" (*About Andrei Tarkvosky* 26). Tarkovsky died of cancer. Vida Johnson and Graham Petrie title the first chapter of their study "A Martyred Artist?" (3–26).

6. According to Johnson and Petrie, Georgii Rerberg, the cameraman for *Zerkalo*, explained that a dearth of color film stock forced Tarkovsky to alternate footage in color and black and white (304).

7. For Tarkovsky's complaints about the Soviet film industry's treatment of him, see the press conference in Milan recorded and summarized by Surkova (*S Tarkovskim i o Tarkovskom* 382). Surkova's chronicle of Tarkovsky's work on his films provides a wealth of specific details (see ibid. passim). Aleksandr Misharin recalls how after a screening of *Zerkalo* Ermash declared, "'Of course, we do have artistic freedom! But not to that degree!'" and how his "statement determined the movie's fate. It was shown only in a few movie theaters, mainly in Moscow" (*About Andrei Tarkovsky* 58). Much may be said for Andrei Mikhalkov-Konchalovsky's sensible position: "It is my conviction that there was no deliberate desire to impede him in his work, at any event in the later years. The film industry officials simply felt that his scripts were too strange and hard to understand. There was never any social protest in them that could have scared the top brass. Andrei was not a dissident" (*About Andrei Tarkovsky* 195).

8. A pupil of Gerasimov, Muratova venerated him instead of dismissing him professionally through pluralization, à la Tarkovsky (see Taubman 2). For the system's considerably more draconian measures against other film directors, see Johnson and Petre 4–6.

9. Surkova justly points out that Tarkovsky was specifically a Soviet director who relied on the system for money, wanted more praise, which would have assured him the privileges others enjoyed, and, despite his disclaimers, felt wounded that the establishment ignored his fiftieth birthday on 5 April 1982 (*S Tarkovskim i o Tarkovskom* 399).

10. Volkova captures Tarkovsky's self-preoccupation in the generously worded formulation, "Andrei zhil s glazami, povernutymi vo vnutr'" ["Andrei lived with his eyes turned inward"] (Volkova 66).

11. The break occurred in 1935–36, when he was three, according to Tarkovsky (interview cited in Boldyrev 46). Critics, however, unanimously claim that he was four years old at the time. See Johnson and Petrie 17.

12. As Bożenna Goscilo penetratingly noted, "Tarkovsky sounds like Kafka crossed with Dostoevsky's *Adolescent*" (personal communication). Indeed, Tarkovsky himself compared his father-son situation to that in *Podrostok* [*A Raw Youth*]. The only opera Tarkovsky staged, Mussorgsky's *Boris Godunov* (with Claudio Abbado in Covent Garden in 1983, the production was shown at the Kirov in 1990), treats filiation and rightful inheritance.

13. For an analysis of loss in both Tarkovsky's and Sokurov's films, see the recent article by Sandler, published while this collection was under review. As Sandler justly observes, "No topic occupies the cinema of Andrei Tarkovsky more relentlessly than that of loss" (127).

14. See, for example, a letter to his father, avowing filial love and strenuously fighting against any expression of resentment: "Ia nikogda ne obvinial tebia v tom, chto ty ushel ot materi" ["I never accused you of abandoning mother"] (cited in Boldyrev 61–62). Yet Arsenii Tarkovsky left not only his wife but his son and daughter—a fact that Tarkovsky suppressed in everyday conversations but projected on screen.

15. P. Volkova contends, "Oni oba byli poetami, otets i syn. Otets pisal stikhi. Syn sozdal poeticheskuiu formy v kinematografe" ["Both father and son were poets. The father wrote poetry. The son created a poetic form in cinematography"] (Volkova 11).

16. On this stratagem, see Boldyrev 23–24.

17. Misharin recalls that the dissolution of Tarkovsky's marriage to his first wife, Irina (Irma) Raush, was "especially hard for him" because of his father's abandonment of the family. Coupled with the frequently reported fact that Tarkovsky's acquaintances mistook a photograph of his *mother, Marina Ivanovna,* for one of Irina, Tarkovsky's choice of wife and the subsequent divorce, initiated by him, suggest his (unconscious?) duplication of Tarkovsky Sr.'s biographical trajectory. See Misharin in *About Andrei Tarkovsky* 52, 56; Volkova 46. Nina Anosova also recalls Tarkovsky's response to her congratulations upon his marriage to Raush with the unexpected remark, "You know, Irma looks like my mother" (*About Andrei Tarkovsky* 47). The wife/mother doubling finds its way into *Solaris* and *Zerkalo*.

18. Noting that Tarkovsky inherited his father's taste for the finer things in life," Johnson and Petrie report the claim by Tarkovsky's sister that he "even imitated his father's handwriting" (19).

19. The director Andrei Mikhalkov-Konchalovsky, who found Tarkovsky's films boring and pretentious in their dialogues, believed that Tarkovsky "increasingly subscribed to Bresson's philosophy. All his heroes became Tarkovskyite. [. . .] For

him [cinema] was a spiritual experience that makes a person better"—true to socialist realism! Konchalovsky emphasizes Tarkovsky's paranoia, which sprang from naïveté and personal problems (*About Andrei Tarkovsky* 190, 191, 196).

20. Upon his mother's death, Tarkovsky lamented, "No one in the world is ever going to love me as she did" (*Time within Time* 208–9).

21. See Lilya Kaganovsky, *How the Soviet Man Was (Un)Made* (Pittsburgh: University of Pittsburgh Press, 2007).

22. Describing Tarkovsky as an "extremely complex individual with sado-masochistic tendencies who fought many of his personal demons on the screen," Johnson and Petrie continue: "His bisexuality, for example, still remains a well-hidden secret in the extremely homophobic Russian society" (17).

23. For a Marxist-Lacanian study of fetish that attempts to reconcile its individual and social operations, see Henry Krips, *Fetish: An Erotics of Culture* (Ithaca, N.Y.: Cornell University Press, 1999).

24. Virtually all reminiscences and biographies dwell on Tarkovsky's introverted remoteness and awkwardness, his inability to achieve any integration, however formal and preliminary, into the social order.

25. In his insightful recent study of Tarkovsky's aesthetics, Bird parenthetically notes that in the film "women are without exception depicted unfavourably, as unwelcome intruders in the male world" (33), but he has little interest in pursuing that fact.

26. It would be crude but perhaps not completely off the mark to identify this female crassness with the two women who kept Tarkovsky and his father apart: Tarkovsky's mother, and his father's new wife, later to be exchanged for yet another woman.

27. "more zhenshchin, priamolineino-trebovatel'nykh, pochti zhestokikh v svoem ogranichitel'nom pafose, zhazhdushchikh sluzhit' sotsial'nomu poriadku, delat' vse 'po pravilam.' Mir poezii vne zhenskoi kompetentsii. [. . .] I voobshche zhenshchiny okazyvaiutsia v fil'me razluchnitsami dvukh muzhchin: 'syna' i 'ottsa."

28. In this respect Sokurov's *Otets i syn* [*Father and Son*] is conceptually Tarkovskian. See José Alaniz's essay in this volume (chapter 11).

29. Sasha's artistic temperament manifests itself not only in his love for the violin but also in his appreciation of statuettes in a store window and his fascination with the ability of mirrors to multiply images—the latter trait allying him with Tarkovsky as filmmaker. Tarkovsky's full-feature films consistently attribute love of art and fascination with visual images to males, who produce art (*Andrei Rublev*), peruse reproductions in books (*Ivanovo detstvo, Zerkalo*) or hang them on their walls (*Solaris*), and so on. He also introduced into his diploma film most of the symbols that recur throughout his features: water and reflections in it, mirrors, apples, horses, birds, endless stretches of space, destruction of buildings, classical music, visions stemming from impassioned desire, and verticality.

30. "Voobshche detstvo svoe vosproizvel v svoikh fil'makh fundamental'no [. . .] ukhod ottsa iz sem'i byl dlia mladentsa [. . .] kosmogonicheskoi katastrofoi, posledstviia kotoroi on zatem, stav vzroslym, neosoznanno stremilsia popravit', ustranit', to est' vosstanovit' iznachal'nuiu kosmicheskuiu v sebe garmoniiu."

31. Josephine Woll rightly notes that the father-son dynamic was peculiar to Soviet cinema and that Tarkovsky's choice of child as protagonist in his first film fit

neatly into the context of Thaw film, which favored the child hero as the embodiment of Thaw values (113). Other directors of such films, however, did not return compulsively to the father-son dyad in terms that were so flagrantly autobiographical in their specifics. Not coincidentally, Ivan's age approximates Tarkovsky's during World War II.

32. Whereas the first sequence unambiguously comprises Ivan's retrospective dream, whose subjectivity produces the contents of the final sequence is unclear: since Ivan, as Gal'tsev learns at this point, is dead, the vision of his "liberation" amid nature can belong only to a fanciful Gal'tsev or, more likely, the director. Tarkovsky's penchant for ending his scenarios with narratively unconvincing but psychologically reassuring fantasies, all too evident in *Katok i skripka, Ivanovo detstvo, Solaris,* and *Zhertvoprinoshenie,* bizarrely parallels Hollywood happy endings and the fairy-tale conclusions of countless socialist-realist verbal and visual texts.

33. The cobweb's dark connotations multiply approximately halfway through the film, when the nurse Masha informs the flirtatious Kholin that cobwebs are the only thing she fears. Vitalii Troianovskii's article on the film makes two excellent points: that Ivan's mother is identified with water throughout and that Ivan's real enemy is not the Nazis but death (108, 109). Certainly Ivan's solitary struggle against, then submission to, death evokes the paradigm of Christ's Passion, which the church/ bunker sequence references via the icon.

34. Additional images of entrapment in tragedy punctuate the mise-en-scène: in a long shot of Ivan's silhouette among protruding remnants of bombed buildings, the ruins seem to enclose Ivan in a cage; once he makes contact with the Russian military unit, claustrophobic shots show him crouching in the semidarkness of the church that serves as a bunker.

35. In Bogomolov's novella, he is shot. Tarkovsky's change here connects Ivan's final fate with the two Soviet scouts prominently hanging along the bank of the swamp. It also brings Ivan's mode of death closer to Christ's crucifixion.

36. The concluding dream, which, unlike the others, obviously cannot be Ivan's, functions as a summation of his fate.

37. As Johnson and Petrie have pointed out, the American translation of the film's title as *My Name Is Ivan* ignores the painful irony of the Russian, which alludes to Ivan's *loss* of childhood owing to the war.

38. While in the novella she is killed at eighteen months (36), in Ivan's dreams and vision she looks approximately Ivan's age.

39. In other words, innocent pleasures are shattered by the military combat that devastates Ivan's childhood. Paradise falls prey to history and, apart from these recollections of "*le temps perdu,*" Ivan's life dwindles to an obsession with vengeance. War's crippling effects on children are further emphasized by the message for help on the wall of the Russians' makeshift headquarters, scratched by eight Soviet adolescents who, one deduces, were executed by the Nazis. This poignant plea intensifies Ivan's hatred of the Nazis and his determination to avenge the dead. The documentary footage toward the end of the film, registering the bodies of German children killed by their fathers before the Allies arrive, generalizes the theme of children's "paying for" their parents' mistakes.

40. The words recall another Thaw orphan—little Fedor in Marlen Khutsiev's *Dva Fedora* [Two Fyodors] (1958).

41. See William Wordsworth, "My Heart Leaps Up When I Behold." A painful episode confirming Ivan's inverted status as caretaker shows an old man crazed by the war's events seeking comfort from the boy.

42. A rehearsal of this scene occurs in Tarkovsky's diploma film, where Sasha points out to Sergei that he should not smoke.

43. On the *puer senex*, see David Lee Miller, "The Father's Witness: Patriarchal Images of Boys," *Representations* 70 (spring 2000): 115–41.

44. The film won both the FIPRESCI and the Jury's Grand Prize at the 1972 Cannes Film Festival. Natal'ia Bondarchuk recalls that Tarkovsky "was upset and offended like a child because the film came in second, not first place, and accused the jury of being fixed" (*About Andrei Tarkovsky* 137).

45. Western readers know *Solaris* in an English translation from the French, whereas Tarkovsky relied on the Russian translation, with subtitles in transliteration. Consequently discrepancies in characters' names proliferate: Berton (in Polish and English) becomes Burton (in Russian/the film); Snaut (in Polish and Russian) becomes Snow (in English); Harey (in Polish) becomes Rheya (in English) and Hari (in Russian). Gibarian, Messenger, and Sartorius undergo no variations in name. My discussion uses the altered, Russian names for comments on Tarkovsky's film.

46. Turovskaia (92), Boldyrev (89), and Volkova (49) also detect the biblical myth of the prodigal son in the film.

47. Some critics refer to Hari simply as Kelvin's lover, but in the chapter titled "Monsters" (in Polish, "Potwory") he introduces her to Snaut as his wife ("moja żona," 129).

48. Although Boldyrev is indentured to the conventions of the hagiographic biographer, he clearly recognizes Tarkovsky's problematic attitude toward gender: "In Tarkovski's cinema, the man *lives* through female energy, but is *saved* by the energy of paternity, the energy of heaven [. . .]. She [the woman—H.G.] is the bosom from which he emerged and to which he cannot be ungrateful. But beyond that it's service to the spirit of the Father, who in essence and status is the Heavenly Father" ["v kinomatografe Tarkovskogo muzhchina *zhivet* zhenskimi energiiami, no *spasaetsia* energiiami ottsovstva, energiiami neba. [. . .] Ona—Iono, iz kotoroi on vyshel i kotoromu ne mozhet ne byt' blagodaren. No dalee—sluzhenie dukhu Ottsa, kotoryi vsegda po suti i statusu Otets Nebesnyi"] (Boldyrev 90). If one interprets the father in Tarkovsky's work as the Heavenly Father, which Tarkovsky's kenotic self-image implies, then the ineluctable question arises: Why would Tarkovsky feel abandoned by God? Tarkovsky's unabating sense of himself as suffering son and divinely endowed artist—credentials that rendered him a kenotic genius who kept recasting his father in myriad roles so as to reconcile himself to the central, devastating event of his childhood—lends credence to Freud's contention in "The Infantile Recurrence of Totemism": "[G]od is in every case modeled after the father and [. . .] our personal relation to god is dependent upon our relation to our physical father [. . .] [G]od at bottom is nothing but an exalted father" (Freud 919–20).

49. The words migrate directly onto the screen from Tarkovsky's diary entries of 8 and 22 October 1979, after his mother's death: "She did not look at all like herself in her coffin"; "I am so lonely. [. . .] I am alone" (*Time within Time* 208–9).

50. The ambiguity of "us" is telling, given the identification of the mother with Hari.

51. Though Johnson and Petrie contend that Kris's "ambiguous relationship" with his "beautiful and remote mother seems to be at the root of the hero's problems" (105), remoteness, in fact, is *Kris's* defining feature, evident in his interactions with his father, Hari, Burton, and the other scientists on Solaris. Here, as in Tarkovsky's life, the mother is the enabler: only after the symbolic scene in which she "purifies" and kisses him can he recover and acknowledge his repressed desire—to bond with his father. If the Ocean materializes the scientists' most deeply rooted but unacknowledged desires, then the film suggests that Kris Kelvin wishes above all to have his loving wife and mother (generational versions of the same female presence) forgive him for the primacy of the father in his (finally recognized) psychological needs.

52. Of course, the indoor rain also serves as a clue for the viewer, indicating that the entire episode is a projection of Kelvin's desire, reified by the Ocean.

53. "It is an autobiographical film" (*Time within Time* 367). Over the years, the script, on which Tarkovsky began work as early as 1968, underwent major revisions and had various titles. For background information and a detailed retelling of the film's narrative, see Johnson and Petrie 111–136. In his diaries, Tarkovsky condescendingly remarked, "[Iusov i]n his lower-middle-class way [. . .] was infuriated by the fact that I was making a film about myself" (*Time within Time* 62). Elements of *Zerkalo* probably could not avoid seeping into *Solaris,* for throughout work on the latter Tarkovsky was battling with his own ever changing ideas for his celluloid autobiography and the Soviet film establishment's lack of support for the film.

54. The adult protagonist lies ailing, presumably on his deathbed, his face never revealed in the film.

55. Sandler also notes that the father's "felt presence offscreen marks paternal absence as the film's theme" (130).

56. See Grigorii Kozintsev's *Hamlet* (1964).

57. Turovskaia likewise reads this sequence as one of the film's several psychological "substitutions" (104–5).

58. With his customary self-contradiction, Tarkovsky claimed that the (allegedly simple) film contained images, which as a category "cannot be deciphered," and not "familiar symbols," which can. In a startling statement that one might sooner have expected from a Soviet official, he observed, "Symbolism is a sign of decadence" (*Time within Time* 369).

59. In an interview M. S. Chugunova, Tarkovsky's assistant, told Maia Turovskaia, "Odin iz rebiat vzial u menia pochitat' ego lektsii i skazal: 'Nu, potriasaiushche, chelovek, kotoryi pishet o teorii, chto nado snimat' zhizn' vrasplokh, delaet sovershenno protivopolozhnoe" ["One of the fellows borrowed his [Tarkovsky's] lectures from me and after reading them said, 'It's simply staggering—the man who writes about the theory that we should film life unawares does completely the opposite'"] (Turovskaia 121).

60. Awarding the film the Special Jury Prize at the Cannes Film Festival likely reflected the jury's human response to Tarkovsky's death rather than its professional assessment of the film's quality.

61. In *Solaris,* for instance, the impulse to self-sacrifice evidenced the loving Hari's gradual metamorphosis into a human being.

62. Tarkovsky's diaries teem with references to the Bible, to which he reportedly was attached during the last year of his life (see Boldyrev).

63. Perhaps that disjunction also troubled Tarkovsky, for the impassioned spokesman for Home and love abandoned his first family for greener pastures in the form of Larisa Egorkina, whom he subsequently married. Boldyrev and Surkova, among others, view Adelaide as a celluloid version of Larisa Tarkovskaia, whom many consider(ed) a bossy philistine.

64. The "family tree" of successive generations doubtless springs from this image.

65. In 1985 Tarkovsky noted, "Without giving the question much thought, I realize that all the fine feelings in the world are worth less than one single good deed" (*Time within Time* 342–43).

REFERENCES

About Andrei Tarkovsky. Compiled by Marina Tarkovskaya. Moscow: Progress, 1990. [Translation of *O Tarkovskom*.]

Bird, Robert. *Andrei Tarkovsky: Elements of Cinema*. London: Reaktion Books, 2008.

Bogomolov, Vladimr. *Roman. Povesti. Rasskazy*. Leningrad: Lenizdat, 1981.

Boldyrev, Nikolai. *zhertvoprinoshenie Andreia Tarkovskogo*. Moscow: Vagrius, 2004.

Dunne, Nathan, ed. *Tarkovsky*. London: Black Dog, 2008.

Eliade, Mircea. *Images and Symbols: Studies in Religious Symbolism*. Translated by Philip Mairet. Princeton, N.J.: Princeton University Press, 1991.

Freud, Sigmund. *Totem and Taboo*. In *The Basic Writings of Sigmund Freud*, trans. and ed. A. A. Brill, 807–930. New York: Modern Library, 1938.

Gorelova, Valeriia. "*Ivanovo detstvo*." In *Rossiiskii illiuzion*, ed. L. M. Budiak, 339–44. Moscow: Materik, 2003.

Johnson, Vida T., and Graham Petrie. *The Films of Andrei Tarkovsky: A Visual Fugue*. Bloomington: Indiana University Press, 1994.

Lem, Stanisław. *Solaris*. Cracow: Wydawnictwo Literackie, 1994 [1961].

———. *Solaris*. Translated from the French by Joanna Kilmartin and Steve Cox. San Diego: Harvest/Harcourt, 1987 [1970].

Lopushanksii, P. M. Trofimenkov. "Tarkovsky v 97-m." *Iskusstvo kino* 10 (1997): 96–99.

Mantsov, Igor'. "Kinoobozrenie Igoria Mantsova: Kosmos. Prishel'tsy." *Novyi mir* 10 (2005). Available at http://magazines.russ.ru/novyi_mi/2005/10/man17-pr.html (accessed 9 June 2007).

O Tarkovskom. Compiled by Marina Tarkovskaia. Moscow: Progress, 1989.

O Tarkovskom. Vospominaniia v dvukh knigakh. Compiled by Marina Tarkovskaia. Moscow: "Dedalus," 2002.

Orlinski, Wojciech. "An Interview with Stanislaw Lem." Summer 1996. Available at http://www.geocities.com/CapitolHill/2594/lem.html (accessed 14 May 2005).

Sandler, Stephanie. "The Absent Father, the Stillness of Film." In *Tarkovsky*, ed. Nathan Dunne, 126–48. London: Black Dog, 2008.

Sokurov, A. "'Kino ne govorit nichego dostatochno vazhnogo. . . .'" *Iskusstvo kino* 10 (1997):100–103. [Interview with N. Sirivlia.]

Surkova, Ol'ga. *S Tarkovskim i o Tarkovskom.* Moscow: "Raduga," 2005.
———. *Tarkovskii i ia.* Moscow: Zebra E, 2005.
Tarkovskii, Andrei. *Arkhivy. Dokumenty. Vospominaniia.* Edited by P. D. Volkova. Moscow: "Podkova," 2002.
Tarkovsky, Andrey. *Time within Time: The Diaries, 1970–1986.* Translated by Kitty Hunter-Blair. Calcutta: Seagull Books, 1991.
Taubman, Jane A. *Kira Muratova.* London: I. B. Tauris, 2005.
Troianovskii, V. "'Mama??!'" *Iskusstvo kino* 10 (1997): 104–9.
Turovskaia, M. *71/2 ili Fil'my Andreia Tarkovskogo.* Moscow: "Iskusstvo," 1991.
Turovskaia, Maiia. *"Soliaris."* In *Rossiiskii illiuzion,* 495–500. Moscow: Materik, 2003.
———. *"Zerkalo."* In *Rossiiskii illiuzion,* 525–30. Moscow: Materik, 2003.
Woll, Josephine. *Real Images. Soviet Cinema and the Thaw.* London: I. B. Tauris 2000.

FILMOGRAPHY

Ivanovo detstvo. [*Ivan's Childhood/My Name Is Ivan*]. Dir. Andrei Tarkovsky. Mosfil'm, 1971.
Katok i skripka. [*The Steamroller and the Violin*]. Dir. Andrei Tarkovskii. Mosfil'm, 1960.
Soliaris. Dir. Andrei Tarkovskii. Mosfil'm, 1972.
Zerkalo. [*The Mirror*]. Dir. Andrei Tarkovskii. Mosfil'm, 1975.
Zhertovoprinoshenie [*The Sacrifice*]. Original title in Swedish, *Offret.* Dir. Andrei Tarkovskii. Swedish Film Institute, Argos Films, Film Four International, 1986.

Figure 10.1. Instant bonding between Sasha and Sergei.

Figure 10.2. Indulgent surrogate father supervising the son.

Figure 10.3. The severe mother distanced via the mirror.

Figure 10.4. The cobweb evoking Ivan's fatal entrapment.

Figure 10.5. Loving mother and son at the well.

Figure 10.6. A bravura shot capturing the fragility of the moment before the mother's violent death.

Figure 10.7. The torments of Ivan's waking nightmare in solitude, his existential condition.

Figure 10.8. The prodigal son's return à la Rembrandt.

ELEVEN

Vision and Blindness in
Sokurov's *Father and Son*

JOSÉ ALANIZ

The supreme achievement of patriarchal
ideology is that it has no outside.

MARY ANN DOANE, "THE VOICE IN THE CINEMA"

Since his 1978/1987 debut with *The Lonely Voice of Man* [*Odinokii golos cheloveka*], Aleksander Sokurov—the "poet laureate" of late-/post-Soviet Russian cinema—has produced a large and critically acclaimed body of work (sixteen features and thirty documentaries of various lengths), in a ponderous, neo-Romantic mode that aspires to nothing less than rendering the unseen *visible*. Linked to other figures of so-called transcendental cinema, such as Robert Bresson, Abbas Kiarostiami, Tsai Ming-liang, and his one-time inspiration, Andrei Tarkovsky,[1] Sokurov makes meticulously crafted films that combine a lush, textured painterliness with richly layered soundscapes and often abstract dialogue, to create an atmosphere of immanence and spiritual longing. Sokurov's metaphysical style, different from film to film but unmistakably his, blurs boundaries between fact and fiction, life and art.[2]

Saturated in warm sunlight-yellows, somber ochers, and Rembrandt reds, Sokurov's feature *Father and Son* (2003) depicts through dreamlike imagery and sound the emotional crisis brought on by the impending separation of Aleksei, a young army cadet, and his father, a retired soldier and war veteran. A meditation on patriarchy and the sacred bonds

of blood, the film forms the second part of a trilogy about family relationships that began with 1997's *Mother and Son*. But we can also read
it as a recapitulation of Sokurov's *The Second Circle* (1990), in which the
hero mourns over the dead body of his (possibly abusive) father and a
soldier—a metonym for the moribund USSR.

Father and Son (explored in more detail below, along with other
recent films) participates in a national project of recuperation, reconstitution, and restoration of the patriarchy after the disasters of the Soviet/
early post-Soviet eras, which had toppled this privileged signifier from
its pedestal. The death of the Symbolic father,[3] exacerbated by the assertion of feminine agency understood as contiguous with late-twentieth-
century Russian consumer culture,[4] would now be followed by His resurrection. For all its "apolitical" hermeticism,[5] then, *Father and Son*, in
fact, bears a heavy ideological burden on its manly shoulders.

All these factors made the film's reception at its Cannes debut especially puzzling and scandalous—to no one more than Sokurov himself.
Critics and reviewers focused (rather obsessively, perhaps) on its presumed homoeroticism and what this might indicate about the filmmaker's rumored identity as a closeted gay man. The widely reported scene
that unfolded at a bizarre press conference had critics returning again
and again to the gay content, with Sokurov by turns berating them for
"decadent" fixations and "vulgar interpretations" ["poshlye traktovki"]
and pleading with them not "to rush to inject [their] own problems and
complexes into the work" ["ne toropites' sobstvennye problemy i kom-
pleksy privnosit' v proizvedenie"]. He compared homosexuality to rac-
ism and nationalism, and spoke darkly of a growing complacency about
filmed violence and cruelty, grumbling that the United States and the
European Union bore responsibility for this "loss to humanity" ["uron
chelovechestvu"] (Kichin "Alexander Sokurov").

This fiasco leads me to explore what follows in this essay: *Father and
Son's* daring (maybe too daring) representation of homosocial, familial
male eros; the role played by Sokurov's appropriation of myth, particularly the Sacrifice of Isaac, and its elaboration in painting (specifically
that of Rembrandt) for his own treatment of an "eternal" patriarchy
and filial duty; and the paradoxical way in which Sokurov couches his
bold, revelatory vision in various forms of blindness—cinematographic,
sexual, and aesthetic. Finally, I touch on how the film's initial, belabored

reception itself might have thrown into relief some critical blinders of contemporary scholarship on cinema.

FATHER, I WANT TO SEE YOU

In a 2005 *SEANS* essay devoted to fatherhood in post-Soviet Russian cinema, Aleksander Sekatskii coined the term *otsepriimstvo* ["patriality"/fatherliness] to denote "the attempt to remove the existential deficit which had emerged where the transformation of a boy into a man traditionally took place" ["popytka ustraneniia eksistentsial'nogo defitsita, voznikshego tam, gde traditsionno proiskhodilo preobrazovanie mal'chika v muzhchinu"] (199). This "deficit" or void, manifest in numerous 1990s films about absent fathers, was now being filled with works in which the fathers returned, to their sons.[6] Crucially, Sekatskii cites a kind of stunned, inarticulate hyper-visuality—exemplified by Aleksandr Zviagintsev's *The Return* (2003)—as central to the idea of *otsepriimstvo*:

> "Did you see what he was like . . ." says one of the boys in the film . . .
> "Yes," answers his younger brother, after a pause. And he finds nothing else to say. Such could be the reaction of an earthbound being to weightlessness: what can you compare it with . . . It's the sweet horror of the unknown: "Did you see what he was like. . ." (199)[7]

Elsewhere Sekatskii compares this astonished act of witness to the sudden sensation of falling, dream visions, and Sartrean vertigo. It is also, I submit, a kind of stupefied blindness, an inability to process and interpret visual stimuli. Producing psychic overload and shock, the overdetermined "father" signifier seems both familiar and unprecedented, uncanny. The sons are petrified, struck dumb before a disruptive sensory abyss/plenitude. We might say that the Father departs (or is toppled) from the Symbolic, but returns as the Lacanian Imaginary: fundamentally indecipherable but emotionally, imagistically laden with haunting significance.[8] He is a kind of reanimated living dead.

Sokurov seems to have anticipated this formulation, figuring the father-son relationship in just these terms—as a kind of horror show— even as the Soviet Union was busy digging its own grave. In the climax to *The Second Circle*, the inept mourner Malianov, a neurotic so overcome by his father's passing that he sits endlessly by his corpse in a dark, disordered apartment and summons the patriarch "back to life."

Malianov's fingers open the corpse's eyes, which stare back at the camera. Moreover, through a series of devices (a slow tilt, lighting, and the strategic use of a mannequin for Malianov *fils*) we arrive at a fascinating overlap: the dead father/live son merge and meld into each other, switching roles. To cement this overlap, Sokurov utilizes an ancient strategy of the *transi*[9] tradition of medieval funerary art: the effigy. For the cadaver, now that we finally see its face, resembles Malianov himself; Sokurov keeps the resemblance slight but undeniable. As Mikhail Iampol'skii and others have pointed out, Sokurov closely supervised the construction of the cadaver mannequin, insisting on a stark realism. In crafting the face, sculptors used the lead actor Petr Aleksandrov's features but did not duplicate them precisely. The effect is thus a distorted "hologram" of Malianov the younger, superimposed on the dead face of Malianov the elder; the grotesque spectacle of a "living" mask imprinted on the visage of a corpse accounts for much of the scene's uncanny, unnerving power. The dead and living share a stark physical likeness, visually enacting further the imbrication of death with life.

Malianov's act of resurrecting the father is *otsepriimstvo avant la lettre*. The father's body, absent and mourned, belongs to the Real, to objecthood. Malianov wants to bring him back to the Symbolic.[10] He "returns" precisely through the agency of vision: his eyes are opened. But this gaze, the evidence of the returned father, petrifies the son: it subjects him to mute, unliving rigidity: fixed in place by the pre-linguistic spectacle of the Imaginary, of otherness that is not otherness. In what Iampol'skii calls "a film with zones of blindness" ("Death in Cinema" 276), Malianov himself is struck blind.

What is it about the father that blinds the son? Why does it resist representation? How does this fundamental unrepresentability short-circuit vision—the son's vision? Why is the father invisible?

In *Dreams of the Burning Child*, David Lee Miller elaborates on these questions in ways both productive and relevant to Sokurov's depiction of *otsepriimstvo*. For Miller, the problem of fatherhood in patrilineal culture is precisely its resistance to representation; there exists no physical link, no "paternal umbilical cord" to tie the father to his (male) issue the way it is so plainly tied to the mother, through biology. This leads to a "structural crisis," an imperative to represent that which does not exist: the "pre-Oedipal father":

> Paternity never has a bodily form. It remains purely testimonial, legal or symbolic (fatherhood is language). The pre-Oedipal father, the *bodily* form of fatherhood, crystallizes, then, only as an excluded possibility, a negated idea, cast out of the symbolic order in the moment that order is instituted. The absence of this body persists, however, as a fundamental embarrassment for patrilineal patriarchy. Any social system that privileges a relation which cannot be seen must of force [*sic*] commit itself to an endless project of representation. It has to go on tirelessly symbolizing the thing it cannot point to. (192; emphasis in original)[11]

At first Real, later Symbolic, the auto-castration of child sacrifice, and especially of sons, plays an important role in this obsessive invention, substantiation, and sustainment of the Father:

> Sacrificial practices, narratives, rhetoric, and imagery have been marshaled in endless combinations to represent this "lost" body as the collective form of social being, in a process that structurally resembles melancholy incorporation: the ego, in this case the self-image of an entire society, identifies with the lost object and substitutes for it. (Miller 214)

In the process, sacrificial sons—"visible stand-ins for the fatherly body" (7)—come to take on "fatherly" traces, represented since Virgil through the *puer senex* ["boy/old man"] tradition. The son, oddly amalgamated and achronal, in a sense "becomes" the father: by giving up his own life, he participates in the greater "truth" of patriarchy upheld by his sacrifice.

Furthermore, the son's shedding of blood fulfills another important paternal function: to reestablish the father as the undisputed "giver of life," a role he seizes from the mother. The Akedah, or "Binding of Isaac" from the Old Testament, is in a way precisely about this seizure from the feminine by the masculine. Abraham, acceding to his heavenly father's wish that he sacrifice his son, takes him up to Mt. Moriah to uphold the rule of fathers, thereby absurdly wiping out his only hope to become "the father of a great nation." The lamb-like son, Isaac, also accedes to *his* father, willingly surrendering himself to slaughter.[12] The gift of death "becomes" the gift of life. In her reading of the Akedah, the religious scholar Nancy Jay notes: "By this act, Isaac, on the edge of death, received his life not by birth from his mother but from the hand of his father as directed by God . . . and the granting of life was a deliberate, purposeful act rather than a mere natural process, a spiritual 'birth' accomplished without female assistance" (102).[13]

The Akedah ends without Isaac actually being killed (thanks to an angel sent by God to intercept the knife at the last minute), but this only transfers the sacrifice from the actual realm into the Symbolic. As the paradigm of both filial love and absolute paternalistic faith, the story of Isaac and Abraham enacts in ritual the symptomatic need to prop up the "invisible" signifier of the father through incessant representation, which, Miller argues, began with child sacrifice. In this way the Akedah is a meta-representation, a self-conscious recounting of the need to represent the fatherly body that details how and why such representations must be sustained.

The various elements of the Akedah myth would be recombined and re-presented centuries later by Rembrandt, a painter of tremendous importance to Sokurov. Critically, he figures the son's inability to "see" the father (and the concomitant self-castration to "substantiate" him) as an act of blinding—a key facet of post-Soviet *otsepriimstvo*.

REMBRANDT'S *SACRIFICE OF ISAAC*

The Dutch master Rembrandt van Rijn's representation of fathers and sons foregrounds ambivalent qualities of blurred identities, separation and reunion, affection and violence.[14] Sons love and want to kill their fathers, fathers weep over and are compelled to destroy their sons—with the device of blindness mediating between them. These various themes are especially apparent in the first version of *The Sacrifice of Isaac* (1635), part of the Rembrandt collection at the Hermitage, with which Sokurov has long been familiar.

For his depiction of the Akedah, Rembrandt chooses the moment when the angel intervenes in the sacrifice, holding back Abraham's arm just as he is about to slice his son's throat. Isaac's long, sinewy body stands out as the brightest object, as if a spotlight were shining on it with a reddish glow. He is stretched out on his back, almost naked; Abraham arches the boy's neck back with this left hand, covering the youth's face completely. The father, crazed with grief, gawks at the angel with "the look of a madman unexpectedly paroled from hell" (Schama 411).

Abraham sees in the angel what he painfully wants to avoid: a boyish face, like his victim's, piercing him with its gaze. Is the angel's face in fact Isaac's? This question touches on Abraham's piece of stage business with his left hand; in Rembrandt's sketches, etchings and paintings of this subject, Isaac always appears with his eyes or face or both covered by his father's hand.[15] Rembrandt's "blinding" of Isaac seems to partake of contradictory motivations; as Schama notes, he paints Abraham's hand as "fully covering, indeed almost smothering, the son's face, at once a gesture of tenderness and suffocating brutality" (410).[16]

The various erasures (imposed blindnesses) enacted by Abraham's act of covering in Rembrandt's various treatments of the Akedah seem quite relevant to Miller's thesis on the fundamental unrepresentability of the "pre-Oedipal father," which leads to a fixation precisely on propping it up (inventing it) through representation. The son, Isaac, thus cannot see the father whom his own shedding of blood will authorize and substantiate. Conversely, in remaining invisible to his son, the father compels the "representation" (of himself, of God) that the sacrifice secures.

Another major erasure, of course, is the feminine. As noted by Jay, the sacrifice amounts to a ritualized symbolic birth whereby the father bestows upon the son the "gift of life" through death, a process filled with intention and meaning that the mother's "merely natural," biological birth processes cannot match. Yet, as it happens, Rembrandt's representation does not wholly erase the feminine; it remains a haunting presence, as mentioned, in Isaac and the angel's sexually ambiguous, quasi-female forms.

Thus the Trinity of Father, Son, and Holy Spirit are caught up in a web of continuities and contradictions. There is ultimately no firm division (physical, spiritual, or sexual) between the three bodies depicted;[17] although some aspects, like the feminine, seem to undergo repression, in Rembrandt's treatment of the Akedah they never fully disappear. The blindness is only ever partial. As I argue below, something similar takes place in Sokurov's restaging of (Rembrandt's restaging of) the Akedah, in which homoerotic, feminine, hyper-masculine and androgynous imagery pervade an at times uneasy visual economy.

FATHER AND SON

Sekatskii in his *SEANS* essay identifies *Father and Son* as "perhaps the first film to have denoted the symptom of *otsepriimstvo* in the full sense of the term" (201) ["vozmozhno, pervym, oboznachivshim v polnuiu silu simptom otsepriimstva"]. Long before this film, much of Sokurov's work contained father imagery, whether the derogating portraits of Hitler (*Moloch* [Molokh] 1999) and Lenin (*Taurus* [Telets] 2000) in his "Great Men of Power" tetralogy or the more reverential treatment in *The Second Circle* and *The Lonely Voice of Man.* Since the late 1990s Sokurov has turned his documentarian's lens to homosocial male communities, particularly in the armed forces: *Spiritual Voices* [*Dukhovnye golosa* 1995] deals with border guards along the Tajikistan-Afghanistan frontier, and *Confession* [*Povinnost'* 1998] solemnizes life in the Russian Navy. His approach to framing the male body in *Father and Son,* in fact, owes much to his work on these documentary projects,[18] as well as his 1988 feature, *Days of Eclipse* [*Dni zatmeniia*].

Yet Sokurov's dolorous opus of paternalist realism is best understood as a companion piece to its predecessor in the "family relationships" trilogy, *Mother and Son.* The two works share many common elements: they both deal with parting and leave-taking (in the earlier film through the mother's death and her son's mourning); show parents and children "telepathically" dreaming the same dreams; invoke mythological motifs; culminate with a circuitous journey on foot by the son, momentarily leaving the parent behind, and arriving at a high vantage point under a gnarled tree overlooking water; touch on tangential strangers whose stories brush up unnoticed against the main narrative; and feature birds and insects that flutter unexpectedly into view. Furthermore, the sometimes radical stylistic departures of *Father and Son* from its "sister" are best appreciated through juxtaposition: the son wanders a "placeless" socium (an unnamed city) rather than a "universal" if isolating nature; he goes not alone but in the company of a domineering companion— significantly, one not enamored of his own father. Also, the latter film has a less tragic mood, as no physical death takes place, and, perhaps most important of all, it has many more edits.[19]

Finally, both *Mother and Son* and *Father and Son* freely evoke, quote, and reimagine paintings by the great masters, especially the German

Romantic Caspar David Friedrich in the former, Rembrandt in the latter.[20] In *Father and Son,* Sokurov appropriates and reconfigures the Akedah, visualizing its motifs partly through Rembrandt's treatment in *The Sacrifice of Isaac.*[21] This cathected mytho-aesthetic schema unlocks the film's otherwise largely opaque dialogue, its characters' strikingly odd, unmotivated actions, and its beautiful but bizarre imagery. Thus the expressionist opening sequence of red-tinged close-ups—flesh struggling, muscles straining and grinding together, hands pressing down limbs, a black mouth gaping, all to the tune of strained breathing—conveys the sacral terror of the Rembrandt work (along with its sexually ambiguous eroticism). Recalling Stan Brakhage in their subjectivized interplay of visual forms, the severe anamorphic distortions of male bodies are ecstatic and hellish. But the conclusion of the scene is, reassuringly, excruciatingly tender: the father is *not,* and never was, killing his child but was rescuing him from those who want to kill him in nightmares ("You saved me, I love you"). More than that: the scene amounts to a fantasy of male parturition, the "gift of life": as in the Akedah, the father has birthed the son.

Aleksei's half-waking dream carries through on this birth motif: the son, half-dressed, like Isaac (but wearing a cross), stands alone in a warm rain within a forest glade by a lonely road. "You'll catch cold," warns the father. Though at first alone, Aleksei is soon joined in the dream by his father ("I see this road, too"); still "umbilically" tied to the "pre-Oedipal paternal body," the son's full independence has not been achieved. Indeed, Aleksei's reluctance to let go forms a major dramatic axis of the film. In a nod to the illusionistic contrivance of the dream imagery, a key shot figures the naked son in his father's arms from a middle distance, forming what Armand White calls a "male pietà," with the father leaning against a wallpaper design of a forest, while the fronds of a houseplant undulate in front of them (the "glade").

The scene concludes with a close-up of the entwined father and son as women's laughter suddenly punctures their male utopia. This laughter forms a sound bridge to the next scene, showing two women in medium shot laughing directly at the camera, at the patent absurdity of "male birth." In this we have the film's sole shot of relaxed heterosexuality: the women are meeting their male soldier friends in the park outside Aleksei's military academy. The marginalized feminine, not for the last time in this work, haunts and ruptures the hermetic world of the father/son dyad.[22]

Sokurov invokes the ritualistic form of the Akedah in various ways throughout the film, but let us focus on the climactic rooftop scene near the end, when the father at last completes the symbolic birth of his son, expressed through a series of precise reversals of the myth. (After this moment Aleksei no longer sees his father in the recurring dream.) The scene opens with the son and father in a tense standoff, with Aleksei still fuming from his last encounter with "the girl," his romantic interest. In medium close-up the son faces the camera, his back to his father, as both aggressively shift their weight from foot to foot. The son fondles a fur coat that belonged to his dead mother (and that is still hanging on the coat rack), while the father recalls Aleksei's childhood: "When you were four. . ." But the son interrupts him, "Look, I'm not at all interested in my childhood," and there is a simultaneous, abrupt cut to a body in army fatigues being slammed to the mat—the image resurrecting the wrestling scene at Aleksei's academy, turning the father/son contest into a metaphor through psychological, "masculinist" montage.

Aleksei suffers painful "birth pangs": he is torn between casting aside his infancy and not wanting to abandon his father. In another quick close-up he unzips his jacket (an echo of his mother's coat, a ripping of the placental sac) and insists that his father accompany him to their building's rooftop, accessed through a plank extended out of their window—another grotesque "phallic birth." Isaac, inverting the myth, *leads his father* up Mt. Moriah. An eager sacrifice, he senses that this ascent will complete his birth: the gift of death will, in fact, mean the gift of life.[23] Indeed, a subsequent medium close-up of the father in Sokurov shows him pleased and smiling at his son's newfound agency.

To the accompaniment of dialogue pertaining to his departure, marriage, and the future, Aleksei mounts his father's shoulders for the iconic *"puer-senex"* image used to advertise the film. A background blur (the neighbor Sasha) calls out to Aleksei, reminiscent of Rembrandt's angel in a nimbus of mist. As the son tells him not to interfere, the father pushes up with his legs and stands up ("Let's fly!"); we cut to a panoramic low-angle long shot of son astride father, against the distant ocean and sky: the "sacrifice" not averted but fulfilled. Aleksei soon falls off—the consummation of the birth—and at last stands before his father as an equal. By way of a public declaration, Aleksei secures his new identity in a three-way embrace (again, the Trinity) as he "introduces" Sasha to his father, even though the two already know each other: "This is my father, and he's my friend. I love him very much." Aleksei speaks with a new voice, reborn, a man.[24]

Father and Son actively, poignantly, strives to reconstitute a heroic, tender, primeval vision, to "re-present" the lost Russian father.[25] Sokurov and his screenwriter, Sergei Potepalov, reinscribe the traditional/mythological markers of patriarchy in a new, quasi-feminine key so that love and intimacy triumph over violence and death.[26] Here, too, as in Rembrandt's *Isaac*, the feminine reasserts its haunting presence. The father tells Aleksei, "You're so much like your mother. God sent you to me."[27] Sokurov's reinscription of the Akedah and Rembrandt's *Isaac*, at its most explicit here, is diffused throughout *Father and Son* through numerous motifs. These motifs relate to some form of blindness on the son's part, which is addressed in the following section.

SHADOWS

In *Savage Junctures: Eisenstein and the Shape of Thinking* Anne Nesbet links the "autonomous" shadow-play in *Ivan the Terrible*, parts 1 and 2, to Eisenstein's concept of "plasmaticness," which formed in part a "unique protest against the metaphysical immobility of the once-and-forever given" (188). In an epic about that most problematic of movie dads, Ivan's shadow is cast onto the walls of his fortress, attaining gargantuan proportions, and towers over his subjects. In the map room scene it expressionistically looms over the globe itself, taking on an unnatural autonomy, something eerily more substantial than symbolic. Assuming a strange half-life, it even comes to dominate the flesh-and-blood man himself.

Shadows in *Father and Son* serve a similar function, though the most significant ones are not necessarily cast by the father. In fact, we often do not see the object (or the light source) producing the shadow—an "abstraction" or "removal" that makes it even more "autonomous" and "plasmatic" than Eisenstein's. Placement, where and what these shadows fall upon, seems key. In the simplest iteration of this motif, the father's shadow literally descends on Aleksei, eclipsing him, and at one point the father's body blocks out the son's shadow, in another form of "blinding." In the scene in the kitchen with Kolia's son, Fyodor, the father's silhouette, cast upon a wall in the background, stands out prominently, running over Aleksei as he enters from the interior of the house.

But it is the shadows cast from some extra-diegetic world, extending into the diegesis, that most preoccupy Sokurov's construction of the mise-en-scène. The wavy shadows of leaves and branches, lit from high above, play over many scenes in the first half of the film. They dance on the father's and son's naked bodies in the opening "Akedah" scene; they shimmer up and down the father's body as he waits for Aleksei at the Academy; and they flicker "plasmatically" in their kitchen and bedrooms. Are these dark speckles produced by the forested glade of Aleksei's recurring dream, the Symbolic border he must cross to achieve adulthood? Are they a visualization of the "dark spots" Aleksei fears he might find in the X-ray of his father's lungs? Do they progressively fade over the course of the film, and ultimately vanish, to signal the son's passage from womb-like darkness to birth-like entry into the light?[28]

The most interesting shadows in *Father and Son* achieve an even greater autonomy: they have disconcertingly real substance, and gaze unseen from the edge of the visible. During an early scene in Aleksei's bedroom, a medium close-up frames son and father in profile as the younger man contemplates the other's face (it is a long take, lasting more than two and a half minutes). "You're so different from me," mutters the son, palpating the father's temple. With attention directed so emphatically to the two men in the foreground, the viewer may not notice a mysterious silhouette, out of focus but recognizably a human figure, in the distant background. It moves and fidgets, looking in through a window. Though centrally located in the frame, the figure is abstracted by the shallow depth of field. This figure reappears later, again framed in a background window, part of a slow tracking shot of the son, as he demands, "Where's Mother?" The figure moves out of sight, to the right, in the direction of the camera's movement. As this mobile frame settles on Aleksei in the foreground, the father enters through a rear(?) door—continuing the motion of the mysterious figure, as if the two were one.

Whatever the identity of the "shadowy stranger," the salient point is that Sokurov keeps these figures *ambiguous* and, characteristically, does everything to (mis)direct the viewer's eye away from them.[29] This "living shadow" is thus plasmatic in the most direct sense: it can comprise all or none of those possible figures: father, Sasha (whom the rooftop "birth" scene equates with the angel), even the young woman, or the Holy Spirit. However we read it, two facts about the shadow seem clear: it belongs in the "watcher" category analyzed below, to which Aleksei remains blind.

WATCHERS

Several onlookers, often unnoticed, inhabit the film at key moments. I have already alluded to the shot of the two women edited as if they were "laughing" at the masculinist opening scene. Yet, as they greet their male friends, these women, in a cutaway, are themselves observed by a lonely soldier apparently hiding in some bushes. Viewers never learn his story.[30] Sokurov establishes a complex economy of surveillance, in part to heighten the theme of the father and son's relationship as beset by outside forces.

In the early military academy scene a number of cadets gaze furtively at the leather-jacketed father, who has come to surprise his son. One cadet stares from behind frosted glass, and another eyes him while pretending to look for something in a coat. When the father confronts him, "Well?" the younger man sheepishly replies, "Nothing." (Tellingly a long shot shows both the voyeur in a mirror and the object of his gaze, staring him down.) Thus, when Aleksei finally emerges to say hello, his explanation seems rather weighty: "I'm sorry I couldn't come sooner. They keep close watch."

What is the source and nature of these men's curiosity? Scenes like this, it must be said, quite readily lend themselves to a homoerotic reading:[31] the sexually interested cadets are checking out "Aleksei's hot dad." Similarly a young man watches from a nearby rooftop as the sweat-drenched, sun-kissed father lifts weights on his own roof—one of the film's more Whitmanesque visions of eroticized male beauty. Could the young soldiers merely be registering that they know this older, retired figure (a war veteran) by reputation? Might the man on the roof simply be bored and have nothing better to look at? In any case, once again Sokurov does not explain his device, though the gazes are clearly marked as significant in the film's overall economy of looking (as I elaborate below).

Of all the gazers, women are the film's most intriguing, precisely because they are often flouted or ignored by the men, and even physically hidden from the viewer. While Aleksei exercises on the rooftop ladder in extreme long shot, Sokurov—through the stylistic oddity of a swish pan—in long shot cuts to a woman standing on her patio. She tells him not to make noise and suggestively asks about "Aleshenka's cat" (while holding a calico in her arms). Is this a reference to the kitten Sasha carries at the end or the woman's snide innuendo about their cats' mating? Aleksei petulantly asks her not to pester him. Laughing, she goes back into her apartment. The woman, whom Aleksei refers to as "tetia Masha," appears only in cutaways; as with the girl, she and the younger man never appear in the same shot. Later she disappears altogether: while the father and son play soccer on the roof, she calls out to them from off-screen, displeased at the noise. This time they fail to register her presence at all. She exists only as a voice, which steadily diminishes in volume before disappearing in laughter.[32]

But the ultimate gazing outsider is the nameless young woman who competes with the father for Aleksei's affections. In several cutaways during the academy scene she stares in through a window; her quick movements and contrast in lighting almost make her look like a shark in an aquarium, a predator staring down prey. One key series of cuts underscores her disruptive role: two straight-on close-ups (one of the father, one of the son) are "punctured," split apart, by a long shot of the girl looking in from outside. These quick edits are bridged by Aleksei telling his father, "I thought you'd be happy." He is clearly disappointed at his inability to cheer his father up with some good news (according to an X-ray, the older man's lungs are healthy). The sequence of shots—Aleksei/girl/father—along with the sudden difference in the men's outlook conveyed through simultaneous dialogue, marks her as an interloper and destabilizing agent.[33] (Aleksei seems to sense as much when he confronts her at the window: "Did you see and hear everything?" "Yes, I saw and heard your father. Yes," she answers, in that odd repetitive cadence that suffuses the film.)[34]

The window scene denotes the young woman's primary function: that of outside see-er. In many shots throughout this dizzyingly edited scene, she is reduced to a staring eye (recalling Eisenstein's depiction of Maliuta Skuratov, the head of the Tsar's Oprichnina or secret police, in *Ivan the Terrible*). In their second scene together, the young woman gazes down upon Aleksei from her balcony; she is depicted from a low angle in fluid, hovering crane shots, while Aleksei appears in medium shots from a high angle, supplicating pitifully in direct address.

This gendered, contrasting shot strategy exemplifies an important aspect of the specific way the "watchers" stare, particularly the women, and especially the young woman. In both the window and balcony scenes, with their crossfire of quick shot/reverse shots, Aleksei appears straight-on, looking predominantly into the camera. But the girl is shot at an angle, and she gazes obliquely; her slippery look never turns directly to the spectator but is always aimed slightly to the side. This is a critical distinction, and not only because it imparts to the girl an untrustworthy, evasive mien.

In an important sense *Father and Son* is a film about looking the beloved in the eye; the mutuality of the gaze, naked and freely chosen, is its moral core. (Recall the angel and Abraham, their gazes locked, in Rembrandt's painting.) Sokurov gives us countless shot/reverse-shots of the father and Aleksei framed in close-up, looking directly into the camera, whispering, with pained or joyous expressions that capture their tormented love for each other. These sequences, which sometimes last several minutes, rival Theodore Dreyer's masterful portraits of the human face; they evoke a stark, nearly unbearable intimacy that transcends the diegesis. For André Bazin, the visage directed at the spectator effects an ontological change: we are no longer spectators but participants (92), extensions of *them*. In these shots we inhabit their subjectivity, witness their astonishing rapture almost as if through their own eyes.

Nothing like this happens in the close-ups of the girl. She is framed slightly askew, and her roaming gaze avoids a straight-on encounter. As I argue in the next section, Sokurov's strategy of filming her has particular repercussions for the nature of Aleksei's own vision. Here we can say that her way of seeing, and that of the other watchers, is voyeuristic, whereas that of the father and son is reciprocal, shared. What the others take without asking, the father and son give freely. This difference explains why the watchers (sexually interested or otherwise) largely remain peripheral, at times even reduced to voices, blind spots: their selfish,

individual gaze[35] excludes them from the father and son's hermetic world
of idealized shared vision.

THE SON'S BLINDNESS

Of all the visual devices Sokurov imports from Rembrandt's *Isaac,* the
son's blindness—the fatherly hand that blots out the child's vision—is
the one he refashions and rearticulates the most; it shows up in numerous guises. These include a full-blown quotation: angry at Aleksei for
risking a dangerous fall, the father violently disciplines him, at one point
by smothering his face with his hand.

Perversely, for all the shadows that elude his sight and all the ogling
onlookers to whom he remains oblivious, Aleksei himself is obsessed
with seeing. He relates vision to penetration, to getting at the essence
of things, but though still a man-child he is symbolically and literally
blocked from seeing at every turn.

Fascinated by an X-ray of his father's chest cavity, Aleksei calls it
a "more revealing" portrait, in which his father cannot hide "behind
clothes or muscles." The celluloid X-ray metaphorizes the movie's own
mode of representation: making the unseen—emotions, spiritual longing, aspects of masculinity usually hidden—nakedly visible. A medium
close-up shoots Aleksei through the X-ray film as he holds it up in front
of him. Behind its veil he appears murky and indistinct, literalizing his
own flawed sense of half-blind vision. The father appears behind him,
ghostlike (in a composition identical to the scene of "fondling the mother's coat" later on), more a hazy reflection of Aleksei's inner thoughts
than a concrete figure.

Sokurov ends this portion of the scene in startling fashion: in a medium shot of both figures showing Aleksei with his back to the viewer,
the younger man abruptly lowers the film, slapping his father in the
face with it. The true, "more revealing" portrait is wielded as a weapon,
a fetish with which to castrate the father at the site of vision. (Recall the
"aggressive" son, Tobias, operating on his father's eye with a needle in
Rembrandt's *Book of Tobit* series.) Later Aleksei again transforms the
X-ray into a weapon, trying to smother Fyodor with it. These actions
isolate the son's problem: he has elevated the father into an image, a totem, and his utter reverence has retarded his growth into a man. Aleksei

prefers the alluring representation of the "pre-Oedipal fatherly body" to the flesh and blood father standing before him. In this, too, he is blind. What happens immediately following this episode literalizes this idea. After Aleksei wraps the X-ray around Fedor's head, the neighbor, Sasha, signals Aleksei from his window, using a mirror's bright reflection. Dazzled, Aleksei yells, "Don't blind me!"

I have described some of the more obvious ways Sokurov figures the son's blindness. Often he works much more subtly. In many shots Aleksei appears with his face/eyes buried in his father's chest, or turned away, or blocked. This is true even in the last waking scene before the final dream, when father and son go to sleep (now in separate beds): they lie in such a way as to occlude their right eyes, equality at last achieved.[36]

Perhaps Sokurov's most nuanced depiction of the son's blindness comes in the girl/Aleksei window scene discussed above. In a showy style, the shots shift rapidly between straight-on close-ups of the young woman and the son,[37] though, as mentioned earlier, she looks slightly askance—unlike Aleksei, who, like his father, stares more "honestly" and directly into the camera. She playfully conceals herself behind the window jamb, the glass, her dangling hair, and an exaggerated mask of facial expressions; she indeed "hides behind clothes and muscles," unlike the father in the X-ray. Futilely Aleksei pursues her with his plodding gaze (figured through back-and-forth pans). This sequence is, in fact, a contest of gazes, which she wins: a final shot shows Aleksei's full face, visible in profile, exposed, whereas hers remains bisected by the jambs, safely hidden. The oblique angles in which she is shot and the way she never looks straight on visualize Aleksei's failure to get a "fix" on her, to dominate her with his half-blind gaze.

Finally, in one of *Father and Son*'s most remarkable coups, the long shot depicting Aleksei, his back to us, as he approaches the young woman's balcony appears broken up into disparate, irreconcilable visual planes. This is the one shot in the entire film in which she and Aleksei appear together (rather than through suturing edits), yet its dreamlike strangeness belies the pedestrian "fact" that the two figures exist in the same world. She materializes on the balcony in the background, a doll-like apparition slightly out of focus, while a sharply defined Aleksei awkwardly inches back from her, his movements strikingly odd, almost as if the footage were being played in reverse. Sokurov then racks focus onto her, throwing Aleksei into indistinctness; they exist in incongruous visual registers.

The shot reads more like a collage or pastiche of different elements, a special effect rather than a mundane treatment of a mundane act (boy meets girl). In technique, if not subject, it announces itself as "defamiliarized." To underscore the sheer oddity of the image, Sokurov intertextually links the film to its companion piece, *Mother and Son,* by having a man with a rucksack walk by, unnoticed by Aleksei, in the foreground. This shot recalls the mysterious, distant "hillside stroller" glimpsed through a window in the earlier film: he walks in the same direction (right to left) and he escapes *that* son's gaze as well.[38]

Indeed, Sokurov often shoots Aleksei as if he were *physically* blind. In one scene, he appears in medium shot against an oft-seen print of an athlete's muscular system, balanced on gymnastic rings (like the ones that hang from the father and son's ceiling). The body's head is left unfinished—in other words, without eyes. But it is Aleksei's attitude that seems striking: he has a downcast expression, his lids heavy and half-closed. His father calls him, unseen, from the other side of a wall. Aleksei slowly turns to the voice and walks as if he cannot see where he is going. The soundtrack here takes on a heightened importance, as the father's off-screen whistling and kitchen noise become crisply audible. Aleksei, responding to the sounds his father makes, walks slowly up to the wall, and caresses a flower print hanging there. His expression is of blind, beatific love for the father he cannot see but senses—invents— behind the partition.

CONCLUSION: THE "ARCHAIC FATHER"

In an important shot of *Father and Son,* a picture of the father's comrade in arms, Kolia, appears in extreme close-up. It is a weathered photo, shown so that its texture of scratches, creases, and reflections plays upon its surface; it goes in and out of focus with the slightest movement. Over this image, the son's voiceover calls, "Father!" ["Otets!"].

As one critic wrote at the film's debut, "Here's an object that you have to decode" ["eto predmet dlia rasshifrovki"] (Kichin "Cannes Laughs Through Its Tears"). In this instance the shot could be decoded as the fabled missing post-Soviet father, summoned back to two-dimensional "life" through filial desire. Conversely we could treat it as a parody of that idea, a tautologous comment on the transparency and fictiveness of his "return." Alternatively it might figure as a fleeting commentary on wars—Afghanistan? Chechnya?—scarcely mentioned in this film about scarred veterans and their sons.[39]

Ultimately the image's tenuous hold on legibility (its constant threat to lapse out of focus) marks the father figure's fragility, its need for constant reinvention and "propping up," in Miller's words, through richly diverse and shifting representational strategies (visual and aural). It is, in short, overdetermined, and in an oddly, *uncannily* familiar way.

In *The Monstrous Feminine*, Barbara Creed advances Julia Kristeva's concept of the "archaic mother"[40] as the source of a particularly male dread in horror cinema. Oceanic, all-encompassing, all-swallowing, the archaic mother "is the parthenogenic mother, the mother as primordial abyss, the point of origin and of end" (17). As figured most starkly in the mise-en-scène of Ridley Scott's *Alien* (1979), the horrific archaic mother functions as the sexual inverse of Miller's "pre-Oedipal father." She requires no great and constant effort at representation to sustain her; rather, her overwhelming, unavoidable presence, the figure par excellence of a "monstrous feminine," serves as the very source of cinematic and extra-diegetic male dread. Moreover, her transcendence of the phallus (her always having preceded it and her ever-present threat to subsume it) leads to the most radically terrifying challenge to male power:

> It is the suggested presence of the gestating, all-devouring womb of the archaic mother which generates the horror. Nor are these images of the womb constructed in relation to the penis of the father. Unlike the female genitalia, the womb cannot be constructed as a "lack" in relation to the penis. The womb is not the site of castration anxiety. Rather, the womb signifies "fullness" or "emptiness" but always it is its *own point of reference.* . . . For the concept of the archaic mother allows for a notion of the feminine which does not depend for its definition on a concept of the masculine. (Creed 27–28; emphasis in original)

Through this negative example, we can see what Sokurov is striving for with his reconstitutive alternative vision of an "archaic father" in *Father and Son*. Where Creed's "monstrous" horror film mother manifests through abysmal voids and gross organic shapes, Sokurov's "revived" father is all flesh tones, warm reds, and soft sunlight streaming through the windows of a (warm-hued, oddly womb-like) apartment. The father is Tchaikovsky's dulcet tones wafting from an old radio, whispered exchanges of love, Shchetinin's beautiful muscles and sensuous torso, his [the father's] face lit in warm colors, the creases of his smile in close-up, his reassuring gaze directed at the viewer. Again, as with Creed, it is a fanciful homosocial realm that "transcends"—destroys—the opposite sex.

Where the archaic mother spectacularly reifies what the male gazer fears—a non-phallic economy of power; going back to mother and hence relinquishing identity—the archaic father embodies (literally) all that he desires and fantasizes for his own image as a man, to the extent of "spilling over" into the homoerotic (indeed, White compares Sokurov's figures to Eisenstein's male portraits). *Father and Son* poses itself an enormous, many-splendored task: to (re)construct, (re)affirm and (re) revivify the post-Soviet father—to rebuild him in palpable, yet "spiritual" flesh,[41] but flesh above all: the warp and woof of the *otsepriimstvo* project. (Lazarus did not rise merely in spirit.)

As in the shot of the photograph depicting Kolia's father, then, Sokurov[42] seeks to incarnate the myth, through every representational strategy at his command. The off-screen voice calling "Otets" over the photograph is summons, herald, pronouncement, wish: "Father, come back. Father; I want to see you; I want to greet you, Father."

"Father (it pleads), blind me."

NOTES

1. Though many sources describe Tarkovsky as Sokurov's mentor or, alternately, Sokurov as Tarkovsky's "heir" (largely because they both make free use of the long take, address metaphysics in their work, and are Russian), this critical shorthand obscures the stark stylistic and ideological differences between the two directors that have existed since the very beginning of the younger man's career. To muddle the patriarchal metaphor, the "son" long ago stepped out of the "father's" shadow, and, in any case, the "father" was more of an uncle or older brother or even cousin. To persist in calling Sokurov "Tarkovsky's heir," to my mind, betrays evidence of superficial viewing. Sokurov himself has noted that his and Tarkovsky's directorial aims "coincide practically in nothing" ["prakticheski ni v chem ne sovpadaiut"] (Sirivlia 102).

2. Compare his "Japanese" films, *A Humble Life* [*Smirennaia zhizn'* 1997] (a documentary about a lonely poet) and *The Sun* [*Solntse* 2004] (a feature about the lonely Emperor Hirohito) to see generic distinctions diffuse like the misty *sfumato*

(painting technique that entails fine shading to produce soft, imperceptible transitions between colors and tones) pervading the mise-en-scène of both works.

3. Hashamova synthesizes the main arguments, especially as they pertain to Russian cinema. See, especially, 216–18.

4. Simpson offers a trenchant analysis of this theme in several permutations spanning East European contemporary art, including that of the Russians Oleg Kulik and Aleksandr Brener (395–98).

5. The film provides only scant clues to the war (presumably Afghanistan or Chechnya) in which the father and (his army friend?) Kolia took part, and it completely forgoes any overt political commentary. And, though the father mentions the "White Nights," he and Aleksei live in a strangely "placeless," ad-free amalgam of St. Petersburg and Lisbon (where the film was shot). One wag dubbed it "Peterbon" (Plakhov).

6. To the list of Russian films of this type drawn up by Sekatskii, Julian Graffy adds Kira Muratova's *Chekhov Motifs* [*Chekhovskie motivy* 2002] and Valerii Todorovskii's *The Lover* [*Liubovnik* 2002].

7. "Vidal, kakoi on," govorit odin iz mal'chikov v fil'me "Vozvrashchenie." "Da," cherez nekotoroe vremia otvechaet mladshii brat. I ne nakhodit, shto eshche dobavit'. Takova mogla by byt' reaktsiia zemnogo sushchestva na nevesomost': s chem ee sravnit' . . . Eto sladkii uzhaz neizvedannogo: "Vidal, kakoi on . . ."

8. This puts my reading of *The Return* at odds with that of Yana Hashamova's essay (chapter 7) in this volume, which argues that the father returns not in the Imaginary but in the Symbolic. Here I will only say that the father in Zviagintsev's film inspires awe through the indecipherability of his motives; his laconic demeanor (though the Symbolic is language) expressed in curt phrases, commands, and surly expressions much more often than "normal" speech; and, in general, through a presence that the boys cannot quite process—until after the father dies and they journey home, at which point the father does indeed reenter the Symbolic realm of all Dead Fathers. As Helena Goscilo argues, his death does secure his sons' rite of passage. Sekatskii and I both focus on the "Imaginary" period before then, however.

9. The *transi* was a representation, usually on a tomb, of the person contained there. As the name implies, the likeness depicted the person not as he had existed in life but in a state of transition, decomposition, sometimes advanced. *Transi* were later used more generally in the *memento mori* tradition, as symbols of the body's inevitable decay. See Ariès 113–14.

10. As Sekatskii notes, here Malianov is operating under the old Aristotelian formula: the father is the cause of his son. In trying to restore the father, Malianov is trying to restore himself. But in the post-Soviet era *otsepriimstvo* demonstrates that the protocol has reversed: the sons have become the cause of the fathers (200).

11. Similarly Kaja Silverman, in her discussion of American postwar cinema, recasts that formula in more classically Lacanian terms, grounding male subjectivity in the disavowal of a fundamental and ever present lack, propped up by "dominant cultural fictions":

> Thus the male subject does not just spontaneously happen to believe that he is not castrated. That belief is instilled in him through the unceasing flow of paternal images and sounds within which he is encouraged to "find"

himself; through the externalizing displacement onto the feminine subject of the losses that afflict him; and last, but by no means least, through his subordination to the dominant fiction by means of which his social formation coordinates its diverse discourses. Since this final operation generally necessitates a series of additional castrations, phallic male subjectivity might also be said to be predicated upon a massive cultural disavowal of the lack upon which it rests. (113)

Certainly I need not recite here the radical shift in "dominant fictions" of all sorts that has taken place in Russia over the last two decades. But I do wish to emphasize the characterization of this shift in the various discursive practices as a largely "masculine" crisis, whether it is the plummeting of male life expectancy to below sixty years of age, the appalling rise in alcoholism and criminality, or the loss of agency in a "free" market for men raised in a moribund Soviet economy. Moreover, as Igor Kon writes, it is precisely in such historical periods of precipitous change, when forms of gender relations grow inadequate, that nostalgia for those forms asserts itself the most, prompting calls to reverse the feminization of *"nastoiashchaia muzhestvennost'"* (563).

12. The mother, Sarah, stays home.

13. The philosopher Kelly Oliver, among others, points out the erasure of the feminine in the Akedah and in several of its philosophical treatments by Soren Kierkergaard, Emannuel Levinas, and Paul Ricoeur. Eliot Borenstein analyzes the strikingly similar misogynistic basis of early Soviet culture and literature in *Men without Women,* and Lynne Atwood and Eric Naiman, among others, have examined the turn from "reproduction" to production in this period. The "unseen" place of women in the paternal exchange of child sacrifice/reproduction bears some relevance for my reading of *Father and Son,* as we shall see.

14. In several major works and countless sketches, Rembrandt (1606–1669) evinced an interest in depicting blindness. Crucially evidence points to this interest having sprung in part from his father's own loss of vision; several portraits show the old man in an attitude indicating sightlessness (Held 127). In works devoted to the apocryphal Old Testament story *The Book of Tobit,* Rembrandt depicts the Tobias restoring his elderly father Tobit's lost vision. Although he executed many different versions, Rembrandt invariably portrays the scene as a medical procedure that almost certainly he had witnessed: the removal of cataracts with a needle-like tool (Held 114). Some have read the episode as a symbolic castration: "Tobias, with his frighteningly sharp instrument, seems to be about to blind his father" (Bal 299); his insistence on the piercing needle would seem to point to an "aggression of the son toward the father, which is acted out through competition and role reversal" (Bal 300). At the same time the tender portraits of Rembrandt's father radiate filial devotion. Julius Held notes that Rembrandt, "with a son's unconscious feeling of guilt," may have associated Tobit with his own sightless father; the series thus becomes a "posthumous tribute to his father and a symbolic form of filial expiation" (128).

15. In his reading of Rembrandt's 1655 sketch, "Abraham's Sacrifice," Peter Schjeldahl notes, "Surely the patriarch is shielding himself from those eyes" (122), and Rabbi Moshe Reiss argues that, in Rembrandt's view, a loving father simply cannot look into his son's eyes and cut his throat.

16. Rembrandt's "smothering" device has repercussions for how we read the story, since, for some commentators on the Akedah (Levinas, Ricoeur, and several midrashim), the sight of Isaac's face (the face of the other) leads to his turning away from the act of sacrifice, away from the law, toward the ethical. We can thus read the curious continuity between Isaac and the angel's body in *The Sacrifice of Isaac* as a visualization of Abraham's own mental image of his son's face, incarnating his new ethical frame of mind. The son/angel's more confrontational posture (raising his hand as if to strike) would, moreover, reflect the latent aggression, competition, and "role reversal" that often limns Rembrandt's depiction of paternal/filial relations.

17. In some sketches Abraham's eyes appeared blurred or blackened in or teared up, a haunting "overlap" with the body of the son. The father is also castrated, his vision compromised too; as Bal notes, he is "not a good see-er either" (300).

18. For example, the handheld subjective shot of the father greeting Kolia's son, Fyodor, at the door (seen from the latter's point of view) recalls a similar setup from *Spiritual Voices,* in which uniformed officers greet Sokurov and his cameraman at their tent along the tense border.

19. In seventy minutes of running time, *Mother and Son* contains only fifty-seven cuts. *Father and Son* burns through that many in the first twenty minutes or so. Some of these are very rapid "showy" cuts, as discussed below.

20. Scholars and interviewers have well documented Sokurov's mission to transform the illusionistic three-dimensionality of cinema into the "flat film image" through the use of distorting anamorphic lenses, shooting through glass, and highlighting the screen's surface texture, the better to arrive at a film's "moral dimension." Iampolskii marvels that Sokurov "works with the reality in front of the camera as if it were painted!" ("Representation—Mimicry—Death" 132). As the filmmaker tells Lauren Sedovsky: "The film image must be created according to the canons of painting because there are no others, and no need to invent them" (126). The Sedovsky interview in *ArtForum* provides an excellent overview of this aesthetic preoccupation, in Sokurov's own words.

21. Rembrandt, in particular, holds a very important place in Sokurov's own visual repertoire. The director has spoken of his regular visits to the Hermitage to see the collection of the Dutch master, whose *Danae* and *The Return of the Prodigal Son* appear in *Russian Ark* (2002). (Fyodor and Aleksei discuss the latter painting on the hilltop near the end of the film.) Sokurov speaks of these works almost as religious relics, as when he told a journalist, "Rembrandt left part of his physical being in his painting—every time you come up to a painting, you feel part of this energy, this sense of something being alive" (Jones).

22. Compare this to Yana Hashamova's arguments on the function of the feminine in Zviagintsev's *The Return* and Khlebnikov/Popogrebsky's *Koktebel* in chapter 7 of this volume.

23. Here the son, paradoxically, rejects his oft-repeated formula: "A father's love crucifies, a son's love is to be crucified." While arguing with his father, he fondles the gymnastic rings that dangle in the corridor; his balancing on them earlier formed a visual symbol of the crucifixion. But he now abruptly turns from them; as he walks toward the roof, they remain suspended in the foreground, pathetically out of focus.

24. Technically Aleksei makes his declaration of manhood in a *four-way* embrace: Sasha is holding a kitten. We can read the animal as a marker of the real, or

"nature," that which escapes human signification. Aleksei's "coming out" as a man is therefore secured not only before the human socius but before the whole universe. Additionally, if in this reinscribed Akedah Sasha is momentarily put in the role of the angel, then his association with a nonhuman being makes sense; after all, Rembrandt draws his angel with bird wings!

25. At the same time, it poses the need for sons to overcome and banish their fathers, as shown by the film's poignant final shot: the father sits half-naked and alone in winter, symbolically abandoned by the grown-up Aleksei on the snow-covered rooftop (the site of generational sacrifice).

26. Citing the father's utterance in *King Lear*, "Nothing will come from nothing," A. O. Scott writes, "[Sokurov] invokes these cruel, canonical visions of paternity to contest them. In the literature of the West, fathers and sons push one another toward tragedy. In its place, *Father and Son* offers romance."

27. This statement seems to refer to the (hetero? homo? pan?) sexual; I would also point out that, in addition to once again blurring the boundaries between identities, the reference to the son's physical resemblance to his mother at this very "sacrificial" moment is important in another respect. The father, we are given to understand, is a widower. The recognition of his dead wife's features in his son enacts her "resurrection" as well.

28. Sokurov's use of these "symbolic" shadows and the film's progressively increasing illumination is comparable to the grotesque birth imagery employed by Leo Tolstoy in *The Death of Ivan Ilyich* (1886). The author figures the dying character falling through a "black sack" and emerging into a dazzling light, like the journey through the birth canal.

29. Sokurov utilizes similarly perverse and complex strategies of misdirection and illusionism in at least three other films, *Mother and Son, The Second Circle*, and *Russian Ark*.

30. This is the same soldier the father later asks to relay to Aleksei that he has come for a visit. When the man hesitates, staring back at him, the father grumbles, "What are you looking at?" ("Chto smotrish'?").

31. Evgenii Bershtein, for example, compares these figures to the homoerotic work of Helmut Berger.

32. The psychoanalytic reading of the cinematic female voice-off is slanted to the maternal, and the woman's superior age, disciplining tone ("I told you not to play soccer here!"), and mocking laughter might indicate some measure of authority. But, as Mary Ann Doane warns, "the voice . . . is also the instrument of interdiction, of the patriarchal order. [T]o mark the voice as an isolated haven within patriarchy, or as having an essential relation to the woman, is to invoke the specter of feminine specificity, always recuperable as another form of 'otherness'" (174.) For different arguments on the female voice-off, and how it might relate to feminine dread, empowerment, and the maternal, see Doane and chapter 4 of Kaja Silverman's *The Acoustic Mirror*.

33. Proceeding from Laura Mulvey's feminine-objectifying "male gaze" in her 1975 essay, "Visual Pleasure and Narrative Cinema," E. Ann Kaplan argues that "to own and activate the gaze, given our language and the structure of the unconscious, is to be in the 'masculine' position" (30). The young woman's bold staring puts her in a position of power vis-à-vis the men, as elaborated further on. She in fact assumes

the gaze position of the sexually ambiguous monster in much horror cinema, as argued by Karen Hollinger, Barbara Creed, and Carol Clover (see their essays in *The Dread of Difference*, ed. Barry Keith Grant, Austin: University of Texas Press, 1996). I conclude this essay with a consideration of Creed's "archaic mother," a related concept of feminine power over the masculine.

34. Her reply opens up an intriguing possibility: Is the girl a hallucination? Is she only able to parrot what Aleksei utters or is thinking or fears? It strikes me as curious that no other character ever sees her or remarks on her visual presence. Just before the academy window sequence, another soldier, his back to us, seems to be leaning over the sill, talking to her, but the extreme long shot leaves this possibility quite ambiguous; the soldier could simply be staring out the window where she happens to "be." In any case, we see this from Aleksei's point of view, as he angrily dismisses the soldier, telling him to vacate the space—out of jealousy? Jealousy of what—a phantom that only he sees? In a similar vein, the father does discuss his son's breakup with the girl, but again he seems to be relying solely on Aleksei's account; the father and the girl never appear in any scenes together. We have no "objective" visual evidence of the girl interacting with other people. Is she "real" or merely Aleksei's mirage?

35. I should clarify that my arguments on blindness in this essay pertain primarily to the son (and to the Akedah as refracted through Rembrandt and "inherited" by this film), not to the various voyeurs and threatening onlookers scattered throughout the movie, who, as already noted, are anything but blind—except that their "prurient" gazes fail to penetrate the "holy" inner sanctum of the father and son's private world.

36. Women especially seem to elude Aleksei's gaze. Apart from an elderly beggar woman to whom he gives charity (in an extreme long shot), he seems to exist on a different visual plane from the opposite gender. In street scenes female passersby appear in the background or foreground. Only Aleksei's male friends recognize him on the tram. Other women, like the aforementioned "cat lady" on the patio, only appear in separate shots (with one exception).

37. Longtime viewers of Sokurov's work will recognize this as a stylistic aberration for a director who has always insisted on long takes and deep space over Eisensteinian montage, and whose best-known film outside Russia is a ninety-minute, edit-free film in one take, *Russian Ark*. One reviewer quipped on the "record number of cuts" in *Father and Son*: "in the context of Sokurov's meditative cinema, this is practically a gripping action thriller" ["v parametrakh meditativnogo kinematografa Sokurova eto prakticheski ostrosiuzhetnyi boevik"] (Plakhov).

38. A *Father and Son* production still shows that the passerby is actually Sasha, who seemingly has been following Aleksei (or perhaps he is the young woman's secret "other man"). But, once more, in the film Sokurov leaves all these possibilities dangling.

39. Sokurov's fabulously rich, polystylistic, and multivoiced text demands an imaginative, flexible, and, above all, open-minded response from those attempting an interpretation—something underscored by the film's one-note reception at Cannes as a "gay film." No one (*pace* Sokurov) can deny the work's intense and radiant homoeroticism. We should not, however, see it as an end but rather as one more sign of the Father signifier's overdetermined status. (For a similar argument on the eros of Michelangelo's equally overdetermined *Pietà* [1499], see Miller 30–36.) It bears repeating: I am of course not arguing that a gay film cannot be a complex or aesthetically

pleasing cinematic experience, or both. I likewise have no "beef" with the notion that *Father and Son* could be read as an "unwittingly gay" film, as Helena Goscilo surmises (personal correspondence). I only caution that any one interpretative schema, queer or otherwise, risks foreclosing too many other hermeneutic possibilities of what is essentially a riotously polysemantic text.

The American critic Armand White expresses this point better than most when he compares the film to more banal Hollywood representations of homosexuality: "[*Father and Son*] isn't gay in the conventional sense. That is, it isn't superficially gay like the drag-queen diminishment of human relations into the supposedly progressive in-jokes of the new *Stepford Wives*. Sokurov has a greater sexual awareness than *Stepfords'* broad, brazen, illogical camp." In "Sokurov's Vision of Intimacy," an essay accompanying the 2004 Wellspring DVD release of the film, he goes further, in part addressing the suggestive closeness in age of the actors playing the leads, which many take as yet more evidence of a homoerotic subtext:

> In exploring the father and son's relationship, Sokurov uses imagery that ingeniously blurs the two men's identities. That nightmare/caress scene [of the film's opening] symbolizes their blood and emotional kinship in an iconographic style that allows their individual personalities to merge. It is erotic, but on an exalted plain that stays consistent with Sokurov's spiritual and artistic endeavor. . . . The father and son are indeed separate characters but Sokurov deals with symbolism as effectively as he utilizes enigma; they are part of Sokurov's language. He means for symbol and enigma to prod a viewer's imaginative investment, to respect life's majesty—the inscrutable mystery of experience—in a non-banal way. This is central to his philosophy about film as a revealing crystal.

Here White seems to be aiming for the stars, but in fairness I think he keys in on an important aspect of Sokurov's daring poetics—very much out of step with most contemporary strategies for representing father/son relationships, to say the least. And all the more exciting for it!

40. It is worth mentioning here, if only briefly, Kristeva's departure from Lacan, particularly her substitution of the Imaginary with the order of the pre-Symbolic semiotic of the "ordered" drives. We can relate the realm of both the "archaic mother" and a putative "archaic father" to her concept of the chora, an aporia-like "non-expressive totality" (35) and "matrix-like space that is nourishing, unnamable, prior to the One and to God" (352). I thank Yana Hashamova for this insight.

41. Another negative example: compare Sokurov's beneficent imagery of Father to that of Nikita Mikhalkov in *Burnt by the Sun* [*Utomlennie solntsem* 1994], in particular the maleficent floating portrait of Stalin, which Mitia salutes near the end.

42. I should address here what some might see as my falling victim to the intentional fallacy. By "Sokurov," however, I mean here not the man, but the organizing principle of the film, its "superego." But there is, of course, another force at work, which in my previous writing on the director I have termed the "Sokurovian unconscious" (the source of the misdirections, tricks, and "perversions" I have noted above). *Father and Son*—I reiterate—is a tremendously rich, productive, and self-contradictory text, precisely why I resist any monolithic or reductive reading. We could, indeed, construct a viable argument for the film as a viciously over-the-top parody on the idea of the

"archaic father." Such an argument might follow that of James L. Rice's essay "Comic Devices in *The Death of Ivan Ilyich*" (*SLEEC* 47, no. 1 [spring 2003]: 77–95), which catalogs the many comic techniques in a novel almost universally read as "serious" and even "depressing." My unpublished essay, "'Death' and 'Nature' in Sokurov's *Mother and Son*," performs a like "contrarian" reading on that similarly (and superficially) dolorous film.

REFERENCES

Ariès, Philippe. *The Hour of Our Death*. Translated by Helen Weaver. New York: Random House, 1980.

Bal, Mieke. *Reading "Rembrandt": Beyond the Word-Image Opposition*. Cambridge: Cambridge University Press, 1991.

Creed, Barbara. *The Monstrous Feminine: Film, Feminism, Psychoanalysis*. London: Routledge, 1993.

Doane, Mary Ann. "The Voice in the Cinema. The Articulation of Body and Space." In *Film Sound: Theory and Practice*, ed. Elisabeth Weis and John Belton, 162–76. New York: Columbia University Press, 1985.

Hashamova, Yana. "Castrated Patriarchy, Violence, and Gender Heirarchies in Post-Soviet Film." In *Gender and National Identity in 20th Century Russian Culture*, ed. Helena Goscilo and Andrea Lanoux, 196–224. Dekalb: Northern Illinois University Press, 2006.

Held, Julius S. *Rembrandt's "Aristotle" and Other Rembrandt Studies*. Princeton: Princeton University Press, 1969.

Iampolskii, Mikhail. "Representation—Mimicry—Death: The Latest Films of Alexander Sokurov." In *Russia on Reels: The Russian Idea in Post-Soviet Cinema*, ed. Birgit Beumers, 127–43. London: Tauris, 1999.

———. "Death in Cinema." In *Re-Entering the Sign: Articulating New Russian Culture*, ed. Anessa Milla-Pogacar and Ellen Berry, 270–88. Ann Arbor: University of Michigan Press, 1995.

Iampol'skii, Mikhail. "The Truth of the Body" ["Istina tela"]. In *Sokurov*, ed. Liubov' Arkus and Vasilii Bertel, 165–67. St. Petersburg: Seans Press, 1994.

Jones, Jonathan. "90 Minutes That Shook the World." *The Guardian*. 28 March 2003. Available at http://film.guardian.co.uk/features/featurepages/0,,923919,00.html (accessed 10 January 2007).

Kaplan, E. Ann. *Women and Film: Both Sides of the Camera*. New York: Methuen, 1983.

Kichin, Valerii. "Alexander Sokurov: Why Such a Garbage Dump in Your Heads?" ["Chto za pomoika u vas v golovakh?"] *Film.ru*. 29 May 2003. Available at http://www.film.ru/article.asp?id=3639.

———. "Cannes Laughs Through Its Tears." ["Kann smeetsia skvoz' slezy"]. *Rossiskaia Gazeta*. no. 98 (3212), 24 May 2003.

Kon, Igor'. "Muzhkie issledovania: meniaiushchiesia muzhchiny v izmeniaiushchemsia mire." In *Vvedenie v gendernie issledovania, chast' I*, ed. Irina Zherebkina, 563–605. Kharkov: Aleteia, 2001.

Kristeva, Julia. *The Portable Kristeva*. Edited by Kelly Oliver. New York: Columbia University Press, 1997.

Miller, David Lee. *Dreams of the Burning Child: Sacrificial Sons and the Father's Witness*. Ithaca, N.Y.: Cornell University Press, 2003.

Nesbett, Anne. *Savage Junctures: Sergei Eisenstein and the Shape of Thinking*. London: Tauris, 2003.

Oliver, Kelly. "Fatherhood and the Promise of Ethics." *Diacritics* 27, no. 1 (1997): 45–57.

Plakhov, Andrei. "The Torments of Interpretation" ["Muki interpretatsii"]. *Iskusstvo kino*, September 2003.

Reiss, Moshe. "Abraham's Moment of Decision." Available at http://www.moshereiss.org/articles/02_abraham_decision.htm .

Schama, Simon. *Rembrandt's Eyes*. New York: Knopf, 1999.

Scott, A. O. "Ties That Bind a Family, Etched in Orange Light." *New York Times*, 14 June 2004. Available at http://movies.nytimes.com/movie/review?res=980DE6D71639F93BA25755C0A9629C8B63 (accessed 27 June 2009).

Sedovsky, Laren. "Plane Songs: Lauren Sedovsky Talks with Alexander Sokurov." *ArtForum* (November 2001): 124–28.

Sekatskii, Andrei. "Otsepriimstvo." *SEANS*, no. 21/22 (2005): 199–205.

Simpson, Pat. "Peripheralising Patriarchy? Gender and Identity in Post-Soviet Art: A View from the West." *Oxford Art Journal* 27, no. 3 (2004): 389–415.

Sirivlia, Natal'ia. "Kino ne govorit nichego vazhnogo . . ." *Iskusstvo kino*, no. 10 (1997): 100–103.

White, Armand. "Beefcake Borscht." *New York Express* 17, no. 6 (2003). Available at http://www.nypress.com/17/26/film/ArmondWhite.cfm .

FILMOGRAPHY

Father and Son [*Otets i syn*]. Dir. Aleksandr Sokurov. Zero Film, Nikola Film, 2003.

Mother and Son [*Mat' i syn*]. Dir. Aleksandr Sokurov. Screen writer, Iurii Arabov. Zero Film, Lenfilm, Roskomkino, 1997.

The Second Circle [*Krug vtoroi*]. Dir. Aleksandr Sokurov. Lenfilm, 1990.

Figure 11.1. Girl. The girl (Marina Zasukhina) often appears as a gazer, shot obliquely through glass and partly obscured by barriers, a predatory eye.

CONTRIBUTORS

José Alaniz is Associate Professor of Slavic Languages and Literatures and Comparative Literature at the University of Washington in Seattle, and author of *Comics and Comic Art in Late/Post-Soviet Russia*. His research interests include death and dying, disability studies, cinema, eco-criticism, and comics studies.

Brian James Baer is Associate Professor of Russian Language and Literature at Kent State University. He has published a number of articles on post-Soviet culture and is author of *Other Russias: Homosexuality and the Crisis of Post-Soviet Identity* (2009) and editor and translator of *No Good without Reward: Selected Works of Liubov Krichevskaia* (forthcoming).

Helena Goscilo, Professor and Chair of Slavic and East European Languages and Literatures at The Ohio State University, writes primarily on gender and contemporary culture in Russia. Her book-length publications since 2000 include *Vzryvoopasnyi mir Tat'iany Tolstoi; Culture in the 1990s* (Special Issue of *20th Century Literature*); *Gender and National Identity in 20th Century Russian Culture* (with Andrea Lanoux); *Poles Apart: Women in Modern Polish Culture* (with Beth Holmgren); *Encyclopedia of Contemporary Russian Culture* (with Tatiana Smorodinskaya and Karen Evans-Romaine), and *Preserving Petersburg: History, Memory, Nostalgia* (with Stephen M. Norris, Indiana University Press, 2008). Her current projects include *Fade from Red: Screening the Cold War Ex-*

Enemy during the Nineties (with Bożenna Goscilo); a volume on glamour and celebrities (with Vlad Strukov); a special journal issue devoted to the mirror in Russian and Soviet culture; and augmentation of the Web site *Stalinka* (with Susan Corbesero).

Seth Graham is a lecturer in Russian at the School of Slavonic and East European Studies, University College London. He has published articles and chapters on literature, film, and humor in the *Russian Review,* the *Dictionary of Literary Biography, Studia Filmoznawcze,* and in several essay collections.

Yana Hashamova is Associate Professor and Director of the Center for Slavic and East European Studies at The Ohio State University. She is also Associate Faculty member of the Departments of Comparative Studies, Film Studies, Women's Studies, and the Mershon Center for International Security. She is author of *Pride and Panic: Russian Imagination of the West in Post-Soviet Film* and has published numerous articles in the areas of Russian film, Russian and West European drama, comparative literature and the arts, critical theory and gender studies in journals such as the *Russian Review,* the *Slavic and East European Journal, Canadian Slavonic Papers,* the *Communication Review, Consumption, Markets, and Culture,* among others. She is currently working on her second monograph, *Screening Trafficking: Prudent or Perilous?,* as well as a volume of essays entitled *Women in War,* and a cluster of articles for *Aspasia* (both edited with Helena Goscilo).

Mark Lipovetsky is Associate Professor of Russian Studies and Comparative Literature at the University of Colorado–Boulder. He is the author of several books on Russian literature and culture, including *Russian Postmodernist Fiction: Dialogue with Chaos* (1999), *Modern Russian Literature: 1950s–1990s* (authored with Naum Leiderman), and *Paralogies: Transformation of (Post)modernist Discourse in Russian Culture of the 1920s–2000s.* He is editor, with Marina Balina, of *Dictionary of Literary Biography: Russian Writers since 1980,* and, with Marina Balina and Helena Goscilo, of *Politicizing Magic: An Anthology of Russian and Soviet Wondertales.* Lipovetsky's current research focuses on cultural discourses of violence in Soviet and post-Soviet culture.

Alexander Prokhorov is Associate Professor of Russian Culture and Film at the College of William and Mary. Author of *Inherited Discourse: Stalinist Tropes in Thaw Literature and Cinema*, he has published many articles and reviews in the *Slavic Review*, the *Russian Review*, the *Slavic and East European Journal*, and *Kinokultura*. His research interests include Russian visual culture, genre theory, and film history.

Elena Prokhorova is Assistant Professor of Russian at the College of William and Mary, where she teaches in the Russian, Film, and Cultural Studies programs. Focusing on identity discourses in late Soviet and post-Soviet television and film, her publications have appeared in the *Slavic Review*, *SEEJ*, *KinoKultura*, and various edited volumes and encyclopedias.

Tatiana Smorodinskaya, Associate Professor of Russian at Middlebury College, is co-editor of the *Encyclopedia of Contemporary Russian Culture* and author of *Konstantin Sluchevsky: Untimely Poet*, as well as articles on contemporary Russian film. She currently is working on a monograph about radio theater and an advanced level textbook on contemporary culture.

Vlad Strukov teaches Russian literature, media, and film at the University of Leeds, as well as digital culture at the Centre for World Cinemas, where he is associate faculty. His publications include the volume *Kul'tura "Post"* and articles on Russian cinema and animation in the *Slavic and Eastern European Journal* and *Animation: An Interdisciplinary Journal*. A member of the editorial board of *Russian Cyber Space*, he is the founding editor of *Static*, an international journal for interdisciplinary debate about paradoxes of contemporary culture.

INDEX

Italicized page numbers indicate illustrations.

Abdrashitov, Vadim, 13, 73, 75
Abuladze, Tengiz, 13, 73, 75, 89
Adomenaite, Nijole, 109n14
Aeschylus, 21n12
Afghanistan, Soviet war in, 15, 16, 66, 116; *Brigada* references to, 19, 219, 221–22, 225; *dukhi* (ghosts) of, 120; *Otets i syn [Father and Son]* and, 300, 302n5
Aigi, Aleksei, 118
Akhmadulina, Bella, 32
Akhmatova, Anna, 248
Alaniz, José, 17, 257
alcoholism, 18, 80, 152, 174, 303n11
Aleksandrov, Petr, 285
Alien (1979), 300
Alov, Aleksandr, 114
American Beauty (1999), 171
The American President (1995), 171
Amerikanskaia doch' [American Daughter] (1995), 138, 139
Anderson, Benedict, 218
Andrei Rublev (1966), 248
Andrei Tarkovsky's Sacrifice [zhertvoprinoshenie Andreia Tarkovskogo] (Boldryrev), 248
Ankor, eshche ankor! [Encore! Again, Encore!] (1992), 14
Anosova, Nina, 269n5, 270n17

anti-Semitism, 227
Antonov, Artem, 110n17
The Apotheosis of War (Vereshchagin painting), 63
Aprel'skii, Sergei, 222
Arcand, Denys, 3
Arnshtam, Lev, 14
Aronovich, Semen, 14
Askol'dov, Aleksandr, 83
Atanesian, Aleksandr, 96
Attwood, Lynne, 170

Backdraft (1991), 171
Baer, Brian, 19, 144
Bakhtin, Mikhail, 36
Balabanov, Aleksei, 16, 117, 121–22, 221
Baltic countries, 100, 116
Balzac, Honoré de, 153
Banderas, Antonio, 138, 156n1
Barbarian Invasions [Les invasions barbares] (2003), 3
Baskakov, Vladimir, 67n13
Bazin, André, 296
Beauvoir, Simone de, 169
Bekmambetov, Timur, 6, 18, 191, 194, 209, 268
Belarus/Belorussia, 100, 101–104
Beliaev, Iurii, 141

Beloe solntse pustyni [White Sun of the Desert] (1969), 13, 51, 67n13, 68n17; character naming in, 63; narrative plot, 61–65; *Ofitsery [Officers]* compared with, 54–55, 60, 61, 63, 64, 65; popularity of, 55, 65; Soviet mythology of civil war and, 60

Beroev, Egor, 149

Besy [The Possessed/Demons] (Dostoevsky), 21n18

Bezhin lug [Bezhin Meadow] (1935–37), 8

Bezrukov, Sergei, 219, 232

Bible/biblical stories, 6, 59, 101, 156, 274n62; Akedah (sacrifice of Isaac), 283, 286–88, 290, 291–92; Bekmambetov's *Dozor* trilogy and, 207; kinship narrative linked to, 74; prodigal son story, 259; Rembrandt's *Book of Tobit* series, 297, 303n14; Tree of Life, 266–67; *Vozvrashchenie [The Return]* and, 173–74. *See also* Jesus Christ, references to; Orthodox Christianity

Bicycle Thieves [Ladri di bicicletti] (1948), 3, 67n4

Bildungsroman, 8, 18, 140, 149, 154

Billington, James, 218

Billy Elliot (2000), 10

Bird, Robert, 249

The Birdcage (1996), 171

Blankenhorn, David, 171

Blokada [The Blockade] (1974–78), 53

Blos, Peter, 90

Bodrov, Sergei, Jr., 121

Bogomolov, Iurii, 63

Bogomolov, Vladimir, 254, 256

Boldryrev, Nikolai, 248, 253, 265, 267, 273n48

Bondarchuk, Fedor, 16, 117

Bondarchuk, Natal'ia, 250

Bondarchuk, Sergei, 12, 73, 105, 127, 249, 268

Boretskii, Iurii, 97

Borneman, John, 15

Boyz n the Hood (1991), 171

Brakhage, Stan, 290

Brashinsky, Michael, 73

Brat [Brother] (1997), 121, 221, 230

Brat 2 [Brother 2] (2000), 121

Brat'ia Karamazovy [The Brothers Karamazov] (Dostoevsky), 21n18, 45n1, 172

Bresson, Robert, 282

Brezhnev, Leonid, 44, 53, 71, 84n4

Brezhnev: Sumerki imperii [Brezhnev: Twilight of the Empire] (2006), 107

Brezna, Irena, 251

Brigada [The Brigade] (TV mini-series), 19, 144, 219–20, 236–37; absent fathers in, 221–28; ethnicity in, 225, 226–28; problems of fraternal governance, 228–30; Rambo references in, 222–25, 238nn4–5; redemption of patriarchy, 231–36; religious references in, 225, 229, 235–36; role of fate in, 232–33; as "Russian *Sopranos*," 220–21, 238n3; stills from, *241–43*

brothers, bands of, 217–18, 219, 224–25, 228–30, 236–37

Bruzzi, Stella, 169

Burliaev, Nikolai, 268n1

Bykov, Rolan, 83, 180

Byl mesiats mai [It Was the Month of May] (1970), 31

cannibalism, 19, 211

capitalism, 185, 219

Carroll, Noel, 54

castration, Symbolic, 7, 172, 176, 303n14; castration anxiety, 300; sons' self-castration, 286, 287; vision and, 297, 304n17

Cattaneo, Peter, 10, 180

Central Asia, 60, 62, 63, 68n17

Chadov, Aleksei, 203

Chapaev (Furmanov novel), 22n19

Chapaev (1934), 57, 252

Character (1997), 10, 181

Chechen War, 15, 16–17, 95, 121–22; *Brigada* references to, 224, 225, 229, 232, 235, 239n13; in *Moi svodnyi brat Frankenshtein [My Stepbrother Frankenstein]*, 118, 132, 144; *Otets*

i syn [*Father and Son*] and, 300, 302n5; Soviet mythology of World War II and, 116, 117, 129; in *Vor* [*The Thief*], 141, 144, 146, 147
chekisty (secret police personnel), 76, 97
Chelovek idet za solntsem [*A Man Walks after the Sun*] (1961), 43
Chernov, Vladimir, 2
chernukha (dark naturalism) films, 85n9, 92
Chernykh, Valentin, 99, 134n3
Chiaureli, Mikhail, 15
Chiginskii, Vasilii, 109n14
Chistoe nebo [*Clear Sky*] (1961), 30
Chkeidze, Rezo, 114
Christianity, 59, 174
Chuchelo [*Scarecrow*] (1984), 83
Chukhrai, Grigorii, 30
Chukhrai, Pavel, 3, 7, 14, 17, 103, 140
Chuliukin, Iurii, 68n17
Chuzhaia belaia i riaboi [*The Wild Pigeon*] (1986), 82
Cimino, Michael, 120
cinema, post-Soviet, 3, 5, 10, 23n37, 52; father-son relations, 172–80; mother relegated to periphery in, 7; prodigal fathers in, 6, 179; war viewed in, 16; women consigned to periphery in, 18; World War II viewed in, 89–108
cinema, Soviet, 5, 15, 20, 73; Brezhnev (stagnation) era, 12–13, 54; civil war Westerns ("Easterns"), 55, 56, 57; de-heroization of, 53; imperial father mythology, 54; mother relegated to periphery in, 7; perestroika period, 13–14, 73–78, 79, 82–84; songs in, 57, 60, 62; Stalinist, 29; war trope and, 51–52. *See also* Thaw period, cinema of
Cinema as Poetry (1989), 250
civil war, Russian, 60, 61, 67n10, 72; class conflict as core issue of, 65; Soviet "Easterns" as film genre, 55, 56, 57
civilization, 4, 7, 206, 213n6

Civilization and Its Discontents (Freud), 1, 4, 138
Clark, Katerina, 30–31, 71
class distinctions, 65, 67n10, 253
"class enemies," 56
Cold War, 15
Collodi, Carlo, 40
communism, 16, 30, 89, 90
Communist Party, Soviet, 9, 34, 42, 101, 170
concentration camps, 9, 151
Conflict Commission, 45n8, 82
consumerism/consumer culture, 53, 228, 283
Coppola, Francis Ford, 220, 229
Corneau, Guy, 169
Corney, Frederick, 29
Cossacks, 96
Creed, Barbara, 300, 301, 306n33
Crenna, Richard, 223
Crime and Punishment (Dostoevsky), 232, 239n16, 258
cult of personality, 12, 34, 71, 142
Czechoslovakia, 116

Daldry, Stephen, 10
Daneliia, Grigorii, 43, 72
Danil'tsev, Ignat, 263
Days of Eclipse (1988), 289
De Sica, Vittorio, 3, 67n4
"Death in Cinema" (Iampol'skii), 285
deep time, 36
The Deer Hunter (1978), 120
Deleuze, Gilles, 185
Delo pestrykh [*The Case of Many Colors*] (1958), 30
Delo Ruminatseva [*Ruminatsev's Case*] (1955), 30, 66n2
democracy, 93, 219, 228, 229, 236, 237
Dennehy, Brian, 223
Derrida, Jacques, 1
Deviataia rota [*The Ninth Regiment*] (2005), 16, 117
direct cinema, 32
Diuzhev, Dmitrii, 224
Diversant [*The Saboteur*] (TV miniseries, 2004), 109n14

Dnevnoi dozor [Day Watch] (2006), 16, 191, 209–12; duality as structural component of, 202–204; ego formation in, 198–202; Oedipus and fate in, 191–93, 197; patriarchy and history in, 208–209; stills from, *215–16;* vampirism in, 204–207

Dni zatmeniia [Days of Eclipse] (1988), 289

Doane, Mary Ann, 282, 305n32

documentaries, 13–14, 79, 107, 155, 282, 289

Dolinin, Dmitrii, 109n14

Dondurei, Daniil, 93

Dontsov, Sergei, 149

Dostal', Nikolai, 30, 97

Dostoevsky, Fyodor, 21n18, 35, 172, 232, 239n16, 270n12

Dozor trilogy, 6, 7, 18

Dreams of the Burning Child (Miller), 285

Dreyer, Theodore, 296

drug trafficking, 225–26

Dubin, Boris, 132

Dubrovskaia, Anna, 193

Dukhovnye golosa [Spiritual Voices] (1995), 289

Durov, Lev, 139

Dva Fedora [Two Fedors] (1958), 12

Dvadtsat' dnei bez voiny [Twenty Days without War] (1976), 104

Dykhovichnyi, Ivan, 14

Dzerzhinskii, Feliks, 97, 107

East of Eden (1954), 3

Eastwood, Clint, 106

ego, in Freudian theory, 172, 198–202, 210, 286

Eisenstein, Sergei, 8, 292, 296, 301

Ekk, Nikolai, 72

Eliade, Mircea, 267

emasculation, 4, 125, 146, 175

Encyclopedia of the Russian Soul [Entsiklopediia russkoi dushi] (radio program), 1–2

"The End of the Century—the End of Chernukha?" discussion, 92–93

"enemies of the people," 91, 108n3, 151

Engels, Friedrich, 71

equality, rhetoric of, 218

Ermash, Filipp, 97, 249, 269n7

Ermler, Fridrikh, 102

Erofeev, Viktor, 1–2, 20n2, 22n18, 170

Eshelon [Echelon] (TV series, 2005), 109n14

Essay on Criticism (Pope), 19–20

Europe, Western, 2, 5, 10

European Union, 283

Evtushenko, Evgenii, 32

Ezhov, Valentin, 68n17

Fadeev, Aleksandr, 22n19, 43

fairy tales, 18

Faludi, Susan, 23

family, nuclear, 37, 44; dismemberment of, 79, 84; dysfunctionality of, 72; in perestroika-era films, 79, 80, 81; rebuilding/reunification of, 39, 40; totalitarian culture against, 115; violence in, 2

"Family Romances" (Freud), 1, 4

Father [Apa] (1966), 3

Father and Son. See Otets i syn [Father and Son] (2003)

Father of the Bride 2 (1995), 171

Fatherless America (Blankenhorn), 171

fathers: absent, 1–5, 52, 221–28, 284; acceptance of, 3, 5, 20n5, 145; alcoholic, 18, 80, 152, 174; "archaic," 299–301; father-daughter relations, 78–81, 139; in Freudian family romance, 5; heroic stature in World War II remembrance, 14; as ideological mentors for sons, 33–34; imperial, 54; infantilized, 75, 79, 80, 82; masculine identities and, 169; Oedipal family drama and, 198; omnipotent versus inept, 172–80; patriotic myths of World War II and, 15; "pre-Oedipal," 286, 288, 290, 298, 300; primal, 217, 237;

recognition of, 5; stability of Great Power and, 56; Symbolic, 176, 180, 283, 302n8; weak/impotent, 127–28, 130, 212

fathers, biological, 8, 13, 103; analogy with divine Father, 155; in Bekmambetov's *Dozor* trilogy, 202, 203; failure as role models, 16; perished in the "Fatherland War," 155; Symbolic father and, 176, 180; in *Tri dnia Viktora Chernysheva [Three Days of Viktor Chernyshev]*, 38, 41

fathers, surrogate, 5, 6, 8, 13; in Bekmambetov's *Dozor* trilogy, 202, 203; in *Beloe solntse pustyni [White Sun of the Desert]*, 62, 63; in *Ivanovo detstvo [Ivan's Childhood]*, 254–57; in *Koktebel'*, 19; orphaned boys and, 12; in *Tri dnia Viktora Chernysheva [Three Days of Viktor Chernyshev]*, 38

Fathers and Sons (Manguel), 1

Father's Day (1997), 171

father-son relations, 4, 20; betrayals under Stalin, 91; in Brezhnev (stagnation) era films, 55; canonical Soviet dynamic, 54; families in film industry, 98, 104–106; Lacan's interpretation of, 7; masculinity as role model and, 170; in *Moi svodnyi brat Frankenshtein*, 128; Oedipus myth and, 192–98; in *Ofitsery [Officers]*, 58; passage of history and knowledge, 77; in post-Soviet films, 172–80, 206; in Sokurov's films, 294; Soviet utopian imagination and, 51; in Tarkovsky's films, 258–68, 262–68, 271n31

Fat'ianov, Vladimir, 97

Federal Security Service (FSB), 96, 107

Fedorov, Nikolai, 260

feminine/femininity, 158n21, 183–84; "archaic mother" and, 300; haunting presence of, 288, 292

feminism, 170

A Few Good Men (1992), 171

filiation, 2, 10, 13, 52, 55, 200

filicide, 3, 4, 7, 21n13; as divine patriarchal prerogative, 19, 211; Oedipal complex and, 193; Russian tsars and, 9

Filipchuk, Misha, 140, 157n8

Film Commission, Soviet, 64

Flags of Our Fathers (2006), 106

Frankenstein (1931), 118, 121, 135n5

Freud, Sigmund, 1, 6, 10, 21n16, 140, 199; on desire and identity formation, 7; on family romance, 7–8, 21n17, 150–51; on God as exalted father, 273n48; Lacan and, 175; on longing for father, 267–68; on mechanisms of language, 213n5; on need for father's protection, 138, 148; on Oedipal complex, 198; on paternal death, 3, 145, 202; on primal parricide, 4, 172, 179, 183; on self-sacrifice and guilt, 267; on superego, 200–201; on totem as substitute for primal father, 237; on the uncanny *(Unheimlich)*, 119; on veneration of father ideal, 217–18

Freudian concepts/themes, 210; in *Beloe solntse pustyni [White Sun of the Desert]*, 63; in *Koktebel'*, 18, 19; unconscious, 199; *Unheimlich* (uncanny), 118–19, 133; in *Zerkalo [Mirror]*, 263–64

Friedrich, Caspar David, 290

Friske, Zhanna, 205

Fukuyama, Francis, 169

The Full Monty (1997), 10, 180

Furmanov, Dmitrii, 22n19

The Future of an Illusion (Freud), 21n16

The Futurological Congress (Lem), 247

Gabriel and Me (2001), 10

Gaft, Valentin, 139

Galich, Aleksandr, 148, 149, 150, 153, 155

gangster films, 220, 229, 238n9

Garmash, Sergei, 120

Gazarov, Sergei, 130

gender studies, 169
generations, succession of, 4, 19–20, 21n9, 160n43; break in, 40; fraternal governance and, 229, 230; in *Ofitsery [Officers]*, 65; in post-Soviet period, 90; in *Solaris*, 262–65; Soviet narratives, 8
Georgia, 74
Gerasimov, Sergei, 15, 30, 43
German, Aleksei, 14, 90, 97; on costume war films, 95; on father in *Khrustalev*, 91; trope of filiation and, 268; World War II films of, 104–105
German, Aleksei, Jr., 15, 104–106
Germans, portrayal of, 15, 39, 102–103, 105–106, 110n17
Ghosts (Ibsen), 159n26
Gladiator (2000), 171
Gladil'shchikov, Iurii, 121
The Godfather (1972), 220, 229
The Godfather Part II (1974), 220, 225, 229, 238n9
Golovnia, Leonid, 102
Goncharov, Ivan, 154
Gorbachev, Mikhail, 13, 71–72
Gorelova, Valeriia, 43
Goscilo, Helena, 11, 302n8, 307n39
Goskino, 67n13, 249
Govorukhin, Stanislav, 92
Graham, Seth, 13
grandfathers, 14, 37, 38, 39, 75
Great Family, trope of Soviet Union as, 8, 11, 14, 71; basic metaphor of Stalinist culture, 30–31; Morozov myth and, 123; nuclear family and, 115; perestroika and, 72; Thaw-era revitalization of, 34, 45n5; in *Tri dnia Viktora Chernysheva [Three Days of Viktor Chernyshev]*, 41, 42, 44; in *Zastava Il'icha [Il'ich's Guard]*, 36
Great Patriotic War. *See* World War II (Great Patriotic War)
Grechko, Andrei, 67n13
Grigor'ev, Evgenii, 37
Guattari, Félix, 185
Gubenko, Nikolai, 36, 73

Gudkov, Lev, 115–16, 117, 129
Guseva, Ekaterina, 222

Happiness (1998), 171
Hashamova, Yana, 17, 18, 158n24, 302n8
Hesiod, 4, 9
history, 72, 73, 91, 211, 214n19, 263
Hitchcock, Alfred, 94
Hitler, Adolf, 15, 84n6, 116, 230, 289
Hollywood cinema, 94, 157n4, 169, 171
Holocaust, 116
home, return to, 153
homoeroticism/homosexuality, 239n12, 283, 294, 301, 306n49
homosocial bonds, 8, 10; father-son relations and, 180; gay readings by Western critics, 17; in *Ivanovo detstvo [Ivan's Childhood]*, 254; mothers/women excluded from, 181, 183, 184, 185; socialist realism and, 252; in Sokurov's films, 289; women in role of bystanders, 12. *See also* male bonding; masculinity
horror films, 300
Horton, Andrew, 73
Hungary, 116
Hunter, Stephen, 147

I lichno Leonid Il'ich [And Personally Leonid Il'ich] (2006), 107
Iakovleva, Elena, 121
Iampol'skii, Mikhail, 283, 304n20
Ia shagaiu po Moskve [I Walk around Moscow] (1964), 43
Ia sluzhil v okhrane Stalina [I Was Stalin's Bodyguard] (1989), 14
Ibsen, Henrik, 159n26
id (Freudian concept), 210
identity/identity formation, 7, 37, 153; Belarusian, 103; Freudian uncanny *(Unheimlich)* and, 119–20; ideological family and, 38; male identity and subjectivity, 263–64, 302n11; masculinity as socially constructed identity, 169; Oedipal complex and,

18, 191; Russian, 66; significance of war in, 56–57; Soviet, 51, 54, 59; stability of, 44
ideology, 70–71, 72, 81, 89, 211
Idi i smotri [Come and See] (1985), 95, 101
Iiul'skii dozhd' [July Rain] (1966), 31
Il'ina, Marianna, 124
Imaginary (Lacanian concept), 7, 19, 182, 210; return of Symbolic father as, 284, 302n8; in *Solaris*, 262; in Tarkovsky's life and work, 251–52
Imagined Communities (Anderson), 218
incest, paternal interdiction of, 64
intelligentsia, Russian, 33, 46n13, 93, 118–19, 125; martyr image and, 248; sociocultural collapse of, 127, 132; split in identity of, 120
Interpretation of Dreams (Freud), 213n5
Irigaray, Luce, 186n13
Ironiia sub'by, ili S legkim parom [Irony of Fate] (1975), 157n5
Iskusstvo kino [The Art of Cinema] (journal), 45n7, 92
Ispytatel'nyi srok [The Probationary Period] (1960), 30
Iumatov, Georgii, 65
Iusov, Vadim, 268n1
Ivan (Bogomolov novella), 254–55, 272n35
Ivan IV (Ivan the Terrible), 9, 221
Ivan the Terrible (1945), 292, 296
Ivanov, Aleksandr, 15
Ivanovo detstvo [Ivan's Childhood] (1962), 12, 96, 135n7, 186n8, 263, 272; competing surrogate fathers, 254–57; *Solaris* compared with, 259, 262; stills from, 278–80; *Zhertvoprinoshenie; Offret [Sacrifice]* compared with, 266
Izobrazhaia zhertvu [Playing the Victim] (2006), 7

Jay, Nancy, 287, 288
Jesus Christ, references to, 207, 267; in *Ivanovo detstvo [Ivan's Childhood]*, 257, 272nn33,35; in *Ofitsery [Officers]*, 59; Tarkovsky's kenotic self-image, 248, 249; in *Vozvrashchenie [The Return]*, 174. *See also* Bible/biblical stories; Orthodox Christianity
Jews, 148, 149, 150, 154, 160n34; in *Brigada* series, 225, 226–27; devastation of World War II and, 151, 153
Josephson, Erland, 265
Jung, Carl, 6
Jungle Fever (1991), 171

Kalatozov, Mikhail, 43, 58, 72
Kalik, Mikhail, 43
Kalinin, Mikhail, 70
Kapitanskaia dochka [The Captain's Daughter] (Pushkin), 21n18, 154
Kaplan, E. Ann, 305n33
Karloff, Boris, 118, 123
Karnaval'naia noch' [The Carnival Night] (1956), 66n2
Katok i skripka [The Steamroller and the Violin] (1960), 252, 261–62, 277–78
Kaufman, Gerald, 158n20
Kavun, Andrei, 98
Kazakevich, Emmanuil, 93
Kazan, Elia, 3
KGB (secret police), 54, 68n20, 96, 107, 236
Khabenskii, Konstantin, 192
Kheifits, Iosif, 30, 66n2
Khlebnikov, Boris, 7, 18, 135n7, 171
Khliustova, Nataliia, 156n1
Khotinenko, Vladimir, 82, 84n3
Khrushchev, Nikita, 29, 33–34, 45n7, 52; as father figure, 71; renewal associated with, 53; Thaw as cultural moment, 72
Khrustalev, mashinu! [Khrustalev, My Car!] (1998), 14, 90–91
Khutsiev, Marlen, 11, 12; on characters in *Zastava Il'icha [Il'ich's Guard]*, 36; cult of personality represented by, 34; documentary effect and, 32; father's death in Stalinist purges, 30; trope of filiation and, 268; World War II films of, 31

Kiarostiami, Abbas, 282
Klimov, Elem, 95, 101
Kogda derev'ia byli bol'shimi [When the Trees Were Tall] (1961), 114
Koktebel' [Koktebel] (2003), 7, 135n7, 171; father-son relations in, 173–74, 176–80; Freudian/Lacanian elements, 18–19; mother's absence and femininity in, 182–84; return of Symbolic father and, 180–81; stills from, *190;* volatility versus stability of father figure, 184–85; weak paternal figure in, 18
Kommissar [The Commissar] (1967), 83
Kommunist [Communist] (1957), 30, 44
Konchalovsky, Andrei, 68n17
Korchagin, Pavel, 122
Korol'kov, Gennadii, 37
Kotcheff, Ted, 120
Kovalov, Oleg, 134n4
Kravchenko, Aleksei, 94–95
Kristeva, Julia, 119, 126, 133, 300, 307n40
Kronos/Chronos (Greek god), 4, 6, 21n9, 156, 160n43, 205
Kryl'ia [Wings] (1966), 108
Kudinenko, Andrei, 101, 102, 103–104
Kukushka [Cuckoo] (2002), 186n11
Kulidzhanov, Lev, 114
Kulish, Savva, 75
Kunin, Vladimir, 96
Kursanty [The Students] (2004), 98–99
Kuznetsov, Pavel, 2–3, 4, 8

Lacan, Jacques, 7, 140, 145, 147, 179; on *Brothers Karamazov,* 172; on father's role in Symbolic order, 172, 182; on Oedipus complex, 201; on the Real, 201
Lacanian concepts/themes, 18, 19, 175, 176, 210, 302n11
Lagutenko, Il'ia, 210
Lamentation over the Dead Christ (Mantegna painting), 174
language, 211, 213n5, 286, 302n8
Lanovoi, Vasilii, 65–66
Larsen, Susan, 144, 159n26, 224

Law of the Father, 7, 10, 11, 13, 19, 156; mother-infant relationship and, 201; in Tarkovsky's life and work, 252; in *Vor [The Thief],* 148
Lebedev, Nikolai, 15, 16, 93–94
legitimacy, 5
Lem, Stanislaw, 247, 250, 257, 258
Lenin, Vladimir, 9, 170; *Brigada* references to, 233; communist utopia and, 30, 34; death of, 45n2; equality associated with, 53; father figures associated with, 30; as "Grandfather," 10, 23n31, 70; as ideological father, 45n3; Mausoleum of, 37; perestroika-era views of, 23n32; prison tattoos depicting, 143; revolutionary ideals and, 11, 36; Soviet leader-cultism and, 71
Leone, Sergio, 220, 237n2
Letiat zhuravli [Cranes Are Flying] (1957), 43, 58, 72
Letters from Iwo Jima (2007), 106
Levy, Dani, 106
Lipovetsky, Mark, 16, 144, 186n11
Liubomirov, Grigorii, 107
Liubshin, Stanislav, 36
Livnev, Sergei, 14, 141
lubok (folk painting), 55, 61
Luk'ianenko, Sergei, 191
Lungin, Pavel, 138

machismo, 12, 15, 138, 155, 170. *See also* masculinity
Magnolia (1999), 171
Makhmudov, Farkhad, 225
male bonding, 51, 54; in *Beloe solntse pustyni [White Sun of the Desert],* 60, 62, 63; in Tarkovsky's films, 253, *277;* war as ultimate space for, 66. *See also* homosocial bonds; masculinity
Malen'kaia Vera [Little Vera] (1988), 73, 80–81, 85n12
Maliukov, Andrei, 109n14
"Mama vykhodit zamuzh" ["Mama Gets Married"] (Moskvina), 146–47
Manguel, Alberto, 1, 4

Mantegna, Andrea, 174
Markov, Pavel, 224
Martirolog (Tarkovsky diaries), 248, 268n2
Martynov, Dmitrii, 193
martyrdom, 35, 135n6; Stalinist, 29, 101, 123; Tarkovsky's self-image and, 248, 257; World War II and, 33, 60
Marx, Karl, 71, 184, 185
masculinism, 291, 294
masculinity, 11, 13, 53, 158n21, 297; authority associated with, 148; biological fathers' failure and, 16; code of honor, 222, 234, 237; crisis of, 169, 170, 211, 221, 223, 303n11; disintegration of Soviet Big Family and, 14; heroic, 55; lonely and repressed, 59; male sexual identity, 169–70; modernity and, 60; perestroika-era views of, 77; symbolic (phallic) birth, 288, 291. *See also* homosocial bonds; machismo; male bonding
Mashkov, Vladimir, 3, 8, 14, 155; as actor, 138, 140, 149, 156n1; multiple roles in connection with *Papa,* 151; on *Papa* as debt to parents, 148; theater and, 156n2
Maslin, Janet, 144, 156n1
Mater' chelovecheskaia [Mother of Humankind] (1975), 102–103
matriarchy, 172
Matrosskaia tishina [Sailors' Rest] (Galich play), 148, 149, 154, 159n33
Meadows, Shane, 10
Medvedev, Dmitrii, 20, 23n28, 24n38
Mein Führer: The Truly Truest Truth about Adolf Hitler (2006), 106
Mein Kampf (Hitler), 230
memory, 41, 46n16, 82, 248
men. *See* fathers; father-son relations; masculinity; sons
Men'shov, Vladimir, 66n2, 96, 192
Meshkiev, Dmitrii, 99, 100, 134n3
Mika and Alfred (Kunin), 96
Mikhalkov, Nikita, 73, 81, 85n13, 307n41

Mikhalkov, V., 175, 186n4
Mikhalkov-Konchalovsky, Andrei, 269n7, 270n19
militarism, 76, 155
military discourse, 14–17
Miller, David Lee, 285, 287, 288, 300
Ming-liang, Tsai, 282
Mir vkhodiahshchemu [Peace to Him Who Enters] (1961), 114
Mironer, Feliks, 30
Mironova, Mariia, 192
Misharin, Aleksandr, 250, 269n7, 270n17
Mishulin, Spartak, 61
Mne dvadtsat' let [I Am Twenty] (1964), 43, 45n7
Moi drug Ivan Lapshin [My Friend Ivan Lapshin] (1986), 97
Moi svodnyi brat Frankenshtein [My Stepbrother Frankenstein] (2003), 5, 16, 144, 184; context of Soviet war mythology, 117–18; Freudian uncanny *(Unheimlich)* and, 118–20, 126–27, 133–34; Great Family myth and, 135n6; inversion of fathering, 127–34, *137*; mimicry of othering, 120–27; psychological trauma of war in, 120–23
Molodaia Gvardiia (Fadeev novel), 22n19, 43–44
Molodaia Gvardiia [The Young Guard] (1947), 15, 43
Molokh [Moloch] (1999), 289
Molotov-Ribbentrop Pact, 100
Mongolians, 81–82
The Monstrous Feminine (Creed), 300
Morozov, Pavlik, 8, 13; Chechen war context and, 16; martyrdom of, 91; *Moi svodnyi brat Frankenshtein* reference to, 122–23; motivation for behavior of, 22n21; perestroika-era reworking of story, 76, 84n1
Moses and Monotheism (Freud), 172
Mosfilm, 94
Moskva slezam ne verit [Moscow Does Not Believe in Tears] (1980), 66n2
Moskvina, Tat'iana, 146–47

Mother and Son (1997), 283, 289, 299, 304n19
mothers and mother figures, 77, 78; absent, 181–84, 203; "archaic mother," 300, 306n33, 307n40; Lacanian Imaginary and, 7; Law of the Father and, 201; in *Moi svodnyi brat Frankenshtein*, 125; Oedipal family drama and, 145, 198; symbolic birth as erasure of, 288; in Tarkovsky's life and films, 242–54, 255, 259, 262, 273n49, 274n51, *278, 279*; unassailable identity of, 5, 286; in *Vor [The Thief]*, 146–47
Motyl', Vladimir, 13, 51, 54, 68n17
Mozart and Salieri (Pushkin), 269n3
Mrs. Doubtfire (1993), 171
Mulvey, Laura, 305n33
Muratova, Kira, 247, 249, 269n8
Muzh i doch' Tamary Aleksandrovny [The Husband and Daughter of Tamara Aleksandrovna] (1988), 73, 78–79
My Name Is Ivan. See Ivanovo detstvo [Ivan's Childhood] (1962)
mythology, ancient Greek, 4, 6, 18–19, 21n12, 156; Kronos, 4, 6, 21n9, 156, 160n43, 205; Oedipus, 193–98, 212n4, 213n7

Name of the Father, 7, 175–76
Narutskaia, Ol'ga, 73, 79, 80
Nashi [Ours] (ultra-conservative group), 10
nationalism, Russian, 116, 121, 218, 226
Naumov, Vladimir, 114
Nazis, 14, 15, 31, 60, 65; cinematic representation of, 105, 106; defeated by Soviet Union, 91; executions of Jews by, 150; in *Ivanovo detstvo [Ivan's Childhood]*, 255, 256, 257, 272n39; Soviet "liberation" from, 117
Neizvestnyi, Ernst, 248
Nesbet, Anne, 292
Nesluzhebnoe zadanie [Unofficial Business] (2004), 96

Neumann, Erich, 154
Nevsky, Alexander, 233
New Year's films, 139
NKVD (secret police), 97, 99, 102, 109n14
Nochnoi dozor [Night Watch] (2004), 6, 16, 191, 209–12; duality as structural component of, 202–204; ego formation in, 198–202; Oedipus and fate in, 191–98; patriarchy and history in, 208–209; vampirism in, 204–207
Nochnoi patrul' [Night Patrol] (1957), 30
Nostalghia (1983), 250

Obyknovennaia istoriia [An Ordinary Story] (Goncharov), 154
October Revolution, 29
Odinokii golos cheloveka [The Lonely Voice of Man] (1978/1987), 282, 289
Oedipal complex, 10, 210, 211; in *Beloe solntse pustyni [White Sun of the Desert]*, 64; civilization and, 206; construction of ego and, 198–202; family romance, 150–51; in *Koktebel'*, 18–19; resolution of, 198, 201, 247; sociocultural transition and, 191; stages of psychosexual development, 198; in Tarkovsky's films, 263, 264; in *Tri dnia Viktora Chernysheva [Three Days of Viktor Chernyshev]*, 43; in *Vor [The Thief]*, 144–45
Oedipus Rex (Sophocles), 7, 192, 193, 197
Officers: The Last Soldiers of the Empire (TV mini-series), 65–66
Offret (1986), 265–68
Ofitsery [Officers] (1971), 13, 54–60, 63, 64; Soviet state involvement in making of, 67; succession of generations in, 65; television sequel/ remake of, 65–66
Okkupatsiia. Misterii [Occupation. Mystery Plays] (2003), 101–103
Okkupatsiia. Pravda i mify [Occupation. Truth, and Myths] (Sokolov), 100

Okudzhava, Bulat, 32, 34, 62, 98
Olen'ia okhota [Deer Hunt] (1981), 97
Oligarkh [Tycoon] (2000), 138
Ona zashchishchaet rodinu [She Defends Her Motherland] (1943), 102
Once upon a Time in America (1984),
220, 237n2
One Fine Day (1996), 171
Oni srazhalis' za rodinu [They Fought
for the Motherland] (1975), 105
origin, myths of, 4, 29
orphans, 3, 12, 30, 58, 96, 102
Orthodox Christianity, 225, 229, 235,
266; in Serbia, 234; sobornost'
(shared leadership) concept,
218; tsars and, 8. See also Bible/
biblical stories; Jesus Christ, references to
Osep'ian, Mark, 11–12, 31, 37, 40
Ostrovskii, Gennadii, 118
Osvobozhdenie [Liberation] (1969–71),
53
Otets i syn [Father and Son] (2003), 6,
7, 184, 282–84; "archaic father" in,
299–301, 307n42; gazes in, 294–97,
298, 299, 309; homoeroticism in,
283, 294, 301, 306n49; Ivanovo
detstvo compared with, 257; Rembrandt's Sacrifice of Isaac and, 290–
92, 296, 297; shadows in, 292–94,
305n28; son's blindness in, 297–99;
strong paternal figure in, 17
Otets soldata [Father of a Soldier] (1965),
114
otherness/othering, 64, 120–27, 130,
135n6, 285, 305n32
Ottoman Empire, 63
ottsepriimstvo ("patriality"), 284, 285,
287, 301, 302n10
"Ottsepriimstvo" (Sekatskii), 3
Ottsy i deti [Fathers and Sons] (Turgenev), 21n18, 154
"Ottsy i synov'ia" ["Fathers and Sons"]
(Kuznetsov), 2–3

Padenie Berlina [The Fall of Berlin]
(1949), 15

Panin, Andrei, 224
Panova, Elena, 222
Papa (2004), 3, 8, 138, 155–56, 184;
family romance and father's ghost
in, 148–55; father-son relations in,
139; Stalin's "paternal" shadow in,
14; stills from, 165–66
Paradzhanov, Sergei, 249
Parfenov, Leonid, 107
paternity, 21n8, 179; as absence, 1–5;
lack of bodily form, 286; real and
Symbolic, 173; sentimental versus
sobering, 138–40; uncertainty of,
21n10
patriarchy, 71, 115, 125, 282; brotherhood (fraternal governance) and,
227, 228–30; deconstruction of, 185;
history and, 208–209; non-Russian
ethnicity and, 226; post-patriarchal
social family, 126; reconstitution
of, 283; redemption of, 144, 221,
231–36; vertical social hierarchies
and, 218
patricide, 3, 4, 8, 150
patriotism, 53, 55, 60, 93–97
Père Goriot (Balzac), 153
Peregon [Transit] (2006), 109n14
perestroika, 13–14, 23n32, 51, 209; generational transition and, 72; male
kinship models, 70; myths of Soviet
history and, 89
Pervyi posle boga [First after God]
(2005), 109n14
Peter the Great, 9
phallocentrism, 187n13
Pichul, Vasilii, 73
Pilikhina, Margarita, 32, 36
Pinocchio (Collodi), 40
Plakhov, Andrei, 121–22
Plato, 6, 8
Platonov, Andrei, 134n1
Pliumbum, ili opasnaia igra [Lead, or
a Dangerous Game] (1986), 13, 73,
75–78, 84n1
Podranki [Orphans] (1976), 73
Podrostok [The Adolescent] (Dostoev-
sky), 21n18

Pokaianie [Repentance] (1984), 13, 76, 77, 80, 84n6; beginning of perestroika/glasnost, 73, 89; reckoning with Stalinist past in, 73–75

Poland, 116–17

Polumgla [Semidarkness] (2005), 110n17

Pope, Alexander, 19–20

Popogrebskii, Aleksei, 7, 18, 135n7, 171

Popov, Valentin, 32

Poroshina, Mariia, 193

Poslednii boi maiora Pugacheva [The Last Battle of Major Pugachev] (2005), 97

Poslednii poezd [The Last Train] (2004), 15, 104, 105–106, *113*

Potepalov, Sergei, 292

Povinnost' [Confession] (1998), 289

POWs (prisoners of war), Soviet, 30, 99, 100, 104

Prasad, Udayan, 10

Predsedatel' [Chairman] (1964), 44

progress, historical, 52, 57

Prokhorov, Alexander, 11, 115

Prokhorova, Elena, 12, 100

Prorva [Moscow Parade] (1992), 14

Proverka na dorogakh [The Trial on the Roads] (1971), 97, 104–105

Prygunov, Lev, 39

psychoanalysis, 6, 150

Ptushko, Aleksandr, 40

Pudovkin, Vsevolod, 32

puer senex (boy/old man), 257, 286, 291, 297

Pushkin, Aleksandr, 20, 21n18, 154, 233, 269n3

Putevka v zhizn' [Road to Life] (1931), 72

Putin, Vladimir, 24n38, 171; "authoritarian democracy" of, 236, 237; *Brigada* series and, 219, 220, 221, 236, 237; election of, 221; Great Patriotic War myth and, 115; Medvedev as "ideological son" of, 20, 23n28; military discourse and, 16; popularity of, 10, 181; restoration of "order" under, 19; Russian cinema and, 23n37; stabilization associated with, 181

Pyr'ev, Ivan, 44n1, 60

Raizman, Yuli, 30, 44

Rambo: First Blood (1982), 120, 222–25, 238nn4–5

Raush, Irina (Irma), 269n4, 270n17

Razgrom [The Rout] (Fadeev novel), 22n19

Real (Lacanian concept), 17, 176, 179, 201–202, 210

Rednikova, Ekaterina, 140

"The Religion of War" (Shpagin), 92

Rembrandt van Rijn, 283, 287; *Book of Tobit* series, 297, 303n14; *Return of the Prodigal Son*, 261; *Sacrifice of Isaac*, 287–88, 290, 292, 296, 297, 303–304nn15–16

Repin, Il'ia, 22n23

The Return. See Vozvrashchenie [The Return] (2003)

Return of the Prodigal Son (Rembrandt painting), 261

Riazanov, El'dar, 66n2, 157n5

A River Runs through It (1992), 171

road movies, 172, 173

Rogovoi, Vladimir, 13, 54, 60

Rogozhkin, Aleksandr, 109n14

Rozendent, Andrei, 149

Rozhdestvenskii, Robert, 32

Russia, Imperial, 12, 54, 63, 82

Russia, post-Soviet: criminal overlap with militarism, 144, 225; crisis of masculinity, 224; gender anxieties in, 170–71; historical amnesia in, 106–107; military actions of, 66; patriotism in, 93–97, 109n9; restoration of patriarchal ideology, 89; Soviet traditions preserved in, 20; stabilization under Putin, 181; State Duma, 19, 221, 224, 236; Yeltsin-era (1990s) chaos, 17, 19, 66, 90, 181, 229. *See also* Chechen War; Putin, Vladimir

Russian Ark (2002), 304n21, 306n37

Russian Idea, 60
Russian War Films (Youngblood), 95
Russo-Japanese War (1904–1905), 82
Rybnikov, Aleksei, 94

Sacrifice (1986), 265–68
The Sacrifice of Isaac (Rembrandt painting), 287–88, 290, 292, 296, 297, 303–304nn15–16
Saltykov, Aleksei, 44
Savage Junctures: Eisenstein and the Shape of Thinking (Nesbet), 292
Saving Private Ryan (1998), 94
Schama, Simon, 288
Schoeberlein, John S., 9, 23n31, 170
Scott, Ridley, 300
SEANS (film journal), 2–3, 52, 284, 289
The Second Circle (1990), 283, 284–85, 289
Sekatskii, Aleksandr, 3, 6, 52; on absence literal and existential, 5; on "patriality," 284; on son's yearning for father, 4–5; on *Vozvrashchenie [The Return]*, 67n5, 179
The Seminar (Lacan), 201
Serbia, 234
Serebrennikov, Kirill, 7
Serezha [A Summer to Remember] (1960), 72–73
Serp i molot [Hammer and Sickle] (1994), 14, 141
sex/sexuality, 79, 80, 198; in Bekmambetov's *Dozor* trilogy, 199; civilization and, 206; Oedipal complex and, 7; repression of desire, 201, 204, 212; vampirism and, 210–11. *See also* homoeroticism/homosexuality
Shakespeare, William, 6, 160n36
Shakhnazarov, Karen, 138
Shakhverdiev, Tofik, 13, 155
Shalimov, Artem, 124
Shelley, Mary, 119, 132
Shepit'ko, Larisa, 108n7
Shevchenko, Elena, 139
Shigarev, Dima, 141
Shnezhkin, Sergei, 107

Sholokhov, Mikhail, 127
Shpagin, Aleksandr, 92, 95, 111n28
Shtrafbat [Penal Batallion] (2004), 97
Shukshin, Vasilii, 42
Sidorov, Aleksei, 19, 144, 219, 268
Silverman, Kaja, 302n11
Simonov, Konstantin, 104
Sirota kazanskaia [Sympathy Seeker] (1997), 138, 139, 157n8, *162–63*
Sleepless in Seattle (1993), 171
Slepyan, Kenneth, 191
Slutskii, Boris, 32
SMERSH counterintelligence agency, 97
Smirennaia zhizn' [A Humble Life] (1997), 301n2
Smirnov, Andrei, 268
Smoktunovskii, Innokentii, 264, 265
Smorodinskaya, Tat'iana, 15
Sochinenie ko dniu pobedy [A Composition Devoted to Victory Day] (1999), 92
socialist realism, 8, 22n20, 76, 252; filial characters of, 29; frustrated ideal of, 41; Great Family myth and, 31, 71; waning canon of, 64. *See also* Stalinism
"social problem" films, 79
Soderbergh, Steven, 258
Sokolov, Boris, 100
Sokurov, Aleksandr, 6, 7, 17; editing style, 295; idealized father and, 18; *Otets i syn [Father and Son]*, 257; *ottseptriimstvo* ("patriality") and, 284, 285, 289, 301; as "poet laureate" of post-Soviet cinema, 282; sexuality of, 283; Tarkovsky and, 248, 250, 301n1
Solaris (Lem novel), 250, 257–58, 259
Solaris (1972), 250, 257–62, 274n53, *281*
Soldaty svobody [Soldiers of Freedom] (1977), 53
Solntse [The Sun] (2004), 301n2
Solntseva, Alena, 153
Solov'ev, Sergei, 82
Solzhenitsyn, Aleksandr, 154

Son and Father: Before and beyond the Oedipus Complex (Blos), 90
songs, in films, 60, 62, 82, 84n6, 231
sons: dispensable, 56; effects of Stalinism on, 11–12; filial betrayal, 8; passage into Symbolic order, 17; patriotic myths of World War II and, 15; post-Soviet search for lost fathers, 90–93; prodigal son in *Solaris*, 257–62, *281;* sacrificial, 6, 64, 286–87; as socialist realist positive heroes, 54; Symbolic order and, 175–79; of Thaw period, 52–53. *See also* father-son relations
Sophocles, 7, 179, 192, 193
The Sopranos (cable TV series), 220, 221, 238n3
Soviet Union (USSR), 8, 9, 54, 75; commemoration of Revolution, 29; constraints on film directors, 248–49; disintegration and collapse of, 89, 219, 284; "fraternal" countries of Eastern bloc and, 70; heroic Russian national history invoked, 12; ideological crisis of Brezhnev era, 44; impotence of geriatric post-Stalin leaders, 9; Master Narrative of, 72; Molotov-Ribbentrop Pact and, 100; Russian Empire linked to, 53–55, 56, 62–64, 107; social reengineering of, 70–71; Spanish Civil War refugees and, 263; Thaw cultural values, 31; victory over Nazi Germany, 91. *See also* Afghanistan, Soviet war in; cinema, Soviet
Sphinx, Oedipus and riddle of the, 195–96, *215*
Spielberg, Stephen, 94
Spivakovskii, Daniil, 119
spy thrillers, 54, 57, 68n20
Stagnation period, 73, 76, 77, 118–19, 144
Stalin, Joseph, 34, 76, 111nn30–31; concentration camps under, 151; cult of personality, 12, 34, 142; death of, 52; as debunked father figure, 114; expansion and protection as-

sociated with, 53; as Father of the Peoples/Nation, 8–10, 23n31, 53, 70, 142, 170; Great Family myth and, 45n2; iconography of, 22n26, 146, 157n15, 307n41; last days of rule, 90–91; mythological status of, 142; "paternal" shadow of, 14; prison tattoos depicting, 143, 146; as protective father, 147–48; purges under, 108n3, 149; Putin compared with, 10; rhetoric of equality and, 218–19; Russian nostalgia for empire and, 11; as "son" of Georgia, 74; victims of, 14, 39, 155; World War II and, 15, 23n27, 31, 142, 157n16
Stalin. Live (TV series, 2006), 107
Stalin s nami? [Is Stalin with Us?] (1989), 13–14, 155
Stalinism, 8, 10, 13; bankruptcy of, 13; camps of, 29, 30, 143, 154; de-Stalinization, 29, 34; father-son relations in context of, 139; Great Family myth, 30–31, 45n5, 115; masculinity/machismo and, 11, 140–48, 155, 224; militarism and misogyny of, 12; Morozov myth and, 84n1, 91; perestroika-era treatment of, 74; recruitment of orphans and, 96; Soviet war mythology and, 104; teleological progressive time and, 36. *See also* socialist realism
Stalin's Guerrillas: Soviet Partisans in World War II (Slepyan), 101
Stalker (1979), 250
Stallone, Sylvester, 223
state service, ideology of, 63
Stishova, Elena, 93, 127–28, 180, 186n4
Stolper, Aleksandr, 14
Strukov, Vlad, 18, 19
Sud'ba cheloveka [Fate of a Man] (1959), 12, 73, 114, 127
Sukhobokov, Vladimir, 30
superego, 21n16, 172, 201, 210, 307n42
Surkova, Ol'ga, 249, 269n3, 270n9
Svetlov, Mikhail, 32
Svoi [Our Own] (2004), 99, 100, 134n3
Svolochi [Bastards] (2006), 96–97

Symbolic order, 7, 17, 19, 210; fall of Soviet system and, 170; father's role in child's development, 172; in *Koktebel' [Koktebel]*, 178; as language and culture, 201, 302n8; model-identification with father and, 145, 147; in *Nochnoi dozor [Night Watch]*, 197; in *Otets i syn [Father and Son]*, 293; *ottsepriimstvo* ("patriality") and, 285; sacrifice of sons and, 286–87; in Tarkovsky's life and work, 251–52; in *Vozvrashchenie [The Return]*, 176, 177, 179; women excluded from, 183

Szabo, Ishtvan, 3, 4

Tabakov, Oleg, 139, 148, 156n2, 157n8
Tadjiks, 225, 226–28
Talankin, Igor', 72
Tarkovsky, Andrei, 6, 12, 13, 96, 179; abandonment of first family, 250, 275n63; as *auteur*, 247–48; on expression of feelings, 247; father's relations with, 249–51, 254, 263, 270n14; sexuality of, 250, 251, 271n22; Sokurov and, 248, 250, 301n1; Soviet film establishment and, 248–49, 269n7, 270n9; transcendental cinema and, 282; views on gender, 251–54, 266, 273n48. *See also Ivanovo detstvo [Ivan's Childhood]* (1962); *Solaris* (1972); *Zerkalo [Mirror]* (1975)

Tarkovsky, Arsenii, 13, 249–50, 254, 265, 270n14; poems of, 264; on *Zerkalo*, 263

Telets [Taurus] (2000), 289

television, 19, 32, 89, 109n9; Brezhnev-era, 54; images in *Tri dnia Viktora Chernysheva*, 40–41; images in *Zastava Il'icha [Il'ich's Guard]*, 35, 48; nostalgic shows about Soviet leaders, 107; *Officers: The Last Soldiers of the Empire*, 65–66; World War II dramas, 90, 97

Telling October (Corney), 29
Terekhova, Margarita, 263

Thaw period, cinema of, 11, 13, 43; bridge to era of stagnation, 44; father-son metaphor and, 52; Great Family myth and, 45n5, 115; nuclear family in, 39, 42; "rebellious" discourse in, 66n2; World War II reimagined, 31

Theogony (Hesiod), 4, 9

time, representation of, 152–53, 193; Greek mythology and, 6, 21n9, 160n43, 205; utopia and, 36

Time within Time (Tarkovsky), 247, 248, 262, 265

Timofeevskii, Aleksandr, 37
Tiunina, Galina, 195
Todorovskii, Petr, 14, 98, 99
Todorovskii, Valerii, 5, 16, 98, 117, 118
Tolstaya, Tatyana, 134n4
Tolstoi, Aleksei, 40, 154
Tolstoi, Leo, 20, 21n18, 305n28
totalitarianism, 9, 59, 93, 114, 115, 170
Totem and Taboo (Freud), 3, 4, 145, 150, 199, 217–18

Tragediia v stile rok [Tragedy in the Style of Rock] (1988), 75

Traktoristy [Tractor Drivers] (1939), 60

Tri dnia Viktora Chernysheva [Three Days of Viktor Chernyshev] (1968), 11–12, 31–32, 45n8; eavesdropping scene, 40, *50*; Great Family myth in, 37, 41, 42, 44; intertitle in, 39, *49*; narrative plot, 37–41; village prose tradition and, 41–42; *Zastava Il'icha [Il'ich's Guard]* parodied in, 42, 43–44

Tri pesni o Lenine [Three Songs about Lenin] (1934), 60

Trifonov, Iurii, 118
tsars, 8–9, 71, 170, 233
Turgenev, Ivan, 21n18, 154
Turovskaya, Maya, 250
Tvoi sovremennik [Your Contemporary] (1967), 44

TwentyFourSeven (1997), 10

Ugriumov, Sergei, 149
Ukraine, 100, 149

Unheimlich (uncanny), 118–19, 133
United States, 93, 139, 171, 227, 239n13, 283
Urga: Territoriia liubvi [Urga: Territory of Love/Close to Eden] (1991), 73, 81–82
Ursuliak, Sergei, 92
Utomlennoe solntsem [Burnt by the Sun] (1994), 85n13, 307n41
utopia, 29, 30, 34, 37, 40; father-son relations and, 51, 52, 290; machines as symbols of, 57; male heroism and, 55; memory of father and, 41; Russian military glory and Soviet utopia, 65; state-endorsed dream of Russian history, 60; time and, 36

V sozvezdii byka [In the Taurus Constellation] (2003), 110n23
vampirism, 18, 19, 194, 195, 198, 209; as form of sexuality, 199, 210–11; as incestuous assault, 204–207; Oedipal complex and, 200, 213n15
Van Diem, Mike, 10, 181
Vasil'ev, Anatolii, 149
Vdovichenkov, Vladimir, 224
Vereshchagin, Vasilii, 63
Verhoeven, Paul, 106
Vernost' [Faithfulness] (1965), 98, 99
Vertov, Dziga, 60
Verzhbitskii, Viktor, 192
Victory Day, 31, 45n6, 91
Vietnam War, 121, 222, 223
village prose traditions, 41–42
Vinogradov, Valentin, 110n28
violence, language of, 129–33
Virgil, 286
"Vladimir's Directors" (Chukhrai), 140
Vlasov, Pavel, 122
"The Voice in the Cinema" (Doane), 282
Voina [War] (2002), 16, 117
Voina i mir [War and Peace] (Tolstoi), 20, 21n18, 154
Volodarskii, Eduard, 97, 104
Vor [The Thief] (1997), 3, 138, *164*, 184; *chernukha* genre and, 92; as critique of Stalinist machismo, 140–48;

father as imitation of Stalin, 11; father-son relations in, 139; Oedipal triangle in, 7; *Okkupatsiia. Misterii* compared with, 103; *Papa* compared with, 152, 154, 155–56; Stalin's "paternal" shadow in, 14; strong paternal figure in, 17
Vorob'ev, Vitalii, 96
Voroshilovskii strelok [Voroshilov's Sniper] (1996), 92
Vostochnyi koridor [Eastern Corridor] (1966), 110n28
voyeurism, 286
"Vozvrashchenie" ["The Return"] (Platonov), 134n1
Vozvrashchenie [The Return] (2003), 3, 17, 67n5, 171; father-son relations in, 172–80; inner evolution to mature self, 18; loss and acknowledgment of father, 145; mother's absence and femininity in, 181–84; *ottsepriimstvo* ("patriality") and, 284; return of Symbolic father, 180, 181; stills from, *189;* volatility versus stability of father figure, 184–85
Vozvrashchenie Vasiliia Bortnikova [The Return of Vasilii Bortnikov] (1953), 32
Vspominai—ne vspominai [Recall—or Not] (P. Todorovskii), 98
Vysotskii, Vladimir, 2

War and Peace (Tolstoi), 20, 21n18, 154
Western culture, representation of, 227–28
Whale, James, 118, 135n5
White, Armand, 290, 301, 307n39
women: *babushka* figure, 20; consigned to peripheral roles, 7, 18; excluded from homosocial bonds, 183, 184, 185; gender roles in Soviet Union and, 170; Mother Russia symbolism and, 225, 238n3; of noble origins, 58; in *Otets i syn [Father and Son]*, 295–96, 306n36, *309;* perceived disloyalty of, 222; sexual difference and identity, 169; Soviet mythology

of civil war and, 60, 61; Tarkovsky's views of, 251–54, 266; World War II and, 102–103, 114. *See also* feminine/femininity; mothers and mother figures

Wordsworth, William, 257

World War II (Great Patriotic War), 3, 54; anniversary victory celebrations, 116; as basic image of Russian national consciousness, 115–16; in Brezhnev (stagnation) era films, 57; *Brigada* reference to, 230; catastrophic loss of (male) life in, 2, 9, 104, 111n30, 114; destruction of Jewish lives in, 153; European and American films about, 106; fathers perished in, 30, 33, 72; generation of martyrs/true fathers, 29; German-occupied territories of USSR, 100; as Great Fatherland War, 70, 71; in *Ivanovo detstvo [Ivan's Childhood]*, 254–57, 278–80; military discourse in cinema and, 14–15; as model of "usable past," 53; partisan guerrillas in, 100–102, 104; penal battalions, 97, 99, 102; in post-Soviet cinema, 89–108, 149; sanctification of father figure and, 114, 115; socialist realism and, 43; sons' search for lost fathers, 90–93; Soviet mythology of, 91–92, 95, 100, 116, 129, 133; Soviet myths challenged, 100–106; Stalin's leadership during, 15, 23n27, 31, 157n16; in *Zastava Il'icha [Il'ich's Guard]*, 33, 37. *See also* Germans, portrayal of; Nazis

World War II veterans, 12, 16, 53, 91, 92; persecution after war, 97; shrinking numbers in post-Soviet Russia, 107

Yakovleva, Irina, 202

Yeltsin, Boris, 17, 84n3, 93, 219, 228

Youngblood, Denise, 95, 101

Yurchak, Alexei, 53

Zakharov, Pavlik, 119

Zakrutkin, Vitalii, 103

Zaslavskii, Grigorii, 155, 159n31

Zastava Il'icha [Il'ich's Guard] (1962), 11, 31, 41; alternate titles, 43, 45n4; critics of, 33–34, 37, 45n7; identity in, 32–33, 34–35; narrative plot, 32, 36–37; naturalizing chronotope of, 37; parodied in *Tri dnia Viktora Chernysheva*, 42, 43–44; Polytechnic Museum sequence, 35, 43, 49; son and father's ghost in, 33–36, 38, 43, 48, 160n36; Stalinism represented in, 34–35; Young Pioneers' chorus, 35, 48

Zasukhina, Marina, 309

Zerkalo [Mirror] (1975), 186n4, 248, 250, 262–65

Zerkalo dlia geroia [A Mirror for a Hero] (1988), 82

Zhdi menia [Wait for Me] (1943), 14

Zhertvoprinoshenie [Sacrifice] (1986), 265–68

Zoia (1944), 14–15

Zolotoi kliuchik [The Golden Key] (1939), 40–41

Zolotukhin, Valerii, 203

Zvezda [The Star] (Kazakevich novel), 93

Zvezda [The Star] (1949), 15

Zvezda [The Star] (2002), 15, 16, 93–95, 113, 117

Zviagintsev, Andrei, 3, 5, 17, 18, 67n5, 145

Zwartboek [Black Book] (2006), 106